T0353454

Advanced Trends in ICT for Innovative Business Management

Advanced Trends in ICT for Innovative Business Management

Edited by

Katarzyna Szymczyk
Ibrahiem M. M. El Emary

CRC Press
Taylor & Francis Group
Boca Raton London New York

CRC Press is an imprint of the
Taylor & Francis Group, an **informa** business

First Edition published 2021
by CRC Press
6000 Broken Sound Parkway NW, Suite 300, Boca Raton, FL 33487-2742

and by CRC Press
2 Park Square, Milton Park, Abingdon, Oxon, OX14 4RN

ISBN: 978-0-367-46062-4 (hbk)
ISBN: 978-1-032-02719-7 (pbk)
ISBN: 978-1-003-02893-2 (ebk)

Typeset in Sabon
by KnowledgeWorks Global Ltd.

Contents

Preface

Nowadays, science, education, technology and business are more closely related than they were a dozen or so years ago. The challenges of today's world force us to undertake changes in business management so that it can meet the expectations of all interested groups. Currently, the most significant emphasis is placed on the implementation of the latest and most advanced technological solutions and digital innovations in business activities that not only improve the functioning of organizations but allow them to develop, become enriched and evolve. An important aspect of this is also education and science aimed at acquiring IT knowledge, competencies and skills in the fields of new computer technologies, digitization and the computerization of entrepreneurial activity in the process of learning. Future generations of employers and employees must follow these trends to be able to achieve modernization of their business activities.

At the beginning of 2020, the world faced another challenge, which was the fight against the pandemic caused by the COVID-19 virus. After less than half of the year, it was noticed how important IT technologies have become for the efficiency of running a business. Enterprises, institutions, schools, universities and any other organizations operating in the markets were forced to transfer their activities to the internet and work by computer, online. Thanks to the implemented IT solutions, these organizations continued to function, and many of them noticed the importance of combining traditional operations in the market with presence in the network and the use of IT tools for management, sales, logistics, transportation or communication with stakeholders. Yet many organizations cannot keep up with the technological revolution and critical differences in access to knowledge, education and technological resources can be observed.

This book is dedicated to discussing the above issues. It is a collection of 18 chapters of valuable scientific studies by researchers from international centers, i.e., universities and technical academies. The authors, based on a number of their research, data analysis, interviews and literature studies, discuss the critical problems and issues related to the implementation and use of advanced IT solutions for the needs of enterprises, organizational development, educational units, markets and the technology itself. It is worth mentioning the most important topics and problems that the authors raise. The discussed issues link to digital transformation, information and communication technologies (ICT), artificial intelligence, the Internet of Things (IoT), and the development of Industry 4.0. These issues complete the argument on effective management systems and the role of technology and ICT in the process of internationalization of business activity of enterprises.

Additionally, some crucial considerations on the subject of digital marketing tools, internet marketing instruments of enterprises and innovative advertising tools and analysis of websites or targeted advertising features in Facebook are discussed. The authors examine the impact of social media on the company's reputation. They focus on the functioning of companies on the internet and the use of digital tools to promote industrial production.

Also, there are considerations on the completeness meter as one of the most crucial elements of logistics customer service, which has been interestingly introduced by an example of commercial cargo motor transport enterprises. Moreover, the book touches upon aspects of the role of immaterial capital in organizational performance, cultural facets of compulsive buying in emerging economies and the impact of higher education on a country's development.

Furthermore, the authors discuss new approaches to agricultural management and advancing technological changes in agriculture, as well as hyperconnectivity and trends towards digital agriculture. They examine the cycle of innovation and investment process at farming enterprises and their production potential and profit. We hope this collection of scientific papers will arouse the interest of researchers, scientists, people in business and market observers.

Katarzyna Szymczyk
Ibrahiem M. M. El Emary

Editors

Katarzyna Szymczyk, PhD, is an Assistant Professor at the Department of Finance, Banking and Accounting at The Faculty of Management, Częstochowa University of Technology in Poland. She graduated from The University of Lodz, The Higher School of Humanities and Economics in Lodz and The University of Warsaw. In 2016, she completed and defended her doctoral thesis titled "Internationalization of Polish enterprises in the Silesian voivodeship and strategic management" and obtained a PhD degree in economics in the discipline of management sciences at Częstochowa University of Technology, Faculty of Management. Her scientific interests focus on issues related to the strategic management, economics, corporate finance, and sustainable development in management and international aspects of entrepreneurship. Since 2017, she has been a member of the Polish Economic Society and The Recruitment Commission at Częstochowa University of Technology, Faculty of Management. She has participated in more than 30 international and state conferences. As a result, she has had numerous publications indexed in the Scopus and Web of Science databases. She has also contributed as a chair of scientific special sessions at the International Conference on Communication, Management and Information Technology (ICCMIT) in Italy (2016), Spain (2018), Austria (2019) and Greece (2020 *online*). In 2016, she took part in the International 2nd Mobility Fair organized by Northeastern Illinois University in Chicago, USA, and the Polish-Hungarian Scientific Symposium on *Contemporary Issues of Enterprise Management in Poland and Hungary* at Szent István University in Gödöllő, Hungary. She is an academic tutor in international finance, monetary policy, banking for entrepreneurs, financial institutions on the capital market or mergers and valuations of enterprises. She has also conducted lectures at Obuda University in Hungary, Valahia University in Targiviste in Romania and Technical University of Madrid in Spain under the Erasmus teachers' mobility program.

Ibrahiem M. M. El Emary, PhD, is a Professor of Computer Science and Systems Information Technology Deanship, King Abdulaziz University, Jeddah, Kingdom of Saudi Arabia. He received his Dr. Eng. Degree in 1998 from the Electronic and Communication Department, Faculty of Engineering, Ain Shams University, Egypt. From 1998 to 2002, he was an Assistant Professor of Computer Sciences in different faculties and institutes in Egypt. From 2002 to 2010, he worked as visiting professor of computer science and engineering in two universities in Jordan. Currently, he is a visiting professor at King Abdulaziz University, Jeddah, Kingdom of Saudi Arabia. His research interests cover various analytic and discrete event simulation techniques, performance evaluation of communication networks, application of intelligent techniques in managing computer communication networks, and performing comparative studies between various policies and strategies of routing, congestion control and subnetting of computer communication networks. He has published more than 200 articles in various refereed international journals and conferences covering computer networks, artificial intelligence, expert systems, software agents, information retrieval, e-learning, case-based reasoning, image processing and pattern recognition, and robotic engineering. Currently, he is also interested in doing scientific research in wireless sensor networks with a view to enhancing its algorithms of congestion control and routing protocols. Also, he has participated in publishing five book chapters in two international books (published by IGI), as well as co-editing two books edited by two international publishers (Springer Verlag and LAP Lampert). He has published 3 books with CRC Press/Taylor & Francis Group and participated as co-editor in publishing a book with John Wiley. He was selected as a member of *Who's Who* from 2015 until 2020.

Contributors

Valentyna Aranchii
Poltava State Agrarian Academy
Poltava, Ukraine

Vitalina Babenko
Department of International E-Commerce
    and Hotel & Restaurant Business
V.N. Karazin Kharkiv National University
Kharkiv, Ukraine

Liudmyla Bezuhla
Department Marketing
Dnipro State Agrarian and Economic
    University
Dnipro, Ukraine

Mariia Danova
Kharkiv Aviation Institute
National Aerospace University
Kharkiv, Ukraine

Anna Derykolenko
Department of Economics,
    Entrepreneurship and Business
Administration, Sumy State University
Sumy, Ukraine

Dmytro Diachkov
Poltava State Agrarian Academy
Poltava, Ukraine

Yamadou Diop
Laboratory of Scientific Engineering of
    Organizations
National School of Business and
    Management
Hassan II University
Casablanca, Morocco

Asmaa Elmortada
Cadi Ayyad University
Sofi, Morocco

Olena Feoktystova
Kharkiv Aviation Institute
National Aerospace University
Kharkiv, Ukraine

Liudmyla Hnatyshyn
Department of Accounting and Taxation
Lviv National Agrarian University
Lviv, Ukraine

Oleksandr Honcharenko
Institute of Information Technologies in
    Economics
Kyiv National Economic University named
    after Vadym Hetman
Kyiv, Ukraine

Yevhen Hrabovskyi
Department of Computer Systems and
    Technologies
Simon Kuznets Kharkiv National University
    of Economics
Kharkiv, Ukraine

Tetiana Ilchenko
Dnipro State Agrarian and Economic
    University
Dnipro, Ukraine

Yasmine Kabli
Management Department
Institut Supèrieur de Commerce et
    d`Administration des Entreprises
    (ISCAE)
Casablanca, Morocco

Marta Kadłubek
Faculty of Management
Czestochowa University of Technology
Czestochowa, Poland

Iryna Koshkalda
Dokuchayev Kharkiv National Agrarian
    University
Ukraine, Kharkiv

Patrycja Krawczyk
Faculty of Management
Czestochowa University of Technology
Czestochowa, Poland

Małgorzata Kuraś
Faculty of Management
Czestochowa University of Technology
Czestochowa, Poland

Piotr Kuraś
Faculty of Management
Czestochowa University of Technology
Czestochowa, Poland

Nataliia Letunovska
Department of Marketing
Sumy State University
Sumy, Ukraine

Viktoriia Makerska
Department of Marketing and Management
    of Innovative Activities
Sumy State University
Sumy, Ukraine

Liudmyla Makieieva
Dokuchayev Kharkiv National Agrarian
    University
Kharkiv, Ukraine

Iryna Markina
Poltava State Agrarian Academy
Poltava, Ukraine

Chams Eddoha Mokhlis
Laboratory of Scientific Engineering of
    Organizations
National School of Business and
    Management
Hassan II University
Casablanca, Morocco

Maryna Nehrey
Department of Economic Cybernetics
National University of Life and
    Environmental Sciences of Ukraine
Kiev, Ukraine

Olena Nihmatova
Lugansk National Agrarian University
Starobelsk, Ukraine

Oksana Prokopyshyn
Department of Accounting and Taxation
Lviv National Agrarian University
Lviv, Ukraine

Sultan Ramazanov
Department of Information Systems in
    Economics
Kyiv National Economic University named
    after Vadym Hetman
Kyiv, Ukraine

Yuliia Romanchenko
Poltava State Agrarian Academy
Poltava, Ukraine

Anna Rosokhata
Department of Marketing
Sumy State University
Sumy, Ukraine

Olena Rybina
Department of Marketing
Head of the Bureau for Quality Assurance
    of Higher Education
Sumy State University
Sumy, Ukraine

Mounia Sbihi
Management Department
National School of Business and
    Management
Hassan II University
Casablanca, Morocco

Ruslan Sheludko
Dokuchayev Kharkiv National Agrarian
    University
Kharkiv, Ukraine

Igor Shostak
Kharkiv Aviation Institute
National Aerospace University
Kharkiv, Ukraine

Nada Soudi
Management Department
Institut Supèrieur de Commerce et
    d`Administration des Entreprises
    (ISCAE)
Casablanca, Morocco

Mykola Syomych
Poltava State Agrarian Academy
Poltava, Ukraine

Aleksandr Teletov
Department of Marketing
Sumy State University
Sumy, Ukraine

Svetlana Teletova
Department of Russian and World
    Literature
Sumy State Pedagogical University named
    after Makarenko
Sumy, Ukraine

Chapter 1

Investments in ICT software and equipment in the process of digital transformation of European Union enterprises

Katarzyna Szymczyk

CONTENT

1.1 INTRODUCTION

In the current reality, companies that implement innovations and modern technological solutions, create internal IT teams and constantly acquire technological competence to respond to market needs faster gain a competitive advantage. Presently, it can be seen that not only organizational culture is important in the company, but also the so-called digital culture, which consists of better and definitely dynamic creation and improvement of technological solutions. The level of digitalization of the company translates into more efficient customer service and facilitates the work of employees. This means that not only employees of IT departments but also senior managers should be able to use and create even simple—but also important for the functioning of the company—applications, IT tools, programs or, for example, reporting solutions. Digitization of manual processes and workflows is an extremely important foundation for the effectiveness of today's enterprises, and in the near future it will affect all spheres of this functioning. In particular, in industrial production the automation of a process is necessary today for the company to be able to keep up with current market trends and competition. It is inevitable this will change the approach to production, in which the use of computer machines, digitized information and automatons will be much more important than human muscles. This is a huge challenge and opportunity for manufacturing companies (Heinze et al., 2018, Reinartz et al., 2019). Digitalization thus brings the need to look for employees with specialized, often narrowed skills such as the ability to learn and manage digital machines and solve complex process problems. This type of qualification will be necessary among the staff for the company to be successful. When it comes to the sphere of customer service, the ability to communicate, build relationships and manage digital solutions will play the biggest role. In the sphere of management and administration of a company, its department or office, the key competences will include the ability to communicate effectively, think critically, possess and use analytical reasoning and practise the skills of effective persuasion.

1.2 METHODOLOGY

The discussion of the topic is based on a comparative analysis of available statistical data, European Commission (EC) reports and scientific literature resources. The author explains the ambiguity of the meaning of digitization, digitalization and digital transformation expressions. She discusses the genesis of digital transformation of enterprises, and compares the access, scope and quality of used technological innovations, ITC solutions, digital software and hardware in companies in various sectors, and of different sizes and scope of functioning.

1.3 DIGITIZATION, DIGITALIZATION AND DIGITAL TRANSFORMATION

The 3Ds (Digitization, Digitalization, and Digital Transformation) are often used incorrectly and interchangeably without proper understanding, especially when one talks about business. First of all, it should be clarified that initially, two decades ago, in the era of the so-called digital age, business used be performed in an analog way, i.e., all information and tasks were done and delivered physically until computers entered business performance. Since then, information has been converted into digital forms (bits and bytes) and business processes became to be digitized, i.e., operated by computers rather than manually (Bounfour, 2016, Vogelsang, 2010, BarNir et al., 2003). So the digitization in business made it faster and more efficient, and today it is hard to imagine an entity using just pen and paper for daily purposes.

Thanks to digitization, business could become digitalized. Digitalization of business should, in fact, be understood as incorporation of digital information and technology, and automation of business processes. Digitalization changes business models, their organization, structure and operations, by using electronic devices, systems, applications and instruments that engender, store or process digitized data. The appearance of computers and introduction of the World Wide Web fundamentally accelerated digitalization of business and changed industry, markets, production, trade and services, life of societies, actions of governments, communication, administration, cultural life and, in general, all aspects of public and private sectors (Collin et al., 2015, Berman and Marshall, 2014, Heinze et al., 2018, Patel & McCarthy, 2000, Roy, 2006, Ramanujam, 2009, Baker, 2014).

Digitization and digitalization are the first and second steps of simplifying business processes and making business performance more effective and satisfactory. These steps are taken within the company. The following step is digital transformation—a holistic transformation of business and its surroundings to focus on the culture and customer experiences. Digital transformation can be understood as a complex process of improving the way of thinking of an enterprise, thanks to which it will be able to create a modern, completely integrated, customer-oriented strategic business. To make this possible, it is crucial to prepare people for the digital transformation. Focusing on customer needs is an essential aspect of this transformation. Understanding the customer's intentions and providing the personalized experience by the company must occur at all times of contact. The data-driven operating model used in the enterprise allows better understanding of the company's condition and increases employee productivity by eliminating the manual business process, and thanks to this the enterprise functions more efficiently, faster and with more agility, and thus is better oriented toward the customer and his/her service. Digital transformation brings a change in the business model focused on providing greater value to the customer (Berman, 2012, Cochoy et al., 2017, Bounfour, 2016, Collin et al., 2015, Vogelsang, 2010). Nowadays, it is

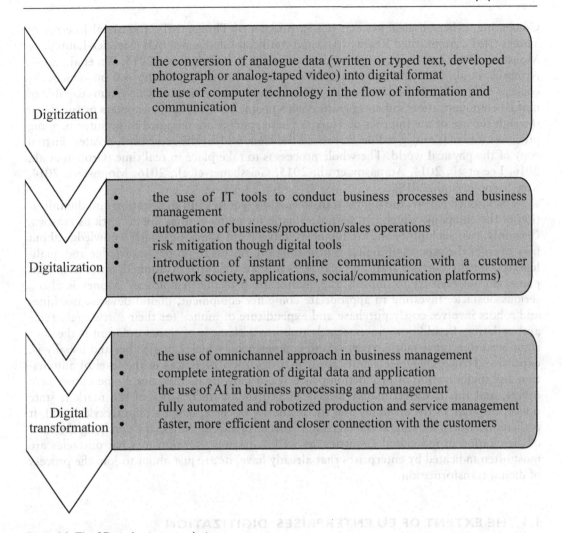

Digitization
- the conversion of analogue data (written or typed text, developed photograph or analog-taped video) into digital format
- the use of computer technology in the flow of information and communication

Digitalization
- the use of IT tools to conduct business processes and business management
- automation of business/production/sales operations
- risk mitigation though digital tools
- introduction of instant online communication with a customer (network society, applications, social/communication platforms)

Digital transformation
- the use of omnichannel approach in business management
- complete integration of digital data and application
- the use of AI in business processing and management
- fully automated and robotized production and service management
- faster, more efficient and closer connection with the customers

Figure 1.1 The 3Ds in business evolution

Source: Own elaboration.

hard to imagine that business could exist without digitization and being digitalized. Often it is claimed business will have to go through the digital transformation in order to be able to exist and function successfully in the digitally connected and integrated network/ecosystem. It should be underlined that digital transformation would not take place (Figure 1.1) without the digitalization of business processes and digitization of company's resources. Nevertheless, not all companies are ready for the third step, many stay behind and some have poor experience even in the first stage of digital evolution due to lack of knowledge, age, scope of business or desire.

Digitalization leads to a digital business, which is essential together with full digitization to start the digital transformation of the society, environment and business itself. We are actually facing the process of creating the global digital ecosystem of business based on the concept of Industry 4.0. The concept intends to reorganize the whole production technologies and processes so that they would become fully automated and include in data exchange such technological innovations as mobile applications, Big Data, Cloud

Computing, cyber-physical systems (CPS), Internet of Things (IoT), Industrial Internet of Things (IIoT), Augmented Reality (AR) and Artificial Intelligence (AI) (Mercier-Laurent & Monsone, 2019, Lasi et al., 2014, Sniderman et al., 2016, Wu et al., 2015, Wu et al., 2014, Armbrust et al., 2010, Bertino et al., 2016, Tan et al., 2019). Industry 4.0 introduces the concept of "intelligent factory", which is basically to use cyber-physical systems capable of mutual communication and co-operation with people (service staff, customers or suppliers) through the use of the Internet of Things. These systems are designed to monitor ongoing processes and make assigned/decentralized decisions and, at the same time, create a virtual copy of the physical world. The whole process is to take place in real time (Gronau et al., 2016, Lee et al., 2014, Atanasov et al., 2015, Geissbauer et al., 2016, Monostori, 2014, Kusi-Sarpong et al., 2018).

As mentioned earlier, the digital transformation requires full digitization and digitalization of the company, which can be problematic for many entities due to various reasons. Certainly, two such problems are financial outlays and a lack of proper knowledge about how to enter the process of digital transformation. Access to proper knowledge and qualified, specifically talented staff and managers in many countries is limited, and often companies do not even try to improve the qualifications of their employees. Money is also a serious obstacle. Investing in appropriate computer equipment, digital devices, machines and robots involves costly purchase and expenditure of money for their software, service and updating. In addition, an extremely important element of transformation is the constant need to acquire more expertise and competences, which can also be, and usually is, expensive. Hence, there are significant disparities and differences in the level of automation and digitalization of production processes in individual countries. Some outperform others, and this is unfortunately largely due to the characteristics of the market, state policy, the state of the economy and the mentality of entrepreneurs (Ślusarczyk, 2018). It is therefore worth looking at the facts and current research results, and verifying the state of digitization in individual countries, as well as paying attention to what obstacles are most often indicated by enterprises that already have, or are just about to join the process of digital transformation.

I.4 THE EXTENT OF EU ENTERPRISES' DIGITIZATION

Commonly, the general level of digitization of individual EU countries is measured by the Digital Economy and Society Index (DESI), which is published by the European Commission. This index quantifies European Union countries by the degree of digitization on the basis of five main DESI dimensions with the weights selected by the user: connectivity, human capital, use of internet, integration of digital technology and digital public services. The dimensions are calculated and presented as the weighted average of them. In 2019 the index showed that EU countries have improved their digital performance in a year's time. The DESI scores are presented in Figure 1.2.

Finland, Sweden, the Netherlands and Denmark obtained the highest scores. These countries are therefore considered to be world leaders in digitization. Countries such as the United Kingdom, Luxembourg, Ireland, Estonia and Belgium can also boast of a high degree of digitization. Such countries as Bulgaria, which is at the end of the ranking with the lowest score, Romania, Greece and Poland or Italy stay far behind the top listed countries (European Commission, 2019a). The degree of digital advancement of companies in the EU is also measured by the Digital Intensity Indicator, which signifies availability at company level of up to 12 different digital technologies. The indicator takes into account factors like internet access for at least 50% of people employed; using the services of ICT

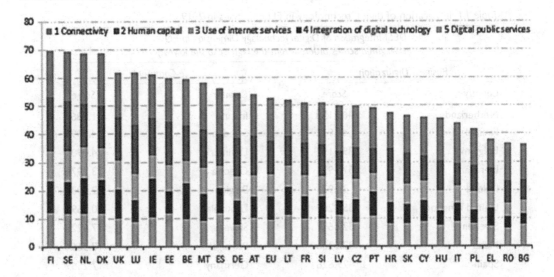

Figure 1.2 DESI index in EU countries in 2019

Source: European Commission, 2019a, The Digital Economy and Society Index (DESI), https://ec.europa.eu/digital-single-market/en/desi.

specialists; high-speed broadband internet (at least 30 Mb/s); mobile devices for at least 20% of workers; owning and running a website, involvement in social media, use of cloud computing, handling e-invoices and their automated processing, e-commerce accounting for at least 1% of total turnover; and online selling for individual clients (B2C) above 10% of total internet sales. Likewise, in examining the level of digitization of enterprises, the Integration of Digital Technology Index is also useful. This index reflects the level of digitization of business and e-commerce (Table 1.1) in EU countries. Nowadays, the importance of incorporating the digital technologies in the functioning of an enterprise is constantly emphasized. The use of digital technologies in the company allows it to increase efficiency; reduce production, service and management costs; and significantly improve the quality of service and communication of the company with clients and contractors.

Furthermore, companies that have decided on e-commerce are more likely to increase sales and attain better, more efficient access to wider markets. As it can be noticed in Table 1.1, e-commerce is best developed in Ireland, Sweden and Denmark (most companies selling online), while in countries such as Bulgaria, Romania and Latvia, e-commerce is still in its infancy, especially in small and medium-sized enterprises. Finns definitely lead the way in implementing e-commerce technologies, followed by the Netherlands. There are also countries where the adoption of e-business technologies is quite slow and they include Bulgaria, Hungary, Romania, Poland and Latvia. The level of digitization of enterprises in EU countries is also reflected in data regarding the number of employees using computers with internet access at work (Figure 1.3).

According to the gathered results, in 2019, Scandinavian enterprises indicated the highest degree of digitization. In Sweden, 82% of employees use computers and the internet in daily business activity, 77% in Denmark and 74% in Finland. A high percentage of employees using computers and the internet was also recorded in the Netherlands (69%), France (62%), the United Kingdom (61%), Belgium (59%) and Germany (59%). Less than 45%, but no more than 40% of EU company employees use computers and the internet at work in countries such as Latvia, Slovakia, Cyprus, Poland and Hungary. In countries like Greece

Table 1.1 Integration of digital technology in EU countries in 2019

DESI Integration of Digital Technology Dimension in EU (in weighted scores ordered from the highest to the lowest)			
Business Digitization		e-Commerce	
Country	Score	Country	Score
Netherlands	46.2158	Ireland	31.7860
Finland	41.932	Sweden	24.5999
Belgium	39.4157	Denmark	24.0909
Denmark	37.1975	Czechia	23.2974
Ireland	36.924	Belgium	22.6934
United Kingdom	35.1267	Lithuania	20.6694
Sweden	32.6607	Slovenia	17.6220
Malta	32.6266	Portugal	17.3664
Spain	29.626	Germany	17.2569
Lithuania	29.0163	United Kingdom	16.8330
Luxembourg	28.5425	Netherlands	16.7862
Cyprus	26.2144	Finland	16.4025
France	26.1419	Malta	16.0588
Portugal	25.4594	Croatia	16.0509
Germany	24.6407	Estonia	15.7247
Estonia	23.4722	Austria	15.4751
Greece	23.3485	Spain	15.0183
Austria	22.6832	France	14.5190
Croatia	22.5128	Slovakia	13.4020
Slovenia	22.4683	Cyprus	11.7522
Italy	21.9975	Hungary	11.2091
Slovakia	21.0583	Italy	10.2756
Czechia	19.1983	Luxembourg	10.1764
Latvia	17.0206	Poland	9.78100
Poland	15.0045	Greece	9.44451
Romania	14.235	Latvia	8.83581
Hungary	14.2163	Romania	6.23195
Bulgaria	13.2805	Bulgaria	4.84688
European Union	25.7941	European Union	15.2584

Source: Own elaboration based on European Commission, 2019b, https://digital-agenda-data.eu/charts/
desi-components#chart={%22indicator%22:%22desi_4_idt%22,%22breakdown-group%22:%
22desi_4_idt%22,%22unit-measure%22:%22pc_desi_4_idt%22,%22time-period%22:%222019%
22} [Note: Calculated as the weighted average of the two sub-dimensions: business digitization
(60%) and e-commerce (40%)].

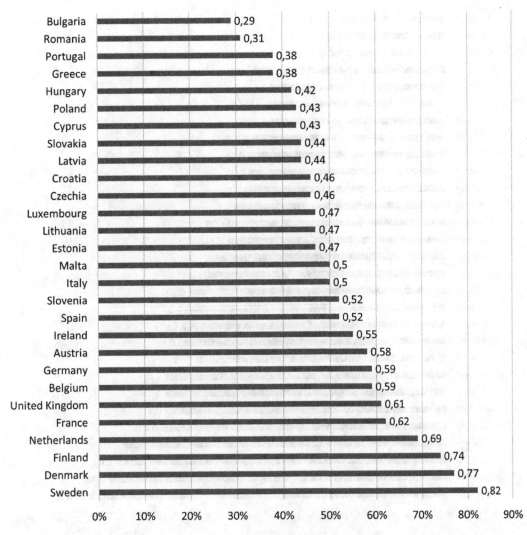

Figure 1.3 Use of computers and the internet by employees in EU enterprises in 2019. (Note: All enterprises, without financial sector [10 persons employed or more)].

Source: Own elaboration based on Eurostat 2019f, https://digital-agenda-data.eu/charts/desi-components#chart={%22indicator%22:%22desi_2b1_ictspec%22,%22breakdown-group%22:%22total%22,%22unit-measure%22:%22pc_ind_emp%22,%22time-period%22:%222019%22}

and Portugal this figure is 38%, and in Romania 31%. The fewest employees, only 29%, use computer equipment and the internet in Bulgaria.

1.5 THE STATE OF DIGITALIZATION OF BUSINESS IN EU COUNTRIES

Considering the level of digitalization of business, DESI calculates such aspects as electronic information sharing and the use of social media and big data, as well as the implementation of cloud computing and the use of the cloud in business performance. In Figure 1.4, there

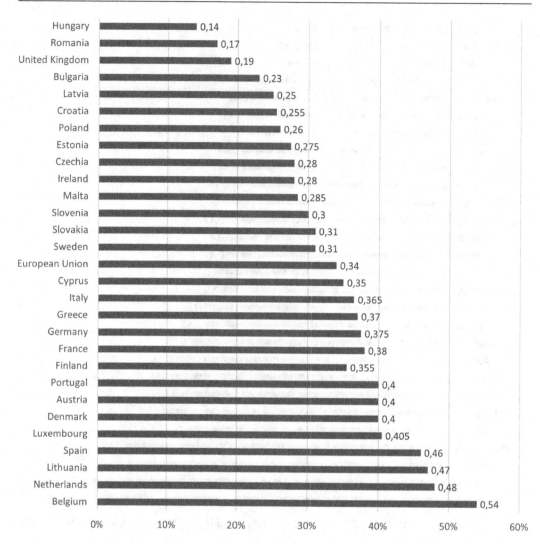

Figure 1.4 Electronic information sharing in business in EU countries in 2019. (Note: Enterprises with 10 or more persons employed. All manufacturing and service sectors, excluding the financial sector. Data rounded to full values).

Source: Own elaboration based on Eurostat (2019e) - Community survey on ICT usage and eCommerce in enterprises (E_ERP1), https://digital-agenda-data.eu/charts/ desi-components#chart={%22indicator%22:%22desi_4a1_eis%22,%22breakdown-group% 22:%22total%22,%22unit-measure%22:%22pc_ent%22,%22time-period%22:%222019%22}

is the percentage of enterprises that use an ERP (enterprise resource planning) software package and they share information amongst operational sections like accounting, planning, production and marketing. The data shows that companies in Belgium (more than a half of companies) or the Netherlands (about 48%) are the leaders in this area, similarly in Lithuania (about 48%) and Spain (48% of companies).

The percentage of companies focused on sharing information through digital tools is very low in Hungary (only 14% of entities in comparison to 54% in Belgium), Romania

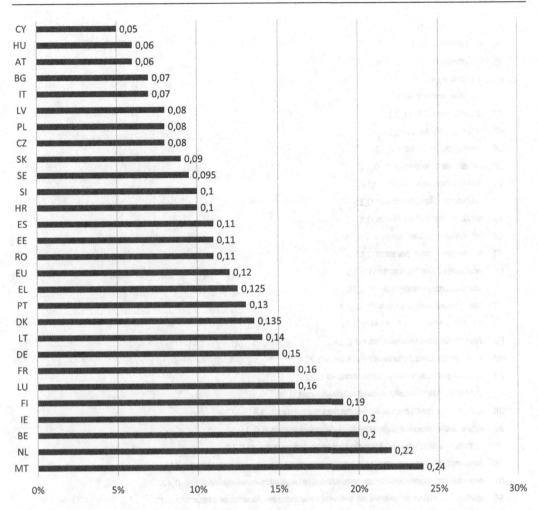

Figure 1.5 Big data analyzed by EU enterprises in 2019. (Note: Enterprises with 10 or more persons employed. All manufacturing and service sectors, excluding the financial sector. Data rounded to full values).

Source: Own elaboration based on Eurostat (2019d) - Community survey on ICT usage and eCommerce in enterprises (E_BD),https://digital-agenda-data.eu/charts/desi-components# chart={%22indicator%22:%22desi_4a3_bigdat%22,%22breakdown-group%22:% 22total%22,%22unit-measure%22:%22pc_ent%22,%22time-period%22:%222019%22}

and Bulgaria, but also in the UK (less than 20%) and Latvia (1/4 of companies use ERP). In modern technologically developed enterprises, analyzing big data should be considered as useful and beneficial as it allows analyzing in large volumes the results from data of various format types. Figure 1.5 presents the results of examining the analyzing the big data from any data source by EU companies.

According to the gathered data, Malta has the biggest number of companies that analyze big data in their business processes (almost a quarter of entities). Also, a high percentage of companies in Belgium and the Netherlands include big data analyses in their operations. Bulgaria, Austria, Hungary and Cyprus are the last in this ranking. Nearly 5% of companies in Cyprus and just over 6% of Hungarian, Austrian and Bulgarian entities analyze

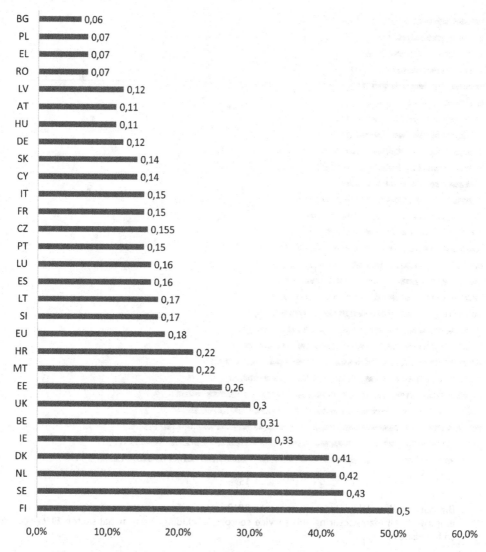

Figure 1.6 Cloud computing in EU enterprises in 2019. (Note: Enterprises with 10 or more persons employed. All manufacturing and service sectors, excluding the financial sector. Data rounded to full values).

Source: Own elaboration based on Eurostat (2019e) - Community survey on ICT usage and eCommerce in enterprises, https://digital-agenda-data.eu/charts/desi-components#chart= {%22indicator%22:%22desi_4a4_cloud%22,%22breakdown-group%22:%22total%22,%22unit-measure%22:%22pc_ent%22,%22time-period%22:%222019%22}

big data. In terms of digital transformation, it is worth mentioning the scores of the DESI index in EU enterprises regarding cloud computing services. DESI checked the use of hosting of the enterprise's database, accounting software applications, CRM software and computing power (Figure 1.6).

Among the surveyed EU companies, this time the best results belong to Finish companies. More than 50% of them rely on cloud computing. Relatively high scores have been achieved by Swedish (almost 44%), Dutch (nearly 42%), Danish (almost 41%), Irish (almost 33%) and Belgian (just above 31%) companies. The digital transformation assumes the change of attitude towards customer service. Therefore, the digital business should include implementing different types of social media like social networks, enterprise's (micro)blog, multimedia content sharing websites, or wiki-based knowledge sharing tools. That may cause certain problems if one takes into account the fact that offering social media means, for the enterprise, acquiring a user profile, an account and permission to use the media by purchasing a usually required user license. The DESI report shows that more or less 43% of British companies and almost 40% of companies in the Netherlands include using social media in their business performance. Interestingly, Cyprus, which was at the end of the big data ranking in incorporating social media in business, remains at the third position among all EU countries with the score of nearly 37% of entities. More than a quarter of companies use social media in Ireland (36%), Denmark and Finland (approx. 29%), Spain (nearly 28%), Malta (26%), and Sweden (approx. 25%). Social media are rather unpopular in business activity in eastern parts of the EU. Less than 13% of companies in Latvia use social media and, approximately, 10% in Poland, and more or less 9% in Romania and Bulgaria (Eurostat, 2019b).

1.6 TOWARDS DIGITAL TRANSFORMATION

Generally in the EU, the countries which are digitally developed the most are the Nordic ones, i.e., Finland, Sweden and Denmark. Also digitally competitive are the Netherlands, the UK, Luxembourg, Ireland and Estonia. Ireland is a leader in business digital development and e-commerce. As well, the Netherlands, Belgium and Denmark have achieved high scores. The least technologically advanced with a low integration of digital technology in business countries are Bulgaria, Romania, Poland and Hungary. E-business technologies that include electronic information sharing, social media, analysis of big data and cloud computing solutions are best developed the Netherlands, Finland and Belgium, whereas such countries like Bulgaria, Hungary, Romania, Poland and Latvia still have plenty work to do in this matter (Chakravorti & Chaturvedi, 2019, European Commission, 2019a). According to the SpotData report (2018), the great financial crisis has contributed to the overall decline in investment in EU countries, but despite this, expenditure on digital assets such as software and ICT equipment has increased by 36% and hardware by 22%. Quoting directly the authors of the report, "digitization is the main megatrend of modern times". However, the use of digital technologies in European enterprises is still relatively low in many countries. The differences are noticeable in the central part of the EU. While in Germany almost 40% of companies use digital technologies in business such as enterprise resource planning (ERP) system, only one in four companies in neighbouring Poland already has such a system (SpotData, 2018).

Digital transformation, in terms of the concept of Industry 4.0, assumes the automation of industrial processes based on high technology solutions. Mainly this involves the introduction of robots and 3D printers in manufacturing processes and management of enterprises. Research indicates that some countries are definitely leading and following the prevailing trend, but there are also those that are still based on traditional production methods and management systems. Regarding the use of 3D printing in EU enterprises (Figure 1.7), one third of enterprises in the EU use 3D printing in the production processes of goods. More than half of companies in the Czech Republic (52%) and almost a half (49%) in Denmark and Cyprus use this technology to facilitate production. Also Hungary (48%) and Estonia (44%) benefit from 3D printing.

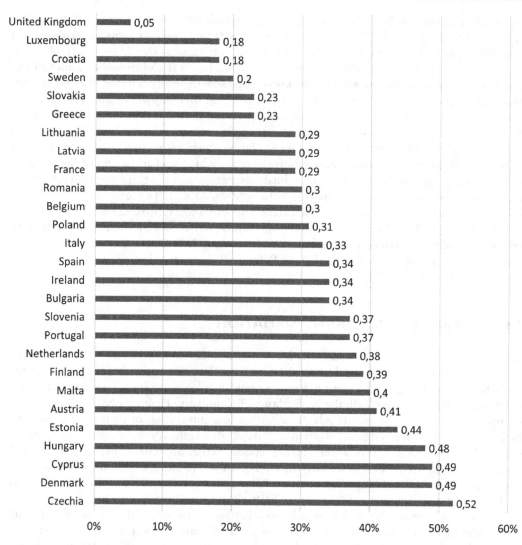

Figure 1.7 Percentage of EU enterprises using 3D printing in 2018. (Note: All enterprises, without financial sector (10 persons employed or more). No data available for Germany).

Source: Own elaboration based on Eurostat (2019a), https://appsso.eurostat.ec.europa.eu/ nui/submitViewTableAction.do

Surprisingly, Sweden, which is regarded as one of the leading countries in digital transformation, recorded in 2018 that only 20% of companies rely on 3D printing in industry. Less than 20% of companies use 3D printing in Croatia and Luxembourg (18%) and a negligible number of UK (5%) entities implemented this innovation in industry. Regarding the use of robots in industry, it is worth analyzing the available data by grouping enterprises by their size. In general, it can be assumed that large enterprises involved in mass production invest the most in robotics. However, in the process of digital transformation, all enterprises, including micro and small, which want to keep up with the competition must adapt to the

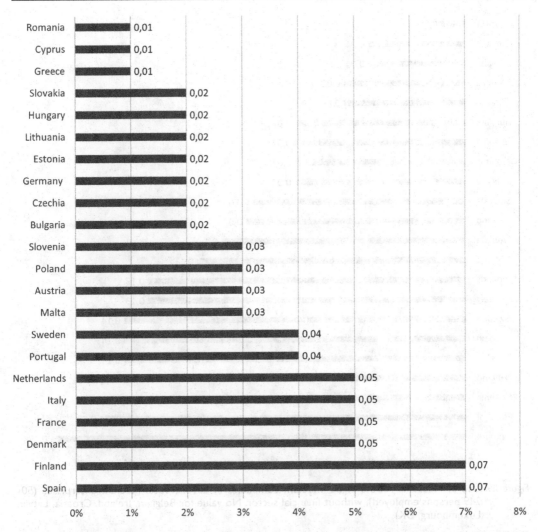

Figure 1.8 Use of industrial robots in EU small companies in 2018. (Note: Small enterprises (10–49 persons employed), without financial sector. No value for Belgium, Ireland, Croatia, Latvia, Luxembourg, UK).

Source: Own elaboration based on Eurostat (2019a), https://appsso.eurostat.ec.europa.eu/ nui/submitViewTableAction.do

prevailing Industry 4.0 trend. As the data shows (Figure 1.8), small companies use industrial robots, although the number is rather small.

The largest number of small companies that use industrial robots are in Spain and Finland (7%). Denmark, France, Italy and the Netherlands have 5% of such companies. Only 2% of enterprises used robots in industry in Bulgaria, the Czech Republic, Germany, Estonia, Lithuania, Hungary and Slovakia. Only 1% of small entities use robots in Greece, Cyprus and Romania (Eurostat, 2019). In the case of medium enterprises (Figure 1.9), Eurostat data from 2018 show that 17% of companies in Denmark use industrial robots, and 15% in Portugal, Slovenia and Finland.

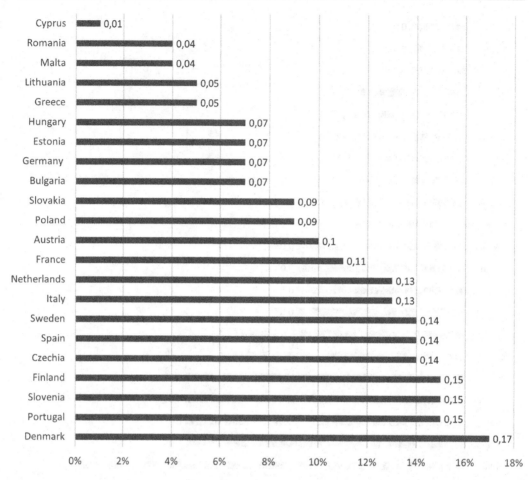

Figure 1.9 Use of industrial robots in EU medium companies in 2018. (Note: Medium enterprises (50-249 persons employed), without financial sector. No value for Belgium, Ireland, Croatia, Latvia, Luxembourg, UK).

Source: Own elaboration based on Eurostat (2019a), https://appsso.eurostat.ec.europa.eu/nui/submitViewTableAction.do

At the end of the ranking there are countries in which less than 10% of business entities use robots in industry. Nine percent of medium enterprises use industry robots in Poland and Slovakia. Bulgaria, Germany, Estonia and Hungary have 7% of such companies, Greece and Lithuania have 5%, and 4% of companies use robots in Malta and Romania. The last in the ranking is Cyprus with 1% of medium companies using industrial robots (Eurostat, 2019a). The data (Figure 1.10) is significantly different in case of large enterprises in EU.

It can be clearly seen that large enterprises are much more willing to invest in industrial robots. This probably results from obvious production needs, but certainly these types of entities have greater opportunities, especially financial ones, to technologically modernize their factories. Robotics in industry can be seen in nearly one third of large enterprises in Slovenia (32%) and the Czech Republic (30%). Good results in digital transformation and following the Industry 4.0 trend can also be seen in Finland, where 28% of large companies use robots in industry, as well as in Austria and Sweden which have 27% of such entities.

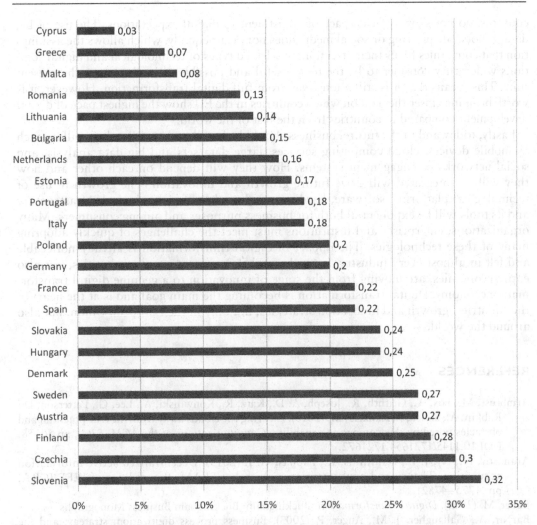

Figure 1.10 Use of industrial robots in EU large companies in 2018. (Note: Large enterprises (250 persons employed or more), without financial sector. No value for Belgium, Ireland, Croatia, Latvia, Luxembourg, UK).

Source: Own elaboration based on Eurostat (2019a), https://appsso.eurostat.ec.europa.eu/nui/submitViewTableAction.do

Less than 20% but more than 10% of large enterprises use industrial robots in Italy and Portugal (18%), Estonia (17%), the Netherlands (16%), Bulgaria (15%), Lithuania (14%) and Romania (13%). Countries in which the use of robots for industrial purposes is below 10% are Malta (8%), Greece (7%) and Cyprus (3%) (Eurostat, 2019a).

1.7 CONCLUSIONS

The level of digitization and digitalization in enterprises of the European Union countries is very diverse. Countries considered to be the most technologically advanced are primarily the countries of the western part of the EU and Scandinavia. However, in some respects, these countries do not show an even pace of adjustment to digital expectations. The use of big data, robots, 3D printing or social media does not occur equally, which allows the assumption that companies focus their attention on selected types of technological and digital solutions which they consider to be the most useful and possible to implement at the present time. This means that it is still a long way from full digital transformation. However, it is worth bringing closer the data on which countries in the EU show the highest pace of digital development compared to countries from the rest of the world.

Lastly, today and in the future, business should be based on key technology pillars such as mobile devices, cloud computing services, large data sets and big data analysis, and social networks or engagement systems. How they will depend on each other and how they will be integrated will drive future growth and innovation. The growth in use of technological platforms, software, hardware and models of technological infrastructure and its tools will be exponential both for business purposes and among consumers. Many organizations, enterprises and institutions must meet the challenges of quickly adopting many of these technologies. The impact of digital transformation is already noticeable and felt in almost every industry. It can be said that current economic entities, but also entire economies, are moving from the stage of innovation to a genuine digital transformation economy. Digital transformation is becoming the main goal and is at the heart of the countries' growth and innovation strategies, not only in the European Union, but also around the world.

REFERENCES

Armbrust, M., Fox, A., Griffith, R., Joseph, A. D., Katz, R., Konwinski, A., Lee, G., Patterson, D., Rabkin, A., Stoica, I., Zaharia, M. (2010). Clearing the clouds away from the true potential and obstacles posed by this computing capability. *Communications of the ACM, 53(4)*, pp 50–58. DOI:10.1145/1721654.1721672.

Atanasov, N., Ny, J. L., Daniilidis, K., Pappas, G. J. (2015). Decentralized active information acquisition: Theory and application to multi-robot SLAM. Proceedings of IEEE ICRA, pp. 4775–4782.

Baker, M. (2014). *Digital Transformation.* Buckingham: Buckingham Business Monographs.

BarNir, A., Gallaugher, J. M., Auger, P. (2003). Business process digitization, strategy, and the impact of firm age and size: the case of the magazine publishing industry. *Journal of Business Venturing, 18*, pp. 789–814.

Berman, S. J. (2012). Digital transformation: opportunities to create new business models. *Strategy & Leadership, 40(2)*, pp. 16–24.

Berman, S., Marshall, A. (2014). The next digital transformation: from an individual centered to an everyone-to-everyone economy. *Strategy & Leadership, 42(5)*, pp. 9–17.

Bertino, E., Choo. K-K. R., Georgakopolous, D., Nepal, S. (2016). Internet of things (IoT): Smart and secure service delivery. *ACM Transactions on Internet Technology, 16(4)*, pp. 1–7. DOI: http://dx.doi.org/10.1145/3013520.

Bounfour, A. (2016). *Digital Futures, Digital Transformation. Progress in IS.* Cham: Springer International Publishing.

Chakravorti, B., Chaturvedi, R. S. (2019). Ranking 42 Countries by Ease of Doing Digital Business. *Harvard Business Review.* Retrieved from https://hbr.org/2019/09/ranking-42-countries-by-ease-of-doing-digital-business (Access: 21.02.2020).

Cochoy, F., Hagberg, J., Petersson McIntyre, M., Sörum, N. (2017). *Digitalizing Consumption. How devices shape consumer culture.* Abingdon: Routledge.

Collin, J., Hiekkanen, K., Korhonen, J. J., Halén, M., Itälä, T., Helenius, M. (2015). *IT Leadership in Transition-The Impact of Digitalization on Finnish Organizations. Research report.* Espoo: Aalto University, Department of Computer Science.

European Commission (2019a). *The Digital Economy and Society Index (DESI)*. Retrieved from https://ec.europa.eu/digital-single-market/en/desi (Access: 21.02.2020).

European Commission (2019b). *Integration of Digital Technology*. Retrieved from https://digital-agenda-data.eu/charts/desi-components#chart={%22indicator%22:%22desi_4_idt%22,%22breakdown-group%22:%22desi_4_idt%22,%22unit-measure%22:%22pc_desi_4_idt%22,%22time-period%22:%222019%22} (Access: 19.02.2020).

Eurostat (2019a). *3D printing and robotics*. Retrieved from https://appsso.eurostat.ec.europa.eu/nui/submitViewTableAction.do (Access:19.02.2020).

Eurostat (2019b). *Community survey on ICT usage and eCommerce in Enterprises (E_SM1_GE2)*. Retrieved from https://digital-agenda-data.eu/charts/desi-components#chart={%22indicator%22:%22desi_4a2_socmed%22,%22breakdown-group%22:%22total%22,%22unit-measure%22:%22pc_ent%22,%22time-period%22:%222019%22} (Access: 21.02.2020).

Eurostat (2019c). *Community survey on ICT usage and eCommerce in Enterprises*. Retrieved from https://digital-agenda-data.eu/charts/desi-components#chart={%22indicator%22:%22desi_4a4_cloud%22,%22breakdown-group%22:%22total%22,%22unit-measure%22:%22pc_ent%22,%22time-period%22:%222019%22} (Access: 21.02.2020).

Eurostat (2019d). *Community survey on ICT usage and eCommerce in Enterprises (E_BD)*. Retrieved fromhttps://digital-agenda-data.eu/charts/desi-components#chart={%22indicator%22:%22desi_4a3_bigdat%22,%22breakdown-group%22:%22total%22,%22unit-measure%22:%22pc_ent%22,%22time-period%22:%222019%22} (Access: 21.02.2020).

Eurostat (2019e). *Community survey on ICT usage and eCommerce in Enterprises (E_ERP1)*. Retrieved from https://digital-agenda-data.eu/charts/desi-components#chart={%22indicator%22:%22desi_4a1_eis%22,%22breakdown-group%22:%22total%22,%22unit-measure%22:%22pc_ent%22,%22time-period%22:%222019%22} (Access: 21.02.2020).

Eurostat (2019f). *Use of computers and the internet by employees*. Retrieved from https://digital-agenda-data.eu/charts/desi-components#chart={%22indicator%22:%22desi_2b1_ictspec%22,%22breakdown-group%22:%22total%22,%22unit-measure%22:%22pc_ind_emp%22,%22time-period%22:%222019%22} (Access: 19.02.2020).

Geissbauer, R., Vedso, J., Schrauf, S. (2016). *Industry 4.0: Building the Digital Enterprise*. 2016 Global Industry 4.0 Survey. What We Mean by Industry 4.0/Survey Key Findings/Blueprint for Digital Success. Retrieved from https://www.pwc.com/gx/en/industries/industries-4.0/landing-page/industry-4.0-building-your-digital-enterprise-april-2016.pdf (Access: 21.02.2020).

Gronau, N., Grum, M., Bender, B. (2016). *Determining the optimal level of autonomy in cyber-physical production systems*. Proceeding of Int. Conference on Industrial Informatics (INDIN), pp. 1293–1299. DOI: 10.1109/INDIN.2016.7819367.

Heinze, A., Griffiths, M., Fenton, A., Fletcher, G. (2018). Knowledge exchange partnership leads to digital transformation at Hydro-X Water Treatment, Ltd. *Global Business and Organizational Excellence*, 37(4), pp. 6–13.

Kusi-Sarpong, S., Moktadir, A., Ali, S. M., Shaikh, A. A. (2018). Assessing challenges for implementing Industry 4.0: Implications for process safety and environmental protection. *Process Safety and Environmental Protection*, 117, pp. 730–741.

Lasi, H., Kemper, H. G, Fettke, P., Feld, T., Hoffmann, M. (2014). Industry 4.0. *Business & Information Systems Engineering*, 4(6), pp. 239–242.

Lee, J., Bagheri, B., Kao, H-A. (2014). *Recent Advances and Trends of Cyber-Physical Systems and Big Data Analytics in Industrial Informatics*. Proceeding of Int. Conference on Industrial Informatics (INDIN). DOI: 10.13140/2.1.1464.1920.

Mercier-Laurent, E., Monsone, C. R. (2019). *Ecosystems of Industry 4.0: Combining Technology and Human Power*. Proceedings of the 11th International Conference on Management of Digital EcoSystems (MEDES '19), pp. 115-119, New York: Association for Computing Machinery. DOI: https://doi.org/10.1145/3297662.3365793.

Monostori, L. (2014). Cyber-physical production systems: Roots, expectations and R&D challenges. *Procedia CIRP*, 17, pp. 9–13.

Patel, K., McCarthy, M. P. (2000). *Digital transformation: the essentials of e-business leadership*. New York: McGraw-Hill.

Ramanujam, R. C. (2009). *Mass communication and its digital transformation*. New Delhi: A P H Publishing.

Reinartz, W., Wieg, N., Imschloss, M. (2019). The impact of digital transformation on the retailing value chain. *International Journal of Research in Marketing, 36(3)*, pp. 350–366. DOI: https://doi.org/10.1016/j.ijresmar.2018.12.002.

Roy, J. (2006). *E-government in Canada: Transformation for the Digital Age*. Ottawa: University of Ottawa Press.

Ślusarczyk, B. (2018). Industry 4.0 – Are We Ready? *Polish Journal of Management Studies, 17(1)*, pp. 232–247.

Sniderman, B., Mahto, M., Cotteleer, M. J. (2016). *Industry 4.0 and manufacturing ecosystems, Exploring the world of connected enterprises*. Deloitte, Retrieved from https://www2.deloitte.com/content/dam/insights/us/articles/manufacturing-ecosystems-exploring-world-connected-enterprises/DUP_2898_Industry4.0ManufacturingEcosystems.pdf (Access: 21.02.2020).

SpotData (2018). *Cyfryzacja to więcej niż technologia*. Retrieved from https://spotdata.pl/research/download/63 (Access: 19.02.2020).

Tan, Y., Yang, W., Yoshida, K., Takakuwa, S. (2019). Application of IoT-Aided Simulation to Manufacturing Systems in Cyber-Physical System. *Machines, 7(2)*. DOI: https://doi.org/10.3390/machines7010002.

Vogelsang, M. (2010). *Digitalization in Open Economies, Contributions to Economics*. Heidelberg: Physica-Verlag HD.

Wu, D., Rosen, D. W., Schaefer, D. (2014). Cloud-Based Design and Manufacturing: Status and Promise. In: D. Schaefer (ed.), *Cloud-Based Design and Manufacturing: A Service-Oriented Product Development Paradigm for the 21st Century*, London: Springer, pp.1–24.

Wu, D., Rosen, D. W., Wang, L., Schaefer, D. (2015). Cloud-based design and manufacturing: A new paradigm in digital manufacturing and design innovation. *Computer-Aided Design, 59*, pp. 1–14. DOI: https://doi.org/10.1016/j.cad.2014.07.006.

Chapter 2

The use of information and communication technologies in small and medium-sized enterprises in Poland

Patrycja Krawczyk

CONTENTS

2.1 INTRODUCTION

Information and communication theories have become a major driver of the economic development of countries in a global world. The information component plays a key role in building the competitive potential of countries and the development of international relations (Petkova et al., 2019). The rapid worldwide progress of Information and Communication Technologies (ICT) in the last three decades has attracted increasing attention from many economists and researchers who have focused on studying the impact of ICT diffusion on business (Bahrini & Qaffas, 2019).

After 1989, Poland transformed its economy from being centrally planned to a market economy. It recovered from a severe economic slowdown in the first half of the 1990s, becoming one of the best-performing countries in the group of post-communist economies. However, as all Central and Eastern European (CEE) countries are at the periphery of the EU economic core. Arendt and Garbowski (2019) devoted themselves to the role of ICT in explaining the innovativeness of Polish enterprises.

Small and medium enterprises (SMEs) are the most numerous group of entities in the contemporary market economy. Their operation is of great significance to owners, employees, local communities and—primarily—for the macroeconomic growth of the country. The problems and challenges they face have been most frequently resolved intuitively, using the achievements of management sciences only to a very minor extent.

Many of those managing SMEs do not have formal, scientific knowledge of finance management, which is necessary to conduct balanced economic activity (Lee, 2012). The specifics of the operation of SMEs, therefore, should be taken into account when designing management mechanisms. The tool that is financial analysis is not reserved only for large economic entities. It does, however, need to be adapted to the size of the entities, due to the limited scope of information provided in their financial reports (Krawczyk & Kokot-Stępień, 2017). There presently exists a range of management techniques that can be efficiently used by small and medium entities. A good way to design and implement them is to confer with a person already experienced in their establishment (Krawczyk, 2017b). ICT components can be introduced into SME structures in a similar manner. Such enterprises should pick those components that are useful to them and that allow further development.

The usage of ICT systems provides enterprises with many diverse advantages, including such fundamentals as more efficient achievement of business objectives, systemic solutions in operations and more efficient reactions to various crises. Many ICT tools can be efficiently used by small and medium entities.

Recent years have brought about an intensification of discourse concerning the development of the SME sector. This issue has been the subject of scientific analyses in various fields and dimensions. This proves that SMEs are of enormous significance for the operation of the contemporary economic market. Digital technologies allow SMEs to improve market intelligence and to access global markets and knowledge networks at relatively low cost. The digital transition facilitates the emergence of "born global" small businesses and provides new opportunities for SMEs to enhance their competitiveness in local and global markets through product or service innovation and improved production processes. Furthermore, Big Data and data analytics provide a wide range of opportunities for SMEs, enabling a better understanding (OECD, 2018). These conclusions suggest the leading question: What is the level of usage of ICT at small and medium enterprises in Poland?

The presented issue shall be verified through the following detailed research inquiries:

- What is the significance of the small and medium enterprise sector for the Polish economy?
- What is the level of use of ICT in Poland compared to other countries?
- Is the level of use of ICT dependent on the enterprise size?
- Do small and medium enterprises in Poland use ICT to the same extent as large ones do?

The following issues related to information and communication technologies will be analysed in detail:

- Computer access within an enterprise
- Internet access
- Computer use by employees
- Access to ICT specialists
- ICT training
- Websites
- Social media
- Cloud computing
- E-invoicing
- Industrial and service robot usage
- ICT security
- Electronic sales
- E-government
- ICT investments
- Use of digital intensity index

The analysis shall be based upon a critical review of the literature and branch-specific reports, as well as the writer's experience, thoughts and observations of practice.

2.2 REVIEW OF THE LITERATURE

In recent years, we have seen increased interest in topics relating to small and medium-sized enterprises. Many scientists from diverse fields of the social sciences have been undertaking research in this area. A better understanding of the context of small businesses, given their less ready access to capital injections, contributes to new perspectives on better development and strengthening at both the national and international levels for these companies (Ferreira de Lara & Neves Guimarães, 2014).

Information and communication technologies are tools used in many areas, including scientific research. Most scientists treat them as basic equipment and use them without even wondering about their significance for their work. Many discuss the significance of ICT from the point of view of their field of research, e.g., engineering, medicine or economics. Regarding the growing importance of ICT and the way it is transforming the world, many academicians and researchers have focused on studying the impact of ICT on economic growth at the industry level, at the national level and between countries (Bahrini & Qaffas, 2019).

The evolution of ICT has been shaped by both innovational complementarities and the sequential appearance of imbalances that have focused innovation activity in discrete phases of industrial development. J. Taalbi draws very important conclusions from the point of view of the importance of SMAE for ICT development. He states that the actors behind ICT innovation have changed from large incumbents with experience in the traditional electrical sector to small entrant firms observing market niches and new opportunities, which stresses the disruptive impact of general-purpose technologies (GPTs) on industrial structure (Taalbi, 2019).

Studies are emerging that link ICT with SMEs. Research on the relationship between IT reliability and the innovation level of organizations has been carried out by Tworek, Walecka-Jankowska, and Zgrzywa-Ziemak (2019). Their empirical analysis shows that there is a relation between IT reliability and the level of innovation. Moreover, information reliability appears as a factor that may influence the organization's ability to create innovations. Service reliability proves to correlate with innovation level, as well, providing additional conclusions that support the realization that service is an important feature. This may also influence employees' ability to employ IT appropriately and efficiently, thereby supporting the generation of innovation (Tworek et al., 2019).

A study by Onyinyi and Kaberuka (2019) examined the moderating role of ICT fusion between resource transformation capabilities and quality management practices among SMEs. They conclude that a firm's efforts to convert resources into inimitable assets have an influence on its ability to deliver quality products that meet customer expectations through creative thinking (Onyinyi & Kaberuka, 2019).

Some studies focus on specific areas of ICT from the point of view of SMEs. One of them explores the process of cloud computing adoption within Romanian small and medium-sized enterprises. Taking into account the findings of this investigation, know-how and experience in cloud computing represents the main components influencing the spreading of cloud computing among Romanian small and medium businesses. Cloud-providing companies can make use of the many social networking companies like Facebook, LinkedIn, Instagram and Twitter to make SMEs more aware about the benefits of cloud computing (Dincă et al., 2019).

Information and communication technologies are effective tools for collecting, storing, processing, sending and presenting information. Unfortunately, entrepreneurs sometimes perceive implementing modern IT solutions as a cost and do not notice that they can be an effective tool to facilitate business management. Other significant barriers in the implementation of new technologies are the high costs of the necessary infrastructure and some applications, as well as security concerns about data (Petryczka, 2017).

Information and Communication Technology can make SMEs capable of capturing potential future markets. Studies show how the use of ICT affects firms' agility and ends in a competitive advantage. ICT capability also affects the firms' competitive agility indirectly by mediating their business agility. If small firms would like to enhance their supply chains and customer relationship management, they should adopt ICT as a tool to transform their businesses. This transformation improves small firms' competitiveness levels because it allows them to manage all their customers (Qosasi et al., 2019).

2.3 A DIAGNOSIS OF THE SITUATION OF SMEs IN POLAND

Reflecting the position of SMEs within the economy is the volume of diverse studies, including scientific and academic ones, concerning this topic. Just as with other issues, we are still missing a clear definition and classification criteria. The key importance of SMEs is also stressed in strategic documents of the European Union, as they make up over 90% of all economic entities; they are the largest employer within the EU economy and most strongly contribute to its development. The qualification criteria for entities within the SME sector were described by the European Commission by way of employment and financial ceilings [Commission Regulation (EU) No 651/2014 of 17 June 2014 (Annex 1)]:

- Medium enterprises include those that employ fewer than 250 people and whose annual turnover does not exceed 50 million euros, or whose annual balance amount does not exceed 43 million euros.
- A small enterprise is defined as an enterprise employing fewer than 50 persons and the annual turnover or annual balance amount of which does not exceed ten million euros.
- A microenterprise is defined as an enterprise employing less than ten persons, with its annual turnover or annual balance sheet sum not exceeding two million euros.

Within the scope of Polish law, a minor entrepreneurship is deemed to be a natural or legal entity that, throughout the previous two financial years, employed fewer than 50 people and achieved a net annual revenue from the sale of goods, services and financial transactions not exceeding the equivalent of ten million euros in PLN. A medium-sized enterprise is considered by law to be any employing up to 250 people over the scope of at least two years, and that achieved annual revenue from sales, services and financial transactions not exceeding the equivalent of 50 million euros in PLN, or whose total assets on the final balance sheet for one of these years did not exceed the equivalent of 43 million euros in PLN (Ustawa z dnia 2 lipca 2004 r. o swobodzie działalności gospodarczej, Dz.U. 2004 nr 173 poz. 1807).

Enterprises within the SME sector, despite their ability to adapt more efficiently and quickly than large economic entities to changing ambient conditions, are exposed to a range of difficulties. They frequently struggle with access to capital and external sources of financing, information and infrastructure, and modern technologies and innovations, particularly early on in their development. Management of small and medium-sized enterprises is characterized by certain specifics that distinguish them from the management of large economic entities. This is stressed by authors of numerous publications (Waśniewski, 2014). The adaptation of selected management tools to their specifics can influence their development.

The development of the small and medium-sized enterprise sector is of significance from the point of view of the economic development of the entire country. An analysis of the situation of Polish SMEs indicates that, in terms of quantity, we do not diverge from the level of the European Union. The qualitative scope of their development, however, merits more attention, particularly in terms of management efficiency, competitiveness and innovation capacity. An enterprise is deemed to be developing if it exhibits the following traits (PARP, 2019):

- Increase in revenue
- Increase in the market turnover share
- Acquisition of new markets
- Introduction of new and modified products to the market
- Increase of financial potential
- Digitalization of registration system
- Ability to adapt to new changes in the environment
- Expansion of technical knowledge
- Expansion of the scope of research and analyses used

Small and medium enterprises stimulate the economy. Their high quality will translate directly to improvements in the economy's competitiveness on a worldwide scale. It is therefore worth analysing the factors that influence their development. What are the barriers against development, and which factors are able to influence dynamic growth? Subject literature establishes that there are both external (macroeconomic) and internal (microeconomic) barriers. Presently, barriers to the development of Polish small and medium enterprises may be deemed to include (Krawczyk, 2017a):

- Barriers due to state policy, including legal provisions, tax rates, unclear regulations
- Financial barriers related to insufficient amounts of material and financial assets, limited access to external sources of financing
- Personnel barriers—insufficient employee qualifications, lack of capacity to acquire qualified personnel, high employee turnover rates
- Education barriers—no efficient and accessible system of education for entrepreneurs within the terms of small business, limited internet usage within business, insufficient access to economic data
- Corruption barriers—related to unfair competition and corruption
- Social barriers—including low business culture, no acceptance or social approval, low social standing of an entrepreneur (frequent negative descriptions of small business owners as "cons" or even "frauds")
- Management barriers—related to insufficient abilities of entrepreneurs in terms of sales and marketing, business planning, financial management as well as those caused by insufficient access to sources of information and market opportunities, etc.

Small and medium entrepreneurship is of enormous importance to the functioning of every country's economy. Both within the EU as well as Poland, the majority of enterprises (99.8%) are micro-, small and medium enterprises (see Table 2.1). On the one hand, SMEs are very flexible; on the other hand, due to their large dispersion, they do not have significant influence on the conditions of doing business. Faced with state administration, their negotiation situation is weaker.

In 2017 in Poland there were two million enterprises, and among these companies the majority (99.8%) were micro-, small and medium enterprises—1.76 million, 59.2 thousand and 15.5 thousand, respectively. Large enterprises numbered 3.4 thousand. The business sector generates 73.5% of the GDP, whereas small and medium enterprises generate over

Table 2.1 Poland against the background of EU countries—comparison of selected areas

	SMEs in Poland	SMEs in EU
Shares in the total number of enterprises	Micro – 96.1%	Micro – 93%
	Small – 2.9%	Small – 5.9%
	Medium – 0.8%	Medium – 0.9%
	SMEs – 99.8%	SMEs – 99.8%
	Large – 0.2%	Large – 0.2%
Share of enterprises in creating gross value added	Micro – 19.6%	Micro – 20.8%
	Small – 13.0%	Small – 17.6%
	Medium – 20%	Medium – 18.0%
	SMEs – 52.9%	SMEs – 56.4%
	Large – 47.1%	Large – 43.6%
Participation in job creation	Micro – 38.4%	Micro – 29.7%
	Small – 11.7%	Small – 20.1%
	Medium – 16.9%	Medium – 16.8%
	SMEs – 67.1%	SMEs – 66.6%
	Large – 32.9%	Large – 33.4%

Source: Own study based on SBA – Annual Report on European SMEs 2018, 2019, European Commission, Brussels 2019; Database estimates for 2018 produced by DIW Econ, based on 2008–2016 figures from the Structural Business Statistics Database (Eurostat), may be different from those published by national authorities.

50% of the GDP, or every second PLN of its amount. Among all groups of enterprises by size, the highest share in the generation of the GDP is held by microenterprises—approximately 30.8% (PARP, 2019).

The Polish business sector is dominated by microenterprises, whose share in the number of all enterprises is a staggering 96.5%. Over the scope of recent years, microenterprise numbers have increased. In 2017 there were approximately two million, 3.5% more than in 2016 and 12% more than in 2008. From among all business entity groups, they have the greatest share in the creation of the GDP PKB—31%, and assuming the GDP value created by the business sector to be 100%—41%. They also significantly influence the job market; within the business sector they generate 40% of workplaces (the number of people employed at such companies is about four million).

There are close to 54 thousand small enterprises, which makes up 3% of the Polish business sector. Over the course of recent years, numbers of small enterprises have been dropping, save for the years 2013–2014, where a record number of over 59 thousand was registered. In 2017 there was 6% less of them than the year before. Among all groups of entities, small enterprises have the lowest share in the generation of the GDP—8%, and assuming the value of the GDP generated by the business sector to be 100%—11%. Their share in job creation is also lowest; within the business sector they generate 12.2% of jobs (about 1.1 million employees). An average small company employs 21 people.

There are presently over fifteen thousand medium-sized enterprises in Poland, which constitutes 0.7% of the Polish business sector. Over the scope of recent years, a drop in the number of small enterprises is noted, and there were close to 1% less of these than in 2016 and 6% less than in 2008. The share of medium-sized enterprises in the generation of the GDP is 11%, and for the years 2007–2016 it rose by 1.9%. Assuming the value of the GDP generated by the business sector to be 100%, this share was 15% (only small enterprises generate less). In addition, they have a share in job creation that is only slightly greater than that of small enterprises—they generate close to 16% of jobs in the business sector (the number of employees of such companies was approximately 1.6 million). An average medium-sized enterprise employs 105 people.

2.4 ICT – THE SIGNIFICANCE OF DEVELOPMENT IN POLAND IN THIS FIELD

Information and communications technology (ICT) is a very broad term, analysed from the standpoint of many areas of science. These technologies are used in all sectors of the economy, and issues related to ICT are the focus of both economists and politicians dealing with the economy and business—in developed as well as in developing countries. The term *ICT* includes all communication media, media allowing the storage of information, and equipment allowing information processing. In addition, ICT also encompasses a range of digital applications and complex IT systems, allowing the actual implementation of higher abstraction-level data processing and storage than the hardware level. It is thus correct to state that information and communications technologies are the circulatory system of the knowledge-based economy, in which the information society is of dominant significance. This significance is confirmed by relevant numbers (ITU, 2019):

- It is estimated that 4.1 billion people used the internet in 2019, reflecting a 5.3% increase compared with 2018. The global penetration rate increased from nearly 17% in 2005 to over 53% in 2019.
- Between 2005 and 2019, the number of internet users grew on average by 10% every year.
- In developed countries, most people are online, with close to 87% of individuals using the internet. In the least-developed countries (LDCs), on the other hand, only 19% of individuals were online in 2019. Europe is the region with the highest internet usage rates; Africa is the region with the lowest internet usage rates.
- In all regions of the world, more men than women are using the internet.
- The percentage of households with internet access at home is generally correlated with a region's level of development. In all regions of the world, households are more likely to have internet access at home than to have a computer because internet access is also possible through other devices. In 2019, more households in many countries had internet access than had computers.
- An important barrier in the uptake and effective use of the internet is a lack of ICT skills.

At the national level, the development of innovative technologies enables a country to take higher ranking positions as measured by the level of information and communication technology development. The assessment is carried out using a number of indicators, calculated with the appropriate index system and applied to analyse problem areas in politics, as well as to monitor progress in introducing innovative technologies (Petkova et al., 2019). Tools to measure the development level in terms of ICT include the ICT Development Index (IDI), the Web Index and the Networked Readiness Index (NRI).

The ICT Development Index (IDI), published annually since 2009, is used to monitor and compare developments in information and communication technology between countries and over time. In the 2017 report, Poland took 49th place (out of 176 ranked states) rising by one level compared to 2016. It was, however, one of the lowest ranked European states (ITU, 2017).

The Web Index was the first measure of the web's contribution to social, economic and political progress, studying countries across the world. Since its launch, the Web Index has become established as a reference point for governments and policymakers internationally, holding governments accountable and driving public debate. In the last full list, Poland was ranked 34th out of 85 states (Web Index 2014).

The World Economic Forum's Networked Readiness Index (NRI) measures the propensity for countries to exploit the opportunities offered by information and communications technology (ICT). It is published in collaboration with INSEAD, as part of its annual Global Information Technology Report (GITR). The report is regarded as the most authoritative and comprehensive assessment of how ICT impacts the competitiveness and well-being of nations. The list is led by Finland and Singapore. According to this report, Poland took 42th place out of 139. Poland's neighbours rank better: Germany – 15, Lithuania – 29, the Czech Republic – 36 (Baller et al., 2016).

On the basis of data from the indicated reports, it must be concluded that Poland still has a lot to do in terms of information and communication technologies. A necessary condition of improved ICT development levels in Poland is support from public administration in bringing legal provisions to order and designating innovative technologies as a priority within state policy.

2.5 RESULTS AND DISCUSSION

In 2019, 96.8% of enterprises used computers. The share of enterprises with access to the internet exceeded 96%. Comparing results of the survey conducted in the EU Member States in 2018, the value of this indicator in Poland was slightly lower than the EU average, and the gap between Polish enterprises and European leaders was 4 percentage points.

The following issues related to information and communication technologies will be analysed in detail: access to computers in enterprises; access to the internet; use of computers by employees; access to ICT specialists and ICT training; usage of websites, social media, cloud computing and e-invoices; availability of industrial and service robots; issues of ICT security, electronic sales, e-government and ICT investments; and the use of a digital intensity index.

The use of modern technologies significantly improves work. Fundamental to this is equipping the enterprise with computers. Their widespread adoption means that the level of computer use in companies remains at a similar and consistently high level, regardless of company size. In 2019, this was 96.1% and 99.5% respectively for small and medium-sized enterprises (Table 2.2).

The percentage of enterprises with internet access exceeded 90%, regardless of the size of the enterprise. This confirms the importance of being able to connect to the global network. The rate of internet access was the lowest in small enterprises. Its level increased steadily in the analysed period from 91.4 in 2015 to 95.6 in 2019. It should be emphasized that the majority of entities had mobile broadband access to the internet. Unfortunately, in the case of small enterprises, this type of connection was only 72.4% in 2019. In the case of medium-sized entities, 88.2% had such a connection in 2019 (Table 2.3).

Table 2.2 Enterprises using computers (as % of total enterprise)

	2015	2016	2017	2018	2019
Total	94.0	94.7	95.6	96.2	96.8
Small	93.0	93.7	94.8	95.5	96.1
Medium	98.7	99.0	99.3	99.3	99.5
Large	99.5	99.8	99.8	99.7	99.9

Source: Own study based on Statistics Poland (GUS) (2019). Information society in Poland. Results of statistical surveys in the years 2015–2019.

Table 2.3 Enterprises with access to the internet by size class (Mobile broadband access to the internet in enterprises by size class (%)

	2015	2016	2017	2018		2019	
				Access to the internet	Mobile broadband access to the internet	Access to the internet	Mobile broadband access to the internet
Total	92.7	93.7	94.8	95.6	67.6	96.3	75.7
Small	91.4	92.5	93.8	94.8	63.7	95.6	72.4
Medium	98.4	98.8	99.1	99.1	82.2	99.2	88.2
Large	99.5	99.7	99.7	99.6	97.1	99.8	97.5

Source: Own study based on Statistics Poland (GUS) (2019). Information society in Poland. Results of statistical surveys in the years 2015–2019.

Mobile devices allow a mobile connection to the internet, which allows people to work outside the enterprise. An employee equipped with such a device has access to email and company applications. no matter where he or she is located, thus increasing performance. In 2019, more than three-quarters of all enterprises provided their employees with mobile devices. In small enterprises, this level is lower and amounted to 63.8% in 2018 and 73% in 2019. For medium-sized enterprises these levels are 82.2% and 88.9% respectively (Table 2.4).

In 2019, as compared to the previous year, the number of employees equipped with computers rose (by 1.6%), as did the number of employees having computers with internet access. The level of usage of computers by employees of SMEs is lower than in larger enterprises. It must be stated that the majority of employees have access to an internet-connected computer at their place of employment. Computers without internet access are held by only 2.4% of small enterprises (small enterprises for 2019: A – B: 42.4% – 40.0% = 2.4%) and 3% of medium-sized enterprises (medium-sized enterprises for 2019: A – B, 44.7% – 41.7% = 3.0%); in the case of larger enterprises, these differences are more significant (Table 2.5).

Company size is related to the share of companies that, within the previous year, employed or tried to employ people in positions requiring special skills within the scope of ICT. In 2018 a third of large enterprises were interested in employing ICT specialists, whereas among small entities this number was only 2.6%, and within medium entities about 7.7%. It must be additionally noted that in 2018 these numbers dropped. This can mean, on the one hand, that the number of open positions in this area dropped. On the other hand, it can be so difficult to find a person to fill this position that entities make no attempts to hire but outsource this function to an external entity. Depending on company size, there is also significant differentiation within the numbers of enterprises employing ICT specialists (Table 2.6).

In 2018, most enterprises outsourced ICT-related tasks to external entities (71.4%); only a third of them employed a specialist in this area. The percentage of entities employing ICT

Table 2.4 Enterprises providing portable devices to employees (%)

	2018	2019
Total	67.7	76.2
Small	63.8	73.0
Medium	82.2	88.9
Large	97.1	97.9

Source: Own study based on Statistics Poland (GUS) (2019). Information society in Poland. Results of statistical surveys in the years 2015–2019.

Table 2.5 Employees using computers in enterprises (%)

	2015		2016		2017		2018		2019	
	A	B	A	B	A	B	A	B	A	B
Total	43.3	38.2	44.0	39.0	45.6	39.7	46.1	40.5	47.7	43.2
Small	37.8	35.2	38.6	35.9	39.9	37.2	39.9	37.0	42.4	40.0
Medium	39.9	36.2	39.2	36.4	42.0	38.4	43.6	40.6	44.7	41.7
Large	48.9	41.2	49.9	42.4	51.3	42.1	51.1	42.5	52.6	46.1

A: employees using computer, B: employees using computer with access to the internet

Source: Own study based on Statistics Poland (GUS) (2019). Information society in Poland. Results of statistical surveys in the years 2015–2019.

Table 2.6 Enterprises that recruited or tried to recruit persons for jobs requiring ICT specialist skills (%)

	2015	2016	2017	2018
Total	5.4	5.3	6.0	4.5
Small	3.2	3.0	3.5	2.6
Medium	10.4	11.3	12.2	7.7
Large	34.6	36.1	36.9	35.3

Source: Own study based on Statistics Poland (GUS) (2019). Information society in Poland. Results of statistical surveys in the years 2015–2019.

specialists was the lowest in small entities (three times smaller than in the case of large entities). These services were outsourced by 68.7% small entities and 81.5% medium-sized ones (Figure 2.1).

The ICT competence of people employed in enterprises must be raised constantly at a pace adapted to the changes taking place in this area. In 2018, 6.4% of companies organized ICT training for specialists, and 11.5% for other employees. In the case of small companies, only 3.2% decided to train for specialists and for other employees it was 7.7%. In the case of medium-sized entities, these values were 14.0% and 21.8% respectively (Table 2.7). These values differ significantly from those for large companies (50.0% and 56.2%).

A company's website is an important marketing communication tool. Websites are becoming more technologically advanced and fulfil many functions. They allow, for example, placing orders and checking their status online, as well as putting up information on employment opportunities. In the year 2019, over two-thirds of companies had their own websites. The leaders in this regard are large companies, with nine out of ten having websites; within the scope of small enterprises this number was 66%, and within medium enterprises it was 87.5%. The growth dynamic is not high. Over the scope of five years the share of small entities having websites rose by 4.7%, and that of medium enterprises rose by 3.6% (Table 2.8)

Use of social media refers to the company's use of internet-based applications or communication platforms to connect, create and exchange content online with clients, suppliers and partners, or within the enterprise. This communication tool can take various forms, for example, social networks, enterprise blogs or microblogs, multimedia content sharing websites, wiki tools. The growing popularity of social media (especially among young users) has meant that they are increasingly exploited by businesses as new communication channels. Social marketing allows companies to create a group of loyal customers and quickly acquire new ones. Through communication in social media, companies encourage consumers to share ideas that they can later use in the creation or development of products and services. Increasingly, social media can be useful when recruiting employees—for example,

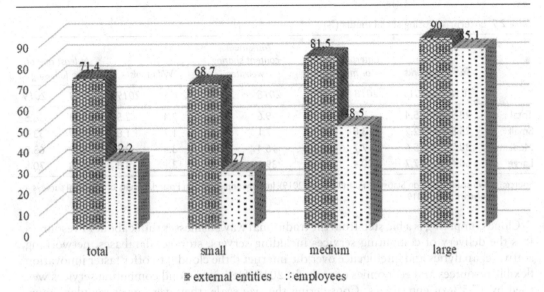

Figure 2.1 Enterprises in which tasks related to ICT were performed by employees or external entities in 2018 (in %)

Source: Own study based on information society in Poland. Results of statistical surveys in the years 2015–2019.

Table 2.7 Enterprises providing training to upgrade ICT skills of their personnel in 2018 (%)

	Training for ICT specialists	Training for other persons employed
Total	6.4	11.5
Small	3.2	7.7
Medium	14.0	21.8
Large	50.0	56.2

Source: Own study based on Statistics Poland (GUS) (2019). Information society in Poland. Results of statistical surveys in the years 2015–2019.

Table 2.8 Enterprises having a website (%)

	2015	2016	2017	2018	2019
Total	65.4	67.0	66.9	66.8	70.2
Small	61.3	62.3	62.6	62.5	66.0
Medium	83.9	86.1	85.3	84.5	87.5
Large	91.2	91.8	91.9	91.1	92.7

Source: Own study based on Statistics Poland (GUS) (2019). Information society in Poland. Results of statistical surveys in the years 2015–2019.

when seeking people with a narrow specialization. They also become a tool for improving communication within the enterprise, enabling the exchange of opinions and ideas between employees.

Every third enterprise in Poland in 2019 used at least one social media channel. The most popular tool was social networking. The use of this type of communication channel is significantly lower in small enterprises (33.2%) compared to medium (63.8%) or large (70.5%). Small enterprises use social networks more often than blogs or wiki tools which are used by only a small percentage (Table 2.9).

Table 2.9 Enterprises using social media (%)

	Social networks		Enterprise's blogs or microblogs		Multimedia, content sharing websites		Wiki tools		At least one of the following	
	2018	*2019*	*2018*	*2019*	*2018*	*2019*	*2018*	*2019*	*2018*	*2019*
Total	28.9	35.4	5.0	5.8	9.6	13.3	2.4	2.5	30.3	36.6
Small	25.8	32.2	3.8	4.7	7.1	10.5	1.7	1.8	26.9	33.2
Medium	38.5	45.6	7.7	7.8	16.4	20.7	3.3	3.7	47.2	63.8
Large	60.1	67.7	20.4	24.0	39.1	46.5	13.1	14.8	63.8	70.5

Source: Own study based on Statistics Poland (GUS) (2019). Information society in Poland. Results of statistical surveys in the years 2015–2019.

Cloud computing is a big step from the traditional way businesses think about IT resources. It is the delivery of computing services including servers, storage, databases, networking, software, analytics and intelligence over the internet ("the cloud") to offer faster innovation, flexible resources and economies of scale. In 2019, fee-based cloud computing services were used by 17.5% of enterprises. Considering the size scale, they were most popular among companies employing at least 250 people, at 52.0%; the lowest interest in these technologies was recorded among small enterprises, at 14.1%; among medium-sized enterprises it amounted to 27.9% (Table 2.10).

In 2018, more than two-thirds of enterprises issued and sent electronic invoices, including those that are not suitable for automatic processing—66.1%—and those that are suitable for automatic processing—18.0%. Electronic invoices were sent mainly by entities employing 250 or more employees—94.0%—and most often they issued invoices suitable for automatic processing—47.6%. Almost two-thirds of small entities issue invoices not suitable for automatic processing and only about 15% that are suitable for automatic processing. In the case of medium-sized companies, these values are almost 80% and slightly more than 25% respectively (Table 2.11).

Table 2.10 Enterprises using cloud computing (%)

	Enterprises using paid cloud computing services		Email (2019)	Hosting of enterprise's database (2019)	Storage of enterprise's files (2019)
	(2018)	*(2019)*			
Total	11.5	17.5	12.9	6.8	9.5
Small	8.8	14.1	10.2	5.3	7.5
Medium	19.0	27.9	20.9	11.1	14.8
Large	42.7	52.0	40.9	22.7	35.3

Source: Own study based on Statistics Poland (GUS) (2019). Information society in Poland. Results of statistical surveys in the years 2015–2019.

Table 2.11 Enterprises sending electronic invoices in 2018 (%)

	Suitable for automatic processing	Not suitable for automatic processing
Total	18.0	66.1
Small	15.5	62.7
Medium	25.2	79.1
Large	47.6	91.3

Source: Own study based on Statistics Poland (GUS) (2019). Information society in Poland. Results of statistical surveys in the years 2015–2019.

Table 2.12 Enterprises using industrial and service robots in 2019 (%)

	Using robots	Using industrial robots	Using service robots
Total	7.5	5.7	2.9
Small	5.7	4.0	2.6
Medium	12.4	10.5	3.5
Large	28.4	25.3	8.1

Source: Own study based on Statistics Poland (GUS) (2019). Information society in Poland. Results of statistical surveys in the years 2015–2019.

Industrial robots are increasingly used in various fields of the economy. In 2019, 7.5% of enterprises used robots in their operations, including industrial robots—5.7%—and service works—2.9%. Of large enterprises, 28.4% used robots. These machines were most rarely used in small companies—5.7%—and in medium-sized companies—12.4% (Table 2.12).

Aware of security threats, enterprises attach great importance to cyber security. With a range of security measures to choose from, they should at least minimize the risk of ICT incidents. In 2019, the percentage of enterprises using any ICT security was 87.2%. Some type of security was used in almost all large enterprises. Almost three quarters of small enterprises required at least strong password authentication, as did nearly 90% of medium companies. Software was updated to current versions by 77.8% of small enterprises and by 92.6% of medium enterprises, and these companies backed up data and transferred it to other locations at a rate of 52.7% and 73.9% respectively (Table 2.13).

E-administration is one of the ICT opportunities that entrepreneurs use more and more willingly. Completing and sending documents online saves time, and posting information on public administration websites makes it easy to track changes in regulations. The high rate of using e-government services confirms the great interest in this activity of entrepreneurs. In 2018, almost all large entities used e-government resources, as did 94.9% of small companies and 98.9% of medium-sized enterprises. This participation rate has remained over 90% for many years (Table 2.14).

Table 2.13 Enterprises using selected ICT security measures in 2019 (%)

	Strong password authentication	Current software updates	Backing up data and transferring it to other locations
Total	76.4	80.2	57
Small	73.4	77.8	52.7
Medium	87.6	92.6	73.9
Large	95.4	97.3	85.7

Source: Own study based on Statistics Poland (GUS) (2019). Information society in Poland. Results of statistical surveys in the years 2015–2019.

Table 2.14 Enterprises using e-government resources (%)

	2015	2016	2017	2018
Total	93.6	94.6	95.1	95.7
Small	92.3	93.5	94.2	94.9
Medium	98.6	98.6	98.9	98.9
Large	99.7	99.6	99.6	99.8

Source: Own study based on Statistics Poland (GUS) (2019). Information society in Poland. Results of statistical surveys in the years 2015–2019.

Table 2.15 Investments incurred by enterprises on selected type of ICT equipment in 2018

	Purchases of IT and communication goods		Purchases of IT goods		Purchases of communication goods	
	% share in general	Value in PLN (millions)	% share in general	Value in PLN (millions)	% share in general	Value in PLN (millions)
Total	37.5	5661.0	34.0	3843.3	19.9	1817.8
Small	31.4	740.8	27.6	578.5	16.3	162.4
Medium	60.1	923.7	57.5	745.9	31.5	177.7
Large	82.3	3996.5	80.6	2518.9	53.8	1477.7

Source: Own study based on Statistics Poland (GUS) (2019). Information society in Poland. Results of statistical surveys in the years 2015–2019.

In 2018, over a third of businesses invested in the purchase of ICT (information and communication) equipment. Over 80% of large companies invested in such equipment. Small and medium-sized enterprises made these investments less frequently. The volumes of such investments were also significantly smaller for small and medium-sized enterprises (Table 2.15).

Statistics, in terms of ICT in businesses, include much detailed data concerning diverse aspects of business. A synthetic indicator that tersely reflects the level of use of ICT in enterprises, taking into account various technologies, is the Digital Intensity Index proposed by Eurostat. It was created on the basis of data obtained from a study of ICT usage in enterprises. The index value estimation assigns every enterprise to one of four digital intensity levels. A point is awarded for every condition fulfilled, with their sum describing the digital intensity index. There are four levels:

- Very low 0–3
- Low 4–6
- High 7–9
- Very high 10–12

In 2018, over half of Polish businesses were included in the group spanning very low digital intensity, with just less than a third being included in the low intensity group. High or very high digital intensity levels were found for 12.5% of enterprises. The largest share of companies having high or very high digital intensity was found for large enterprises, at 42.5%, with the lowest being found for small enterprises, 10.0%. For medium companies the share was 19% (Table 2.16).

Table 2.16 Enterprises classified by digital intensity index (%)

	Very low	Low	High	Very high
Total	56.3	31.3	11.0	1.5
Small	60.9	29.2	9.1	0.9
Medium	40.9	40.1	16.3	2.7
Large	15.6	41.9	32.7	9.8

Source: Own study based on Statistics Poland (GUS) (2019). Information society in Poland. Results of statistical surveys in the years 2015–2019.

2.6 CONCLUSION

Analyses of numbers concerning small and medium enterprises in Poland regarding information and communications technologies allow the following conclusions:

- Over the course of recent years, many developed and developing countries have become aware of the significance of small and medium enterprises. This sector creates the most jobs in the market and is characterized by creativity and engagement. After the period of dominance of state-owned companies and later transnational corporations, the time of SMEs is beginning in Poland. Fundamental statistical data shows their key role for the development of the economy. The development level of the Polish SME sector is close to the EU level, as proven by statistical data.
- Poland had transformed its economy from being centrally planned to a market economy and is becoming one of the best-performing countries in the group of post-communist states. However, as all CEE countries, Poland is at the periphery of the EU economic core. One mode by which to attain a higher level is increased implementation of ICT.
- The usage of ICT will allow businesses to develop dynamically, to achieve business objectives more efficiently, to implement systemic solutions in business and to more efficiently react in the event of a crisis. Small and medium enterprises cannot afford to forgo the broad range of options offered by ICT.
- Polish companies mostly use computers and mobile equipment; furthermore, the majority of these have internet access. Practically all large companies use computers (99.9%), while among medium-sized enterprises this number is 99.5%, with 96.1% among small ones. Data on internet access are very similar (large enterprise: 99.8%, medium enterprises: 99.2%, small enterprises: 95.6%).
- Considering the individual areas of ICT (including employees using computers, access to ICT specialists, ICT training, use of websites, social media, cloud computing, e-invoices, industrial and service robots, implementation of ICT security, electronic sales, use of e-government resources, ICT investments, the Digital Intensity Index), the scope of implementation depends on the enterprise size. The level of usage of ICT by large enterprises is higher than that of medium-sized companies and is significantly higher than in small enterprises.
- There are great differences, and they depend on the analysed issue and on the company size.

The conclusions allow an answer to the initial question: What is the level of usage of ICT at small and medium enterprises in Poland? The numbers show that the scope of usage of ICT is lower in medium-sized enterprises and significantly lower in small enterprises. Considering the number of companies in this group as a whole, top-down action is needed to support enhanced implementation of ICT by this class of enterprise.

The study has certain limitations due to the data that was analysed. The analysis is based on results of studies conducted by Statistics Poland (GUS) (2019) and presented within information society in Poland. Results of statistical surveys are from the years 2015–2019. This study encompassed enterprises with ten or more employees. This means that ICT implementation in microenterprises was not analysed. However, such an analysis may be conducted at a later time on the basis of statistical data published by the institution. This could also be the vantage point for additional research by the author.

REFERENCES

Arendt, Ł., Grabowski, W. (2019). The role of firm-level factors and regional innovation capabilities for Polish SMEs. *Journal of Entrepreneurship, Management and Innovation (JEMI), 15(3)*, pp. 11–44.

Bahrini, R., Qaffas, A. A. (2019). Impact of Information and Communication Technology on Economic Growth: Evidence from Developing Countries. *Economies 7(21)*, pp. 1–13. DOI:10.3390/economies7010021.

Baller, S., Dutta, S., Lanvin, B. (2016). *The Global Information Technology Report 2016. Innovating in the Digital Economy.* World Economic Forum, Cornell University, INSEAD. Retrieved from: http://www3.weforum.org/docs/GITR2016/GITR_2016_full%20report_final.pdf (Access:10.02.20).

Commission Regulation (EU) No 651/2014 of 17 June 2014 (Annex 1).

Dincă, V. M., Dima, A. M., Rozsa, Z. (2019). Determinants of cloud computing adoption by Romanian SMEs in the digital economy. *Journal of Business Economics and Management, 20(4)*, pp. 798–820. DOI: 10.3846/jbem.2019.9856.

Ferreira de Lara, F., Neves Guimarães, M. R. (2014). Competitive Priorities and Innovation in SMEs: A Brazil Multi-Case Study. *Journal of Technology Management & Innovation, 9(3)*, pp. 51–64.

ITU (2017). *IDI 2017 Rank.* Retrieved from: https://www.itu.int/net4/ITU-D/idi/2017/index.html (Access: 10.02.20.).

ITU (2019). *Measuring digital development: Facts and figures 2019.* Switzerland, Geneva. Retrieved from: https://www.itu.int/en/ITU-D/Statistics/Pages/facts/default.aspx (Access: 10.02.2020).

Krawczyk, P. (2017a). Kapitał ludzki i innowacyjność jako determinanty dalszego rozwoju sektora MSP w Polsce. *Zeszyty Naukowe Politechniki Śląskiej. Organizacja i Zarządzanie, 113*, pp. 207–2018. DOI: 10.29119/1641-3466.2018.113.16.

Krawczyk, P. (2017b). Zarządzanie w małych i średnich przedsiębiorstwach – adaptacja wybranych technik. In: Wielgórka, D. (ed.) *Wybrane problemy zarządzania nowoczesną organizacją we współczesnej gospodarce.* Częstochowa: Wydawnictwo Wydziału Zarządzania Politechniki Częstochowskiej, pp. 24–33.

Krawczyk, P., Kokot-Stępień, P. (2017). Specyfika analizy finansowej w sektorze małych i średnich przedsiębiorstw. *Marketing i Rynek, 7*, pp. 367–376.

Lee, B. (2012). *Financial Guide for Small and Medium Enterprises.* Singapore: CPA Australia Ltd.

OECD (2018). *Strengthening SMEs and entrepreneurship for productivity and inclusive growth*, OECD 2018 Ministerial Conference On SMEs. Retrieved from: https://www.oecd-ilibrary.org/docserver/c19b6f97-en.pdf?expires=1600087426&id=id&accname=guest&checksum=8291D CF0932E2EDA92F1F31DC1D1400E (Access: 10.02.2020).

Onyinyi, B., Kaberuka, W. (2019). ICT fusion on the relationship between resource transformation capabilities and quality management practices among SMEs in Uganda. *Journal Cogent Business & Management, 6(1)*. DOI: 10.1080/23311975.2019.1586063.

PARP (2019). Raport o stanie sektora małych i średnich przedsiębiorstw w Polsce. Retrieved from: https://www.parp.gov.pl/storage/publications/pdf/2019_07_ROSS.pdf (Access: 10.02.2020).

Petkova, L., Ryabokon, M., Vdovychenko, Y. (2019). Modern systems for assessing the informatization of countries in the context of global sustainable development. *Baltic Journal of Economic Studies, 5(2)*, pp. 158–170. DOI: 10.30525/2256-0742/2019-5-2-158-170.

Petryczka, I. (2017). Wykorzystanie technologii informacyjno-komunikacyjnych w przedsiębiorstwach z branży logistycznej. *Zeszyty Naukowe Uniwersytetu Przyrodniczo-Humanistycznego w Siedlcach. Seria: Administracja i Zarządzanie, 113*, pp. 83–93.

Qosasi, A., Permana, E., Muftiadi, A., Purnomo, M., Maulina, E. (2019). Building SMEs' Competitive Advantage and the Organizational Agility of Apparel Retailers in Indonesia: The role of ICT as an Initial Trigger. *Gadjah Mada International Journal of Business, 21(1)*, pp. 69–90.

SBA – Annual Report on European SMEs 2018/2019, European Commission, Brussels 2019.

Statistics Poland (GUS) (2019). *Information society in Poland. Results of statistical surveys in the years 2015–2019*, Warszawa, Szczecin.

Taalbi, J. (2019). Origins and pathways of innovation in the third industrial revolution. *Industrial and Corporate Change, 28(5)*, pp. 1125–1148. DOI: 10.1093/icc/dty053.

Tworek, K., Walecka-Jankowska, K., Zgrzywa-Ziemak, A. (2019). IT Reliability and Innovation in SMEs: Empirical Research. *Journal of Management and Business Administration. Central Europe*, 27(2), pp. 83–96.

Ustawa z dnia 2 lipca 2004 r. o swobodzie działalności gospodarczej, Dz.U. 2004 nr 173 poz. 1807 [*in English*: Act of 2 July 2004 on freedom of establishment, OJ C 104, 11.12.2004, p. 1. 2004 No. 173 item 1807].

Waśniewski, P. (2014). Pomiar wyników finansowych w małych i średnich przedsiębiorstwach. *Zeszyty Naukowe Uniwersytetu Szczecińskiego. Finanse. Rynki finansowe. Ubezpieczenia*, 66, pp. 525–534.

Web Index (2014). Retrieved from: ttps://thewebindex.org/data/?indicator=INDEX&country=ALL (Access: 10.02.20.).

Chapter 3

Approach to the voice control of IoT objects in "smart house" systems

*Igor Shostak, Vitalina Babenko, Mariia Danova
and Olena Feoktystova*

CONTENTS

3.1 INTRODUCTION

The creation of language interfaces could be used in a variety of systems: voice control for people with disabilities, reliable control of combat vehicles, "understanding" only the voice of the commander, answering machines, automatically processing hundreds of thousands of calls per day (for example, in the sales system for air tickets), etc. (Gaida et al., 2014; Alcantud et al., 2006). In this case, the speech interface should include two components: a system of automatic speech recognition to receive a speech signal and convert it into text or command, and a speech synthesis system that performs the opposite function—converting messages from machine to speech.

However, despite rapidly growing computing power, the creation of speech recognition systems remains an extremely difficult problem (Gaida et al., 2014; Yu, 2013; Dong and Li, 2015). This is due to its interdisciplinary nature (it is necessary to have knowledge in philology, linguistics, digital signal processing, acoustics, statistics, pattern recognition, etc.) and the high computational complexity of the developed algorithms.

There are areas of application of automatic speech recognition systems, where the described problems are particularly acute due to severely limited computing resources, for example, at IoT facilities (AlHammadi et al., 2019). The current development of IoT is associated not only with new technologies, but also with the creation of a technological ecosystem and the development of a number of proposals for the collection, transmission and aggregation of data, and a platform that allows you to process this data and use it to implement "smart solutions" (Malche & Maheshwary, 2017; Hoque & Davidson, 2019; Ghaffarianhoseini et al., 2017).

The most common example of IoT is the technology of the "Smart House", in which security, energy saving and comfort are monitored by software that combines household appliances into a single system using data transfer technology (Al-Kuwari et al., 2018; Vinay Sagar & Kusuma, 2015). "Smart House" is a modern tool to increase comfort and living standards; part of the process takes place automatically, and the rest can be controlled remotely, which makes it relevant for study and improvement, especially with regard to regulating its parameters via voice control.

The aim of this article is to describe the approach to voice control of IoT objects, which are part of the "Smart House" system, providing high accuracy of speech recognition by set of special means of artificial intelligence.

3.2 MATERIALS AND METHODS

The idea of the proposed method of constructing information features, which are adapted from the speaker and acoustic conditions of a deep neural network with a narrow neck, is to use an adapted deep neural network to extract features (Nielsen, 2019; Vesely et al., 2013). The basis for this idea was the following conclusion: the better the recognition accuracy provided by a deep neural network with a narrow neck, the better the recognition accuracy will be able to provide a system built on the basis of features extracted from this neural network (Xue, 2014; Yu et al., 2013).

Analysis of deep neural network adaptation algorithms has shown that deep neural network adaptation using i-vectors significantly increases recognition accuracy by providing the deep neural network with additional phonogram information (Saon, 2013). Thus, the proposed method is based on the assumption that the features extracted from a deep neural network with a narrow neck, adapted by i-vectors, will have greater resistance to acoustic variability and better discriminative ability than similar features derived from an adapted neural network.

The complete algorithm for constructing features, according to the proposed method, consists of the following steps:

1. Construction of capital signs (for example, MFCC) for training of the GMM-HMM model
2. Training of GMM-HMM model tryphons
3. Formation of marking of educational data on the connected states of tryphons by means of the GMM-HMM model
4. Construction of features for learning deep neural network (these features may differ from those used in learning a GMM-HMM model)
5. Reduction of input data for deep neural network training to zero mean and unit variance
6. Initialization of deep neural network training with L hidden layers
7. Training of a deep neural network according to the criterion of minimizing mutual entropy (see Figure 3.1(a))
8. Construction of i-vectors for the training base
9. Reduction of the constructed i-vectors to zero mean and unit variance, or normalization in any other way
10. Expansion of the input layer of the trained deep neural network with the initialization of the corresponding coefficients of the weight matrix with zero values
11. Additional training of a deep neural network with an extended input layer according to the features to which an i-vector is added in each frame, which corresponds to this part of the phonogram (see Figure 3.1(b)). This uses a lower learning speed, and the objective function is added to the term R(W), the fine deviation of the weights W^l of the trained model from the values of the weights W^l of the original model, which is determined by the formula

$$R(W) = \lambda \sum_{l=1}^{L+1} \left\| vec(W^l - W^l) \right\|_2 = \lambda \sum_{l=1}^{L+1} \sum_{i=1}^{N_l} \sum_{j=1}^{N_{l-1}} (W_{ij}^l - W_{ij}^l)^2, \tag{3.1}$$

where vec(W) means the vector obtained by combining all the columns of the matrix W, and λ—the value of the fine, usually selected in the range between 10^{-8} and 10^{-6}.

12. Splitting the layer l of the deep neural network (for example, the last hidden layer) into two layers as follows:

$$v^l = f(W^l v^{l-1} + b^l) \approx f(W_{out}^l (W_{bn}^l v^{l-1} + 0) + b^l). \tag{3.2}$$

Here, the first layer is a small layer with a linear activation function, a matrix of W_{bn}^l weights, and a zero shift vector; the second layer is a non-linear layer with a matrix of weights W_{out}^l and a displacement vector b^l, having the dimension of the original broken layer. Breakdown is carried out by means of (Singular Values Decomposition, SVD) of a matrix of weights W^l,

$$W^l = USV^T \approx \tilde{U}_{bn} \tilde{V}_{bn}^T = W_{out}^l W_{bn}^l, \tag{3.3}$$

where the lower index bn means a reduced dimension. Thus, the original deep neural network with L hidden layers is transformed into a deep neural network with (L + 1) hidden layers with a linear thin layer l. Adding a narrow layer in front of the source layer DNN, allowed the number of parameters of the acoustic model to be reduced several times without compromising the quality of its work.

13. Additional training of the obtained deep neural network with a narrow neck (see Figure 3.1(c)) with a lower speed and a penalty for the deviation of the weights from the weights of the original model

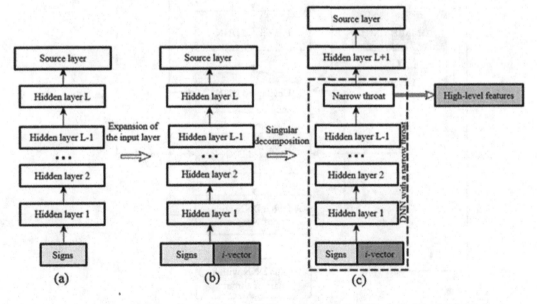

Figure 3.1 The main stages of learning a deep neural network with a narrow neck, adapted using i-vectors: Learning non-adapted deep neural network (a), learning adapted deep neural network (b), learning adapted deep neural network with a narrow neck (c)

14. Rejection of the layers of the deep neural network that occur behind the narrow throat
15. The use of the obtained neural network with a narrow neck to build high-level features

Because the markup quality generated by the GMM-HMM model has a significant effect on DNN learning, it makes sense to repeat the steps of the algorithm for the best results, starting with the second, using GMM-HMM learning features constructed using a deep neural network with a narrow neck. The scheme of the proposed algorithm for constructing features is presented in Figure 3.2.

The features built on this algorithm can be further used for training both GMM-HMM models and for training DNN-HMM models.

The following algorithm of training of acoustic models on the basis of the signs constructed according to the offered method is offered:

- Training of GMM-HMM model tryphons on the basis of the constructed signs
- Marking of educational data on the connected states of tryphons by means of the GMM-HMM model constructed by tryphons
- Training of DNN-HMM model using constructed features taken from a wide temporal context (for example, in 31 frames). One of the advantages of such deep neural learning is the ability to effectively take into account the broader temporal context, compared to deep neural networks trained on "raw" features (Zhang, 2014).

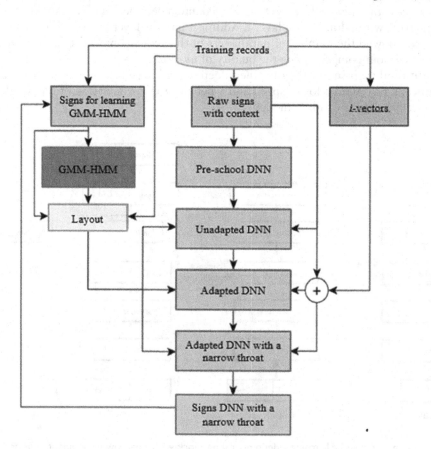

Figure 3.2 Scheme of the algorithm for constructing features using a deep neural network with a narrow neck, adapted using i-vectors

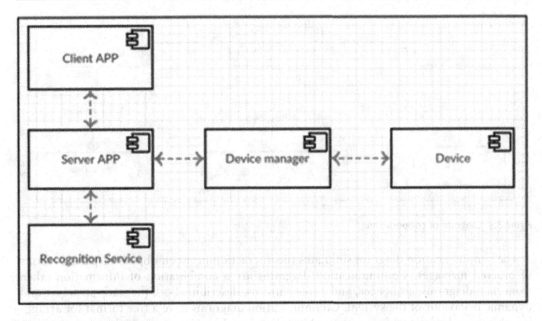

Figure 3.3 Component diagram

The system has a multilevel architecture, which consists of the following parts:

- Client application that reads speech signals
- Speech signal processing server
- Command recognition server
- Signal transmission module on the device
- Devices connected to the system

The structure of the system can be seen in more detail on the component diagram (see Figure 3.3). The component diagram shows the relationships between software components, including source code components, binary components, and executable components. The software module can be presented as a component. The component diagram represents the encapsulated classes along with their interface shells, ports, and internal structures (which can also consist of components and connectors). Components are connected through dependencies when the required interface of one component is connected to the existing interface of another component. This illustrates the client-source relationship between the two components. Dependency shows that one component provides the service needed by another component. The dependency is represented by an arrow from the client interface or port to the imported interface, when a component diagram is used to show the internal structure of the components provided and the required interfaces of the composite component can be delegated to the corresponding interfaces of the internal components.

The cooperation diagram shows the interaction between the parts of the system "Smart House" (see Figure 3.4). The user sends a language request in the client application. The client application sends a language request to the logic server, which in turn sends a request to the recognition service. Upon receiving the recognized signal, the logic server sends a command to the device manager, which in turn gives a command to the device to which the command corresponds.

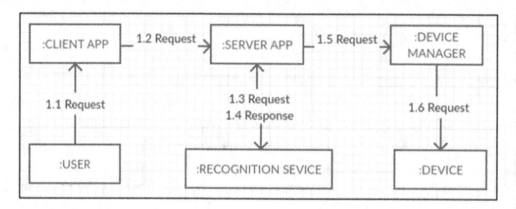

Figure 3.4 Diagram of cooperation

The communication diagram simulates the interaction between objects or parts in terms of ordered messages. Communication diagrams are a combination of information taken from class diagrams, sequences, and usage patterns, describing both the static structure and dynamic behaviour of the system. Communication diagrams have a free format for arranging objects and relationships as in an object diagram. To maintain the order of messages in this free format, they are numbered chronologically. Reading the communication diagram begins with message 1.0 and continues in the direction of forwarding messages from object to object. A communication diagram shows much of the same information as a sequence diagram, but because of a different way of presenting information, some things on one chart are easier to see than on another. The communication diagram more clearly shows which elements each element interacts with, and the sequence diagram more clearly shows the order in which the interactions take place.

With the help of these diagrams you can observe the basic structure of the system and the stages of interaction of parts of the system with each other.

JavaScript development language was used to develop the application. JavaScript is a dynamic, object-oriented prototype programming language. Implementation of the ECMAScript standard is most often used to create web page scripts, which allow the client-side (end-user devices) to interact with the user, control the browser, asynchronously exchange data with the server, and change the structure and appearance of the web page.

JavaScript is classified as a prototype (subset of object-oriented) scripting programming language with dynamic typing. In addition to prototyping, JavaScript also partially supports other programming paradigms (imperative and partially functional) and some relevant architectural features, including dynamic and weak typing, automatic memory management, prototype inheritance, functions as first-class objects.

The client application does not have a user interface, but only runs in the background on the user's device. This allows us to scale our system. The application can be placed in a container for use on a page in a browser or on a mobile application. Requests and transmission of voice commands are performed using the HTTP protocol.

Thus, having received a language command from the user, the application sends it to the logic server. An example of receiving a voice signal from the user is shown in Figure 3.5.

Once the command is written, it must be passed to the business logic server for further processing and execution. Thus, Figure 3.6 shows the principle of sending a command to the logic server using the jQuery AJAX library. jQuery is a popular open source JavaScript library. It was introduced in January 2006 at BarCamp NYC by John Resig. According to research by W3Techs, JQuery is used by more than half of the million most-visited sites.

```
var session = {
    audio: true,
    video: false
};
var recordRTC = null;
    navigator.getuserMedia(session, function (mediastream) {
        recordRTC = RecordRTC(MediaStream);
        recordRTC.startRecording();
    }, onError);
```

Figure 3.5 Receiving a user voice message

```
recordRTC.stopRecording(function(audioURL) {
    var  formData = new FormData();
    formData.append('edition[audio]' recordRTC.getBlob())
    $.ajax({
        type: 'POST',
        url: 'some/path'
        data: formData,
        contentType: false,
        cache: false,
        processData: false,
    })
})
```

Figure 3.6 Language command transmission

jQuery is the most popular JavaScript library used extensively today. jQuery is free software under the MIT license (until September 2012 there was dual licensing under the MIT and GNU General Public License of the second version).

The jQuery syntax is designed to make navigation easier to navigate by selecting DOM elements, creating animations, handling events, and developing AJAX applications. jQuery also provides opportunities for developers to create plugins at the top of the JavaScript library. Using these objects, developers can create abstractions for low-level interaction and create animations for high-level effects. This helps to create powerful and dynamic web pages.

After the language command is received by the business logic server, this command must be passed to the recognition service. To do this, the request is saved in a WAV file and sent to the recognition service (see Figure 3.7).

WAV is an audio file format developed by Microsoft and IBM. WAVE is based on the RIFF format, extending it to information about audio parameters such as the codec used, sampling rate, and number of channels. WAV as well as RIFF was provided for IBM PCs, so all variables are written in little endian format. The WAV equivalent for PowerPC computers is AIFF. Although WAVE files can be recorded using any audio codec, uncompressed PCM is commonly used, which results in large file sizes (about 172 KB per second for CD quality).

```
fetch('/api/speech-to-text/token').then(function(response) {
  return response.text();
}).then(function (token) {

  stream = WatsonSpeech.SpeechToText.recognizeFile({
    token: token,
        file: document.querySelector('#audiofile').files[0],
        play: true, // play the audio out load
        outputElement: '#output' // CSS selector or DOM Element (optional)
  })

  stream.on('error', function(err){
    console.log(err);
      });

}).catch(function(error){
    console.log(error);
  });
};
```

Figure 3.7 Transfer the file to the recognition service

Another disadvantage of the file is the limit of up to 4 GB, due to the 32-bit variable. The WAV format has been partially supplanted by compressed formats, but due to its simplicity, it continues to be widely used in audio editing and on portable audio devices such as players and digital voice recorders.

After the command has been recognized, a response with the recognized command arrives at the logic server. The logic server analyzes the correspondence and belonging of the recognized command in the dictionary of commands that are available in the system. This analysis uses a search tree—a dynamic non-linear data structure, each element of which contains its own information (or a link to the place in computer memory where information is stored) and a link to several (at least two) other similar elements. Search trees are used to represent dictionaries as an abstract data type. It is believed that each element of the dictionary has a key (weight) that takes values from a linearly ordered set. Such a set may be, for example, a numerical set or a set of words in a language. In the latter case, the lexicographic order can be considered linear. Thus, the search tree can be used both as a dictionary and as a priority queue. The time of the main operations is proportional to the height of the tree. If each internal node of the binary tree has exactly two descendants, then its height and time of basic operations are proportional to the logarithm of the number of nodes. Conversely, if a tree is a linear chain of n nodes, this time grows to $O(n)$. It is known that the height of a random binary tree is $0(\log n)$, so in this case, the execution time of the main operations is $0(\log n)$. Of course, binary search trees that occur in practice can be far from random. However, by taking special measures to balance the trees, you can ensure that the height of trees with n nodes will be $O(\log n)$.

After analyzing the command and obtaining a successful result, the command is encoded in a special sequence of characters, which are then passed to the device manager. After receiving a command from the business logic server, the device manager performs the necessary actions on the device to which this command belongs.

3.3 RESULTS

The Switchboard database was used to train the acoustic models, and the Switchboard sub-base of the HUB5 Eval 2000 test database was used to evaluate the results. The swbd (s5c) recipe from the Kaldi ASR tool was used as a basis for the experiments (Kaldi, 2016).

To build i-vectors, we used a system based on UBM (Universal Background Model) with 512 Gaussians, trained on 13-dimensional MFCC features, supplemented by the first and second derivatives. With its help, vectors of dimension 100 were extracted for training and test records.

3.3.1 Training on fMLLR-adapted features

In this series of experiments as a basic model was taken a deep neural network dnn5b with 6 hidden layers of 2048 neurons and sigmoids as activation functions from the prescription swbd (s5c), trained on fMLLR-adapted using GMM-HMM triphon model tri4 40-dimensional features, taken with a temporary context of 11 frames (central frame and 5 frames left and right).

The adapted dnn5b_iv model was trained on the input features of the base model, supplemented by an i-vector of dimension 100. The training was initialized to the base model with an extended input layer, using a learning speed of 0.002 and a penalty $4 \cdot 10^{-8}$ for deviating weights from the base model.

A linear layer of dimension 80 was added to the adapted model by means of singular decomposition of the weight matrix of the 6th hidden layer. The neural network with a narrow neck thus obtained was used to initialize the training of the dnn5b_iv_bn6-80 model, with training at a rate of 0.002 and a penalty $4 \cdot 10^{-8}$ for deviation weights from the values of the initializing neural network. This model, after removing the last hidden layer and the source layer, was used to construct 80-dimensional features (SDBN).

The triphone GMM-HMM model tri_sdbn with the same number of Gaussians (200000) and related states (11500) as the basic trifon model tri4 was trained on SDBN features. Also SDBN traits, taken with a context of 31 frames, liquefied over time after 5 frames (that is [-15 -10 -5 0 5 10 15]), were used to train DNN-HMM model dnn_sdbn with 4 hidden layers of 2048 neurons with sigmoids, with the initialization of training using limited Boltzmann machines. To train all of the above models, the marking on the bound states of the tryphones made using the basic GMM-HMM model tri4 was used.

The DNN-HMM model dnn_sdbn_smbr_i1lats was trained according to the sMBR-criterion of sequence separation, according to the training scheme, similar to the model dnn5b_smbr_i1lats from the recipe swbd (s5c).

Finally, the DNN-HMM model dnn_sdbn_sdbn-ali_smbr_i1lats was trained in a similar manner using triphone bound state markup made using the GMM-HMM tri_sdbn model. The results of the experiments are shown in Table 3.1.

Table 3.1 The results shown by models trained on the features built using the proposed method in a subset of the Switchboard test base HUB5 Eval 2000

Acoustic model	WER, %	AWER, %	WERR, %
tr/4	21,3	–	–
tr/ sdbn	15,6	5,7	26,8
dnn5b	14,6	–	–
dnn5b /v	14,1	0,5	3,4
dnn5b /v bn6-80	14,3	0,3	2,1
dnn sdbn	13,6	1,0	6,8
dnn5b smbr /llats	12,9	–	–
dnn sdbn smbr /llats	12,4	0,5	3,9
dnn sdbn sdbn-al/ smbr /llats	12,1	0,5	6,2

The DNN-HMM model dnn5b_iv, adapted to the speaker and acoustic environment using i-vectors, showed a 0.5% absolute and 3.4% relative reduction in recognition error, compared to the baseline DNN-HMM model.

Adapted with i-vectors DNN-HMM model with a narrow neck dnn5b_iv_bn6-80 gave the expected deterioration compared to the model dnn5b_iv, but still proved to be better than the baseline DNN-HMM model by 0.3% absolute and 2.1% relative.

The triphonic GMM-HMM model on SDBN tri_sdbn features showed a 5.7% absolute and 26.8% relative reduction in recognition error, compared to the basic triphonic GMM-HMM model.

The DNN-HMM model dnn_sdbn showed a 1.0% absolute and 6.8% relative reduction in recognition error compared to the baseline DNN-HMM model, and a 0.5% absolute and 3.5% relative reduction in recognition error compared to the baseline adapted DNN-HMM model dnn5b_iv.

The DNN-HMM model dnn_sdbn_smbr_i1lats, trained using the sMBR criterion, was 0.5% absolute and 3.9% relative better than the base model dnn5b_smbr_i1lats, trained on the same criterion.

The DNN-HMM model dnn_sdbn_sdbn-ali_smbr_i1lats, trained using the sMBR criterion and markup from the GMM-HMM model tri_sdbn, was 0.9% absolute and 6.2% relative better than the base model dnn5b_smbr_em1lats.

The results allow us to conclude about the high efficiency of the developed method in the problem of the recognition of English as a spontaneous language.

3.3.2 Raw training without the use of fMLLR adaptation

In the above experiments, training was carried out on the features already adapted to the speaker, using the fMLLR transformation. However, the use of i-vectors adapts to the speaker, as well as fMLLR adaptation. The use of fMLLR-adapted features reduces the growth that would be provided by the use of adaptation using i-vectors. Therefore, there is reason to expect that without the use of fMLLR-adaptation, the developed method of constructing features will demonstrate even greater efficiency (Saon, 2013).

To evaluate the performance of the proposed method of constructing signs in the absence of fMLLR-adaptation, another series of experiments was performed. The same marking on the bound states of tryphones made with the help of the tri4 model was used for model training, and raw spectral features—logarithms of signal energies in 23 triangular Mel-frequency filters—were used as signs for training deep neural networks (FBANK), supplemented by the first and second derivatives and taken with a temporal context of 11 frames (central frame and 5 frames left and right). Similarly, as in experiments on fMLLR-traits, the following models were taught:

- Basic DNN-HMM model dnn-fbank with 6 hidden layers of 2048 neurons with sigmoids
- DNN-HMM model dnn-fbank_iv, adapted using i-vectors (used the same 100-dimensional i-vectors as in experiments on fMLLR-signs)
- Adapted DNN-HMM model dnn-fbank_iv_bn6-80 with a linear thin layer of dimension 80, located in front of the last hidden layer. Next, a deep neural network with a narrow neck dnn-fbank_iv_bn6-80 was used to construct 80-dimensional features (SDBN-FBANK), which were trained triphonic GMM-HMM model tri_sdbn-fbank and DNN-HMM model dnn_sdbn-sham with 4 2048 neurons with sigmoids as activation functions (as in the previous experiment, the features for this DNN-HMM model were taken with a temporary context of 31 frames, liquefied after 5 frames). Table 3.2 presents the results obtained during these experiments.

Table 3.2 The results shown by the models trained on the features built using the proposed method without the use of fMLLR-adaptation in a subset of the Switchboard test base HUB5 Eval 2000

Acoustic model	WER, %	AWER, %	WERR, %
tri4	21,3	–	–
tri_sdbn-fbank	16,3	5,0	23,5
dnn-fbank	16,4	–	–
dnn-fbank_iv	14,9	1,5	9,1
dnn-fbank_iv_bn6-80	14,9	1,5	9,1
dnn_sdbn-fbank	14,2	0,7	13,4

The results indicate the following:

The dnn-fbank_iv DNN-HMM model, adapted to the speaker and acoustic environment using i-vectors, showed a 1.5% absolute and 9.1% relative reduction in recognition error, compared to the baseline DNN-HMM dnn-bank_iv.

The i-vectors adapted to the DNN-HMM model with the dnn-fbank_iv_bn6-80 bottleneck showed the same results as the adapted DNN-HMM model dnn-fbank_iv.

The triphonic GMM-HMM model tri_sdbn-fbank on SDBN-FBANK features showed a 5.0% absolute and 23.5% relative reduction in recognition error, compared to the basic triphonic GMM-HMM model.

The DNN-HMM model dnn_sdbn-fbank showed a 2.2% absolute and 13.4% relative reduction in recognition error, compared to the baseline DNN-HMM model, and a 0.7% absolute and 4.7% relative reduction in recognition error, in comparable to the adapted DNN-HMM model dnn-fbank_iv.

To experimentally evaluate the effectiveness of the proposed two-stage algorithm for initializing learning with it, deep neural networks were trained in the following configurations:

- fMLLR-adapted using GMM-HMM triphones models tri4 40-dimensional features, taken with a temporal context of 11 frames (center frame and 5 frames left and right); 6 hidden layers of 2048 neurons with sigmoids
- Logarithms of signal energies in 23 triangular Mel-frequency filters (FBANK), supplemented by the first and second derivatives and taken with a time context of 11 frames (central frame and 5 frames left and right); 6 hidden layers of 2048 neurons with sigmoids
- Constructed 80-dimensional features of SDBN, obtained from adapted using i-vectors deep neural network and taken with a context of 31 frames, liquefied over time after 5 frames

As before, the marking on the bound states from the triphonic GMM-HMM model tri4 was used. In the first stage, retraining was performed using limited Boltzmann machines; in the second stage, training was on the criterion of minimizing mutual entropy at a speed of 0.008 on a training sample, from which 98% of the examples corresponding to the pause were randomly dropped. The thus obtained deep neural networks for fMLLR, FBANK, and SDBN configurations were used to initialize the full training sample. The learning speed was reduced to 0.0004, an accelerated Nesterov gradient with a value of 0.7 was used, and a penalty $4 \cdot 10^{-8}$ for deviation of weights from the values of the initializing deep neural network was used.

The result was DNN-HMM models dnn5b_2step, dnnfbank_2step and dnn_sdbn_2step for fMLLR, FBANK and SDBN configurations, respectively. The results demonstrated by these models are shown in Table 3.3.

Table 3.3 Results demonstrated by models trained using a two-step initialization algorithm in the Switchboard sub-sample of the HUB5 Eval 2000 test base

Acoustic model	WER, %	AWER, %	WERR, %
dnn5b	14,6	–	–
dnn5b_2step	14,5	0,1	0,7
dnn-fbank	16,4	–	–
dnn-fbank_2step	15,9	0,5	3,0
dnn_sdbn	13,6	–	–
dnn_sdbn_2step	13,5	0,1	0,7

From these data it is possible to draw a conclusion about the advantage of the proposed two-stage algorithm of initialization of training over the algorithm of retraining by means of limited Boltzmann machines on 0,1–0,5% absolute and 0,7–3,0% relative, depending on the used configuration. It should be noted that the efficiency of the algorithm is high for "raw" unadapted features (FBANK) and decreases with the transition to more complex adapted features (fMLLR or SDBN).

The aim of the next experiment was to find out which of the three proposed methods of learning a deep neural network adapted with the help of i-vectors using a two-stage learning algorithm shows the best results. The experiment was performed on the FBANK configuration. The dnn-fbank_iv model adapted using DNN-HMM i-vectors, trained without the application of the proposed two-stage initialization algorithm, was chosen as the basic model (see Table 3.4).

Three models adapted using DNN-HMM i-vectors were trained using the proposed two-stage learning initialization algorithm:

1. The model dnn-fbank_sil2_iv was trained according to the data with an uninterrupted pause. An unadapted deep neural network trained with pause thinning up to 2% was used as initializations.
2. The model dnn-fbank_sil2_sil100_iv was trained according to the data with an uninterrupted pause. To initialize the training, an unadapted deep neural network dnn-fbank_2step was used, trained on data with an uninterrupted pause using a two-stage algorithm.
3. The model dnn-fbank_sil2_iv-sil2_sil100 was trained according to the data with an uninterrupted pause. To initialize the training, an i-vector–adapted deep neural network trained with pause thinning up to 2% was used, the training of which was initialized with an adapted deep neural network trained with pause thinning up to 2%.

Table 3.4 Comparison of three methods of learning adapted using i-vectors of deep neural networks using a two-stage initialization algorithm on a subset of the Switchboard test base HUB5 Eval 2000

Acoustic model	WER, %	Δ WER,%	WERR, %
dnn-fbank_iv	14,9	–	–
dnn-fbank_sil2_iv	14,7	0,2	1,3
dnn-fbank_sil2_sil100_iv	14,7	0,2	1,3
dnn-fbank_sil2_iv-sil2_sil100	14,7	0,2	1,3

3.4 CONCLUSION

The study reviewed methods for adapting acoustic models based on deep neural networks designed to compensate for inconsistencies in learning and operating conditions and thus increase the resilience of the recognition system to the acoustic variability of the speech signal.

A method was developed to construct features that are from a deep neural network with a narrow neck, adapted to the speaker and the acoustic environment with the help of i-vectors. An algorithm for training acoustic models based on deep neural networks using the constructed features is proposed. A two-stage algorithm for initializing the training of acoustic models based on deep neural networks has been developed to reduce the influence of speech-containing segments on the training of the acoustic model. Experimental studies have been conducted to confirm the effectiveness of the proposed method and algorithm in the problem of English language recognition by the Internet of Things that are part of the "Smart Home" system.

Promising areas for further development of the topic include, first, improving the method of constructing informative features extracted from the adapted to the speaker and acoustic conditions of the deep neural network, by training a deep neural network with a narrow neck using sequence criteria. Second, improving the accuracy of command recognition through the use of acoustic models based on wrapping and recurrent neural networks. Third, improving the accuracy of command recognition through the use of approaches to building language models that allow effective consideration of the distant semantic context, as well as morphological, syntactic, and semantic information. And, first of all, increase the speed of the command recognition of the "Smart House" system.

REFERENCES

Alcantud, F., Dolz, I. Gaya, C., Marcoset, M. (2006). The voice recognition system as a way of accessing the computer for people with physical standards as usual. *Technology and Disability*, *18(3)*, pp. 89–97. DOI: 10.3233/TAD-2006-18301.

AlHammadi, A., AlZaabi, A., AlMarzooqi, B., AlNeyadi, S., AlHashmi, Z., Shatnawi, M. A. (2019). *Survey of IoT-Based Smart Home Approaches*. Proceedings at Advances in Science and Engineering Technology International Conferences (ASET), Dubai, United Arab Emirates, pp. 1–6. DOI: 10.1109/ICASET.2019.8714572.

Al-Kuwari, M., Ramadan, A., Ismael, Y., Al-Sughair, L., Gastli, A. and Benammar, M. (2018). *Smart-home automation using IoT-based sensing and monitoring platform*. Proceedings at IEEE 12th International Conference on Compatibility, Power Electronics and Power Engineering (CPE-POWERENG 2018), Doha, 2018, pp. 1–6. DOIoi:10.1109/CPE.2018.8372548.

Dong, Y., Li, D. (2015). *Automatic Speech Recognition: A Deep Learning Approach*. London: Springer-Verlag.

Gaida, Ch., Lange, P., Petrick, R., Proba, P., Malatawy, A., Suendermann-Oeft, D. (2014). Comparing Open-Source Speech Recognition Toolkits. Retrieved from: http://suendermann.com/su/pdf/oasis2014.pdf (Access: 23.06.2020).

Ghaffarianhoseini, A., Ghaffarianhoseini, A., Tookey, J., Omrany, H., Fleury, A., Naismith, N., and Ghaffarianhoseini, M. (2017). The Essence of Smart Homes: Application of Intelligent Technologies towards Smarter Urban Future. In: Information Resources Management Association (IRMA) (ed.), *Artificial Intelligence: Concepts, Methodologies, Tools, and Applications*, Hershey: IGI Global, pp. 79–121. DOI:10.4018/978-1-5225-1759-7.ch004.

Hoque, M.A., Davidson, C. (2019). Design and Implementation of an IoT-Based Smart Home Security System. *International Journal of Networked and Distributed Computing*, 7(2), pp. 85–92.

Kaldi (2016). Kaldi ASR Toolkit. Retrieved from: http://kaldi-asr.org/. (Access: 30.11. 2019).

Malche, T., Maheshwary, P. (2017). Internet of Things (IoT) for building Smart Home System. Proceedings at International Conference on I-SMAC (IoT in Social, Mobile, Analytics and Cloud) (I-SMAC), Palladam, pp. 65–70. DOI: 10.1109/I-SMAC.2017.8058258.

Nielsen, M. (2019). *Neural Networks and Deep Learning.* Retrieved from: http://neuralnetwork-sanddeeplearning.com/ (Access: 12.12.2020).

Saon, G. (2013). *Speaker adaptation of neural network acoustic models using i- vectors.* Proceedings at IEEE Workshop on Automatic Speech Recognition and Understanding (ASRU), pp. 55–59.

Veselý, K., Ghoshal A., Burget L., Povey, D. (2013). *Sequence-discriminative training of deep neural networks.* Proceedings at Interspeech 2013. ISCA, 14th Annual Conference of the International Speech Communication Association, Lyon, France, August 2013. Retrieved from: http://www.cstr.ed.ac.uk/downloads/publications/2013/is13-dnn_seq.pdf (Access: 26.06.2020).

Vinay Sagar, K. N., Kusuma, S.M. (2015). Home Automation Using Internet of Things. *International Research Journal of Engineering and Technology, 2*(3), pp. 1965–1970.

Xue, J. (2014). *Singular value decomposition based low-footprint speaker adaptation and personalization for deep neural network.* Proceedings at IEEE International Conference on Acoustics, Speech and Signal Processing (ICASSP), pp. 6359–6363.

Yu, D., Seltzer, M. L., Li, J., Huang J.-T., Seide F. (2013). Feature Learning in Deep Neural Networks - Studies on Speech Recognition Tasks. arXiv:1301.3605v3 [cs.LG] 8 Mar 2013. Retrieved from: https://arxiv.org/pdf/1301.3605.pdf (Access: 10.09.2020).

Zhang, Y. (2014). *Extracting deep neural network bottleneck features using low- rank matrix factorization.* Proceedings at IEEE International Conference on Acoustics, Speech and Signal Processing (ICASSP), pp. 185–189.

Chapter 4

ICT as a component of the internationalization strategy of the enterprise

Piotr Kuraś

CONTENTS

4.1 INTRODUCTION

A distinctive feature of the contemporary world economy is the increasing level of uncertainty of the business environment of enterprises (Baker et al. 2016). For enterprises, this means the need to seek new methods of building a competitive edge, since classical concepts and methods of management are insufficient (Binns et. al., 2014; Kaplan & Orlikowski, 2015). This is mainly related to the phenomenon of a discontinuity of the development of markets and their globalization. Strategic management attempts to tackle these challenges; it may be generally understood as an information/decision-making process supported by classical management functions (Stabryła, 2000). Strategic management aims to deal with solving key problems in the business of enterprises, which are decisive in terms of the company's going concern and development, in the account of the influence of the surroundings and key factors of its production capacity. In terms of action, strategic management constitutes a set of methods that allow testing, assessing and projecting the future of the entire enterprise or its individual elements in the account of the perspective of the company's going concern and development.

Strategic management does not yet have a homogeneous definition. It seems that it is not possible, due to different conditions of operation, and different resources as well as goals. In addition, it is prevented by the unpredictable business environment, which directly translates to the verifiability of all forecasts. Their accuracy gets lower as the time horizon of planning is longer. These elements affect the level of effectiveness of strategic planning. This mainly results from the fact that the planning approach requires foreseeing the conditions of operation of the enterprise in the long term (Stonehouse & Pemberton, 2002). The more distant the perspective, the less effective and reliable the forecast. These circumstances mean that for the management of the enterprise to be effective it must be expanded by additional elements. Firstly, the enterprise must increase its strategic flexibility, understood as an ability to adjust to changes in the environment (Shimizu & Hitt, 2004). All these elements and many others must be taken into account while selecting the proper strategy for development and competition (Bingham et al., 2015; Sull, 2015). The selection of a proper strategy for the enterprise constitutes one of the key choices in deciding about its functioning in the future, because the strategy defines the long-term perspective of activities in terms of competitors as well as the manner of managing resources. In these conditions, the enterprise's orientation on resources seems an interesting alternative to the planning approach (Barney et al., 2001). A resource-based approach to managing the enterprise may give better effects that management based on long-term forecasts, which are exposed to a high risk of error, in particular in light of the high market uncertainty.

The resource-based approach has a firm position in the strategic management trend (Barney et al., 2001). It concentrates on explaining the dependencies between the enterprise's resources and its competitive advantage. It especially notes the conditions of the permanent nature of this advantage, and the related consequences for the process of formulating a competing strategy (Godziszewski, 2006). In accordance with the assumptions of the resource-based approach, an enterprise constitutes a set of resources and skills, which contribute to its power and differentiate it from other entities (Obłój, 2007). The type, size and the nature of resources and skills constitute the principal factors affecting the company's competitive position, profitability and development.

Regardless of the above considerations, the enterprise can apply various basic strategies as well as supporting functional strategies (Porter, 1980). The possibility of selecting from among various and often mutually exclusive strategies requires the enterprise to conduct a detailed review of the close and more distant competitive environment as well as possessed resources and competencies. A properly conducted analysis of competition allows effective implementation and efficient performance of the adopted strategy. Apart from classical development strategies, the enterprise may also consider an internationalization strategy. This is related to a requirement to partially move selected or all types of business: trade, production, research and development etc., abroad.

The internationalization process is the most significant at the level of enterprises because they constitute the main group of entities whose business activity affects the general flow of the globalization process (Tallman, 2002). Going global directly triggered the trend to internationalize other areas of economies and markets. These trends are aggregated and transformed at the highest level—meaning the world economy. These observations allow formulating the conclusion that there are still areas of extreme importance for enterprises which require continuous improvement of knowledge.

4.2 RESEARCH METHODOLOGY

The aim of the research was to present the role of ITC in the process of internationalization of the business activity of enterprises. The initial study of source literature, as well as own observations and experience, indicated the huge influence of ITC on processes of internationalizing certain enterprises, industries, markets and, in consequence, the entire world economy. It should be considered that internationalization processes have the most significance in relation to enterprises, because these processes are aggregated and transformed to higher levels and, in consequence, to the globalization of the world economy. In the last decades, these processes have become more intensive. In addition, they are supported by technical progress as well as changes in the area of collection, processing and distribution of information and knowledge, which become the accelerators of change. Undoubtedly, these accelerators include ICT. Increasing the scope, significant reduction of the duration of information flow, and enriching information with previously unavailable elements contribute to speeding up the process of internationalizing enterprises and what follows, the globalization of the world economy. An example of this may be the contribution of ITC to the process of transmitting the context of information. For example, the global progress in this area resulted in the possibility to hold teleconferences. They allow real-time communication and the ability to interact, but also tracking of nonverbal messages sent by the caller. These messages may include more information than communication in codified and formalized form. These observations are the main motives for undertaking this study. The reasons mentioned above were deemed sufficient to attempt to better understand the discussed phenomena to broaden the scope of the discussion in this area.

The scientific perspective is related to the need to apply appropriate research methods. For the purpose of this article, the most frequently used methods of processing study material were used: analysis and synthesis. The subject of the analysis was the process of internationalization of business activity of enterprises and the ICT. The analysis aimed at disassembling the problem into smaller elements to detect the existing conditions, attributes or cause-and-effect relations. Mental analytical operations refer to deductive conclusions. The study process also included synthesis methods with the use of the inductive reasoning assumption. For this purpose, the author took advantage of the available source literature, in particular in the area of the theory on the internationalization of enterprises. Therefore, the procedure has the form of literature studies, and the approach itself has an -epistemological nature.

4.3 BASIC STRATEGIES OF DEVELOPMENT OF ENTERPRISES

There are two basic methods of international enterprise development (Lee & Lieberman, 2009). The first method is the internal development, which happens without the participation of other entities. The second method is the external development, where the enterprise undertakes various forms of cooperation with other entities. Apart from various forms of co-operation, the external development strategy may be executed through co-operation with actual or potential competitors, meaning through a strategic alliance (Albers et al., 2016; Kuraś, 2012).

Apart from answering the question on the general development strategy, the enterprise must also select the manner of behaviour towards market competitors. The selection of a product development strategy is related to the requirement to solve a dilemma on whether the enterprise will go for specialization or diversification (Kaulich, 2012). Another issue is the scale of activity. This means the need to choose between businesses on a regional, national or global scale (Verbeke & Asmussen, 2016). Selecting a competitive strategy is also connected with the need to adopt a certain manner of approach towards clients and markets, which may generally be put down to competing on the basis of costs or differentiation (Banker et al., 2014).

A strategy may be understood as an integrated and coordinated set of actions undertaken in order to use principal competencies and to obtain competitive advantage (Hitt et al., 1995; Johnson et al., 2010). This allows distinguishing the two basic types of strategies (Zorska, 1998; Stabryła, 2000; Janasz et al., 2010):

- Base
- Functional

Base strategies define the general manner in which the enterprise competes. They include the following strategies:

- Cost leadership strategy
- Quality leadership strategy
- Lead strategy
- Market niche strategy

The cost leadership strategy assumes that it is necessary to achieve higher cost-effectiveness than competition (Gehani, 2013). This allows offering the product at a price lower than competitors, without any disadvantage for the enterprise's profitability. The effect of the economy of scale contributes to achieving the cost advantage. In the case of an increase in production, the unit cost of the product is decreasing, which makes production more profitable from the economic point of view. The increase of the production volume translates to a growth of work performance and a relative reduction of the costs of work. This phenomenon is referred to as the effect of specialization. Whereas the effect of innovation results from collecting experiences. This allows implementing modifications of products, technologies and production processes, which translate to a decrease in costs related to delivering products to the market, in particular costs connected with production or provision of services.

The quality leadership strategy (Choon Tan et al., 2000) assumes that the standard product cannot satisfy the needs of all clients. There is a group of consumers on the market who are ready to incur larger costs of purchase to receive a product which is better adjusted to their needs or which has unique characteristics that make it stand out on the market. There are also clients on the market who are ready to pay a much higher price than typical clients are ready or willing to pay in exchange for the effect of prestige. Higher sales in turn allow using better materials and solutions, and financing the costs of work of better-qualified staff. This strategy is often referred to as the differentiation strategy.

The lead strategy is related to the need to compete in all or most segments in the industry in which the enterprise is operating. This strategy consists of a confrontation with market rivals by way of delivering a typical product at a typical price. Competing on the basis of this strategy is substantially hindered if the enterprise has at its disposal substantially smaller resources. If this manner of competing is difficult, enterprises often apply the market niche strategy.

The market niche strategy (Noy, 2010); Schot & Geels, 2008) consists of concentrating the activities around the selected group of products (industry concentration), the geographical market (geographical concentration) or a defined group of buyers (market concentration). This type of strategy is often used by enterprises which do not want to confront much stronger rivals or do not want to compete in a highly competitive market. It requires identifying a relevant gap in the market and then managing it. As a rule, this strategy is applied by micro, small and medium enterprises, satisfied with the size of this market. This strategy allows applying a peculiar evasion from the competition, thus enabling the enterprise to operate in an area where competition is small or does not exist at all. Larger enterprises are usually not interested in the market of this size, or smaller organizational flexibility does not allow them to manage such niche.

Apart from the above-mentioned types of base strategy, there are also various functional strategies consisting of concentrating activities and programs executed inside the enterprise (Sharma & Fisher, 1997). Adopting these strategies is related to a change in the activity of the enterprise, mainly in the area of research, procurement, production and sales. However, they are usually executed with the use of advanced technologies as well as knowledge and experience. Strategies are applied to improve products and processes as well as the information infrastructure in the enterprise, which allows not only communication but also learning within the organization. The application of functional strategies leads to four effects:

- Raising effectiveness
- Raising quality
- Increasing innovativeness
- Increasing adjustment to the market

Adopting and executing functional strategies or, more precisely, functional programs, allows reduced costs and/or increased diversity of products, therefore they constitute the basis for executing base strategies.

4.4 EVOLUTION OF THE INTERNATIONALIZATION STRATEGY

Internationalization consists of expanding the business of an enterprise to foreign markets in order to ensure better development possibilities and a better competitive position (Tallman, 2002). This process is favoured by, amongst others, the advancement of science and technology, the development of economies of certain countries and the international market, and the growing investment potential of enterprises. The resulting strong increase of the size, geographical range and forms of expansion of enterprises caused the integration of numerous markets. As a result, there are new trends visible in the economy, namely treating the entire world as one common market on which the enterprise is operating (Boon, 2017). The selection of the internationalization strategy means managing the enterprise in a global environment, i.e., oriented to foreign markets, global competition and the ability to use the globally dispersed production factors. This strategy requires a high level of engagement in operations on foreign markets and is connected with developing intensive, multilevel international relations.

At the stage of planning the internationalization strategy, the enterprise must choose between standardization and differentiation of the method for gaining and maintaining the competitive advantage on individual foreign markets. The model of enterprise development prepared by Ansoff, 1985) is based on the above criteria. He distinguishes the following strategies:

- Penetration – consists of investing in current business, mainly in the scope of products and markets
- Product development – aims at implementing new products on the markets where the enterprise currently operates
- Market development – consists of expanding to new markets, using existing products for this purpose
- Diversification – consists of diversifying the business, thanks to simultaneously investing in new products and new markets

Development strategies executed on the world market consist of diversification in two dimensions: industry dimension and international dimension (Zorska, 1998). In the industry dimension, activities are undertaken in a horizontal, vertical, concentrical or conglomerate system (Pierścionek, 1997) and are related to the selection and management of various products on different markets. Strategies executed in the international dimension are related to locating the business outside of the border of the home country, and coordination of these activities on the world scale.

The source literature usually mentions four principal models of the behaviour of enterprises. These strategies are generally referred to as cross-border (Zorska, 2002) or global (Yip, 1995). In addition, another used term is *international strategies*; however, this may be confusing because this term also refers to a specific type of a cross-border (global) development strategy. These include the following strategies:

- Multinational
- International
- Global
- Transnational

A multinational (Brock & Birkinshaw, 2004) strategy requires a decentralization of decision-making and a de-location of resources. The activity of foreign branches of an enterprise is based on a significant level of autonomy as well as the independent use of key competencies and resources transferred from the mother company. This strategy is based on a strong differentiation of foreign outlets handled by individual branches. The purpose of these strategies is to adjust the production to the needs of the markets in hosting countries.

An international strategy (Hitt et al., 2016) consists of a diversification of the product dimension and the national (market) dimension. Product diversification consists of manufacturing various groups of products in individual foreign branches, adjusted to regional requirements. National or market diversity assumes using different locations for different operating activities (different for purchases, production, sales). In this strategy, the enterprise coordinates and standardizes activities performed in certain countries or regions. The difference between a multinational and international strategy consists of the scope of independence in the performance of tasks. Foreign multinational branches have a higher level of independence (Zorska, 1998).

A global strategy is characterized by strictly integrated and coordinated activities on a global scale. Products offered by the global enterprise have standard nature and relatively low prices. This strategy is applied to markets where the pressure to adjust to local requirements does not exist or is minor, and the pressure on low costs is high. Sales of a unified product are executed on as many foreign markets as possible (Yip, 1995; Stonehouse et al., 2000). The effect of low costs may be strengthened, thanks to obtaining the effect of scale in combination with access to cheap production factors offered by target countries. In this strategy, the effectiveness of each foreign branch is not as important as in the case of an international strategy. The strategic contribution to the effectiveness of an enterprise as a whole is more important. In this strategy, it is allowed to maintain even unprofitable branches if their existence is important for maintaining or strengthening the position of the enterprise on the market.

A transnational strategy (Donaldson, 2009) constitutes a combination of an international strategy and a global strategy. It consists of an attempt to coordinate and standardize activities both in the product dimension and in the national markets dimension. Since these conditions are hard to meet, a substantial part of decisions and activities must be de-localized onto individual markets. Transnational strategies demonstrate a better adjustment to local requirements than global strategies.

In the opinion of Yip (1995), the strategy should be adjusted to each of the four groups of factors: market, cost, and competitive and government factors. This is possible at all stages of the overall global strategy, which include (Stonehouse et al., 2000):

- Development of the key strategy – which constitutes the basis of the enterprise's competitive edge

- Internationalization of the key strategy – expanding the activity to an international scale
- Globalization of the international strategy – integration of the strategy in various countries

Certain elements of the same strategy (e.g., the level of participation in the world market, global location of the business, standardization of products, marketing and integrated competitive moves) may have a global nature, whereas others have a local nature. Their scope and level of globalization depends on the force, effect and direction of influence of individual groups of globalization factors. Combining the ability to react locally in accordance with the assumptions of the global strategy configuration and a high level of coordination allows developing multiple strategic skills, which facilitate adjusting to local and global needs. The strategy, which meets the criteria of a global strategy and takes account of the local conditions, is referred to as a transnational strategy.

4.5 INTERNATIONALIZATION IN THE RESOURCE-BASED APPROACH

In the strategic management theory, various approaches to managing an enterprise may be distinguished. These approaches may be used in various manners to manage an enterprise which is executing an internationalization strategy. According to McKiernan (1997), the following approaches may be singled out:

- Planning approach
- Evolution (learning) approach
- Positioning approach
- Resource-based approach

The planning approach assumes the need to plan long-term activities on foreign markets to achieve an "alignment" status between the general strategy of the enterprise and the environment of the target country (Ansoff, 1965; Andrews, 1987). Management in this approach is understood as a systemized and a deterministic process, which covers defining goals, (internal and external analysis), as well as implementing an overall strategy of the enterprise. The benefits of this approach include, in particular, formalization of goals and defining control tools, which allow measuring results. Whereas weaknesses include limited possibilities in an unstable and unforeseeable environment. Uncertainty and inaccuracy of data and information, on the basis of which the strategy is planned, may lead to wrong decisions (Stonehouse et al., 2000). To limit the risk, the enterprise analyses and assesses risk factors in the host country, which constitutes one of the most significant factors of selecting the location country.

The evolution (learning) approach assumes that along the passage of time the strategy in the enterprise will start to emerge and take form. In this approach, it is assumed that the enterprise somehow "handles itself" on the market (Mintzberg & Waters, 1985; Mintzberg & Quinn, 1996). In reality, enterprises often adjust their strategies to the changing conditions of the environment. Therefore, the strategy evolves in a rational manner as a reaction to changes in the environment (Quinn, 1978). The strategy may, therefore, be recognized as a combination of goal plans and on-going adjustments made with time. This means that substantial deviations may occur between the planned strategy and the executed strategy (Mintzberg, 1987). This approach only explains the phenomenon of internationalization to a small extent. It is difficult to execute foreign expansion without informed purposeful decisions. However, the expansion may take effect in circumstances, where it is not a result of an intended activity but, for example, cooperation with a larger internationalized partner or foreign entity.

The positioning approach is mainly based on concepts presented by Porter (1980; 1985), in particular the general strategy concept, the five forces model and the value chain model. In accordance with the assumptions in this approach, strategic management begins with an analysis of the competitive environment using the five forces model. It aims at defining the profitability of the given sector. Then, an analysis is performed regarding activities aiming at increasing the added value of the enterprise and mutual relations between these activities—with the application of the value chain model. The results of these analyses constitute the basis to formulate a general strategy of the enterprise. This approach is also referred to as an external–internal approach due to the subjects of analyses (McKiernan, 1997). Critics of this approach (Rumelt, 1991) note that it is a static approach, profitability of the sector does not have to define the profitability of the enterprise, it is concentrated on competition (without regard for cooperation), and emphasis is placed on the environment rather than on competencies of the company. This approach may be applied without any restrictions for the purpose of foreign expansion. Restrictions may include hindered access to information and a risk of incomplete understanding of legal, economic and social conditions of functioning on foreign markets.

The last one of the above-mentioned approaches is the resource-based approach. The basic difference between the positioning approach and the resource-based approach is that the positioning approach emphasized the position of the enterprise in its sector, and the resource-based approach concentrates on the manner of managing input resources to develop key competencies and differentiating abilities. This approach dominated strategic thinking in the 1990s (Prahalad & Hamel, 1990; Kay, 1993). A resource-based approach should be treated not as an alternative but rather as a supplement of the positioning approach. Studies performed by various researchers, e.g., Hamel and Prahalad (1994), demonstrate that the activity of the enterprise must be subordinated to the market and must be sensitive to the needs of customers (Krupski, 2006). Therefore, an external analysis applied in the positioning approach is essential. The discussed approach is also referred to as an internal–external approach because it firstly concentrates on the enterprise's resources, and only then analyses the environment (McKiernan, 1997).

A resource-based approach attempts to explain the dependencies between the enterprise's resources and its competitive advantage. It notes the conditions of sustainability of this advantage and the related consequences for the process of formulating a competing strategy (Godziszewski, 2006). This approach assumes that the enterprise is a set of resources and creative skills, which prove its power and differentiate it from other entities (Obłój, 2007). The type, quantity and nature of resources and skills are the basic factors which shape the competitive position and the development potential of the enterprise. This approach assumes the need to conduct an external–internal analysis of the enterprise, and in this scope it does not constitute an alternative but rather a supplement of the positioning approach.

In the resource-based approach, the resource category is at the centre. Resources mean a group of manufacturing factors, held or controlled by the enterprise, which are transformed and configured in various processes, as a result of which final goods or services are created. Four types of resources are mentioned most frequently (Barney, 1997):

- Financial resources
- Physical resources
- Human resources
- Organizational resources

More detailed classifications additionally cover a division into technological resources, image (reputation), and relations with clients and suppliers (Hunt & Morgan, 1995). Resources are also often divided into tangible and intangible resources. Tangible resources have a physical form and include, for example, real estate, devices and financial means. Intangible resources do not have a physical form and include, mainly, the brand, reputation and intellectual property rights (Grant, 1991).

The *capabilities* category is characteristic of the resource-based approach. This should be understood as a possibility related to a group of resources to execute certain tasks. These possibilities depend not only on the state of resources but also on their configurations created in the enterprise and manners of their use. An important concept related to resources is also a *competence*. This may be defined as the enterprise's ability to use all the possessed resources. From the perspective of competitiveness, we may distinguish a *distinctive competence*, thanks to which the enterprise uses its resources better than the competition, or a *core competence* related to an ability to learn, in particular in the scope of coordinating various manufacturing skills and integrating numerous technology streams (Prahalad & Hamel, 1990). The most important assumptions of the resource-based approach are as follows (Barney, 1991):

- Resources are unevenly distributed amongst companies, which is the cause of their heterogeneity
- Resources cannot be freely transferred amongst companies

To be able to achieve a competitive advantage based on resources, they must have defined characteristics. Barney (1991) distinguished the following characteristics:

- Valuable
- Rare
- Imperfectly imitable
- Non-substitutable

The strategic value of a resource results from its usability to build a competitive advantage. The more valuable the resource, the better its usability. This value changes with time. As time passes by, defined resources and their configuration become disseminated, hence losing their strategic value. It should be highlighted that the strategic value of resources is contextual, which prevents defining an objective list of these values or determining which resources are more valuable than others.

Scarcity of resources means that the quantity of resources is not sufficient for all enterprises. Possessing scarce resources allows taking a better market position than competitors. The more scarce the resource, the longer the period of obtaining these resources and evening out by competitors. When most of the market participants are equipped with defined resources, their strategic attractiveness decreases.

The difficulty of imitating resources results from their characteristics, as a result of which, obtaining or manufacturing resources is very difficult or very expensive. Frequently, resources or their combinations are created within a defined organizational and environmental context in the long term. Attempts to recreate them in different conditions and in the short term may turn out impossible. Additional hardship results from the fact that defined combinations of resources are generated within a specific social context, which comprises organizational culture, company reputation, relations with employees, suppliers, clients, etc. This element may be used in the internationalization process when the enterprise, which undertakes a foreign expansion, has at its disposal certain resources that allow delivering a product unique in the target market, a product of much higher quality or a product cheaper than the competition's.

A lack of substitutes means that resources cannot be replaced. Possessing such resources—in particular those generated within the organization and well protected—may constitute an important source of competitive advantage for a long time. This attribute of a resource has a similar scope and effect in the internationalization process as in circumstances described above. However, this allows gaining a stronger effect in the form of an even more sustainable competitive advantage.

A diversity of resources gives a possibility to build a competitive advantage based on this element. The diversity of resources allows combining them in various configurations. This allows companies which apply foreign expansion strategies to obtain a unique effect on the target market in the form of a distinguished product or service, which may constitute an important element in building a competitive advantage. Limited availability of resources results from the fact that resources are not equally available to all enterprises. This results in asymmetry, which provides enterprises with easier access to these resources, and allows building an advantage on this element. Frequently, the reason behind the company's expansion, related with better resources (machines, devices, human capital, know-how, experience, reputation, capital) provided by companies operating in the given target market and/or higher effectiveness of using these resources, results in a situation where resources are not equally accessible to all enterprises.

Summing up, in the resource-based approach it is assumed that there is a connection between the described characteristics and the possibility of building a competitive position. Resources which are diversified, rare and valuable may generate a competitive advantage. If, in addition, they are difficult to imitate and immobile as well as irreplaceable, they have the potential to generate a sustainable competitive advantage (Głuszek, 2006). However, it should be underlined that for permanent market success, possessing resources is not sufficient. It is essential to skilfully manage resources, as this process, combined with resources, may give the enterprise an advantage in the market.

4.6 TECHNOLOGY AS AN ELEMENT OF A STRATEGIC RESOURCE OF THE ENTERPRISE

In general terms, technology may be understood as a method of processing natural resources into usable resources, such as knowledge about this process or, more broadly, an area of technology dealing with preparing and conducting processes of manufacturing or processing resources, semi-finished products and goods in the most efficient conditions. Technology has great significance for the overall strategy of the enterprise, whereas its influence is multidirectional (Itami & Numagami, 1992). Certain technologies, within the scope of communication techniques—in particular development of the internet—substantially contribute to unifying tastes of consumers worldwide. This leads to a unification of the product range on the global scale. However, global unification has extremely serious consequences for technologies applied by the enterprise. The best technological solutions spread very quickly, thus setting new quality, functional and aesthetic standards (Koźmiński, 1999). However, full product unification on all world markets is not possible, because in the case of many products we are still faced with diversified demand in various countries. This results from cultural diversity and sustained consumption habits (Strategor, 1997).

The spread of new advanced technologies substantially contributed to the change of base development strategies applied by the enterprise. A good example of this is an increasingly widespread use of computer-aided design—CAD (Hirz et al., 2013)—and computer-aided manufacturing—CAM (Abduo et al., 2014). The integration of CAD with CAM—CAD/CAM (Alghazzawi, 2016)—allows for computer-integrated manufacturing—CIM (Lewoc et al., 2018). These systems have significantly contributed to the change in the conditions of competing on the market. An example of this is the significant shortening of the product life cycle in recent years. At the beginning of the 1990s, a given vehicle model was produced, on average, for about a decade. During this time, the model went through *face-lifting* twice at most. This usually consisted of introducing small stylistic changes without significant technical innovations. Currently, models are replaced after just five years on average, and this period in many cases is reduced to even three years; the offering of manufacturers includes an increasing number of versions of the same vehicle, in technological and construction terms. In consequence, enterprises must make strategic decisions in a shorter time, in a less and less stable business environment.

Technology is usually identified with knowledge on the possibilities of using and manners of combining resources in the production process. Since possessing appropriate technologies may translate to improving the competitive position, they should be treated as an element of the strategic resource. The skillful use of technology may become one of the key competencies of an enterprise. In such a case, this often translates to increasing abilities to introduce innovation.

Technologies are often used in competitive struggle because they allow improving the group of products. This may be carried out in several ways, for example, through (Stonehouse et al., 2000):

- Assigning new functions
- Assigning new attributes
- Increasing reliability

Advanced technologies allow the creation of a product with unprecedented functions. Examples include mobile phones, satellite phones and satellite navigation. Developing products with different functionalities has changed the rules of communication and the functioning of entire economies and communities. Another effect of using technology consists of assigning new attributes to existing products, as a result of which the products become more usable and universal. For example, equipping the mobile phone with faster processors, more memory and larger screens initiated the creation of the smartphone segment. As a result, contemporary phones are, in fact, microcomputers and have become more personal communication and entertainment centres than just phones.

Relations between technologies and products have been presented above. On a similar basis, relations between technologies and the manufacturing process may be identified. The use of technology to improve the competitive advantage may result from:

- Shortening the time between implementing the new product concepts
- Improving the quality
- Reducing the cost

The use of modern design systems (CAD/CAM) translates to substantial reductions in the time required to prepare the concept of a new product and implement its production. Increasing the level of automation allows improvements in the quality of the product by way of reducing the number of errors occurring in complex repeatable processes. Simplifying the product, and increasing the production volume and reliability of manufacturing processes allows reducing the cost.

Technology may be manifested in various forms. It may be tangible or intangible. In the case of certain products (e.g., mobile phones, computer software), applied technologies, due to their tangible nature, are available to the competition to a certain extent. Detailed research on the competition's products allows applying proven solutions in a company's own products. However, a real competitive advantage comes from technologies in intangible forms. In such a case, the same product in no way reveals technologies applied during production, because they are not materialized in this product. An example of this may be the production of *float* type glass. The traditional technology consists of rolling liquid glass until the desired thickness is reached. However, this requires further processing. In the process of manufacturing *float* type glass, the glass is continuously flowing into a tub with liquid tin. The result is a perfectly flat sheet, without the need for polishing (Stonehouse et al. 2000).

Technologies used to build competitive advantage may be further divided into:

- Design technologies
- Manufacturing technologies

In the first case, an enterprise with defined competencies (e.g. electronic systems and programming) may concentrate on marketing products based on joint solutions. For example, Samsung is one of the world's largest producers of consumer electronics. It is active in many market segments and manufactures, amongst other things, televisions, mobile computers, photo cameras and music players. A common characteristic of these products is that they are based on the competencies of the company in terms of designing electronic systems and programming. Competitive advantage may also be built around manufacturing processes. Implementing unique manufacturing and organizational solutions may substantially increase competitiveness. A model example is Ford's mass production system, which revolutionized and forever changed the face of industry worldwide and the entire global economy.

4.7 TECHNOLOGICAL STRATEGY OF THE ENTERPRISE

The enterprise's overall strategy includes functional strategies. One of them is the technological strategy. It is formed to use market opportunities and prevent threats related to using technology in the competitive struggle. The implementation of the technological strategy is carried out in several stages. These include:

- An analysis of the technological potential
- Obtaining new technologies
- Using technology
- Protecting technology against competition

In the first stage, the potential of the enterprise to build a competitive advantage with the use of technology should be assessed. For this purpose, it is essential to distinguish key competencies of the company in the area of technology and confront them against opportunities and market threats. It is also significant to recognize technological gaps in order to undertake appropriate corrective activities. The analysis of the technological potential requires defined systemized activities, which consist of revising (Goodman & Lawless, 1994):

- The process of technological innovations
- The innovative potential
- Technologies, in terms of their competitiveness

Firstly, the company's competences and experience in creating and implementing technological innovation should be assessed. This helps to work out a risk profile of current and future undertakings in order to select the areas of technology with the largest potential for building a competitive advantage. This potential is then compared with the innovative potential of competitors. In particular, the analysis should cover the research and development potential, the number and level of innovativeness of new products and the moment of marketing the new product, as well as dependencies between these numbers and the market position of the competitor. Next, technologies should be verified in terms of their competitiveness. This criterion allows properly grouping technologies demanded by the enterprise and formulating a proper implementation policy. Technologies may be divided into those that may be included in the technological portfolio in the future, technologies in the early development stage, technologies key for building competitive advantage and mature technologies, commonly applied both in the analysed company and in competitor companies.

The next stage of formulating a technological strategy requires deciding whether the enterprise will prepare its own technologies or if they will be obtained from the outside. In the case of transnational corporations, technologies are usually developed in the organization. Companies have their own R and D centres and incur substantial expenditures on developing their own unique and distinguishing technologies. Another method of obtaining technology is a purchase of a licence, establishing a joint-venture company, or a non-capital strategic alliance with a partner possessing relevant technologies. Entities which cannot develop an appropriate budget for R and D works often apply a technological imitation strategy. This consists of implementing technologies which proved to work well in competitor companies and may be copied due to broad availability.

For the technological strategy to make a significant contribution to the development of the enterprise, obtained technologies must be used in the most effective manner. The key issue is the vision of using the technology and creating appropriate organization conditions for the proper use of technologies. At this stage, a decision must be made on the location of the technological centre in the organizational structure of the enterprise, and sufficient support must be ensured.

Possessed technologies, in particular those prepared in the enterprise, should be protected from competition. It is easier to protect intangible technologies, related to manufacturing processes, than tangible processes reflected in the final product. In principle, there are two ways to proceed. Particularly valuable technologies may be patented. The patent procedure, however, is long, costly and requires a detailed description of the patented technology, which will be available to competitors. Therefore, their own innovative technologies may be developed on the basis of the patent documentation of the competition. The enterprise may also attempt to keep the technology secret. This is a better solution in case of small innovations, or innovations that require immediate implementation due to technological progress and quick ageing of technology.

4.8 THE POSITION OF ICTs IN THE TECHNOLOGICAL STRATEGY

The development of technology has a substantial influence on the functioning and the layout of competition forces in the world economy (Ford, 2014; Ahmad & Schroeder, 2011). The radical transformation of production systems in the world was initiated by the mass production system prepared by H. Ford. The system was based on the decentralization of manufacturing activities and the standardization of subassemblies. Thanks to specialization and standardization of activities, and revolutionary work organization consisting of a precise division of tasks, Ford ensured a record pace of production and low prices for offered products. The shape of the current economy was also greatly affected by further organizational improvements. *Just-in-time* systems, *flexible manufacturing systems* and *lean production* concepts developed in their factories ensured a competitive advantage to Japanese manufacturers of vehicles for many years. These systems were popularized worldwide (see: Monden, 2011).

The aforementioned systems are based on product standardization. This allows offering the same or only slightly modified products worldwide. The cost of adjusting products to the requirements of regional markets is reduced significantly. Therefore, technological development constitutes one of the most important factors of globalization. However, a special role in this regard is played by information and communication techniques.

In the past decades, many technologies were created and developed, which gave rise to irreversible changes in the society. The development of television, in particular satellite television, mobile and satellite telephony, and the internet mostly put a stop to restrictions resulting from distance and cultural differences. As a result, tastes and needs of consumers around the world are becoming unified. This process is in the interest of companies operating on an international scale, since it allows the creation of a global product, which can be offered to any client around the world without the need for any changes. Enterprises are creating this process themselves, as a result of informed decisions and activities. Examples include global marketing programs, which contribute to unifying consumer tastes. Apart from changes on the demand side, ICT techniques significantly increased possibilities available to enterprises in terms of coordinating activities worldwide and facilitated quick reactions to the changes happening in certain regional markets

ICT techniques allow many companies to be successful on the global market. They play an important role in the process of learning and knowledge management. They also enable better coordination of tasks and constitute an effective tool in the competitive struggle. ICT techniques constitute an important link to the process of building and strengthening key competencies and cost reduction. However, apart from the undoubted benefits of the discussed techniques, they also bring certain threats. The spread of ICT techniques intensifies the competitive struggle in defined sectors as well as the entire world economy and increases the uncertainty of the environment (Chakravarthy, 1997).

The development of ICT techniques has triggered radical changes in information architecture. There has been a transition from a centralized to a dispersed data processing system as resources, information and knowledge have become cheaper and easier to access. Managers have at their disposal a huge arsenal of tools supporting collection, processing and presentation of data and information. At present, the problem is not so much a lack of data but the enormous volume available for selection.

Various systems have an important role in today's management of an enterprise. These include mainly *decision support systems (DSS)*, *expert systems*, *neural networks*, multimedia and intelligent databases. Software development allowed creating *executive information systems* (EIS) and *strategic information systems* (SIS). Based on complex and often inconsistent and incomplete data, these systems help obtain information and knowledge. They allow making more effective decisions and improve the organization's ability to react in an increasingly chaotic and competitive environment.

The contribution of ICT techniques in a global strategy results from the change of the methods of knowledge management, coordination of tasks, increase of flexibility and ability to react to change. These techniques play a principal role in information collection, processing, interpretation and coding, as well as developing new organizational knowledge, which forms the basis of key competencies. ICT techniques formed the basis of the infrastructure, which supports the network organizational structures that may become a significant element of the learning organization process (Stonehouse & Pemberton, 1999).

ICT techniques allow building a network of relations between enterprises. They are the condition of establishing virtual companies. This business configuration allows concentrating on key competencies, which are strengthened as a result of operating within a network. Thus, the effect of synergy is obtained.

Competitive advantage of companies that apply the global strategy results from the configuration and coordination of activity. ICT techniques have substantially contributed to an increased coordination of activity conducted in geographically dispersed centres. They also increased the number of available configurations. These effects are obtained with a simultaneous increase of flexibility and the pace of reaction to change.

4.9 CONCLUSION

Individual national economies are becoming increasingly related to economies of other countries, forming one huge common market in which the enterprise must compete. These processes are intensifying, along with the dynamics of the relations. The issue of internationalization of enterprises is, therefore, still valid and requires continuous improvement of knowledge. In spite of the unchanged mechanism of internationalization, defined as expanding the company's activity in order to ensure better development possibilities, the conditions of this process are changing. These conditions mainly include external circumstances, which result from changes in the legal, economic, technical and social areas. The force of influence of individual areas and individual factors is changing. Examples include technologies, in particular ICT, which have completely changed the standards of communication as well as obtaining, processing, collecting and distributing knowledge over the course of the past years. This equips enterprises with a completely different set of tools essential to compete on the market. Foreign expansion of companies is becoming increasingly available for medium, small or even micro-enterprises, since various ICT channels, tools and techniques allow undertaking certain activities on foreign markets at small or even marginal cost, which was impossible not so long ago and constituted one of the principal barriers of entering foreign markets.

This article is theoretical and discussed methods of analysis and synthesis constitute elements of the mental process, in particular induction and deduction, without the support of empirical studies. This article is to contribute to the author's further studies and provides suggestions for other authors interested in internationalization as well as technological and ICT strategies, and in continuous research in this area, in particular empirical studies.

REFERENCES

Abduo, J., Lyons, K., Bennamoun, M. (2014). Trends in Computer-Aided Manufacturing in Prosthodontics: A Review of the Available Streams. *International Journal of Dentistry, 2014,* pp. 1–15. Doi: https://doi.org/10.1155/2014/783948.

Ahmad, S., Schroeder, R.G. (2011). Knowledge management through technology strategy: implications for competitiveness. *Journal of Manufacturing Technology Management,* 22(1), pp. 6–24.

Albers, S., Wohlgezogen, F., Zajac, E. J. (2016). Strategic Alliance Structures: An Organizational Design Perspective. *Journal of Management,* 42(3), pp. 582–614.

Alghazzawi, T. F. (2016). Advancements in CAD/CAM technology: Options for practical implementation. *Journal of Prosthodontic Research,* 60(2), pp. 72–84.

Andrews, K. R. (1987). *The concept of corporate strategy.* Homewood: Irwin.

Ansoff, H. I. (1965). *Corporate strategy; an analytic approach to business policy for growth and expansion.* New York: McGraw-Hill.

Ansoff, H. I. (1985). *Zarządzanie strategiczne*, Warsaw: PWE.

Baker, S. R., Bloom, N., Davis, S. J. (2016). Measuring Economic Policy Uncertainty. *The Quarterly Journal of Economics, 131(4)*, pp. 1593–1636.

Banker, R. D., Mashruwala, R., Tripathy, A. (2014). Does a differentiation strategy lead to more sustainable financial performance than a cost leadership strategy? *Management Decision, 52(5)*, pp. 872–896.

Barney, J. (1991). Firm Resources and Sustained Competitive Advantage. *Journal of Management, 17(1)*, pp. 99–120.

Barney, J. (1997). *Gaining and sustaining competitive advantage*. Reading: Addison-Wesley.

Barney, J. B., Ketchen, D. J., Wright, M. (2001). The Future of Resource-Based Theory: Revitalization or Decline? *Journal of Management, 37(5)*, pp. 1299–1315.

Barney, J., Wright, M., Ketchen, D. J. (2001). The resource-based view of the firm: Ten years after 1991. *Journal of Management, 27(6)*, pp. 625–641.

Bingham, Ch. B., Eisenhardt, K. M., Furr, R. (2015). Which Strategy When? *MIT Sloan Management Review. Special Collection. "Top 10 Lessons on Strategy"*, pp. 20–27.

Binns, A., Harreld, J. B., O'Reilly, C.A., Tushman, M. L. (2015). The Art of Strategic Renewal. *MIT Sloan Management Review. Special Collection. "Top 10 Lessons on Strategy"*, pp. 1–3.

Boon, M. (2017). Business Enterprise and Globalization: Towards a Transnational Business History. *Business History Review, 91(3)*, pp. 511–535.

Brock, D., Birkinshaw, J. (2004). Multinational Strategy and Structure: A Review and Research Agenda. *Management International Review*, pp. 5–14.

Chakravarthy, B. (1997). A new strategy framework for coping with turbulence. *Sloan Management Review, 38(2)*, pp. 69–82.

Choon Tan, K., Kannan, V.R., Handfield, R.B., Ghosh, S. (2000). Quality, manufacturing strategy, and global competition: An empirical analysis. *Benchmarking: An International Journal, 7(3)*, pp. 174–182.

Donaldson, L. (2009). In search of the matrix advantage: A reexamination of the fit of matrix structures to transnational strategy. In: J.L.C. Cheng, E. Maitland, and S. Nicholas (eds.), *Managing, Subsidiary Dynamics: Headquarters Role, Capability Development, and China Strategy (Advances in International Management)*. Bingley: Emerald Group Publishing Limited, 22, pp. 3–26.

Ford, S.L.N. (2014). Additive Manufacturing Technology: Potential Implications for U.S. Manufacturing Competitiveness. *Journal of International Commerce and Economics*. Retrieved from: https://usitc.gov/publications/332/journals/vol_vi_article4_additive_manufacturing_technology.pdf (Access: 16.05.2020).

Gehani, R. R. (2013). Innovative Strategic Leader Transforming From a Low-Cost Strategy to Product Differentiation Strategy. *Journal of Technology Management & Innovation, 8(2)*, pp. 144–155.

Głuszek, E. (2006). Formułowanie strategii w nurcie zasobowym – ograniczenia i wyzwania. In: R. Krupski (ed.), *Zarządzanie strategiczne. Ujęcie zasobowe*. Wałbrzych: WWSZiP, pp. 75–90.

Godziszewski, B. (2006). *Istota zasobowego podejścia do strategii przedsiębiorstwa*, In: R. Krupski (ed.), *Zarządzanie strategiczne. Ujęcie zasobowe*. Wałbrzych: WWSZiP, pp. 9–24.

Goodman, R. A., Lawless, M. W. (1994). *Technology and strategy: conceptual models and diagnostics*. New York: Oxford University Press.

Grant, R. M. (1991). *Contemporary strategy analysis: concepts, techniques, application*. Cambridge: Blackwell.

Hamel, G., Prahalad, C. K. (1994). *Competing for the future*. Boston: Harvard Business School Press.

Hirz, M., Dietrich, W., Gfrerrer, A., Lang, J. (2013). *Integrated Computer-Aided Design in Automotive Development*. Berlin: Springer-Verlag.

Hitt, M. A., Ireland, R. D., Hoskisson, R. E. (1995). *Strategic management: competitiveness and globalization Concepts*. Minneapolis/St. Paul: West Publishing.

Hitt, M. A., Li, D., Xu, K.(2016). International strategy: From local to global and beyond. *Journal of World Business, 51(1)*, pp. 58–73.

Hunt, S. D., Morgan, R. M. (1995). The comparative advantage theory of competition. *Journal of Marketing, 59(2)*, pp. 1–15.

Itami, H., Numagami, T. (1992). Dynamic interaction between strategy and technology. *Strategic Management Journal, 13(S2)*, pp. 119–135.

Janasz, K., Janasz, W., Kozioł, K., Szopik-Depczyńska, K. (2010). *Zarządzanie strategiczne. Koncepcje, metody, strategie.* Warsaw: Difin.

Johnson, G., Scholes, K., Whittington, R. (2010). *Podstawy strategii.* Warszawa: PWE.

Kaplan, S., Orlikowski, W. (2015). Beyond Forecasting: Creating New Strategic Narratives, *MIT Sloan Management Review. Special Collection. "Top 10 Lessons on Strategy"*, pp. 14–19.

Kaulich, F. (2012). Diversification vs. specialization as alternative strategies for economic development: Can we settle a debate by looking at the empirical evidence? United Nations Industrial Development Organization (UNIDO), Vienna. Retrieved from: https://open.unido.org (Access: 16.05.2020).

Kay, J. A. (1993). *Foundations of corporate success: how business strategies add value.* Oxford/New York: Oxford University Press.

Koźmiński, A. K. (1999). *Zarządzanie międzynarodowe.* Warsaw: PWE.

Krupski, R. (2006). Kierunki rozwoju ujęcia zasobowego zarządzania strategicznego. In: R. Krupski (ed.), *Zarządzanie strategiczne. Ujęcie zasobowe.* Wałbrzych: WWSZiP, pp. 53–64.

Kuraś, P. (2012). Alians jako model współdziałania strategicznego przedsiębiorstw. In: A. Stabryła and T. Małkus (eds.), *Strategie rozwoju organizacji.* Kraków: Mfiles.pl., pp. 57–71.

Lee, G. K., Lieberman, M. B. (2009). Acquisition vs. internal development as modes of market entry. 2009. *Strategic Management Journal, 31(2)*, pp. 140–158.

Lewoc, J. B., Izworski, A., Skowronski, S. (2018). Performance Modelling of a Computer-integrated Manufacturing and Management System. *Journal on Developments and Trends in Modelling and Simulation, 28(2)*, pp. 67–74.

McKiernan, P. (1997). Strategy past; strategy futures. *Long Range Planning, 30(5)*, pp. 790–798.

Mintzberg, H. (1987). The Strategy Concept I: Five Ps For Strategy. *California Management Review, 30(1)*, pp. 11–24.

Mintzberg, H., Quinn, J. B. (1996). *The strategy process: concepts, contexts and cases.* London: Prentice-Hall.

Mintzberg, H., Waters, J. A. (1985). Of strategies, deliberate and emergent. *Strategic Management Journal, 6(3)*, pp. 257–272.

Monden, Y. (2011). *Toyota Production System. An Integrated Approach to Just-In-Time.* 4th Edition. Boca Raton: CRC Press.

Noy, E. (2010). Niche strategy: merging economic and marketing theories with population ecology arguments. *Journal of Strategic Marketing, 18(1)*, pp. 77–86.

Obłój, K. (2007). *Strategia organizacji. W poszukiwaniu trwałej przewagi konkurencyjnej*, Warsaw: PWE.

Pierścionek, Z. (1997). *Strategie rozwoju firmy.* Warsaw: PWN.

Porter, M. E. (1980). *Competitive Strategy: Techniques for Analysing Industries and Competitors.* New York: The Free Press.

Porter, M. E. (1985). *Competitive Advantage.* New York: The Free Press.

Prahalad, C. K., Hamel, G. (1990). The Core Competence of the Corporation. *Harvard Business Review.* May–June, pp. 79–90.

Quinn, J. B. (1978). Strategies for change: logical incrementalism. *Sloan Management Review, 20*, pp. 7–21.

Rumelt, R. P. (1991). How much does industry matter? *Strategic Management Journal, 12(3)*, pp. 167–185.

Schot, J., Geels, F. W. (2008). Strategic niche management and sustainable innovation journeys: theory, findings, research agenda, and policy. *Technology Analysis & Strategic Management, 20(5)*, pp. 537–554.

Sharma, B., Fisher, T. (1997). Functional strategies and competitiveness: an empirical analysis using data from Australian manufacturing. *Benchmarking for Quality Management & Technology, 4(4)*, pp. 286–294.

Shimizu, K., Hitt, M. A. (2004). Strategy flexibility: Organizational preparedness to reverse ineffective strategic decisions. *Academy of Management Executive, 18(4)*, pp. 44–59.

Stabryła, A. (2000). *Zarządzanie strategiczne w teorii i praktyce firmy*. Warsaw: PWN.

Stonehouse, G., Hamill, J., Campbell, D., Purdie, T. (2000). *Global and transnational business: strategy and management*. New York: Wiley.

Stonehouse, G., Pemberton, J. (1999). Learning and knowledge management in the intelligent organization. *An International Journal*, 7(5), pp. 131–144.

Stonehouse, G., Pemberton, J. (2002). Strategic planning in SMEs – some empirical findings. *Management Decision*, 40(9), pp. 853–861.

Strategor (1997). *Zarządzanie firmą. Strategie, struktury, decyzje, tożsamość*. Strategor Group, Warsaw: PWE.

Sull, D. N. (2015). Closing the Gap Between Strategy and Execution. The Art of Strategic Renewal. *MIT Sloan Management Review. Special Collection. "Top 10 Lessons on Strategy"*, pp. 52–60.

Tallman, S. (2002). Internationalization, Globalization, and Capability-Based Strategy. *California Management Review*, 45(1), pp. 116–135.

Verbeke, A., Asmussen, Ch. G. (2016). Global, Local, or Regional? The Locus of MNE Strategies. *Journal of Strategies Studies*, 53(6), pp. 1051–1075.

Yip, G. S. (1995). *Total global strategy: Managing for worldwide competitive advantage*. Englewood Cliffs, N.J: Prentice Hall.

Zorska, A. (1998). *Ku globalizacji? Przemiany w korporacjach transnarodowych i w gospodarce światowej*. Warsaw: PWN.

Zorska, A. (2002). Strategie KMN na rynku wyrobów przemysłowych w Polsce. In; A. Zorska (ed.), *Korporacje międzynarodowe w Polsce. Wyzwania w dobie globalizacji i regionalizacji*. Warsaw: Difin, pp. 79–109.

Chapter 5

Automation of forming complex advertising products

Yevhen Hrabovskyi

CONTENTS

5.1 INTRODUCTION

The modern production and commercial activities of any entity cannot be imagined without the use of advertising and promotional products. Advertising is a kind of engine for the economic activity of the enterprise. The creation of promotional products greatly facilitates the process of contacts with potential customers and clients, and creates the necessary prerequisites for expanding the target market segment. Automation of the process of creating an advertising product provides wide opportunities for distribution of advertising in large editions and the creation of high-quality and bright advertising, and as a result of this, the achievement of the enterprise of significant competitive positions in the market.

The specialized literature (Leach, 2017; Sonntag & Xing, 2013; Hrabovskyi et al., 2018) offers techniques and technologies for the creation of various types of advertising using 3D installations and separately analyzed the general features and perspectives of 3D printing for the creation of advertising printed products.

In scientific articles (Hafiz et al., 2011; Meillier et al., 2018) methods and technologies are discussed that increased efficiency and persuasiveness of stereoscopic 3D advertising. These works offer the basic parameters to determine the effectiveness and potency of creating a 3D advertising product.

Visual advertising technologies that provide a positive effect to consumers in the form of persuasion, preferences and recall of advertising posters are offered in studies (Simola et al., 2015; Shelly & Esther, 2017; Hopp & Gangadharbatla, 2016). The technology of digital advertising production is also analyzed in these studies.

Visual technologies for the creation of promotional products are proposed and systematized in the studies (Debbabi et al., 2010; Hrabovskyi et al., 2020). These studies provide opportunities to determine the appropriate conditions for improving the quality of visual advertising products.

Methodical bases of color-tint formation and optimization of color schemes are proposed in scientific articles (Mulisch, 2014; Urbas & Stankovič, 2015). These articles offer factors that improve the image of advertising.

Modelling of the process of creation of effective advertising products is considered in the studies of Babenko et al. and Malyarets et al. (Babenko et al., 2019; Malyarets et al., 2019).

However, specialized literature does not provide the ability to support the processes of creating a comprehensive technology for the automation of complex advertising products.

5.2 RESEARCH PROBLEM AND DISCUSSION

The purpose of this study is to develop an automation technology for advertising products formation. No advertising subject can afford to use all advertising tools simultaneously and distribute it on an unlimited scale.

The success of an advertising message depends on where and when it was published. Before choosing one or another type of advertising, you need to determine the purpose of the advertising event. Goals can be very different; they depend on the submission of the advertiser.

Practice shows that in one advertising event, as a rule, goals intersect. In this regard, all advertising goals can be grouped into 3 groups.

The first group includes goals that form the company's image. The second group can include goals related to stimulating advertising. The third group consists of goals which allow using advertising tools to ensure stability in the sale of goods, as well as customer retention.

The right choice of advertising means is to take away exactly the ones that allow to solve this advertising goal most effectively.

Advertising cannot be effective if there is no market analysis (economic environment, competitors, etc.), no specifics of the advertised product (general characteristics of the product, life cycle, etc.) and no understanding of the consumer audience (demographic characteristics, motives and needs, consumer benefits from the use of the goods, etc.). Without clear planning, the advertising campaign will not be able to segment the audience of consumers. Proceeding from the foreign and domestic experience of advertising, it can be argued that the complex and consistent conduct of promotional events gives a much greater effect than the individual, unrelated to each other common purpose and separated in time measures.

To efficiently select channels of advertising distribution, is specialized work that requires a lot of time. As a rule, this work is done by humans. At the same time, the authors present their own developments based on their own experience. As a result, one question may have several different answers and very often they are false. That is why the theme "Automation of forming a complex of advertising products" is relevant to the present day.

Every enterprise sooner or later becomes a pre-choice of a means of advertising. It should take into account the criteria for the effectiveness of advertising, the function of one kind or another, as well as direct advertising goals, which seek to reach the company. The solution of such a problem is quite complex and troublesome, because the question is rather unstructured. The probability of mistakes is quite large. The problem should be considered from a scientific point of view.

To solve poorly structured and unstructured problems quite well, a method of analysis of hierarchies (MAI) is suited. The methodology for solving such problems is based on a systematic approach, in which the problem is considered as a result of interaction and, moreover, the interdependence of many dissimilar objects, and not simply as their isolated and autonomous aggregate.

The complexity, as already noted, is characterized by a large number of interactions between many subjective and objective factors of different types and extent of importance, as well as groups of people with different purposes and contradictory interests. These factors determine the likelihood or inability to choose one of the alternatives that is acceptable to all with a certain degree of compromise.

To deal with this complexity, you need a systematic procedure for submitting groups, their goals, criteria and behaviour, due to these objectives, alternative results and resources, distributed over these alternatives. At MAI, this procedure is reduced to building a hierarchy of problems.

The decisive advantage of MAI over most existing methods of evaluating alternatives is a clear expression of judgment and a contribution to the analysis of the structure of the problem.

Inherent in humans are two characteristic features of analytical thinking: one is the ability to observe and analyze observation, the other is the ability to establish relationships between observations, assessing the level (intensity) of relationships, and then synthesize these relations in the overall perception of the observable.

On the basis of these properties of human thinking, three principles have been formulated:

1. The principle of identity and decomposition
2. The principle of discrimination and comparative judgments
3. The principle of synthesis

Mathematical eligibility, the decisive rule in MAI, is transparent and is based on the method of own values and principle of the hierarchical composition, which have a clear mathematical justification.

Thus, MAI satisfies the basic criteria to provide comprehensive scientific validity of the decision-making method.

So, at the first stage of solving the problem we will construct a hierarchy of problems. The overall objective (focus) of the problem is usually the highest level of hierarchy. Focus should be the level of the most important criteria. Each of the criteria may be divided into subcriteria. The subcriteria should be the level of alternatives, whose number can be very large. In some hierarchies, the level of active forces (actors) that is located below the level of common criteria may be included.

The hierarchy of advertising choice problems is shown in Figure 5.1:

1. Choice of advertising
2. Coverage
3. Availability
4. Value
5. Controllability
6. Authority
7. Server
8. Informing
9. Exhortations
10. Reminders
11. Report on the emergence of a new product/service
12. Mark new ways of using the known product/service
13. To form the company image
14. To describe the goods or services provided by the company
15. To form advantages with respect to a certain brand
16. Convince consumers to make a purchase immediately
17. Recall that the product may take the nearest time
18. To support awareness consumer about goods
19. Remind consumers where the goods are sold
20. Advertising in the press
21. Advertising on television

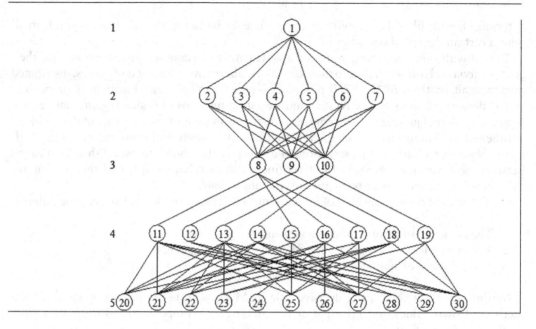

Figure 5.1 The hierarchy of advertising choice problems

22. Radio advertising
23. Outdoor advertising
24. Transit advertising
25. Advertising in cinemas
26. Exhibitions and fairs
27. Printed (printing) advertising
28. Advertising on the internet
29. Advertising souvenirs
30. Direct postal advertising

Once hierarchical, the problem is to set prioritize criteria and evaluate each of the alternatives by criteria. In MAI the elements of the task are compared in pairs with respect to their influence on a common characteristic for them. The paired information system results in a result that can be presented as a back symmetrical matrix. An element of a matrix A (i, j) is the intensity of the manifestation of the hierarchy element i for the j hierarchy element monitored on the intensity scale from 1 to 9, proposed the author of the method where evaluations are the following meaning:

1 – Equal importance
3 – Moderate advantage of one above the other
5 – Significant advantage of one above the other
7 – Significant advantage of one over another
9 –A very strong advantage to one over another
2, 4, 6, and 8 are corresponding intermediate values

Priorities are synthesized from the second level downwards. Local priorities are multiplied by the priority of the corresponding criterion at the highest level and summed up on each element according to the criteria affected by the element.

A highly useful byproduct of the theory is the so-called consistency index (CI) that gives information about the degree of disruption of consistency. Together with the matrix of paired comparisons, we have a method of measuring the degree of deviation from consistency. If such deviations exceed the limits set, then the one who holds the judgment should be rechecked in the matrix. The consistency index is calculated according to Formula (5.1).

$$CI = (lmax - n) / (n - 1), \tag{5.1}$$

where lmax is the maximum eigenvalue of the matrix,

n – number of elements (dimension) of the matrix.

If we divide the CI by a number corresponding to the random consistency of the matrix of the same order, we obtain the consistency ratio (CR). The value of CR should be about 10%, and not more than 30%, otherwise you need to check your judgments.

Constructing the hierarchy of relations and weight coefficients was carried out taking into account the results of a questionnaire. Ten people have been delivered as experts, 60% of whom are experts in the field of advertising and marketing in general and regard their knowledge in these areas as high and medium. The remaining 40% of experts regard the level of their knowledge in marketing as basic.

Since the first level of the hierarchy is the purpose of advertising, the weight of this node is taken as a unit. Next, for each factor sets a weighting factor and constructs a matrix of pairwise comparisons. The best task is to flatten the table. The table dimension is determined by the number of arcs that are included in this vertex.

Thus we can compile a report on a built hierarchy.

Level 1.

Node: The choice of advertising. Weight: 1.000.

Factors:

1. Coverage. Weight – 0.330.
2. Availability. Weight – 0.163.
3. Cost. Weight – 0.159.
4. Handling. Weight – 0.046.
5. Authoritative. Weight – 0.166.
6. Server. Weight – 0.135.

Matrix Paired Comparisons (5.2):

$$M = \begin{pmatrix} 1.000 & 5.000 & 1.000 & 3.000 & 1.000 & 5.000 \\ 0.200 & 1.000 & 3.003 & 4.000 & 1.000 & 0.500 \\ 1.000 & 0.333 & 1.000 & 5.000 & 1.000 & 0.000 \\ 0.333 & 0.250 & 0.200 & 1.000 & 0.000 & 0.333 \\ 1.000 & 1.000 & 1.000 & 0.000 & 1.000 & 0.000 \\ 0.200 & 2.000 & 0.000 & 3.000 & 0.000 & 1.000 \end{pmatrix} \tag{5.2}$$

lmax = 6.919. CI = 0.184. RC = 0.148.

Level 2.

Node: Reach. Weight: 0.330.

Factors:

1. Informing. Weight – 0.430.

2. Exhortations. Weight – 0.311.
3. Reminder. Weight – 0.259.

Matrix Paired Comparisons (5.3):

$$M = \begin{pmatrix} 1.000 & 3.000 & 1.000 \\ 0.333 & 1.000 & 3.003 \\ 1.000 & 0.333 & 1.000 \end{pmatrix} \tag{5.3}$$

lmax = 3.562. CI = 0.281. RC = 0.185.
Node: Accessibility. Weight: 0.163.
Matrix Paired Comparisons (5.4):

$$M = \begin{pmatrix} 1.000 & 1.000 & 1.000 \\ 1.000 & 1.000 & 1.000 \\ 1.000 & 1.000 & 1.000 \end{pmatrix} \tag{5.4}$$

lmax = 3.000. CI= 0.000. RC = 0.000.
Node: Cost. Weight: 0.159.
Matrix Paired Comparisons (5.5):

$$M = \begin{pmatrix} 1.000 & 1.000 & 1.000 \\ 1.000 & 1.000 & 1.000 \\ 1.000 & 1.000 & 1.000 \end{pmatrix} \tag{5.5}$$

lmax = 3.000. CI = 0.000. RC = 0.000.
Node: Steer. Weight: 0.046.
Matrix Paired Comparisons (5.6):

$$M = \begin{pmatrix} 1.000 & 9.000 & 7.000 \\ 0.111 & 1.000 & 0.200 \\ 0.143 & 5.000 & 1.000 \end{pmatrix} \tag{5.6}$$

lmax = 3.210. CI = 0.105. RC = 0.181.
Node: Authority.
Weight: 0.166.
Matrix Paired Comparisons (5.7):

$$M = \begin{pmatrix} 1.000 & 0.500 & 1.000 \\ 2.000 & 1.000 & 2.000 \\ 1.000 & 0.500 & 1.000 \end{pmatrix} \tag{5.7}$$

lmax = 3.000. CI = 0.000. RC = 0.000.
Node: Server.
Weight: 0.135.
Matrix Paired Comparisons (5.8):

$$M = \begin{pmatrix} 1.000 & 6.000 & 4.000 \\ 0.167 & 1.000 & 0.333 \\ 0.250 & 3.000 & 1.000 \end{pmatrix} \qquad (5.8)$$

lmax = 3.054. CI = 0.027. RC = 0.047.
Level 3.
Node: Informative. Weight: 0.430.
Factors:

1. Report on the emergence of a new product/service. Weight – 0.108.
2. Mark new ways to use a known product. Weight – 0.108.
3. To form company image. Weight – 0.108.
4. Description provided by company services or sold goods.

Weight – 0.108.
Assembly: Weight: 0.311.
Factors:

1. To form an advantage with respect to a particular brand. Weight – 0.155.
2. Convince consumers to make a purchase immediately. Weight – 0.155.

Node: Reminders. Weight: 0.259.
Factors:

1. Remind consumers that a product may need in the near future. Weight – 0.086.
2. Support Awareness consumer about the product. Weight – 0.086.
3. Remind consumers where the goods are sold. Weight – 0.086.

Level 4.
Node: Report on the emergence of a new product/service. Weight: 0.108.
Factors:

1. Advertising in the press. Weight – 0.059.
2. Advertising on television. Weight – 0.199.
3. Advertisement in cinemas. Weight – 0.069.
4. Printed (printing) advertising. Weight – 0.189.
5. Advertising on the Internet. Weight – 0.093.
6. Direct postal advertising. Weight – 0.060.

Matrix Paired Comparisons (5.9):

$$M = \begin{pmatrix} 1.000 & 0.000 & 0.000 & 0.000 & 0.111 & 0.000 \\ 0.000 & 1.000 & 0.000 & 0.000 & 0.000 & 0.000 \\ 0.000 & 0.000 & 1.000 & 0.000 & 0.111 & 0.000 \\ 0.000 & 0.000 & 0.000 & 1.000 & 0.200 & 0.000 \\ 9.000 & 0.000 & 9.000 & 5.000 & 1.000 & 0.000 \\ 0.000 & 0.000 & 0.000 & 0.000 & 0.000 & 1.000 \end{pmatrix} \qquad (5.9)$$

lmax = 6.000. CI = 0.000. RC = 0.000.
Node: To form a preference in relation to a particular brand. Weight: 0.155.
Factors:

1. printing (printing) advertising. Weight – 0.189.
2. Advertising souvenirs. Weight – 0.199.

Matrix Paired Comparisons (5.10):

$$M = \begin{pmatrix} 1.000 & 0.000 \\ 0.000 & 1.000 \end{pmatrix} \tag{5.10}$$

lmax = 2.000. CI = 0.000. RC = 0000.
Node: Remind consumers that goods may be needed in the near future. Weight: 0.086.
Factors:

1. Advertising in the press. Weight – 0.059.
2. Advertising on television. Weight – 0.199.
3. Advertising on the radio. Weight – 0.087.
4. Outdoor advertising. Weight – 0.102.
5. Advertisement in cinemas. Weight – 0.069.
6. Printed (printing) advertising. Weight – 0.189.
7. Direct postal advertising. Weight – 0.060.

Matrix Paired Comparisons (5.11):

$$M = \begin{pmatrix} 1.000 & 0.000 & 0.111 & 0.000 & 0.000 & 0.000 & 0.000 \\ 0.000 & 1.000 & 3.000 & 0.000 & 0.000 & 0.000 & 0.000 \\ 9.000 & 0.333 & 1.000 & 1.000 & 9.000 & 2.000 & 0.000 \\ 0.000 & 0.000 & 1.000 & 1.000 & 0.000 & 0.000 & 0.000 \\ 0.000 & 0.000 & 0.111 & 0.000 & 1.000 & 0.000 & 0.000 \\ 0.000 & 0.000 & 0.500 & 0.000 & 0.000 & 1.000 & 0.000 \\ 0.000 & 0.000 & 0.000 & 0.000 & 0.000 & 0.000 & 1.000 \end{pmatrix} \tag{5.11}$$

lmax = 7.009. CI = 0.002. RC = 0.001.
Node: Maintain consumer awareness about the product. Weight: 0.086.
Factors:

1. Advertising in the press. Weight – 0.059.
2. Advertising on television. Weight – 0.199.
3. Advertising on the radio. Weight – 0.087.
4. Printed (printing) advertising. Weight – 0.189.
5. Advertising on the Internet. Weight – 0.093.
6. Direct postal advertising. Weight – 0.060.

Matrix Paired Comparisons (5.12):

$$M = \begin{pmatrix} 1.000 & 0.000 & 0.143 & 2.000 & 0.111 & 0.000 \\ 0.000 & 1.000 & 0.000 & 5.000 & 1.000 & 0.000 \\ 7.000 & 0.000 & 1.000 & 5.000 & 0.500 & 0.000 \\ 0.500 & 0.200 & 0.200 & 1.000 & 0.111 & 0.000 \\ 9.000 & 1.000 & 2.000 & 9.000 & 1.000 & 9.000 \\ 0.000 & 0.000 & 0.000 & 0.000 & 0.111 & 1.000 \end{pmatrix} \qquad (5.12)$$

lmax = 6.121. CI = 0.024. RC = 0.019.
Node: Mark new ways of using a known product/service.
Weight: 0.108.
Factors:

1. Advertising on television. Weight – 0.199.
2. Advertisement in cinemas. Weight – 0.069.
3. Printed (printing) advertising. Weight – 0.189.

Matrix Paired Comparisons (5.13):

$$M = \begin{pmatrix} 1.000 & 5.000 & 0.000 \\ 0.200 & 1.000 & 0.000 \\ 0.000 & 0.000 & 1.000 \end{pmatrix} \qquad (5.13)$$

lmax = 3.002. CI = 0.001. RC= 0.001.
Node: to form company image. Weight: 0.108.
Factors:

1. Advertising on television. Weight – 0.199.
2. Advertising on the radio. Weight – 0.087.
3. Transit. Weight – 0.022.
4. Exhibitions and fairs. Weight – 0.022.
5. Advertising souvenirs. Weight – 0.099.

Matrix of paired comparisons (5.14):

$$M = \begin{pmatrix} 1.000 & 0.000 & 0.000 & 0.000 & 0.000 \\ 0.000 & 1.000 & 0.000 & 0.000 & 0.000 \\ 0.000 & 0.000 & 1.000 & 0.000 & 0.000 \\ 0.000 & 0.000 & 0.000 & 1.000 & 0.000 \\ 0.000 & 0.000 & 0.000 & 0.000 & 1.000 \end{pmatrix} \qquad (5.14)$$

lmax = 5.000. CI = 0.000. RC = 0.000.
Node: Describe the products or services provided by the company. Weight: 0.108.
Factors:

1. Advertising in the press. Weight – 0.059.
2. Advertisement in cinemas. Weight – 0.069.
3. Printed (printing) advertising. Weight – 0.189.

Matrix of paired Comparisons (5.15):

$$M = \begin{pmatrix} 1.000 & 3.000 & 1.000 \\ 0.333 & 1.000 & 0.000 \\ 1.000 & 0.000 & 1.000 \end{pmatrix} \tag{5.15}$$

lmax = 3.001. CI = 0.001. RC = 0.001.
Node: Convince consumers to make a purchase immediately. Weight: 0.155.
Factors:

1. Advertising on television. Weight – 0.199.
2. Advertising on the radio. Weight – 0.087.
3. Outdoor advertising. Weight – 0.102.
4. Advertisement in cinemas. Weight – 0.069.
5. Direct postal advertising. Weight – 0.060.

Matrix of paired comparisons (5.16):

$$M = \begin{pmatrix} 1.000 & 0.000 & 0.000 & 0.000 & 0.000 \\ 0.000 & 1.000 & 0.000 & 0.000 & 0.000 \\ 0.000 & 0.000 & 1.000 & 0.000 & 0.000 \\ 0.000 & 0.000 & 0.000 & 1.000 & 0.000 \\ 0.000 & 0.000 & 0.000 & 0.000 & 1.000 \end{pmatrix} \tag{5.16}$$

lmax = 5.000. CI = 0.000. RC = 0.000.
Node: Remind consumers where the product is sold. Weight: 0.086.

1. Outdoor advertising. Weight – 0.102.
2. Printed (printing) advertising. Weight – 0.189.
3. Direct postal advertising. Weight – 0.060.

Matrix of paired comparisons (5.17):

$$M = \begin{pmatrix} 1.000 & 0.000 & 5.000 \\ 0.000 & 1.000 & 0.000 \\ 0.200 & 0.000 & 1.000 \end{pmatrix} \tag{5.17}$$

lmax = 3.002. CI = 0.001. RC = 0.001.
Level 5.

Node: Advertising in the press. Weight – 0.059.
Node: Advertising on television. Weight – 0.199.
Node: Advertising on the radio. Weight – 0.087.
Node: Outdoor advertising. Weight – 0.102.
Node: Transit advertising. Weight – 0.022.
Node: Advertising in cinemas. Weight – 0.069.
Node: Exhibitions and fairs. Weight – 0.022.
Node: Printed (printing) advertising. Weight – 0.189.

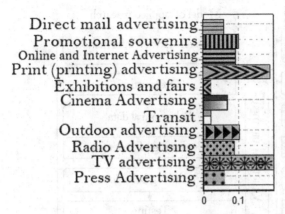

Figure 5.2 The resulting chart on the results of the research of goods advertisement

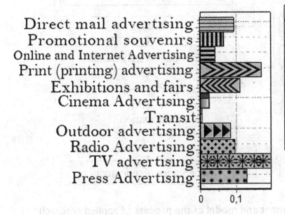

Figure 5.3 The resulting chart based on the study of service advertising

Node: Advertising on the internet. Weight – 0.093.
Node: Advertising souvenirs. Weight – 0.099.
Node: Direct mail. Weight – 0.060.

The resulting chart on the results of the research of goods advertisement is shown in Figure 5.2. The resulting chart based on the study of service advertising is shown in Figure 5.3.

As you can see from the results of the study and the resulting diagrams, the TV and print (printing) advertising lead to much greater weight. Also, it should be noted that considering the ways of making all examined types of advertising it can be seen that most of it takes printing. In this case, the development of the automated system for the formation of complexes of advertising products should take into account the printing features of a particular type of advertising.

CONCLUSIONS

The peculiarity of the modern design is first of all connected with heavily developed design units, significantly weaker—methodical and science only began to develop. The relationship between theory and practice in the design can, at best, be called tense. However, we can say

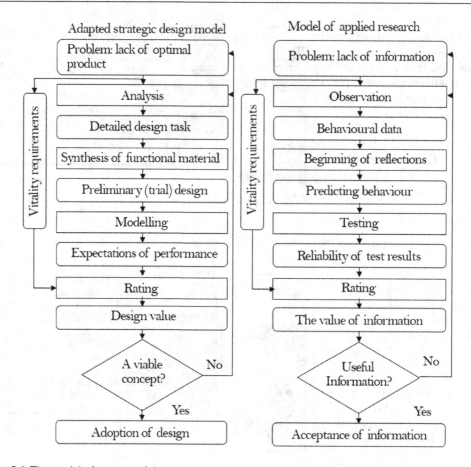

Figure 5.4 The model of process of design development and model of the process of applied research

that the practice is considered to be a kind of research, as the product of the designer's work embodies the information and therefore is actually a result of the study, and it means that it is possible to formulate his or her theoretical findings.

We use the comparison of the two models—the model of process of design development and model of the process of applied research (Figure 5.4).

The similarity is obvious: both design and research involve identifying the problem, exercising the intended sequence of steps to study this problem and finding the most suitable solution. Each step involves a study, i.e., the process of finding information necessary as a basis for each stage of the product creation process. So, for practitioners of design research is a search process in three areas: search for insight, search ideas, and search solutions.

Search for insight. For efficient design, the designer must have a deep understanding of the context in which it should work. But these researches are not necessarily and are not always conducted deliberately. Many designers tend to the innate ability to be on the same wavelength with the environment, people and their needs, and with color, shape, and material; this peculiar indentity in the material world allows them to use the acquired knowledge in the design process. However, more often there is also the need to collect information about the markets and all sides interested in the appearance of the product (including customers, users, manufacturers), and for this there are special facilities, techniques, and disciplines.

Search for ideas. During the design, the designer seeks ideas that can help provide the product a certain form, which includes the features of the product, the materials from which it should be manufactured, and its aesthetics. In this situation designers once again use their intuitive knowledge, but intuition tends to be in need of help from a conscious research endeavour. It all depends on the creative giftedness of the designer and his or her ability to use the available knowledge to expand your imagination. Having defined the context of the design task, the designer begins to look for ideas. To stimulate the creative process are used some of the methods of procreation creative ideas. They are also called design methods.

Techniques for finding creative ideas:

1. Brainstorming: The methodology of group participation in ideas generation to find a solution for a particular problem
2. Tree goals: The methodology is to enumerate the goals of design and project objectives and to build a diagram of hierarchical relations between them.
3. Counter-planning: This technique requires the analysis of the preconditions and substantiation of the problem, decision, plan, or design through the process of the proposal and reviewing opposite preconditions, which results in the final, revised decision, plan, or understanding
4. Interaction matrix: Research and drawing up the interaction between several elements within the solved problem
5. Network interaction: Transformation of a matrix of interaction into a representation of spatial or other links between elements of the problem
6. Forced links: The way to spawn innovation is to find possible links, at the moment, clearly not existing between the components of a product or system
7. New combinations: Search for new, previously non-existent combinations from alternative components

Search for solutions. Finally, in the process of working directly on design concepts and solutions, the designer conducts (formally or informally) a study that implies not only the application of various creative techniques, but also a methodical search for processes, materials, technologies, and ideas.

It is clear that all three categories of search are interdependent and mutually complementary. Understanding context, finding ideas, and testing concepts intersect.

Design process. The designer seldom conducts these searches consistently: first understanding, then ideas, and at the end, decision. The design process resembles a constant alternation, which can be illustrated on the example of four main categories of the design process: formulation, development, migration, and reaction.

The formulation is connected to identifying needs and planning the formulation of a task. Such a beginning of the design process and development of a new product often defines the term "fuzzy beginning": At this stage, the designer and other participants of the product development process are trying to understand the needs, requirements, and wishes of all interested parties, and the result is a determination of incentives for further ideas.

In this process, you can select two parts. One of them is the study of the environment in general, when the designer and representatives of other functions of the company, such as sales and marketing, study trends, gather general information about the market, monitor the users and consumers, track the use of the product, and obtain feedback. Very often, the designer assumes only observation of trends and consumers, which is conducted formally or, which happens much more often, informally. Designers can go to exhibitions, attend retail outlets, watch TV, and purposefully collect information on the market and users. The Market Research Department and the trade staff also collect such information, but at the

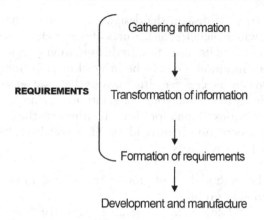

Figure 5.5 The process of presentation requirements

official level. The purpose of the designers is to intuitively understand the world in which they are going to work to make it possible to spawn ideas and start a creative process. In other words, they are in search of understanding and ideas.

As soon as the task or concept is defined, the search becomes more focused, apply special methods of research, which is often called the process of presentation requirements (Figure 5.5). In the procedure of collection and transformation of information for the development of requirements, formal techniques are applied, usually borrowed from the sphere of market research, but with the advent of ethnographic techniques, the most important aspect was the fixation of the research results and control of their use and values throughout the development of the product, i.e. process of requirements management.

The "development" stage is connected with idea threshold, concept, and detailed development of design. At this stage, the designer searches for ideas, using the available knowledge, information, and creative techniques to develop concepts; decides which technologies, materials, and processes will contribute to the rise of ideas and solutions; tests design concepts, and reviews designed design taking into account context and user reaction to this design.

The foldings covers the introduction of design into production and product release to the market or its delivery to the user or the consumer. Here the research is concerned solely with ensuring a smooth transfer of design to production—most of the research has already been carried out in the previous stages of planning. But at this stage the designer receives some knowledge and experience in the field of understanding of production and implementation processes. The information obtained is extremely useful in solving future design problems.

During the reaction stage, the designer appeals to the results of the work, evaluating them in terms of reaction of users and other interested parties, and also gives an estimation to the whole process and the obtained knowledge. All this is part of the process of training the designer and the organization as a whole. The aggregate obtained as a result of knowledge and information collected will help in search of understanding the impression created by the design.

Thus, the research, design searches, and design process itself are interconnected and repeatedly cross. It is a constant learning and knowledge management process. Conducting research is mainly the field of the designer, especially in the beginning of the design process.

The Automated System (AS) of forming of the promotional products complexes must meet the following functional requirements:

1. Data entry: AS must necessarily allow to set the default values for the data being entered, where it is desirable
2. Transactions AS must be projected so that they can be completed in the smallest number of operations
3. Direct transition to the tools of practical implementation of the system recommendations
4. Computational operations: AS should contain modules for intermediate calculation of some indicators
5. The automated system must provide operative assistance throughout the system
6. Operational assistance in the AS must be context-dependent

All error messages referenced by the system must necessarily be meaningful in order to get their users to do the proper actions.

At any stage in the development interface, the program can run the runtime. After compiling, a program form appears on the screen that behaves like a normal Windows tab. The form is usually hosted by components that make up the program interface, and the developer's task is to assign a response to them to specific user actions, such as pressing the button or selecting a switch. Such reactions determine the functionality of the application.

To function the automated system of formation of complexes of advertising products will be as follows: Choose the type of enterprise and advertising budget, as well as the necessary advertising goals. Then, when you click on "Suggest Options" in the tab below will be shown the recommended types of advertising. Next, go to the second system unit. Choose the age category of consumers, uniqueness of the goods and accent attention and press the button "Create recommendations". The following recommended options appear in the tab below: In Block 3, "Additional features", the user has the ability to click on the appropriate buttons to move to graphics programs, calculator, and database managers, as well as view reports of marketing companies about the status of various industries.

Before you run the program, you must ensure that the program text contains no syntax errors. To detect syntax errors, the program is compiled and composed. In the Delphi stage compilation and layout are not separated and executed sequentially.

It is possible to compile the project at any stage of development. It is convenient to check the appearance and correctness of the individual function of the form, as well as to test fragments of the code.

When you compile a project, you create a ready-to-use file, which can be a dynamically loaded program or library. The name of the application after compiling matches the filename of the project, and the program itself is standalone and does not require additional Delphi files for its operation. However, if you use other files in the process of executing the program, such as images or help files, these files should be presented to the program.

Compiling an app can be done in several ways. You are compiling a program with the main menu, such as Run/Run or F9, and then running the program. If the compilation was successful, an executive file (.exe) that runs on execution is created. If a project consists of several modules, only those that have been modified since the last compilation have been compiled, which saves time significantly.

Another way to compile a program is to run the Home menu command.

By the command Project/Compile < The project name, >, or Ctrl + F9. In this case, all project files are compiled, where changes occurred after the last compilation. Compile also files that depend on these changes. Additionally, the project program is always recompiled in this case.

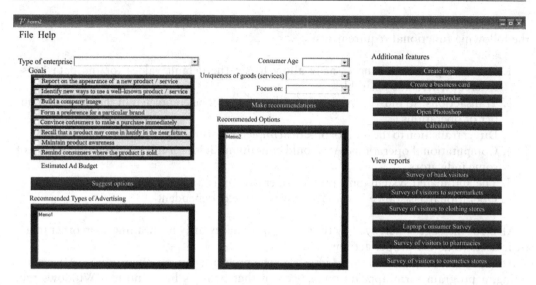

Figure 5.6 The tab of the automated system of forming a complex of advertising products

Compiling all project files without exception is done by using the Project/Build command < the project name >. This compiles all files that are included in the project, regardless of whether the changes were made.

In addition to applying the above methods, you can use the Project/Compile and Project/Build All Projects commands to compile projects, which apply when working with project groups.

The tab of the automated system of forming a complex of advertising products, which is run for execution, but even with unfilled fields is shown in Figure 5.6.

The interface and content of the automated system of advertising products formation are very simple and understandable, that is, they are available to understand almost every user. This is very important, because in this way the system can use both a regular user and a specialist. The system's content modules are not tied to one another.

Thus, in this study it is proposed the automation technology of forming advertising complexes and formed methodological bases of advertising complexes formation. A hierarchical model of advertising selection based on a defined number of indicators to evaluate the effectiveness of advertising is developed. The final product was received in the course of solving practical tasks—the automated system of formation of advertising production complexes.

The practical result of this study is also the recommendations of the developer of advertising, which can be used in the process of forming complexes of advertising products and their direct development.

REFERENCES

Babenko, V., Kulczyk, Z., Perevosova, I., Syniavska, O., Davydova, O. (2019). *Factors of the development of international e-commerce under the conditions of globalization*. SHS Web of Conferences, pp. 10–16. DOI: https://doi.org/10.1051/shsconf/20196504016.

Debbabi, S., Daassi, M., Baile, S. (2010). Effect of online 3D advertising on consumer responses: the mediating role of telepresence. *Journal of Marketing Management, 26 (9–10)*, pp. 967–992. DOI: https://doi.org/10.1080/02672570903498819.

Hafiz, D. A., Sheta, W. M., Bayoumi, S., Youssef, B. A. (2011). A new approach for 3D range image segmentation using gradient method. *Journal of Computer Science, 7*, pp. 475–487. DOI: https://doi.org/10.3844/jcssp.2011.475.487.

Hopp, T., Gangadharbatla, H. (2016). Novelty Effects in Augmented Reality Advertising Environments: The Influence of Exposure Time and Self-Efficacy. *Journal of Current Issues & Research in Advertising*, *37*(2), pp. 113–130. DOI: https://doi.org/10.1080/10641734.2016.11 71179.

Hrabovskyi, Y., Brynza, N, Vilkhivska, O. (2020). Development of information visualization methods for use in multimedia applications. *EUREKA: Physics and Engineering*, *1*, pp. 3–17.

Hrabovskyi, Y., Yevsyeyev, O, Pandorin, A. (2018). Development of a method for the creation of 3D advertising printing products. *Eastern-European Journal of Enterprise Technologies*, *6/2* (96), pp. 6–18. DOI: 10.15587/1729-4061.2018.147325.

Leach, N. (2017). Size Matters: Why Architecture is the Future of 3D Printing. *Architectural Design*, *87*(6), pp. 76–83. DOI: https://doi.org/10.1002/ad.2241.

Malyarets, L. M., Babenko, V. O., Nazarenko, O. V., Ryzhikova, N. I. (2019). The Modeling of Multi-criteria Assessment Activity in Enterprise Management. *International Journal of Supply Chain Management*, *8*(4), pp. 997–1004.

Meillier, C., Ammanouil, R., Ferrari, A., Bianchi, P. (2018). Distribution strategies for very large 3D image deconvolution algorithms. *Signal Processing: Image Communication*, *67*, pp. 149–160. DOI: https://doi.org/10.1016/j.image.2018.06.012.

Mulisch, M. (2014). Tissue-Printing. Springer, p. 24. DOI: https://doi.org/10.1007/978-3-658-03867-0.

Shelly, R., Esther, T. (2017). *Digital Advertising: Theory and Research*. London: Routledge, Taylor & Francis Group, p. 496.

Simola, J., Hyönä, J., Kuisma, J. (2015). *Perception of visual advertising in different media: from attention to distraction, persuasion, preference and memory*. Lausanne: Frontiers Media SA, p. 124.

Sonntag, S., Xing, N. (2013). *An investigation of the effectiveness and persuasiveness of stereoscopic 3D advertising*. International Conference on 3D Imaging, *Liège*, 3-5 Dec, pp. 1–7. DOI: https://doi.org/10.1109/IC3D.2013.6732080.

Urbas, R., Stankovič, U. (2015). Color differences and perceptive properties of prints made with microcapsules. *Journal of graphic engineering and design*, *1*, pp. 15–21.

Chapter 6

Digital agriculture innovation
Trends and opportunities

Vitalina Babenko and Maryna Nehrey

CONTENTS

6.1 INTRODUCTION

Nowadays, the agricultural sector faces many challenges. The main requirements by society of agriculture are to provide people with quality food, to manage the environment properly, to effectively adapt to climate change and agricultural risk management, and to maintain the viability of rural areas. Although agriculture in 2020 produces enough to feed 7.8 billion people (worldometers.info), 820 million people worldwide still suffer from hunger (FAO, 2019). To meet the growing demand for agricultural products, it is necessary to increase production and increase production efficiency. In addition, the availability of fresh water and productive arable land is declining, which will create new challenges for agriculture. Agriculture provides jobs for about 28% of the total workforce (OECD, 2019). There are more than 570 million farms in the world (Lowder et al., 2016). Urbanization processes can significantly affect the structure of employment in agriculture and negatively affect the development of rural areas. All these problems require the transformation of the agricultural sector and rapid adaptation to global change.

Digitization of agriculture can be part of solving these problems. Today, digitization is spreading everywhere, in every science and industry. Production is becoming increasingly dependent on hardware connected to the software. Agriculture is being transformed by innovative technologies, and even traditionally similar methods of agricultural production are finding it difficult to resist disruptions.

6.2 THE IMPACT OF GLOBAL MEGATRENDS ON AGRICULTURE

The Megatrends Hub estimated the next fourteen global megatrends for future (Megatrends hub):

1. Diversifying inequalities
2. Climate change and environmental degradation
3. The increasing significance of migration
4. Growing consumerism
5. Aggravating resource scarcity
6. Increasing demographic imbalances
7. Expanding the influence of the East and South
8. Accelerating technological change and hyperconnectivity
9. Changing nature of work
10. Diversification of education and learning
11. Shifting health challenges
12. Continuing urbanization
13. The increasing influence of new governing systems
14. Changing the security paradigm

How do these megatrends affect agriculture?

1. Diversifying inequalities. The number of people living in extreme poverty is declining. Global inequality between countries is also declining. However, the issue of the gap between the richest and poorest segments of the population within the country is still relevant. Poor access to education, health care, and technology is most pronounced in rural areas.
2. Climate change and environmental degradation are significant problems for agriculture. They are shifting agricultural production and reducing land resources. Agriculture is also affected by sudden changes in temperature, changes in precipitation, and sudden weather events. Even if we stop all human activity and stop all emissions, the climate will continue to change. Therefore, agriculture must become less vulnerable to climate change. In particular, it is necessary to create resistance to harsh circumstances in varieties of agricultural plants and to develop appropriate agronomic measures and approaches to land use. Adapting to climate change is a real challenge for agriculture.
3. Increasingly the significance of migration can cause a shortage of labor in agriculture. In addition, migration processes can change the structure of demand for agricultural goods, which will force agricultural producers to change the structure of agricultural production.
4. Growing consumerism. It is estimated that in 2050 the population will be about 9 billion people. In addition, this growth will be exacerbated by an increase in people with increased purchasing power. This will increase the demand for agricultural products. As the increase in land resources is significantly limited, farmers need to increase productivity and use available resources efficiently.
5. Aggravating resource scarcity. Increasing demand for land, minerals, materials, energy, water, and food is exacerbated by climate change, making natural resources even more expensive and scarce. Therefore, agriculture's access to natural resources is becoming increasingly limited.
6. Increasing demographic imbalances. Structural population shifts are an increase in the urban population and, consequently, a decrease in the rural population. In addition,

there is a trend of population aging. This will negatively affect the development of rural areas and the availability of labor resources for agriculture.

7. Expanding the influence of the East and South. The shift of global economic and political influence from the Group of 7 (Canada, France, Germany, Italy, Japan, the United States, and the United Kingdom) to the E7 (Brazil, China, India, Indonesia, Mexico, Russia, and Turkey) is likely to cause significant changes in prices and the structure of agricultural production.

8. Accelerating technological change and hyperconnectivity. The active development of big data analysis, drones, 3D printing, IoT, artificial intelligence, robotics and other technological changes are leading to the emergence of new concepts of agriculture: Smart Farming, Precision Agriculture, Decision Agriculture, Agriculture 4.0 and Digital Agriculture. All of this significantly changes the nature of agricultural production and causes structural changes in the agricultural sector.

9. Changing nature of work. The development of modern technologies and automation of production require new skills from agricultural workers. In addition, agriculture includes new generations and the older generation works longer. The requirements and tasks for the workforce are changing accordingly.

10. Diversification of education and learning. Access to information, new approaches to learning, and the development of the concept of lifelong learning change access to education and lead to the diversification of learning. How global education trends will affect agriculture remains an unexplored question.

11. Shifting health challenges. The development of science and medicine has led to an increase in the duration and quality of life, reducing the incidence of infectious diseases. However, some diseases (cardiovascular, diabetes, cancer, obesity) increase the burden on health. Requirements for the quality of agricultural products are increasing as the link between food and health grows.

12. Continuing urbanization. Increasing the share of the urban population can negatively affect the development of rural areas and reduce the labor force for agriculture.

13. The increasing influence of new governing systems. Globalization, rapid digitalization and the increased influence of social media are creating new management systems; traditional management systems are becoming used less and less. In agricultural management, the goal is to achieve not only economic and production goals but also social and environmental goals, in particular maintaining nature and biodiversity, securing safe labor circumstances, guaranteeing animal welfare and others.

14. Changing the security paradigm. Facilitating access to powerful weapons, military conflicts and violent extremism have indirect effects on agriculture. However, in the long run, this may also be a challenge for agriculture.

These megatrends characterize changes in agriculture, food, agribusiness, biotechnology and chemistry, and can be used to identify specific development paths for a region and specific conditions to address major challenges for the future food situation.

6.3 DIGITAL AGRICULTURE DEVELOPMENT

The development of agriculture has been accelerating rapidly for the last 100 years. At the beginning of the last century, the basis of agriculture was the use of manual labor—Agriculture 1.0. This model of agriculture is characterized by adaptation at the local level, high labor intensity and small production volume. Although the time frame of this form of agriculture is essentially from ancient times to 1920, Agriculture 1.0 can still be seen on family farms (Babenko, 2014; Tucker, 2017).

Agriculture 2.0 was the impetus for the development of agribusiness and industrial agriculture. This stage began in 1920 when fertilizers, pesticides and agricultural machinery began to be actively used in agriculture. New approaches have helped increase efficiency and produced many cheap foods (Rungsuriyawiboon, 2004).

Today we are in the process of transition from Agriculture 1.0 and Agriculture 2.0 to Agriculture 3.0 and Agriculture 4.0.

Agriculture 3.0 began its development in the 1990s with the introduction of innovations. Agriculture began to use high-tech sensors, cloud computing and specialized software, and big data analysis took agriculture to a new level (Rabbinge, 2012; Shorikov and Babenko, 2014; Babenko, 2017; Rose and Chilvers, 2018; Serraj and Pingali, 2019; Trukhachev, et al., 2019; Plieninger, et al., 2019).

Further development of technologies contributed to the emergence in the early 2010s of a new model. Agriculture 4.0 is digital agriculture. This model is characterized by the presence of a large amount of information in digital form about agricultural production. A significant number of agricultural processes are automated and use modern, innovative approaches.

The main trend in Agriculture 3.0 and Agriculture 4.0 is digitalization. There are new concepts of agriculture, which are based on the processes of digitization: Smart Farming, Precision Agriculture or Precision Farming, Decision Agriculture, Agriculture 4.0, Digital Agriculture (Klerkx, Jakku, and Labarthe, 2019). In this study, we will use the term *digital agriculture* for all these concepts.

Smart farming is a management concept focused on providing the agricultural industry with the infrastructure to leverage advanced technology—including big data, the cloud and the Internet of Things (IoT)—for tracking, monitoring, automating and analyzing operations (Wolfert, et al., 2017; Weltzien, 2016; Ozdogan, et al., 2017; Blok and Gremmen, 2018; Chernyakov, et al., 2019; Vaganova, et al., 2020). Smart farming is software-managed and sensor-monitored.

Precision agriculture is a technology-enabled approach to farming management that observes, measures and analyzes the needs of individual fields and crops (McKinsey & Company Report, 2016). By allowing farmers to apply tailored care and manage water more effectively, it boosts productivity, improves economic efficiency, and minimizes waste and environmental impact. Its development is being shaped by two technological trends: big data and advanced-analytics capabilities on the one hand, and robotics—aerial imagery, sensors, sophisticated local weather forecasts—on the other.

The use of precision farming over a long period of time makes it possible to move to the following model of agricultural management—Decision Agriculture. The collected large amount of data allows agricultural production to be organized in a new way. Decision Agriculture gives farmers the opportunity to manage inputs by every foot and optimize each field's performance, extending well beyond the obvious regions of drainage tile needs or the basic data used to evaluate seed varieties (Leonard, et al., 2017; Sakhno, et al., 2019).

Digital agriculture is the use of new and advanced technologies, integrated into one system, to enable farmers and other stakeholders within the agriculture value chain to improve food production (Project Breakthrough, 2017; Trendov, et al., 2019).

Technologies used include sensors, communication networks, Unmanned Aviation Systems (UAS), artificial intelligence (AI), robotics and other advanced machinery, and often draws on the principles of the Internet of Things. Each one of these brings something valuable to farming from data collection, through to management and processing, as well as guidance and direction. This integrated system offers new insights that enhance the ability to make decisions and subsequently implement them (Sundmaeker, et al., 2020; Anshari, et al., 2019).

The main digital agriculture technology is next (Pedersen & Lind, 2017):

- Data collection technologies: global satellite navigation systems used for driving, mapping; mapping technologies (field topography, soil supply with nutrients, yield); technologies for obtaining information on the properties of vegetation and soil (based on cameras and sensors), working with big data; machines and software for data collection technologies (tractors using the international ISOBUS protocol, unmanned aerial vehicles, unmanned ground vehicles, information systems for managing an agricultural enterprise, software for monitoring and forecasting yields, etc.).
- Data transmission technology: mobile connection; LPWAN communication; internet (wireless, broadband).
- Data analysis and evaluation technologies: data analysis techniques to isolate homogeneous zones within the field; decision support systems; agricultural enterprise information management systems
- Work with big data, cloud computing.
- Precision application technologies: driving technologies (controlled movement on the field, auto-piloting); technologies of differentiated use (differential application of mineral, organic, lime fertilizers, chemical plant protection products, differentiated sowing, accurate physical destruction of weeds, precise irrigation, etc.).
- Complex solutions: technical vision; Internet of Things; robots; unmanned aerial vehicles, unmanned ground vehicles; artificial intelligence.
- Technologies in the field of agricultural economics: blockchain.

The map of technologies and maturity has been presented in Table 6.1.

There are a number of barriers to the introduction of new technologies in agriculture. The high cost of modern technologies and the delayed effect of their implementation can make the effect of the introduction of modern technologies unviable. Also, certain problems in the introduction of new technologies may be the result of established habits of farmers and the lack of new skills and abilities.

Obstacles to the introduction and development of digital agriculture:

- Employment in the agricultural sector. Agriculture provides perhaps the largest number of jobs in the world economy. The introduction of digital agriculture and the use

Table 6.1 Map of technologies and maturity (De Clercq et al., 2018)

Produce differently using new techniques	Hydroponics bioplastics algae feedstock	Desert agriculture seawater farming
Use new technologies to bring food production to consumers, increasing efficiencies in the food chain	Vertical/Urban farming	Genetic modification 3D printing Cultured meats
Incorporate cross-industry technologies and applications	Drone technology Internet of Things Data analytics Precision agriculture	Nanotechnology Food sharing and crowdfarming Artificial intelligence Blockchain
Today	Readiness to "grow" to market Time	

of modern technologies can significantly reduce employment. This effect can be most negative in those regions where a significant proportion of the population is employed in agriculture and can lead to a significant increase in unemployment.

- Significant costs for technology development. Modern technological solutions for agriculture are much cheaper than before. However, the initial costs of developing and implementing digital agriculture, especially on a large scale, can be very costly, which will stifle innovation. To implement an efficient digital agriculture system, technologies need to be developed, tested, researched, implemented, scaled and controlled. Therefore, the initial cost of modern technologies, especially in those areas where there is little research and development, may be a significant obstacle to implementation in the coming years.
- Data protection. The application of digital agriculture technologies produces a lot of data. The efficiency of their use increases when data is exchanged and joint solutions are developed. However, access to data can exacerbate inequalities, impede competition and create economic barriers. In addition, the use of data raises issues of intellectual property. It will be unprofitable for successful farmers to develop common technologies that will increase competition.
- Security. Digital agriculture will remove obstacles as well as the whole digital society - security issues. If the technology is not reliable enough and accessible to attackers, danger may arise for crop production, animal husbandry and other areas of agriculture. This can even lead to large-scale catastrophes: the inability to provide humanity with food, water pollution, water supply damage, interruption of crop growth and even provoke an agricultural war.
- Readiness for change. Established traditions and habits of agriculture can be a significant obstacle to the introduction of digital agriculture technologies. In addition, there is currently insufficient information on the effectiveness of digital agriculture technologies and so far there are few studies showing the impact of digital technologies on the efficiency of agricultural production.

Different digital agriculture technologies may have different results in different conditions; for example, in developed countries as opposed to developing countries. This is because the technologies are used in different initial conditions, in combination with different technical developments of the regions and are not context neutral, and are also associated with certain configurations of political and economic power.

6.4 AGRICULTURAL PRODUCTIVITY ANALYSIS

In recent years, increasing the productivity of agricultural production has led to increased supply and increased food security. However, there are significant differences in the efficiency of agriculture in different countries. We will evaluate the productivity of agriculture in different countries, using Data Envelopment Analysis.

An important stage in the evolution of approaches to measuring productivity was the study of M. Farrell (Farrell, 1957) on the concept of economic efficiency, the essence of which is the ratio of actual productivity to the maximum possible.

According to this interpretation, each set of resources (market inputs) is characterized by a maximum of production, and the actual values of market outputs represent the degree of achievement of this maximum. Productions that provide the maximum market output per unit of market input acquire the status of "standard" and form the "limit of productivity". The task of the analysis is to compare industries in terms of efficiency of their resource base and determine the distance between the enterprise and the "productivity limit". To do this, use the following methods:

- Parametric - provide for the formation of the production function for production standards by methods of mathematical statistics (construction of the stochastic limit of production capacity; adjusted least squares);
- Non-parametric - determine the limits of production capacity (maximum market yields) for any combination of resources (Data Envelopment Analysis [DEA]).

The Data Envelopment Analysis (DEA) model was developed by Michael Farrell in 1957. In his study, Farrell evaluated the effectiveness of one unit of the final product with one input and one output.

The problem of limited use of parametric methods is actualized (Rungsiriyawiboon and Coelli, 2004): first, the method of stochastic marginal production function limits the scope of research only to mono-product productions, while the DEA method allows determining the remote function for the multiproduct system; second, unlike the DEA method, parametric methods require a specification of the type of production function or cost function.

Data Envelopment Analysis is based on the use of a linear programming apparatus. This method eliminates the influence of the performer on determining the level of the weight of each market entry and exit, which eliminates the risk of subjectivity in the assessment. The criteria of efficiency in the DEA methodology is the achievement of Pareto's optimum, which is determined by the maximum possible volume of production at the existing technological level and resource provision. The DEA method allows us to: determine the aggregate indicator for each studied object in the framework of the use of market inputs to market outputs; take into account environmental factors; not be limited to the functional form of dependence between inputs and outputs; identify priority areas for productivity growth; and assess the necessary changes in market inputs/outputs that would allow bringing the object to the limit of efficiency.

The first DEA model was developed by Charnes et al. (1978). Further development of DEA-models is characterized by two-vector according to the influence of production scale. If the productivity of enterprises increases in proportion to the number of resources expended, then the line on which the surveyed enterprises should be sets a limit for them with a constant return on resources (CRS). However, if with an increasing amount of resources its return decreases, the limit of production capacity will look like a curve. In this case, it is a variable-return-to-scale VRS model. The first vector is represented by CCR models, according to which productivity is measured on the basis of an optimally weighted ratio between market inputs and market outputs. The evaluation is performed in coordinates from 0 (minimum efficiency) to 1 (maximum efficiency). The diagnosis of productivity growth reserves involves the search for alternatives to maximize efficiency to 1 (Malmquist, 1953).

Formally, this algorithm involves solving the optimization problem (6.1):

$$
e_0 = \frac{\sum_{j=1}^{s} u_j y_{j0}}{\sum_{i=1}^{r} v_i x_{i0}} \rightarrow max
$$

$$
\frac{\sum_{j=1}^{s} u_j y_{jm}}{\sum_{i=1}^{r} v_i x_{im}} \leq 1, \quad m = \overline{1,n} \tag{6.1}
$$

$$
e_0 = \frac{\sum_{j=1}^{s} u_j y_{j0}}{\sum_{i=1}^{r} v_i x_{i0}} \rightarrow max
$$

$$uj \geq 0, \quad j = 1, 2, \ldots, s,$$

$$vi \geq 0, \quad i = 1, 2, \ldots, r.$$

where e_0 is the efficiency of the researched enterprise; n is the number of studied objects; r is the number of objects included in the comparison range; s is the number of objects that were selected for the latter after comparison; x_{i0} - the value of the i-th market range of the studied object; y_{j0} - the j-th market type of the studied object; x_{im} - the i-th input factor of the m-th object; y_{jm} - the j-th output of the m-th object; v_i is the value of the range of different objects; and u_j is a significant number of analyzed objects j.

BCC model was developed by Banker et al. (1984). It identifies increasing or decreasing scale effects for each object. The mathematical form of the variable scale effect can be represented to add a new modified y_0 to the objective function of the original model (6.2):

$$e_0 = \frac{\sum_{j=1}^{s} u_j y_{j0} + u_0}{\sum_{i=1}^{r} v_i x_{i0}} \rightarrow max$$

$$\frac{\sum_{j=1}^{s} u_j y_{jm} + u_0}{\sum_{i=1}^{r} v_i x_{im}} \leq 1, \tag{6.2}$$

$$u_j, v_i \geq 0.$$

where u_0 is the scale effect:

if $u_0 < 0 \rightarrow$ decreasing output scale
if $u_0 > 0 \rightarrow$ increasing output scale
if $u_0 = 0 \rightarrow$ constant output scale

Production productivity management involves the implementation of alternative approaches: increasing the volume of sold products in the case of a constant amount of resources spent; reducing of resource costs with a constant volume of sold products; providing conditions for outstripping the growth of sales over the growth rate of resource costs. The use of tools for the DEA model allows us to solve these management problems. Different DEA models are used for this purpose.

In the first model, the target function is aimed at proportionally increasing the market outputs of the studied enterprise to the limits of efficiency, a variant of this model is called the output-oriented model. A feature of the second, input-oriented model is the proportional reduction of market inputs to the limits of efficiency. The third model is defined as total efficiency model.

Technological changes in the DEA model are estimated using an index (Malmquist, 1953), the essence of which is to compare market inputs for two different periods so that the number of resources spent in the base period could be reduced at a constant level of production in the planning period. Later, Caves et al. (1982) substantiated the feasibility of using this index to assess performance, and Fare et al. (1994) proposed methods for calculating the Malmquist performance index based on an analysis of the operating environment. The calculation of the Malmquist index allows you to determine: change in the positioning of the object in accordance with the efficiency limit; displacement of the limit in time; efficiency fluctuations in accordance with the change in the scale of management; the dynamics of the total productivity of factors of production.

The application of DEA results in dynamics that allow us to investigate the movement of the efficiency limit in time and to draw a conclusion about the trajectory of development of objects (industry as a whole): progressive or regressive. This method allows us to determine the reasons for changes in performance: improving quality of management, optimizing the scale of the object, improving technology, and so on.

6.4.1 Data

In this study, the productivity of agriculture is calculated for 35 countries from two groups: Euro-28 and CIS, and advanced economies. The status of a country with a developed economy was determined according to the standard list of the IMF. The composition of local groups is as follows.

Not all data are available for Turkmenistan and Tajikistan. From the dataset were also excluded Cyprus, Luxembourg and Malta as countries with small agriculture areas.

For all represented countries we calculated the efficiency of agriculture based on the Net Production Index Number, employment in agriculture, Gross Fixed Capital Formation (GFCF), nutrient nitrogen, nutrient phosphate P2O5, nutrient potash K2O, agricultural land (1000 ha) (Figure 6.1). Input data represents in Table 6.2.

VRS technology and input orientated efficiency is shown in Table 6.3, whereas Table 6.4 presents CRS technology and input orientated efficiency.

Analysis of agricultural productivity in different countries has shown that there is great potential for productivity increases. Therefore, implementation of innovations in agriculture are promising.

The effective implementation of innovations in agriculture requires a comprehensive approach, which includes the following:

- Informing key agricultural actors about new products and processes, ensuring the development of relevant new skills and intensifying the introduction of innovations
- Providing access to databases, digital technologies and online platforms to expand the potential of agriculture
- Facilitating access to financial resources and venture capital in agriculture

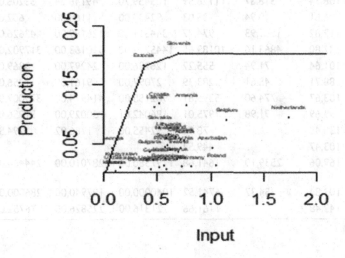

Figure 6.1 Graphical interpretation of productivity calculations

Table 6.2 Data for productivity calculation

Country	Net Production Index Number (Int, $)	Employment in agriculture (1000 persons)	GFCF	Nutrient nitrogen N (tonnes)	Nutrient phosphate P_2O_5 (tonnes)	Nutrient potash K_2O (tonnes)	Agricultural land (1000 ha)
Armenia	135,39	338,06	91,52	146292,20	324,00	914,70	1676,80
Austria	101,24	183,50	2091,18	117840,00	32304,00	37709,00	2670,17
Azerbaijan	141,78	1729,60	199,09	26370,60	501,00	1300,00	4773,00
Belarus	133,67	472,79	1148,08	348508,00	76252,00	408591,00	8532,70
Belgium	85,52	57,39	1256,59	171826,00	18757,00	59833,00	1350,80
Bulgaria	126,21	203,74	564,58	333620,00	65231,00	34012,00	5021,00
Croatia	127,73	120,65	261,18	72320,00	13241,00	18477,00	1546,00
Cyprus	79,07	13,23	16,59	7968,00	5380,00	3302,00	111,88
Czechia	102,28	149,08	1610,07	404184,00	47446,00	37561,00	3489,00
Denmark	103,33	71,18	1351,81	228139,00	33987,00	64127,00	2625,63
Estonia	129,47	25,04	288,48	36390,00	7889,00	10909,00	1003,00
Finland	97,26	94,29	1592,86	138128,00	22524,79	32869,00	2275,00
France	96,14	753,59	12003,96	2191727,00	409585,00	393256,00	28718,02
Georgia	70,40	602,71	104,10	51000,00	5360,19	2406,06	2394,00
Germany	107,90	539,86	10551,58	1658837,00	231079,00	430080,00	16657,00
Greece	92,80	454,52	1516,92	173123,00	51914,00	43865,00	6136,00
Hungary	87,15	219,14	929,15	366043,00	91655,00	96866,00	5282,00
Ireland	110,13	112,34	1006,06	302390,51	113165,90	141024,06	4446,00
Italy	92,32	884,00	10058,02	602730,00	162260,00	115670,00	12812,00
Kazakhstan	140,57	1383,40	757,25	91532,00	33111,00	2507,00	216992,00
Kyrgyzstan	113,97	633,30	33,26	35217,00	5089,00	151,00	10541,10
Latvia	151,57	68,67	494,20	78285,00	25447,00	30468,00	1931,00
Lithuania	136,45	108,58	784,12	160237,00	50884,00	71413,00	2953,90
Luxembourg	109,78	2,38	149,65	13731,00	1124,00	1359,00	130,52
Malta	90,29	2,43	20,91	2122,40	127,79	148,87	10,38
Netherlands	119,54	175,12	4838,31	261053,00	9134,00	26827,00	1796,00
Poland	117,55	1707,80	4220,27	1150600,00	343400,00	555800,00	14374,00
Portugal	108,34	318,37	1128,59	105459,70	49146,24	33206,04	3619,03
Moldova	96,81	410,94	35,03	92438,00	1168,00	602,00	2317,90
Romania	112,82	1951,93	974,77	344311,00	126189,00	43626,00	13521,00
Russia	147,80	4863,16	10183,65	1445212,00	510163,00	317902,00	216249,00
Slovakia	101,64	71,94	555,22	126236,00	24297,00	18869,00	1886,00
Slovenia	88,71	45,61	283,39	27097,00	9161,00	11356,00	617,48
Spain	103,67	774,60	5395,81	982155,00	414974,00	379007,00	26265,70
Sweden	99,69	91,98	1975,01	186042,81	30029,00	31956,00	3031,50
Tajikistan	138,48		78,84	52455,00	1786,92	294,50	4734,70
Turkmenistan	103,47		449,52				33838,00
Ukraine	169,06	2539,10	1641,68	1197380,00	287010,00	244460,00	41515,00
United Kingdom	103,86	354,37	6741,52	1040000,00	197940,00	286000,00	17349,98
Uzbekistan	143,48		1161,66	721316,00	225826,00	76752,00	25545,00

Table 6.3 VRS technology and input orientated efficiency

Efficiency range	%	Countries
0<= E <0.1	31.4	Azerbaijan, Ukraine, Belarus, Romania, Spain, Great Britain, France, Italy, Germany, Poland
0.1<= E <0.2	37.1	Finland, Bulgaria, Russia, Belgium, Denmark, Sweden, Austria, Portugal, Czechia, Greece, Ireland, Netherlands, Hungary
0.2<= E <0.3	8.6	Kyrgyzstan, Lithuania, Moldova, Uzbekistan
0.3<= E <0.4	5.7	Armenia, Slovakia
0.4<= E <0.5	5.7	Latvia, Croatia
0.5<= E <0.6	0	
0.6<= E <0.7	0	
0.7<= E <0.8	0	
0.8<= E <0.9	0	
0.9<= E <1	0	
E ==1	11.4	Estonia, Georgia, Kazakhstan, Slovenia

Table 6.4 CRS technology and input orientated efficiency

Efficiency range	%	Countries
0<= E <0.1	40.0	France, Germany, Poland, Russia, Italy, Spain, United Kingdom, Romania, Ukraine, Belarus, Hungary, Azerbaijan, Kazakhstan
0.1<= E <0.2	34.3	Greece, Ireland, Uzbekistan, Netherlands, Czechia, Austria, Portugal, Belgium, Denmark, Sweden, Bulgaria, Kyrgyzstan, Finland
0.2<= E <0.3	5.7	Moldova, Lithuania
0.3<= E <0.4	5.7	Slovakia, Armenia
0.4<= E <0.5	5.7	Croatia, Latvia
0.5<= E <0.6	0	
0.6<= E <0.7	2.9	Slovenia
0.7<= E <0.8	0	
0.8<= E <0.9	0	
0.9<= E <1	2.9	Estonia
E ==1	2.9	Georgia

- Ensuring the active introduction of ICT in agriculture, which will increase the efficiency of the entire production process,
- Ensuring transparency in agriculture, improving legislation, and reducing bureaucracy.

6.5 INNOVATION IN DIGITAL AGRICULTURE

Innovations in agriculture involve changing the established ways of farming and creating new production processes. Innovations differ in the level of costs, the complexity of implementation, the level of risk, etc.

The spread of agricultural innovations is a process through which new methods of agricultural production are spreading in agriculture. Novelty creates a certain degree of uncertainty, so quite often innovations are not accepted by farmers.

Table 6.5 The agriculture innovation challenge top innovators

Company	Proposed Solution
Arable, San Francisco, CA	Actionable field intelligence and seasonal insights using microclimate and crop health IoT sensors.
CropIn, India	CropIn's AI and ML powered platform collects farm-level data using the mobile application, enables farmers with accurate, timely, prescriptive advisories, and provides agribusinesses with a rich data platform.
Satelligence, Netherlands	Satelligence provides a solution for Fall Armyworm (FAW) destruction. FAW risk maps are created and inform farmers their farms are at risk.
Injini LLC, Delaware, USA	The company uses farmers' contributions to social media platforms. AI algorithms applied on the social media content can create deduced intelligence from the input, after which it can be graded and applied to the data platform.
eSusFarm®, South Africa	Collecting/tracking the agronomic activities of smallholder/subsistence farmers on a real-time basis.
Saillog, Israel	Based on images of crop problems, farmers receive instant identifications of the problems, locally relevant guidance on integrated pest management techniques and direct communication with crop protection experts.
Aerobotics, South Africa	Technology "Drone Scouting" captures high-resolution video to detect and measure the size and color of the fruit. Aerobotics provides reports throughout the season which estimate the count of fruits, and size distribution and estimations up until harvest.
AIGROEDGE, India	Edge IoT and artificial intelligence–based expert system (SAAS) provides real-time data and personalized suggestions to farmers to enhance yield and high profit margins.
AgriProject, Namibia	Establishing the "Internet of Bees" to monitor and support the growth of honey-producing beehives by setting up data transmitting beehives and local weather stations to monitor the environment.
IFAM, Taiwan	Intelligent monitoring, analysis and early warning system for FAW in Africa. A built-in infrared sensor accurately counts the number of FAW trapped in a smart pheromone trap box and sends that information to the farmer through the instant messaging application.
Carpe Diem Solutions, Israel	Innovative Extreme Weather understands weather in real time with unmatched precision, and interference-free, long-range and automatic recognition of meteorological formations providing a step-change in disaster prediction efficiency.
RVF-Zero, Senegal	The device detects Rift Valley Fever (RVF)–carrying mosquitoes and informs authorities as soon as a new wave of RVF-carrying mosquitoes appears. This allows farmers to avoid losing their entire herd to RVF by allowing authorities to take rapid action to limit the impact of the virus.
Jaguza Tech, Uganda	Detecting the vectors of RVF. The device consists of a photocatalytic mosquito lamp with an integrated mini surveillance camera connected to Wi-Fi and a tripod that can be fixed to the ground to withstand flooding and high winds.
Yuktix, India	ICT system that uses an indigenous knowledge database and accurate weather information to predict onset of crop diseases. This system comprises Yuktix IoT sensor devices, a mobile app and software for dispensing advisories.
Satyukt, India	The scalable algorithms combine multi-satellite data, and leverage big data analytics and physical and machine learning algorithms to estimate real-time, finer and high frequency of data at the desired scale across the globe in different climatic conditions.
Innosapien Agro Technologies, India	The multimodal artificial intelligence in the platform automatically detects pests, diseases and deficiencies prior to any visible symptoms right on the field, within a few seconds, while also providing automatic farm-specific customized advisories in real time.

(Continued)

Table 6.5 (Continued) The agriculture innovation challenge top innovators

Company	Proposed Solution
Biome Makers, USA	BeCrop is an all-in-one functional soil test that determines the biological quality of arable soil. The combination of the most advanced technologies of DNA sequencing and Intelligent Computing allows Biome Makers to use the soil microbiome as bioindicator of land status and value.
OpenAgri.ai, Indonesia	Uses spectral information from freely and abundantly available cloud masks to enhance the current traditional prediction method. This spectral information will be used to enhance historical weather information available publicly, often in near–real time for any area in the world.
ARC, South Africa	The Community Based Extreme Weather Portal is a crowd-sourcing app to assimilate hail data, combining weather station and cell signal data into an archive to support farmers and the insurance industry.
mPower Social Enterprises Ltd., Bangladesh	GEOPOTATO is an ICT that provides farmers with timely alerts about the risk of blight. GEOPOTATO combines satellite and local weather data with an epidemiological and crop growth model to forecast blight pressure at a high geographic and temporal resolution.

Less risk-averse farmers take innovation early, reap "innovation rents", resulting in lower unit costs and increased profits. An active introduction of innovations increases the total volume of production, which causes lower prices. This situation disproportionately affects farmers. Small farmers are the first to face challenges, and accordingly, this situation can bring greater benefits to large farmers and consumers. Accordingly, it is necessary to manage the innovation process in such a way as to take into account the interests of all stakeholders.

The World Bank's Agriculture Observatory identified the Agriculture Innovation Challenge Top Innovators. They are presented in Table 6.5 (World Bank, 2020).

Managing innovation in digital agriculture is still imperfect. For an effective innovation process, it is necessary to develop a long-term strategy for digital agriculture, to establish a permanent dialogue with stakeholders, taking into account the functions and tasks of different organizations, to improve coordination between scientific, governmental and agricultural producers and to implement integrated systems.

Public funding for research and digital agricultural activities plays an important role. Ongoing public funding for research, enhanced by private funding, will allow for active innovation in digital agriculture.

International cooperation is also important. International projects, exchanges of researchers, students, and research infrastructures, will allow faster and more efficient implementation of innovative solutions in agriculture.

6.6 CONCLUSIONS

Global megatrends are manifested all over the world, but with different intensities and speeds in different regions. However, they can be seen as typical trends in agriculture. Analyzing a wide range of global trends and studying their implications for the future of agriculture, it is necessary to take into account their implications and evaluate the possible results in the formation of the agricultural management system.

More and more modern technologies are used in agriculture, and as a result, production conditions are changing, so that agricultural production systems can be optimized and meet modern societal needs. The development of digital agriculture will contribute to the provision of sufficient food of good quality and composition, which will meet the needs of a constantly growing world population. It will also reduce the side effects of the environment, saving many hectares to ensure biodiversity.

For the effective development of digital agriculture, it is very important to make basic technologies available as widely as possible for all agriculture and to implement them with a minimal negative impact on farmers.

Improvements in technology will make agriculture a more profitable, efficient, safer and friendlier environment. However, agricultural operations must take a very different path with the advancement of technology.

In this new era of agriculture, modern technology is becoming crucial. The data collected will be used to help farmers use their land, water and other resources more efficiently. Much of the data collection will be done by agricultural drones, satellites, and "smart" agricultural equipment. Crop and livestock management will be significantly automated, which will significantly increase the efficiency of agricultural production.

Innovation in agriculture is not just about technology. Innovation in agriculture must also include social, organizational and institutional processes. The success of innovation in agriculture depends not only on key stakeholders but also on government, science and society as a whole.

REFERENCES

Anshari, M., Almunawar, M. N., Masri, M., & Hamdan, M. (2019). Digital marketplace and fintech to support agriculture sustainability. *Energy Procedia*, *156*, pp. 234–238.

Babenko, V.O. (2014). *Management of innovation processes of processing enterprises of agrarian and industrial complex (mathematical modeling and information technologies)*: monograph. [Upravlinnya innovatsiynymy protsesamy pererobnykh pidpryyemstv APK (matematychne modelyuvannya ta informatsiyni tekhnolohiyi): monohrafiya], Dokuchaev Kharkiv National Agrarian University, KhNAU, Kharkiv: Machulin, 380 p. [in Ukraine].

Babenko, V. O. (2017). Modeling of factors influencing innovation activities of agricultural enterprises of Ukraine. *Scientific Bulletin of Polissia*, 1(9), 2, pp. 115–121. DOI: 10.25140/2410-9576-2017-2-2(10)

Banker, R. D., Charnes, A., & Cooper, W. W. (1984). Some models for estimating technical and scale inefficiencies in data envelopment analysis. *Management science*, *30*(9), 1078–1092.

Blok, V., & Gremmen, B. (2018). Agricultural technologies as living machines: toward a biomimetic conceptualization of smart farming technologies. *Ethics, Policy & Environment*, *21*(2), pp. 246–263.

Caves, D. W., Christensen, L. R., & Diewert, W. E. (1982). Multilateral comparisons of output, input, and productivity using superlative index numbers. *The economic journal*, *92*(365), pp. 73–86.

Charnes, A., Cooper, W. W., & Rhodes, E. (1978). Measuring the efficiency of decision making units. *European journal of operational research*, *2*(6), pp. 429–444.

Chernyakov, M., Chernyakova, M., & Akberov, K. (2019, January). Innodiversification model of the digital economy of the agricultural sector. In *2nd International Scientific conference on New Industrialization: Global, national, regional dimension (SICNI 2018)*. Atlantis Press.

De Clercq, M., Vats, A., & Biel, A. (2018). Agriculture 4.0: The future of farming technology. *Proceedings of the World Government Summit, Dubai, UAE*, pp. 11–13.

Fare, R., Grosskopf, S., & Knox Lovell, C. A. (1994). *Production frontiers*. Cambridge University Press.

Farrell, M. J. (1957). The measurement of productive efficiency. *Journal of the Royal Statistical Society: Series A (General)*, *120*(3), pp. 253–281.

Klerkx, L., & Rose, D. (2020). Dealing with the game-changing technologies of Agriculture 4.0: How do we manage diversity and responsibility in food system transition pathways? *Global Food Security, 24*, 100347.

Leonard, E., Rainbow, R., Laurie, A., Lamb, D., Llewellyn, R., Perrett, E., ... & Wood, G. (2017). Accelerating precision agriculture to decision agriculture: Enabling digital agriculture in Australia.

Lowder, S. K., Skoet, J., & Raney, T. (2016). The number, size, and distribution of farms, smallholder farms, and family farms worldwide. *World Development, 87*, pp. 16–29.

Malmquist, S. (1953). Index numbers and indifference surfaces. *Trabajos de estadística, 4*(2), pp. 209–242.

McKinsey & Company Report (2016). How big data will revolutionize the global food chain. Retrieved from: https://www.mckinsey.com/business-functions/mckinsey-digital/our-insights/how-big-data-will-revolutionize-the-global-food-chain# (Access: 15.07.2020).

Megatrends hub. Retrieved from: https://ec.europa.eu/knowledge4policy/online-resource/mega-trends-hub_en (Access: 15.07.2020).

OECD (2019), *Innovation, Productivity and Sustainability in Food and Agriculture: Main Findings from Country Reviews and Policy Lessons*, OECD Food and Agricultural Reviews, OECD Publishing, Paris. Doi: https://doi.org/10.1787/c9c4ec1d-en.

Ozdogan, B., Gacar, A., & Aktas, H. (2017). Digital agriculture practices in the context of agriculture 4.0. *Journal of Economics Finance and Accounting, 4*(2), pp. 186–193.

Pedersen, S. M., & Lind, K. M. (2017). Precision agriculture–from mapping to site-specific application. In *Precision agriculture: Technology and economic perspectives* (pp. 1–20). Cham: Springer.

Plieninger, T., Torralba, M., Hartel, T., & Fagerholm, N. (2019). Perceived ecosystem services synergies, trade-offs, and bundles in European high nature value farming landscapes. *Landscape Ecology, 34*(7), pp. 1565–1581.

Project Breakthrough. (2017). Digital Agriculture: Feeding the future. Retrieved from: http://breakthrough.unglobalcompact.org/disruptive-technologies/digital-agriculture/   European Commission, (Access: 15.07.2020).

Rabbinge, R., & Bindraban, P. S. (2012). Making more food available: promoting sustainable agricultural production. *Journal of Integrative Agriculture, 11*(1), pp. 1–8.

Rose, D. C., & Chilvers, J. (2018). Agriculture 4.0: Broadening responsible innovation in an era of smart farming. *Frontiers in Sustainable Food Systems, 2*, p. 87.

Rungsuriyawiboon, S., & Coelli, T. (2004). Regulatory reform and economic performance in US electricity generation. *Centre for Efficiency and Productivity Analyisis*.

Sakhno, A., Salkova, I., Broyaka, A. & Priamukhina, N. (2019). Methodology for the Impact Assessment of the Digital Economy on Agriculture Development. *International Journal of Recent Technology and Engineering 8, no. 3C*, pp. 160–164.

Serraj, R., & Pingali, P. L. (Eds.). (2019). *Agriculture & Food Systems to 2050: Global Trends, Challenges and Opportunities*. World Scientific Publishing Company Pte. Limited.

Shorikov, A.F., & Babenko, V.A. (2014). Optimization of assured result in dynamical model of management of innovation process in the enterprise of agricultural production complex. *Economy of Region*, 1, pp. 196–202. Doi: 10.17059/2014-1-18.

Sundmaeker, H., Verdouw, C., Wolfert, S. & Pérez Freire, L. (2016). Internet of food and farm 2020. *Digitising the Industry-Internet of Things connecting physical, digital and virtual worlds* 2.

Trendov, N. M., Varas, S., & Zeng, M. (2019). *Digital Technologies in Agriculture and Rural Areas. FAO: Rome, Italy*.

Trukhachev, V., Bobrishev, A., Khokhlova, E., Ivashova, V., & Fedisko, O. (2019). Personnel training for the agricultural sector in terms of digital transformation of the economy: Trends, prospects and limitations. *International Journal of Civil Engineering and Technology, 10*(1), pp. 2145–2155.

Tucker, C. (2017). *Advances in cattle welfare*. Woodhead Publishing.

Vaganova, O. V., Solovjeva, N. E., Aulov, Y. L., & Prokopova, L. I. (2020, April). Transformation of Agriculture Through Digitalization, Innovative Solutions, and Information Technologies. In: *III*

International Scientific and Practical Conference "Digital Economy and Finances"(ISPC-DEF 2020), Atlantis Press, pp. 65–68.

Van Criekinge, T., & Calenbuhr, V. (Forthcoming). *Sustainable food systems: Towards*

Weltzien, C. (2016). Digital agriculture or why agriculture 4.0 still offers only modest returns. *Landtechnik*, 71(2), pp. 66–68.

Wolfert, S., Ge, L., Verdouw, C., & Bogaardt, M. J. (2017). Big data in smart farming–a review. *Agricultural Systems*, 153, pp. 69–80.

World Bank. (2020). Innovation challenges for food security & agriculture risk financing in Southern Africa. Retrieved from: https://www.worldbank.org/en/events/2020/03/09/agriculture-risk-innovation-challenge#1 (Access: 15.07.2020).

Chapter 7

Relevance of the completeness meter of transport services

Marta Kadłubek

CONTENTS

7.1 INTRODUCTION

Nowadays, the company gaining superiority over the competitive market is not only about implementing innovative technologies or introducing modern product solutions to the offer, but on efficient and effective logistics service, which gives the opportunity to keep old customers and acquire new ones. According to Ballou (2004) in order to gain a competitive advantage, business entities use various strategies to achieve it, but one of the most important is the customer service strategy. In reference to customer service strategy can be considered as a well-thought-out perspective action plan, whose goal is systematic progress up to the achievement of the assumed customer service pattern, which should allow maintaining or taking a specific position on the market.

There is no single recognized and commonly used definition of customer service in the literature. However, many statements show that it is a multidimensional and difficult to explain term. As emphasized by Christopher (2010), it is because of the multidimensional nature of customer service and due to the large diversity of needs of individual markets that in each business activity it is necessary to identify elements of customer service before, during and after sales, as well as their measures. One of the most important measures is the service completeness meter, which is the subject of the article. The purpose of this paper is assessment of relevance of the completeness meter as perceived by the recipients of services on example of commercial cargo motor transport enterprises using a multiple discriminant analysis.

7.2 THEORETICAL BACKGROUND

The sphere of customer service includes all activities aimed at the proper implementation of the order process and service standards, as well as before- and after-sales customer service (Kempny, 2001). The definition of customer service contains all areas of contact with the customer, including tangible and intangible elements. Due to its broad approach, it is a sphere of both marketing and logistics. Analysing customer service areas, it is possible to separate tasks that strictly belong to the marketing department, as well as those that are in the area of logistics competence.

Customer service is one of the crucial terms in modern logistics (Kisperska-Moroń and Krzyżaniak, 2009). This is due to the very principles of logistics management and the objectives, which in the simplest way expresses the 7R rule (Christopher, 2010), which includes the following elements: the right product, the right consumer, in the right quantity, in the right quality, in the right place, at the right time and at the right price.

Logistics customer service can be interpreted in many ways depending on the point of view of manufacturers, suppliers, sellers or customers (Florez-Lopez and Ramon-Jeronimo, 2012; Price and Harrison, 2013). Basically, logistics customer service can be interpreted as the appropriate ability to operate in the area of a company's logistics system that strives to meet the needs of customers, including ensuring optimal delivery time, high efficiency of operations and a properly high level of communication with the customer (Lambert et al., 2008).

The process of logistics customer service is divided into three clearly dependent phases (Kempny, 2001). The pre-transaction phase refers to all of the activities that are designed to examine the preferences of customers, set the standards and determine the appropriate logistics customer service policy. Defining contract performance standards is an essential element of this phase. Service standards must be tailored to the real and actual preferences of the recipients. Thus, setting logistics customer service standards should be preceded by research that focuses on the identification of customers' needs within the logistics activities. These preferences can be different to potential groups of customers. Then it may be profitable to separate individual customer segments and different service policies for separate groups. The company should be able to adapt to different customer expectations and should use the procedures in the event of exceptional situations. The company must also take into account the need to adapt to the unusual requirements of customers, which may bring relatively high profits (La Londe, 1985). In organizations focused on providing a high quality of logistics customer service, special communication systems are designed and systems are introduced to support the construction of customer relations, tracking shipments, and placing and handling orders, as well as giving the possibility to control the process of order fulfilment. An important element of the whole process is also to present the consumer with a service declaration that will enable the company to present its real possibilities.

The transaction phase mainly relates to the order processing process (Blanding, 1982). The transactional elements of logistics customer service allow for efficient and consistent with customer expectations transaction conducting—from the moment the order is placed until the product or service is received. They relate to direct contact with the consumers, and their proper implementation significantly determines their satisfaction. The basic elements that make up the process may include delivery time as the time that passes from the moment the order is placed until the customer receives the product or service. Another crucial components are (Lambert and Stock, 1993): the availability of the product from stocks, flexibility of deliveries, frequency of deliveries, reliability of deliveries, completeness of deliveries, accuracy of deliveries, convenience of placing orders, convenience of documentation and others.

The post-transaction phase is the stage at which customer satisfaction is measured. It consists of post-transaction elements that guarantee consumers proper use of purchased products. However, they give the manufacturer the opportunity to determine whether the product sold performs its functions as intended. These include warranty, installation, repair, replacements and delivery of parts. The consumer receives full access to necessary parts or repairs, after-sales guarantees and operating instructions, as well as dismantling and reinstalling the product after repair or replacement. The following elements of after-sales service standards include return policies and complaints. This is a very important issue, as handling returns is a very expensive element for producers. It also affects the load on the logistics system and disrupts its proper operation.

Satisfying the above criteria can be considered in reference to a variety of meters for assessing the logistics customer service in the enterprise (Byrne and Markham, 1991; Chen et al., 2009). The assessment system, which allows for consistent opining regarding inaccuracies and accomplishments, is particularly significant for the quality of logistics customer service. The parameters of measurement should be continuously modified due to the requirements of the enterprise (Nogalski and Ronkowski, 2007). The right approach seems to be both to indicate the level of logistics customer service within the enterprise, and to monitor and control its measurement of the quality of logistics service using proper logistics categories. They are presenting procedures and essentials in the area of management in the enterprise (Borowiecki and Siuta-Tokarska, 2009), articulated in sufficient components of measurement, meters of logistics customer service. The major assignment of the meters is to register events from the logistics system which will comprise the foundation for measurement of the level of logistics customer service (Nowicka-Skowron, 2001).

Due to the subsequent definition of logistics meter presented by Fertsch (2006), it is the value specified in units of measure, expressing events and facts of the flow of materials and information in the logistics system of the enterprise or supply chain. Meters are diverse in terms of categories, ranges and areas of impact. In logistics terms, meters empirically present some observable and measurable actual states, are expressed in relative units, and are evaluative and comparative in their nature (Kisperska-Moroń, 2006).

The meters for measuring logistics customer service can be chosen due to the specificity of the performed logistics tasks. The most completely developed is the system of measurement and evaluation of logistics customer service of delivery and procurement in terms of management of material resources: materials, raw materials, finished products. In practice, there is an extensive variety of meters for evaluation of the results and opportunities incorporating logistics functions in the area of the flow of resources (Chaberek, 2002). Amongst the most commonly used meters identifying the level of logistics customer service and its monitoring and control, among others, Ballou (2004), Coyle et al. (2013), and Kempny (2001) list completeness meter.

The completeness meter is specified as one of the most imperative elements of logistics customer service, in dependence on the availability of stocks, associated to time and accuracy. It is one of the transaction components of logistics customer service influencing a successful transaction, in line with customer requirements – from the point of placing an order to the point of receiving the goods. Gołembska (2009) understands completeness of deliveries as the supplier's ability to entirely complete the order and, in the occurrence of not assembly the standards as to deliverance completeness, there are so called underdeliveries. Baraniecka et al. (2005) identifies the completeness of deliveries as the determination of the supplier's aptitude to perform the general arrangement of products ordered. In reference to the extensive assortment of products, it is connected with the preservation of a high level of stocks. In comparison, completeness meter indicates the percentage of orders fulfilled due to their arrangement (Twaróg, 2005).

7.3 METHODOLOGY OF THE RESEARCH

Exploration on the achievement of logistics customer service in the view of the recipients of the services of commercial cargo motor transport enterprises (Rydzkowski, 2011; Rucińska, 2015; Wojewódzka-Król and Rolbiecki, 2013) in the Silesian Voivodeship (southern Poland), which was realized using the SERVQUAL method (Parasuraman et al., 1988; Zhou and Pritchard, 2009), made it obtainable to evaluate the quality of logistics customer service components of business entities involved in the research sample. The questionnaire forms were completed by 294 customers of 147 surveyed commercial cargo motor transport companies in the Silesian Voivodeship, i.e., by two customers of each entity. Analyzing of the medium level of divergence between the assumptions and experiences of 294 customers of the companies in the area of logistics customer service components, on the basement of the possessed primary data, in the next stage of the research on the significance of the quality of logistics customer service was made for those components, which were recognized by the recipients of the transport services as the most essential. One of these most crucial components was the completeness of the services. In consideration of the assignment of chosen components of logistics customer service in the surveyed companies, a trial was made to explore the influence of the quality of chosen components of logistics customer service on the completeness of services, which presents the relevance of the completeness meter as recognized by the recipients of transport services.

In reference to indication of the above-mentioned connotation, the multiple discriminant analysis was employed. The discriminant model which was planned to be developed, as suggested by Triola (2012), in the space of k-dimensional inhomogeneous random vectors of finite values of mathematical expectations, variances and covariances, hyperplanes can be approved, which will separate this space into subspaces of more homogeneous vectors. The research sample is found in p-dimensional sample of normal distribution with expected value of vector x and the same covariance matrix, S.

In reference to the related variance of the observed variables, as the subsequent stage of the research, the assessment of the discriminant function was made. Important decisive and infuencial issues refer to the coefficients of a discriminant function, which intend is to icrease the percentage of the inter-group variability of the input data to their intra-group variability (Jajuga, 1993). The decisive factor was the Anderson's classification statistics according to the following formula (Statsoft, 2020):

$$W = (\overline{x}_1 - \overline{x}_2)^T S^{-1} x - 0,5 \cdot (\overline{x}_1 - \overline{x}_2)^T S^{-1} (\overline{x}_1 + \overline{x}_2), \tag{7.1}$$

where: x shiuld be classified into population 1 (with low rated results) when W<0, and into population 2 (with high rated results), when W > 0.

As the principle of disseverance of the endogenous variables, arbitrary values of results for variable X were introduced as follows:

- the 1-st group is for: X<–3
- the 2-nd group is for: –3 ≤ X< 0
- –3 ≤ X_i < 0; the 3-rd group is for: 0≤X<3
- 0 ≤ X_i < 3; – the 4-th group is for: X≥3

X_i ≥ 3. Respective values were allocated and classifyied into the groups: 1, 2, 3, 4 for each company category, so the entities with: very good logistics customer service, good logistics customer service, poor logistics customer service and very poor logistics customer service. The dependent variable is X—completeness of the services of the transport enterprises examined.

The assessment sample refers to 294 complete questionnaire forms received from the customers of commercial cargo motor transport companies, which were the basis for categorization. Nine input variables were recommended for the above-mentioned potential output variable. The independent variables are presented in Table 7.1.

Table 7.1 Independent variables

Variable number	Variable name
V1	Meeting the environmental requirements by the fleet of the transport enterprises examined
V2	Inquiry response time in the transport enterprises examined
V3	Terminal protection in the transport enterprises examined
V4	Reliability of the logistic consultancy of the transport enterprises examined
V5	Extensiveness of the services of the transport enterprises examined
V6	Geographic coverage of the services of the transport enterprises examined
V7	Meeting the environmental requirements by the infrastructure of the transport enterprises examined
V8	Competencies and expertise of the logistic consultancy of the transport enterprises examined
V9	Round-the-clock servicing offered by the transport enterprises examined

Source: Own elaboration.

In the introduced discriminant function the determination of all independent variables is considered. First of all, the interference was presumed that at least the first k discriminant variables were significant, and the hypothesis of the significance of the last $s - k$ discriminant variables was settled in the test. The inquiry was performed progressively in the following order, due to the interference that the level of significance for particular parameters should be lower than 0.05 (Statsoft, 2020). The estimations were realized using the *STATISTICA 10.0* programme.

7.4 RESEARCH RESULTS

Performed discriminant function specifies the determination of the nine independent variables on the dependent variable X, which is completeness of the services of the transport enterprises examined. To present the most important features of this function, the subsequent assessment effects tabularized are submitted.

In reference to the data presented in Table 7.2, the discrimination of the determined categories by the dependent variable X indicated in the model has immense value of Wilks' Lambda: $\Lambda = 0.6469$, F = 7.652, p < 0.0000. The level of Wilks' Lambda has been reduced from 0.6652 to 0.6617 after adding the final variable to the model and specifying the raise

Table 7.2 Attributes of independent variables: A review of the discriminant function analysis for the dependent variable X—completeness of the services of the transport enterprises examined

Variable Number	Wilks' Lambda	Part. Wilks'	Elim. F (4,21)	p Level	Toler.	1-Toler. (R-square)
V1	0,6931	0,9333	10,1084	0,0001	0,7888	0,2112
V2	0,7028	0,9203	12,2462	0,0000	0,9465	0,0535
V3	0,7010	0,9228	11,8317	0,0000	0,7567	0,2433
V4	0,6622	0,9769	3,3447	0,0367	0,7991	0,2009
V5	0,6762	0,9566	6,4173	0,0019	0,7246	0,2754
V6	0,6767	0,9560	6,5180	0,0017	0,7284	0,2716
V7	0,6701	0,9654	5,0736	0,0068	0,8933	0,1067
V8	0,6652	0,9724	4,0208	0,0190	0,8156	0,1844
V9	0,6617	0,9776	3,2381	0,0407	0,7786	0,2214

Source: Own elaboration using the *STATISTICA 10.0* package.

Table 7.3 Determination of the standardized and raw discrimination function coefficients for the variable X—completeness of the services of the transport enterprises examined

Variable Number	Standardized values		Raw values	
	1-st function	*2-nd function*	*1-st function*	*2-nd function*
V1	−0,6044	−0,1257	−0,5031	−0,1047
V2	−0,5988	0,1503	−0,5328	0,1337
V3	0,2131	0,7431	0,1736	0,6054
V4	−0,3393	0,1364	−0,2811	0,1130
V5	−0,4089	−0,3671	−0,4036	−0,3624
V6	0,5098	0,1146	0,2650	0,0595
V7	−0,0669	−0,4765	−0,0452	−0,3219
V8	0,0010	0,4515	0,0008	0,3588
V9	−0,2893	−0,2449	−0,1588	−0,1344
Constant	–	–	−0,4833	0,9107
Eigenvalue	0,2890	0,1993	0,2890	0,1993
Accumulated proportion	0,5918	1,0000	0,5918	1,0000

Source: Own elaboration using the *STATISTICA 10.0* package.

in its discrimination capability. The rejection of the F value for the independent values is considerable, and also the decisive level of significance approved for the whole variables, so $p < 0.05$, without a doubt, presents an important donation of all results to the discrimination. The values of tolerance vary between 0,7246 and 0.9465, which confirms that the new information brought in by these variables are of high value. The introduced assessments prove the significant but rather parallel importance of the whole input variables in the considered model.

The settlements introduced in Table 7.3 prove that the independent variable V1, which is meeting the environmental requirements by the fleet of the transport enterprises examined, determined maximum influence on the discrimination of the dependent variable X. Also the results presents the tendency of the distances of successive variables from one another, which diversify definitely. The strong determinants are independent variables in the following order:

- V2: inquiry response time in the transport enterprises examined
- V6: geographic coverage of the services of the transport enterprises examined
- V5: extensiveness of the services of the transport enterprises examined
- V4: reliability of the logistic consultancy of the transport enterprises examined
- V3: terminal protection in the transport enterprises examined
- V9: round-the-clock servicing offered by the transport enterprises examined

Independent variables: V8, which are competencies and expertise of the logistic consultancy of the transport enterprises examined, and V7, which is meeting the environmental requirements by the infrastructure of the transport enterprises examined, despite their significance, have much lower influence. Among the two functions recommended in the previous approach, the first function was selected because of its noticeably highest eigenvalue. In addition, this fact is proved by the chi-square test assessments, presented in Table 7.4.

Table 7.4 Assessments of the significance test of discriminant variables for the variable X—completeness of the services of the transport enterprises examined

	Eigenvalue	Canonical R	Wilks' Lambda	chi-square	df	p level
0	0,2890	0,4735	0,6469	125,0224	18	0,0000
I	0,1993	0,4077	0,8338	52,1687	8	0,0000

Source: Own elaboration using the STATISTICA 10.0 package.

In reference to Table 7.4, both functions are identified as of properly high significance, however the results imply more advanced usage of the first function.

The consecutive columns of the acquired Table 7.5 include the mean values of discriminant variables designated for each company category, so the entities with very good logistics customer service, good logistics customer service, poor logistics customer service and very poor logistics customer service. The dissimilarities in the area of the mean values of the discriminant variable for estimation are considerably more immense, principally for the second and third group. The first discriminant function differentiates the whole estimations, which are in a systematized appearance. Also it should be noted that estimations of the mean value of the first discriminant function are not analogous to the other appraisals.

In reference to the data presented in Table 7.6, the settlements concern the conclusion that the dependent variable characterizes in the first model mainly the discrimination values of the input value V1—meeting the environmental requirements by the fleet of the transport enterprises examined, then V2—inquiry response time in the transport enterprises examined and V5—extensiveness of the services of the transport enterprises examined. In the second approach, the variable V3_terminal protection in the transport enterprises examined, would have been considered.

Due to the data presented in Table 7.7, more than 77.89% of the commercial cargo motor transport companies have been properly classified to the assessment scores. This result is a satisfactory achievement, which is noticeable in both the second group of scores with 90.41% accuracy and in the first group with 44.44% accuracy. The maximum accuracy was reached for the companies assessed negatively (93.9%), therefore, as a consequence, the function is classified as an optimistic one.

The simulation of theoretical values as well as empirical values for the variable X—completeness of the services of the transport enterprises examined, are presented in Figure 7.1. The graphic illustration demonstrates a reasonably high level of matching the results of discrimination to the real results. The function that treats the considered dependent variable as a criterion seems to be of high relevance for logistics customer service based on analysis of the reserach data.

Table 7.5 Numerical estimation of the prospective functions for the dependent variable X– completeness of the services of the transport enterprises examined

	I-st function	2-nd function
G I:I	1,5139	2,1603
G 2:2	0,2099	–0,1928
G 3:3	–0,9030	0,3452

Source: Own elaboration using the STATISTICA 10.0 package.

Table 7.6 Assessment of the correlation coefficients of the
input variables with the discriminant variables for
the dependent variable X—completeness of the
services of the transport enterprises examined

Variable number	1-st function	2-nd function
V1	−0,5363	−0,1174
V2	−0,5229	0,1689
V3	−0,1739	0,5807
V4	−0,2436	0,3981
V5	−0,3678	−0,1998
V6	0,2439	−0,1960
V7	−0,2380	−0,3956
V8	−0,2777	0,4582
V9	−0,0926	−0,1134

Source: Own elaboration using the *STATISTICA 10.0* package.

Table 7.7 Gradation accuracy matrix for the estimation of companies
for the dependent variable X—completeness of the services
of the transport enterprises examined

	Percent	G 1:1	G 2:2	G 3:3
G 1:1	44.4444	4	5	0
G 2:2	90.4110	7	198	14
G 3:3	40.9091	0	39	27
Total	77.8912	11	242	41

Source: Own elaboration using the *STATISTICA 10.0* package.

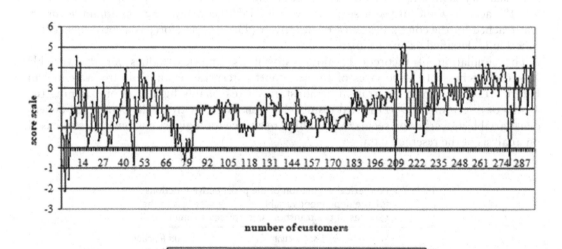

Figure 7.1 Theoretical and empirical values settled for the variable X—completeness of the services of the
transport enterprises examined

Source: Own elaboration.

7.5 CONCLUSIONS

The logistics customer service policy established in transport companies should include a commitment to meet customer requirements and continually improve developed service standards, on the basis of creation of the framework for establishing indicators that measure service quality.

The prerequisite to offering logistics customer service of high quality is its regular verification. The primary difficulty which occurs in reference to this matter is appropriate choice of such measures that would allow for the complex control of the logistics service elements which are important from the perspective of the enterprise's customers. Despite the fact that the assessment of the quality of logistics customer service, managers should pay attention to the meters that give perspective to evaluate the company's ability to fulfil orders. In the area of logistics, the measures are established in the enterprise typically to realize operational controlling, present information about the occurrences of processes and make effective improvements.

In the set of meters of logistics customer service, essential for the perception of services providers of the surveyed commercial cargo motor transport companies is the completeness meter. This meter specifies significant statistical relations with the chosen determinants of the scope of logistics customer service in the surveyed enterprises, although it is in correlation with the three variables of the discussed subject matter. The results of the research seems to confirm the importance of logistics customer service based on analysis of the research data. At the same time, however, due to the low values of the achieved statistical assessments, the considerations restricted in the concluding remarks are relatively hypothetical, and the oversimplification statements they are based on can be regarded as valid research theses, which may bring on areas of advanced basic research.

REFERENCES

Ballou, R. H. (2004). *Business Logistics. Supply Chain Management*. USA: Prentice Hall.

Baraniecka, A., Rodawski, B., & Skowrońska, A. (2005). *Logistyka: ćwiczenia*. Wrocław: Wydawnictwo Akademii Ekonomicznej we Wrocławiu.

Blanding, W. (1982). *Blanding's practical physical distribution. A handbook for planning and operations*. Washington: Traffic Service Corporation.

Borowiecki, R., & Siuta-Tokarska, B. (2009). *Problemy funkcjonowania i rozwoju małych i średnich przedsiębiorstw w Polsce. Synteza badań i kierunki działania*. Warszawa: Wyd. Difin.

Byrne, P. M., & Markham, W. J. (1991). *Improving quality and productivity in logistics process – Achieving customer satisfaction breakthroughs*. USA: Council of Logistics Management.

Chaberek, M. (2002). *Makro- i mikroekonomiczne aspekty wsparcia logistycznego*. Gdańsk: Wyd. Uniwersytetu Gdańskiego.

Chen, K.K., Chang, C.T., & Lai, C.S. (2009). Service quality gaps of business customers in the shipping industry. *Transportation research Part E*, 45, pp. 222–237.

Christopher, M. (2010). *Logistics and Supply Chain Management*. London: Financial Times/Irwin Professional Pub.

Coyle, J. J., Langley, C. J. Jr., Novack, R. A., & Gibson, B. J. (2013). *Supply Chain Management. A Logistics Perspective*. Nashville: South Western College Pub.

Fertsch, M. (2006). *Słownik terminologii logistycznej*. Poznań: Biblioteka Logistyka.

Florez-Lopez, R., & Ramon-Jeronimo, J. M. (2012). Managing logistics customer service under uncertainty: An integrative fuzzy Kano framework. *Information Sciences*, 202, pp. 41–57.

Gołembska, E. (2009). *Logistyka w gospodarce światowej*. Warszawa: Wyd. C. H. Beck.

Jajuga, K. (1993). *Statystyczna analiza wielowymiarowa*. Warszawa: PWN.

Kempny, D. (2001). *Logistyczna obsługa klienta*. Warszawa: PWE.

Kisperska-Moroń, D. (2006). *Pomiar funkcjonowania łańcuchów dostaw.* Katowice: Wyd. Akademii Ekonomicznej im. Karola Adamieckiego w Katowicach.

Kisperska-Moroń, D., & Krzyżaniak, S. (2009).*Logistyka.* Poznań: Instytut Logistyki i Magazynowania.

La Londe, B. J. (1985). *Customer service. The Distribution Handbook.* New York: The Free Press.

Lambert D. M., & Stock J. R. (1993). *Strategic Logistics Management.* R. D. Boston: Irwin.

Lambert, D.M., Stock, J.R., & Elram, L. (2008). *Fundamentals of Logistics Management.* Singapore: McGraw Hill.

Nogalski, B., & Ronkowski, R. (2007). *Współczesne przedsiębiorstwo. Problemy funkcjonowania i zatrudniania.* Warszawa: TNOiK.

Nowicka-Skowron, M. (2001). *Efektywność systemów logistycznych.* Warszawa: PWE.

Parasuraman, A., Zeithaml, V., & Berry, L. (1988). SERVQUAL: a multiple-item scale for measuring consumer perceptions of service quality. *Journal of Retailing,* 64(1), pp. 12–40.

Price, P.M., & Harrison, N.J. (2013). *Looking at Logistics: A Practical Introduction to Logistics, Customer Service, and Supply Chain Management.* USA: Access Education.

Rucińska, D. (2015). *Rynek usług transportowych w Polsce: teoria i praktyka.* Warszawa: PWE.

Rydzkowski, W. (2011). *Usługi logistyczne: teoria i praktyka.* Poznań: Instytut Logistyki i Magazynowania.

Statsoft (2020, February 11). *Analiza dyskryminacyjna w STATISTICA Help.* http://www.statsoft.pl.

Triola, M.F. (2012). *Elementary Statistics.* London: Pearson.

Twaróg, J. (2005). *Mierniki i wskaźniki logistyczne.* Poznań: Instytut Logistyki i Magazynowania.

Wojewódzka-Król, K., & Rolbiecki, R. (2013). *Polityka rozwoju transportu.* Gdańsk: Wydawnictwo Uniwersytetu Gdańskiego.

Zhou, R., & Pritchard, A. (2009). Using SERVQUAL to measure the service quality of Ravel agents in Guangzhou. *Journal of Services Research,* 9, pp. 129–143.

Chapter 8

Innovative and investment direction of farming enterprise development

Liudmyla Hnatyshyn, Ruslan Sheludko,
Oksana Prokopyshyn and Liudmyla Makieieva

CONTENTS

8.1 INTRODUCTION

Transformations, which have occurred in the economic development of leading countries, confirm their transition to the innovative model of development. Moreover, the existing theoretical approaches, methods and instruments of practical implementation of the innovative and investment process in the operation of farming enterprises of Ukraine have not always been relevant to the growing needs and expectations of the innovative development. It is forced both by the small size of the enterprises of a farming type and by peculiarities of operation of those organizational–legal forms in agriculture. It deals with the problems of financing, imperfect institutional environment, seasonal character of production, operation mainly on leased land that motivates interest of the farmers to introduce innovations, on one hand, and prevents introducing the innovations and investing in those processes of the sector of farming enterprises on the other hand.

The positive dynamics of farming enterprises development should be influenced by innovations, which are closely connected with the production potential of farming activity. Under conditions of severe competition with foreign producers of agricultural products and domestic agroholdings, only farming enterprises which efficiently organize their innovative activity and introduce eco-innovations (Lesakova, 2019), can be successful and competitive. Thus, particular attention should be currently paid to detection of the innovative factors of farming enterprises development, their analysis and diagnostics.

The aim of the research is to examine the innovative constituent of farming enterprises development, which is based on determination of the impact of elements of the resource component of production potential on the profit of farming enterprises. Such approach will secure determination of the factors of impact on the profit growth as a principal financial source for introduction of innovations in the activity of farming enterprises. The next task of our research is to argue effective innovative and investment ways of reproduction of the production potential of farming enterprises based on application of innovative alternative investment mechanisms under conditions of a limited access of the farming enterprises to investment resources. It will create preconditions for innovative activity, modernization, economic growth and improvement of the competitive capacity of farming enterprises.

8.2 LITERATURE REVIEW

In Ukraine, the majority of farming enterprises operate on the fundamentals of self-sufficiency. Thus, introduction of innovations is mainly fulfilled by means of reinvesting of their profit (Hnatyshyn, 2018). In this context, Siekelova et al. (2019) stress the importance of profit as a principal motivating factor of small enterprises operation. Other scientists (Liubkina et al., 2019) argue the considerable value of innovations as a key factor of impact on competitiveness of enterprises. However, they point at the necessity to use financial tools of stimulation of the innovative activity of enterprises. While assessing efficiency of management of the innovative development of enterprises, it is proposed to consider the impact of resource and financial factors (Grynko & Gviniashvili, 2017).

Fedonin, Riepina and Oleksiuk (2004) consider innovations that make an immediate impact on current and future capabilities of the economic system to transform the incoming resources for maximum satisfaction of corporative and social interests. According to Rossokha (2005), innovative decisions secure the ability of enterprises to develop. For farming enterprises, innovations serve as a crucial factor of development, because Shumpeter (1982) considers that innovations secure an increase of the efficiency of use of the production factors, which are getting more expensive. Moreover, the innovative way of development is principally intended to increase income, contrary to the extensive and intensive ways of development, which are focused on growth of the output and reduction of costs respectively (Lutsiv, 2008). Thus, the authors of the work consider that innovative development of farming enterprises is an efficient instrument to create production potential, because the enterprises, introducing innovation in production, have significant competitive advantages due to improvement of product quality, extension of their consumption properties and increase of efficiency of the enterprise's performance generally (Zubar 2015). Innovation activity is a key area for achievement of the strategic goals of enterprises (Karpenko et al., 2019). Thus, the innovative way of development is focused on the increase of earning of farming enterprises (Koshkalda et al., 2019). It is particularly true in the current conditions, when the access to credits is limited because of high interest rates. Hence, Hoang (2017) argues a negative impact of the limited crediting on the income of family farms and proposes to simplify access to the system of microcrediting and microfinancing.

In spite of the numerous scientific works examining statistically significant relations between the labour and financial resources and efficiency of use of the innovative instruments in the enterprise activity by means of economic–mathematic methods (Malyarets et al., 2019), there is still little research on the problems of use of the methodic approaches to determination of the factors of impact on the increase of profit. The value of profit characterizes the capability of farming enterprises to develop on the base of innovations. Not much attention is paid to argumentation of the stimuli of the innovative way of development, which is focused on the increase of profit of farming enterprises.

8.3 RESEARCH METHODOLOGY

The methodological base of the research is supplied by a set of methods of scientific comprehension. A complex use of those methods secured establishment of theoretical and applied aspects of the research as to reproduction of the production potential of farming enterprises on the innovative and investment base. The following methods were used, particularly, a system method—to determine general regularities of the innovative and investment way of reproduction of the production potential of farming; induction and deduction—to consolidate phenomena and processes, connected with development of farming enterprises on the innovative and investment fundamentals; abstract and logical—to develop an investment mechanism of reproduction of the production potential of farming enterprises on the innovative base; monographic—to detect the tendencies of production potential reproduction on the example of chosen farming enterprises; and graphic—for visual presentation of the research materials. Econometric modelling, particularly methods of correlation–regression analysis, is the key element of the research. Those methods were used for evaluation of the impact of elements of the resource component of production potential on the profit of farming enterprises. The information base of the research is supplied by the official data of the State Statistics Service of Ukraine concerning development of farming enterprises.

At the preparatory stage of economic–mathematic modelling, the authors determined that profit generation is influenced by geographical conditions of the location of the farming enterprise, as well as its specialization. Thus, generally in Ukraine, as well as in the zones of Steppe and Forest Steppe, the farming enterprises with less than 20 ha of land use are primarily specialized in animal breeding. Farming enterprises with a larger area of land use are engaged in crop production. In the zone of Polissia, farmers holding 30 ha of arable land are engaged in animal breeding. However, at the farming enterprises with about 900 ha of arable land, the trend is to combine crop production and animal breeding.

8.4 RESULTS AND DISCUSSION

Reproduction of the production potential of farming enterprises, particularly intensive ones, can be secured by introduction of an investment and innovative model. The authors of the work consider that investments are closely connected with the strategy of farming enterprises, because such a model upgrades the production potential of farming enterprises. It is a crucial feature of the move forward to development. Reproduction of the production potential of farming enterprises on the innovative base requires an appropriate level of the resource base and additional money and material investment, which normally are intended for qualitative improvement of the production potential of farming enterprises, not their quantitative upgrading. Thus, in the system of reproduction of the production potential of farming enterprises, innovations should be considered in their relations with investments, supporting their introduction.

Nowadays, there are specific requirements for operation of farming enterprises, which are determined by imperfect industrial structure and quality of production potential, as well as high level of competition in the agrarian sphere. From the innovation position, the category of "production potential" should be considered as actually possible and expedient production of agricultural products under reasonable use of production factors and the least possible harm to environment (Hnatyshyn, 2018). Thus, innovative improvement of production, the ability to supply agricultural products and goods of a new, ecologically safe and nutritive balanced type to consumers, has become a general law not only of the competitive fight, but also as a precondition for a healthy diet and environmental protection.

The diversity of conditions of farming enterprises operation, different degrees of their engagement in the innovative process, and not identical stages of the life cycle of innovation at each separate enterprise or the organization in general require creation of the appropriate managerial support for development of the innovative process, adopted to the branch requirements and particularities of farming performance, securing strengthening of the strategic platform and competitive capacity of farming enterprises. Particularly, upgrading of the technical constituent of production potential, as well as introduction of new, innovative forms of production management and management of the enterprise generally are the crucial factors of the last. However, lack of financing means that the volume of investments in the fixed capital of agricultural enterprises and direct investments in the agrarian sphere are still at a very low level.

Currently, the agrarian sector is attractive neither to domestic nor to foreign investors. Statistical reports mark that in 2010–2018, the share of resources intended for agriculture, constituted from 6.1 to 14.1% of the total investments in the economy of Ukraine. One of the reasons for such a situation, as scientists say, is the absence of the institutional environment for inflow of investment in the AIC. The situation is forced by a set of institutional problems of the national economy. The research confirms that, in spite of the positive dynamics, in the last five years the level of investment support for farming enterprises constituted 8–10% of the total need for investment resources. The index is extremely low and does not secure extended reproduction of the production potential of farming enterprises, preventing the enterprises from coming out of the recession. In Lviv region, the investment base of agriculture differs from the other regions of Ukraine by a higher level of some indices. Thus, in 2018, the share of direct investments in the stock capital of agricultural enterprises of Lviv region was 2.5 times higher, compared to the national index. First, a common frontier of Lviv region with the European Union contributes to activation of the processes of foreign investment, and second, a foreign investor, avoiding business risks, often prefers small projects, which are successfully implemented by land-poor farming enterprises of the Carpathian area. An example is presented by the amalgamation of farmers in the Stryi district of Lviv region into a farming servicing cooperative, Stryiskyi Yas, within the framework of the project "Improvement of the awareness and assessment of the potential of valorization of high-quality food products in Lviv region", which is funded by the French government. It is also worth noting that the Canadian project "Development of dairy business in Ukraine" is intended to eliminate the difficulties faced by small and medium-size milk producers.

Efficiency indices are the main moving force of investment processes activation in the farming environment. Considering a simple payment system and criterial base, a farming enterprise should take a profit rate as the index, i.e., a ratio of the profit amount in the reporting year to the amount of the advance capital, or in other words, to the currency of the balance assets. The profit rate demonstrates the degree of capital growth, advanced for production of agricultural products to obtain profit by the farming enterprise. Thus, the index can be considered as a criterion of investment attractiveness of farming enterprises. The performed calculations demonstrate that the profit rate is higher at the farming enterprises engaged in crop production, because grain products, along with fewer risks, secures comparatively faster capital turnover, higher profitability of products and, thus, a shorter payback period in the reproduction cycle. Moreover, the authors of the research have not found any impact of the enterprise size on the profit rate level, i.e., it is also at the same level both at small and larger enterprises. However, a higher recoupment of investments is achieved when not raw material, but products of its processing are sold. Available processing capacities increase the economic stability of farming enterprises, as well as supporting the solution of the problem of employment for rural populations. It is particularly important for the branches with a relative excess of internal production and/or insufficient export channels, mainly vegetable growing and horticulture (Moldavan & Shchubravska, 2015).

Farming enterprises are currently at a new stage of their development. However, their competitive capacity and investment attractiveness are significantly lower than those of the large enterprises of agrarian business. Nevertheless, rise in efficiency of the sector of farming enterprises and accelerated reproduction are possible only due to transfer to the innovative model of development. Thus, the important precondition for reproduction of their production potential is in the exceeding of income over expenditures, supplying a share of funds for investments. It is necessary to speed up the process of development of the institutional support concerning regional and interregional investments. The authors of the work suggest that, under conditions of such common tendency, farming enterprises are not ready to take any radical measures concerning reconstruction and reorganization of their production because the attracted investments are primarily used for completion of the earlier started projects. However, there are few classic cases when, under conditions of appropriate management and a well-argued strategy of development, farming enterprises are able to support reproduction processes on the fundamentals of attraction of foreign investments. The large farming enterprise Hadz, in the Buchach district of Ternopil region, holding 600 ha of gardens, cooperate with some Polish and Italian companies. The enterprise has built fruit storage facilities, and installed a sort line and a drying line for production of dried fruit and apple chips.

To analyse the impact of cost elements of the production factors, which create the base of production potential, it is proposed to make grouping of farming enterprises of Ukraine by the level of land use in 2018. To determine some dependences, farming enterprises are grouped into 31 groups considering the area of arable land (from 0 to above 2000 ha of arable land per one enterprise).

Considering the mentioned reasons, the further research needs creation of three categories of farming enterprises:

1. Category I, which includes enterprises from eight to 28 groups (from 20 to 1499 ha of arable land per one farming enterprise); in that category, crop production specialization prevails;
2. Category II, which includes enterprises from the first to the seventh groups (family farms from 0 to 19 ha of arable land per one farming enterprise); animal husbandry specialization prevails here;
3. Category III, which includes enterprises from eight to 31 groups. In contrast with Category I, it includes 29–31 groups of enterprises with the range of land use from 1500 and above 2000 ha of arable land. They are the groups of farming enterprises with non-typical areas of land use. Moreover, one can observe sharp fluctuations of values of the indices, which will be used for modelling. It is obvious that it can be connected with the impact of redistribution of agroholding capital, in case large farming enterprises are *de facto* included in their organizational structure. Thus, the groups 29–31 were excluded from Category I. Nevertheless, the creation of Category III is forced by the attempt to reach the appropriate quality of the regression model and interpretation of the obtained results. Thus, for the analysis, the authors used the mean values of the indices in terms of 1 ha of agricultural lands. The prevalence of animal breeding specialization (above-described) at some farming enterprises is the reason for the analysis of the indices of economic efficiency and elements of costs to be performed per head of livestock, as it is methodically better. Thus, the authors of the research decided to combine the groups 29–31 with the groups of enterprises of mixed specialization for the analysis of the impact of operation of large farming enterprises, engaged in crop production, on the models of Category I. Theoretically, such an approach can balance and smooth the tendencies in the large category, which includes farming enterprises of different branches.

The research studies the dependence of profit y (dependent variable) on the following values (independent variables) for the groups of enterprises of different categories: payment for labour x_1; material costs (costs of seed, mineral fertilizers and fodder) x_2; payment for services and work of outsourcing organization x_3; payment for lease of land plots x_4; depreciation x_5.

To examine regional differences, the appropriate research was conducted both for Ukraine generally and for natural zones, i.e., Steppe, Forest Steppe, and Polissia. The calculations were performed with the use of the statistical package R.

On the example of Ukraine and groups of enterprises of Category I, the authors made a detailed analysis of development of a regression model.

1. Ukraine
   a. Category I
      First, it is necessary to develop a linear model of multiple regression, which considers the impact of all five factors $x_1,...,x_5$ on the value of profit y and includes the constant:

$$y = b_0 + b_1 x_1 + b_2 x_2 + b_3 x_3 + b_4 x_4 + b_5 x_5 \qquad (8.1)$$

Based on the data of the analysis of Ukraine generally, the following results were obtained:

- assessment of the model coefficients $b = [b_0, b_1, b_2, b_3, b_4, b_5]^T$:

  $b = [-644.46; -0.8370; 1.3821; -0.0533; -0.2976; 0.8516]^T$

- regression model (composed on the base of assessed coefficients b):

  $y = -644.46 - 0.8370 x_1 + 1.3821 x_2 - 0.0533 x_3 - 0.2976 x_4 + 0.8516 x_5 \qquad (8.2)$

- Student statistic for each of the coefficients $t = [t_0, t_1, t_2, t_3, t_4, t_5]^T$:

  $t = [-0.8571; -0.4703; 3.5613; -0.2038; -0.3009; 0.4121]^T$

- coefficients of multiple correlation $\hat{R}^2 = 0.874$
- Fisher statistic $F = 20.8$

The coefficients of the model were assessed on the base of 21 observations. Number of the degrees of freedom of the model was equal to 6. The significant points of the statistics of Student and Fisher by 0.05 level of significance account for $t_* = t(0.025; 5) = 2.1314$, $F_* = F (0.05; 5; 15)$ respectively.

According to the Fisher statistic, one can declare that the profit (value y) depends on the aggregate of the values $x_1,...,x_5$, $(F>F_*)$. The value of the coefficient of multiple correlation $\hat{R}^2 = 0.874$ confirms that the model explains 87% of dependence of the variable y on the aggregate of the values $x_1,...,x_5$. The values of the Student statistic demonstrate that the coefficient is significant only under the variable x_2: $|t_2| > t_*$, 3.5613>2.1314. The other coefficients are insignificant. Such results are often connected with multicollinearity between independent variables. It is necessary to calculate the matrix R of the coefficients of pair correlation for different values of enterprises of the groups 8–28 (Category I). The values of the coefficients of pair correlations for that model are presented in Table 8.1.

Table 8.1 demonstrates that the variable y is considerably influenced by the variables x_2, x_4 and x_5 (material costs, lease payment for land plots and depreciation), i.e., coefficients of pair correlation $r(y, x_2) = 0.9330$, $r(y, x_4) = 0.8353$, $r(y, x_5) = 0.8709$.

Table 8.1 Matrix of dependence between the variables of grouped farming enterprises of Ukraine (coefficients of pair correlation of Category I)

Index	y	x_1	x_2	x_3	x_4	x_5
y	1.0000	0.2374	0.9330	0.0171	0.8353	0.8709
x_1	0.2374	1.0000	0.2991	0.5653	0.0232	0.2848
x_2	0.9330	0.2991	1.0000	0.0460	0.8809	0.9231
x_3	0.0171	0.5653	0.0460	1.0000	−0.2008	0.0818
x_4	0.8353	0.0232	0.8809	−0.2008	1.0000	0.9262
x_5	0.8709	0.2848	0.9231	0.0818	0.9262	1.0000

On the other hand, those variables strongly correlate with one another (the values of the coefficients of pair correlation $r(x_i, x_j)>0{,}75$): $r(x_2, x_4) = 0.8809$, $r(x_2, x_5) = 0.89231$, $r(x_4, x_5) = 0.9262$. It means that those variables cannot simultaneously enter the regression equation. To get rid of multicollinearity, the authors used the method of a gradual selection of variables. It has resulted in a regression equation, which includes one independent variable, x_2, i.e., material costs. The research presents the obtained characteristics of the model:

- regression model

$$y = -1066.9 + 1.4255x_2 \tag{8.3}$$

- Student statistic for each of the coefficients $t = [t_0, t_2]^T$

$$t = [-4.1391; 11.299]^T$$

- coefficient of multiple correlation $\hat{R}^2 = 0.87$
- Fisher statistic $F = 128$

Critical points of the Student and Fisher statistics by the 0.05 level of significance account for: $t_* = t(0.025; 1) = 2.0930$, $F_* = F (0.05; 1; 19)$ respectively.

The analysis of the model (8.3) demonstrates that it provides explanation of 87% [almost similar to the model (8.2)] of the relation between the dependent and independent variables. The (8.3) argues that the size of profit is primarily dependent on material costs. A positive value of the coefficient concerning costs confirms an increase of the profit in case of material costs growth. It is worth noting that inclusion of quadratic additive components in the model does not cause improvement of the model quality. Such a phenomenon is possible under the increased level of mechanization and use of innovative technologies in production. The aspect of profit reinvesting in the fixed assets can be considered as a substitution of one element of production potential by another.

It is also necessary to study a linear model of multiple regression, which concerns the impact of all five factors $x_1, \ldots, x_5$ on the size of profit y, and does not include a constant:

$$y = b_1 x_1 + b_2 x_2 + b_3 x_3 + b_4 x_4 + b_5 x_5 \tag{8.4}$$

The gradual selecting of variables has produced the following linear model:

$$y = -2.425 x_1 + 1.416 x_2 \tag{8.5}$$

with characteristics like:

- Student statistic for each of the coefficients $t = [t_1, t_2]^T$:

$t = [-3,7512; 10,381]^T$, $t_* = 2,0930$

- coefficient of multiple correlation $\hat{R}^2 = 0.85$
- Fisher statistic $F = 53.489$; $F_* = 3.5219$

The model (8.5) explains 85% [almost similar to the model (8.3)] of the relation between the dependent and independent variables. The size of the profit in that model depends on labour payment (variable x_1) and material costs (variable x_2). A positive value of the coefficient under the variable x_2 confirms the profit growth in case of increased material costs. A negative value of the coefficient under the variable x_1 argues that an increase of the labour payment influences the profit negatively. Thus, it is possible to conclude that a farming enterprise is a unique structure, which has to secure self-employment of the farmer's family in the way of innovative development; as well, it should be the place of employment for peasants and employed workers. Similar to the previous case, inclusion of quadratic additive components in the model does not provide improvement of the model quality.

b. Category III

Table 8.2 demonstrates the figures of the coefficients of pair correlation for the studied values of the enterprises, included in groups 8–31 (Category III).

Similar to the group of enterprises of Category I, the variable y is considerably influenced by the variables x_2, x_4 and x_5, i.e., material costs, payment of the lease of land parcels and depreciation.

As in the previous case, those variables strongly correlate with one another. The value of the corresponding coefficients of correlation between the variables y, x_2, x_4 and x_5 are smaller as compared to the corresponding values in the Table 8.1. The research has distinguished two models among the linear ones. Those models are presented in the Table 8.3.

In both models, the value of the Fisher statistic confirms that generally profit depends on the aggregate of the studied factors. In the model with a constant in the farming enterprises of Category III, the crucial impact on profit is made by payment for the land lease (in other words, increase of the area of land use), i.e., variable x_4. (It is worth remembering that at the enterprises of Category I, the crucial impact is made by material costs.)

Table 8.2 Matrix of dependence between the variables of grouped farming enterprises of Ukraine (coefficients of pair correlation of Category III)

Index	y	x_1	x_2	x_3	x_4	x_5
y	1.0000	0.1691	0.7366	0.2369	0.7429	0.7534
x_1	0.1691	1.0000	0.3774	0.6102	−0.0658	0.4172
x_2	0.7366	0.3774	1.0000	0.1144	0.8075	0.8772
x_3	0.2369	0.6102	0.1144	1.0000	−0.1687	0.2393
x_4	0.7429	−0.0658	0.8075	−0.1687	1.0000	0.7902
x_5	0.7534	0.4172	0.8772	0.2393	0.7902	1.0000

Table 8.3 Statistical characteristics of the regression model of dependence of the profit from 1 ha of agricultural land on the aggregate of factors (farming enterprises of Ukraine, Category III)

Model	Characteristics of the model		
	Student statistic and its significance point, t, t_*	Fisher statistic and its significance point, F, F_*	Coefficient of multiple correlation $\hat{R}^2$
$y = 787.59 + 2.014 x_4$	$t : 3.55; 5.20$ $t_* = 2.07$	$F = 27.1$ $F_* = 4.30$	$\hat{R}^2 = 0.55$
$y = 0.464 x_2 + 2.717 x_5$	$t : 2.10; 2.18$ $t_* = 2.07$	$F = 152$ $F_* = 3.44$	$\hat{R}^2 = 0.58$

The world experience proves that advantages of the land lease relations are determined by the fact that the lease secures release of the financial resources for investing in innovative machinery, new technologies, construction of new premises, etc. In the model with no constant included, the main impact on profit is made by material costs and depreciation costs, i.e., variables x_2 and x_5 (at the enterprises of Category I, profit is influenced by material costs and labour payments).

The coefficients of multiple correlation $\hat{R}^2$ demonstrate that the mentioned models explain the relation between the dependent and independent variables by 55% and 58% respectively. Thus, it is recommended to modify them by inclusion of additional explanatory variables in the model and/or selection of other types of regression equations.

Table 8.4 presents the regression models, which include quadratic additive components.

Table 8.4 demonstrates that all coefficients of the models are significant. The models provide appropriate explanation of the relation between the dependent and independent variables by 91% and 92% respectively.

c. Category II

Table 8.5 supplies values of the coefficients of pair correlation for the studied indices of the enterprises of the groups 1–7 (Category II). The variable y is considerably influenced by the variables x_2 and $x_{5,}$ i.e., material costs and depreciation. Those variables strongly correlate with each other, similar to the variables x_1 and x_3.

Table 8.4 Statistical characteristics of the quadratic regression model of dependence of the profit from 1 ha of agricultural land on the aggregate of factors (farming enterprises of Ukraine, Category III)

Model	Characteristics of the model		
	Student statistic and its significance point, t, t_*	Fisher statistic and its significance point, F, F_*	Coefficient of multiple correlation $\hat{R}^2$
$y = 7949.3 - 43.013 x_1 + 0.811 x_2 +$ $+ 4.392 x_3 + 1.719 x_4 + 0.039 x_1^2 -$ $- 0.001 x_3^2$	$t : 3.10; -3.74; 2.45;$ $7.34; 3.70; 3.53;$ -6.41 $t_* = 2.11$	$F = 28.9$ $F_* = 2.70$	$\hat{R}^2 = 0.913$
$y = -12.74 x_1 + 7.164 x_3 +$ $+ 12.523 x_4 - 12.657 x_5 -$ $- 0.014 x_1 x_4 - 0.013 x_4 x_5 +$ $+ 0.013 x_1^2 - 0.002 x_3^2 +$ $+ 0.034 x_5^2$	$t : -4,36; 5,70; 4,05;$ $2,98; 2,59; 2,33; 3,42;$ $5,07; 3,09$ $t_* = 2,13$	$F = 19.3$ $F_* = 2.58$	$\hat{R}^2 = 0.923$

Table 8.5 Matrix of dependence between the variables of grouped farming enterprises of Ukraine (coefficients of pair correlation of Category II)

Index	Y	x_1	x_2	x_3	x_4	x_5
Y	1.0000	0.6842	0.9368	0.3211	0.0455	0.9059
x_1	0.6842	1.0000	0.4255	0.9026	−0.4286	0.4223
x_2	0.9368	0.4255	1.0000	−0.0017	0.3010	0.9751
x_3	0.3211	0.9026	−0.0017	1.0000	−0.6320	0.0022
x_4	0.0455	−0.4286	0.3010	−0.6320	1.0000	0.4438
x_5	0.9059	0.4223	0.9751	0.0022	0.4438	1.0000

Table 8.6 demonstrates that all coefficients of the models are significant. The models provide appropriate explanation of the relation between the dependent and independent variables, by 98%, 93% and 99% respectively. In all presented models for farming enterprises of Category II, depreciation (variable x_5) makes a positive impact on the profit. Thus, the suggestion is that depreciation costs mostly influence the maintenance of current activity but not reproduction of the fixed assets, as well as not contributing to innovative development of the enterprises.

The research results have distinguished two linear models and one quadratic model which supply the best explanation of the behaviour of the effective feature. Coefficients of those models are significant. Those models are presented in Table 8.6. However, the authors stress that the number of observations (number of the groups of farming enterprises which are included in Category II is equal to 7) is too small compared to the number of explained variables. Thus, such models (as well as conclusions based on them) should be carefully treated.

Natural Zones of Ukraine.

The research was conducted concerning farming enterprises in the natural zones of Ukraine. Tables 8.7–8.9 present short results from that research.

Innovations secure new features and priorities in activity of farming enterprises. Investigation of the cycle of innovation and investment process makes the basis for the specification of the mainly self-reproductive type of that process at farming enterprises. Moreover, foreign investments secure introduction of innovations and the dynamic character of reproduction. Innovative forms of management of production and enterprise in total are not just features of modernization of the technical constituent of production potential, but also crucial factors of the competitive capacity of farming enterprises.

Nowadays, farming business in Ukraine is a rather risky form of private agrarian business. That is not only because of the impact of natural factors, but also due to strengthening

Table 8.6 Statistical characteristics of the regression model of dependence of the profit from 1 ha of agricultural land on the aggregate of factors (farming enterprises of Ukraine, Category II)

Model	Characteristics of the model		
	Student statistics and the significance point, t, t_*	Fisher statistic and their significance point, F, F_*	Coefficient of multiple correlation $\hat{R}^2$
$y = 5175.1 - 72.965x_4 + 1.4124x_5$	$t : 5.99; -5.50; 13.66$ $t_* = 2.78$	$F = 93.4$ $F_* = 6.94$	$\hat{R}^2 = 0.979$
$y = 0.385x_1 + 0.952x_5$	$t : 3.19; 5.86$ $t_* = 2.57$	$F = 32.3$ $F_* = 5.79$	$\hat{R}^2 = 0.928$
$y = 0.728x_3 - 1.955x_5 -$ $-1.37/10^5 x_3^2 + 2.4/10^4 x_5^2$	$t : 4.45; -3.11; -3.40; 5.11$ $t_* = 2.13$	$F = 101$ $F_* = 9.12$	$\hat{R}^2 = 0.993$

Table 8.7 Statistical characteristics of the regression model of dependence of the profit from 1 ha of agricultural land on the aggregate of factors (farming enterprises of the Forest Steppe zone)

Model	Coefficient of multiple correlation $\hat{R}^2$
Category I, Groups 8–28 Correlation: the variable y is considerably influenced by the variables x_2, x_4, x_5: $r(y, x_2) = 0.8078$, $r(y, x_4) = 0.7542$, $r(y, x_5) = 0.821$. Explanatory variables don't correlate with one another, x_4, x_5: $r(x_4, x_5) = 0.8412$	
$y = 0.389x_2 + 2.835x_5$	$\hat{R}^2 = 0.727$
$y = -5.710x_1 - 3.198x_4 + 13.232x_5 +$ $\quad + 0.0083x_1^2 + 0.0037x_4^2 - 0.0132x_5^2$	$\hat{R}^2 = 0.903$
Category III, Groups 8–31 Correlation: the variable y is mostly influenced by the variable x_5: $r(y, x_5) = 0.7928$ Explanatory variables do not correlate with one another	
$y = 0.364x_2 + 3.144x_5$	$\hat{R}^2 = 0.669$
Category II, Groups 1–7 Correlation: the variable y is considerably influenced by the variables x_1, x_3, x_4, x_5: $r(y, x_1) = 0.9567$, $r(y, x_3) = 0.9326$, $r(y, x_4) = 0.7737$, $r(y, x_5) = 0.9005$ Explanatory variables x_1, x_2, x_3, x_5 correlate with one another: $r(x_1, x_3) = 0.9328$, $r(x_1, x_5) = 0.9206$, $r(x_3, x_4) = 0.7857$, $r(x_3, x_5) = 0.8092$	
$y = 2.453x_1$	$\hat{R}^2 = 0.863$

of competition with large agricultural enterprises, particularly both for the sale markets and for resources. In the conditions of self-sustainability, farming enterprises introduce innovations by means of profit to secure continuity of operation. Thus, it is possible to conclude that farming enterprises with 20–1499 ha of arable lands, generate rather large figures of profit in the process of reproduction on the innovative base. In Category III, which includes enterprises with land use above 1500 ha of arable lands per one enterprise, the opportunity of innovative development by means of internal sources of financing is also observed. Location and organizational-branch structure immediately influence the combination of the

Table 8.8 Statistical characteristics of the regression model of dependence of the profit from 1 ha of agricultural land on the aggregate of factors (farming enterprises of the Polissia zone)

Model	Coefficient of multiple correlation $\hat{R}^2$
Category I, Groups 8–28 Correlation: explanatory variables do not correlate with the effective feature and with one another. The greatest value of the coefficient of pair correlation is between y and x_5: $r(y, x_5) = 0.5596$	
$y = 4.172x_5$	$\hat{R}^2 = 0.348$
Category III, Groups 8–31 Correlation: explanatory variables do not correlate with the effective feature and with one another. The greatest value of the coefficient of pair correlation is between y and x_2, x_5: $r(y, x_2) = 0.6051$, $r(y, x_5) = 0.5594$	
$y = 0.233x_2 + 0.952x_5$	$\hat{R}^2 = 0.4274$
Category II, Groups 1–7 Correlation: the variable y is considerably influenced by the variables x_2, x_5: $r(y, x_2) = 0.9475$, $r(y, x_5) = 0.8214$. Explanatory variables x_1, x_2, x_5 correlate with one another: $r(x_1, x_2) = 0.8070$, $r(x_1, x_5) = 0.9364$, $r(x_2, x_5) = 0.9586$	
$y = 3082.3 - 2.548x_5 + 0.0002x_5^2$	$\hat{R}^2 = 0.988$
$y = 0.16x_2 - 1.635x_5$	$\hat{R}^2 = 0.990$
$y = 0.263x_3 - 2.004x_5 + 0.00017x_5^2$	$\hat{R}^2 = 0.991$

Table 8.9 Statistical characteristics of the regression model of dependence of the profit from 1 ha of agricultural land on the aggregate of factors (farming enterprises of the Steppe zone)

Model	Coefficient of multiple correlation $\hat{R}^2$
Category I, Groups 8–28 Correlation: the variable y is considerably influenced by the variables x_4: $r(y, x_4) = 0.7797$ Explanatory variables do not correlated with one another	
$y = 790.38 + 1.861x_4$	$\hat{R}^2 = 0.608$
$y = 0.514x_2 + 1.445x_4$	$\hat{R}^2 = 0.690$
$y = -1324.6 + 2440.8x_3 + 3.804x_4 - 918.49x_5 -$ $\quad - 2.070x_3x_4 + 0.779x_4x_5 - 1.241x_3^2 + 0.176x_5^2$	$\hat{R}^2 = 0.968$
Category III, Groups 8–31 Correlation: the variable y is mostly influenced by the variable x_4 : $r(y, x_4) = 0.7797$ Explanatory variables do not correlate with one another, but for x_4, x_5: $r(x_4, x_5) = 1$	
$y = 3.247x_4$	$\hat{R}^2 = 0.544$
$y = -223.5 + 5.942x_4 + 1.263x_5 - 0.0017x_4x_5$	$\hat{R}^2 = 0.703$
$y = 1563.5x_3 + 1.712x_4 - 588.45x_5 - 1.334x_3^2 +$ $\quad + 0.189x_5^2$	$\hat{R}^2 = 0.781$
Category II, Groups 1–7 Correlation: the variable y is considerably influenced by the variables x_3, x_5 : $r(y, x_3) = 0.9295$, $r(y, x_5) = 0.9295$ Explanatory variables x_1, x_3, x_5 strongly correlate: the coefficients of pair correlations are close to 1.	
$y = -2172.6 - 6.812x_1 + 1.293x_2 - 2515.3x_3 -$ $\quad - 18.43x_4 + 948.34x_5$	$\hat{R}^2 = 0.99$
$y = 0.173x_3$	$\hat{R}^2 = 0.860$
$y = -79021.6x_3 - 2976.5x_5 + 1.067x_3^2 - 0.151x_5^2$	$\hat{R}^2 = 0.99$

elements of a resource constituent of production potential, which defines the amount of the farms' profit. Positive impact on the principal source of reproduction of production potential of farms, i.e., profit, is done by intensification of production and extension of innovative activity.

Results of the economic–mathematic modeling demonstrate the essential impact of material costs and depreciation on the increase of profit. It argues the common thesis about the impact of intensification on efficiency of production. An increase of depreciation costs in the structure of expenditures confirms use of new and more efficient kinds of machinery. For family farming in the Steppe zone, the priority of innovations should be focused on the reproduction of material and resource bases. The increase of costs for livestock fodder makes a considerable impact on the increase of the profit of family farms of Polissia in the structure of their material costs.

Thus, application of innovations influences efficiency of reproduction of the production potential of farming enterprises, appearance of scientific–technical, social, ecological and economic effects. Farming enterprises, introducing innovations for activation of their production potential reproduction, simultaneously secure changes of the organizational–technical and social–economic levels of development of the territory in which they are placed, and contribute to growth of the national economy. In the end, innovations force the appearance of new technologies (change of technologies can create opportunities for development of a commodity, new ways of marketing, production or delivery, as well as improvement of the related services); change of product cost; a new segment of the branch (tapping into a new segment of the market, a farming enterprise significantly changes the chain of values).

Thus, one can conclude that innovation is a change of production technology, immediately influencing productivity of production factors and the way of their combination, and thus, supports transformation of production processes (Lutsiv, 2008). Hence, innovation is a way to more efficient, more rational and more safer use of production potential for creation of competitive advantages of farming enterprises (Figure 8.1).

The degree of introduction of innovations into production potential depends on the innovative activity of farmers, primarily on the enterprises' capability to introduce innovations into their production processes. Thus, the focus on innovations in the production potential is a principal factor of formation of highly technological production, which can produce knowledge-intensive products with high benefit and competitive capacity, both in the domestic and foreign markets. The focus of innovations in the production potential of farming enterprises is on a new quality, obtained from interaction of the elements of production potential and innovations.

To attract innovations to the reproduction process, it is reasonable to use the notion of "innovative activity of farming enterprises". In the opinion of the article's authors, innovative activity is the activity focused on the search for opportunities to intensify operation activity and production in order to satisfy social needs for the competitive capacity of agricultural products, goods and services due to use of scientific–technological and intellectual

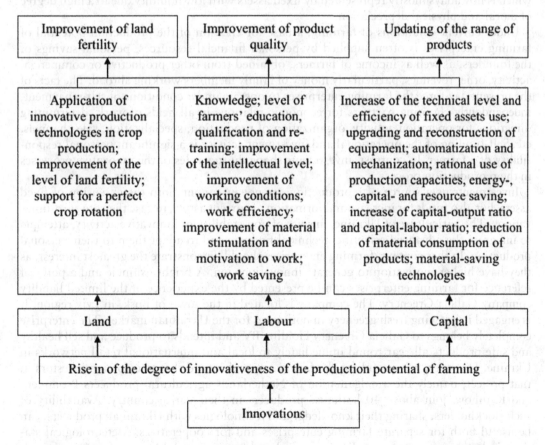

Figure 8.1 Impact of innovations on raising the degree of innovativeness of the production potential of farming enterprises (composed by the authors)

potentials. It is connected with obtaining new, radically improved products, the technologies of their production, the organizational forms and methods of economic activity and a system of management. In other words, innovative activity, focused on use and commercialization of the findings of scientific research and development, forces the appearance of new competitive goods and services in the market. From the economic position, innovative activity is a process, focused on the capital raise (its reproduction), implemented through the capability of a farming enterprise to create new products, objects, technologies, processes. A legal aspect of innovative activity suggests approval of the right of ownership and the right of use of the objects of intellectual property (Bratchuk, 2016). Considering that interpretation, as well as ideas of the scientists and results of personal findings, the authors of the article suggest that innovations should be reasonably included in non-material assets with the subsequent achievements and determination of the effect from sale of the innovative products.

Innovations supply new features and priorities in the activities of farming enterprises. Old energy- and material-consuming productions are gradually dying out. They are being replaced by new, resources-saving production. However, innovations cannot be fulfilled without investments. Examination of the cycle of the innovative and investment process gives the reasons for specification of primarily self-reproductive type of that process at farming enterprises. Low attractiveness of farming to potential investors is caused by complicated financial conditions of the most enterprises, narrow or even no subject of pledge, which is nowadays mostly represented by fixed assets with low liquidity due to a high degree of moral and physical depreciation.

Under current conditions of farming, a base for creation of the production potential of farming enterprises is often supplied by personal financial resources, personal savings of the founders, as well as income of farmers, obtained from other productive or commercial activity, other revenues, particularly money of family members working abroad. The facts of the present day force the farming enterprises to operate under conditions of self-repayment, independently choosing partners for economic relations in all fields of work, determining directions for operation activity, organization of production, specialization, sale channels, etc. Self-funding of the operational and investment activity is a significant personal responsibility of a farmer. In contrast, investments shape the key roles of the innovative processes in the reproduction process.

Investments as a source of reproduction are not just inputs into the extension of fixed assets, but also funds for increase and formation of current assets, in case they are agro-innovations. The agriculture of Ukraine, in spite of non-stability of innovative activity, attempts to integrate the advanced scientific–technical findings and to adapt them to their personal production. In that context, farming enterprises should demonstrate the greatest interest, as they have higher motivation to generate innovations ion. A bright example and a point of reference for farming enterprises can be presented by the experience of the limited liability company Galicia Greenery. The company is located in the town of Busk, in Lviv region. It is engaged in growing fresh greenery in hothouses for the Ukrainian market. The enterprise completely belongs to Galicia Greenery Holding BV and intends to produce and sell healthy and safe products all year round immediately to local and international retail networks in Ukraine. However, it is useful for the farmers to understand that two foreign investors in that project, namely the amalgamation of Netherlands agricultural producers Prominent and Rainbow, join above 40 hothouse producers in their native country. Availability of such stockholders, sharing their knowledge and technologies with Ukrainian producers, can be useful both for separate farming enterprises and for cooperatives. Meteorological stations in hothouses, automatic climate control and "smart" sprinklers are features of modern vegetable growing, particularly growing of lettuce, in the hothouses with Netherlands investments. For our domestic agricultural producers, such technologies are still innovations, while for the foreign producers, it is no longer so.

Considering the fact that "in agriculture, the output from investment resources use is considerably higher than totally in the economy of Ukraine" (Mazniev, 2014), there is an obvious need to focus effective innovative and investment mechanisms on reproduction of the production potential of farming enterprises and, consequently, to propose an alternative variant under conditions of a limited access of the farming enterprises to investment resources (Figure 8.2). Such an approach supports optimization of the investment supply

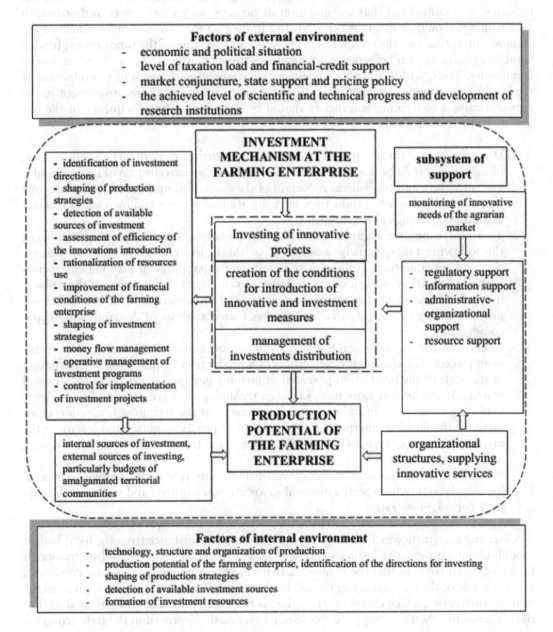

Figure 8.2 Investment mechanism of reproduction of the production potential of farming enterprises on innovative base (composed by the authors)

for extended reproduction of the production potential of farming enterprises on the base of advanced resource-saving technologies concerning achievement of a maximum result from employment of the engaged resources. Normally, internal reserves, particularly profit, significantly restrict capabilities of the farming enterprises as to innovations. Introduction of innovations as an effective instrument of production potential reproduction requires a farmer to accumulate some profit for several years. It considerably stagnates the reproduction processes and reduces efficiency of production potential employment.

Among the sources of investment in the innovating projects of farming enterprises, the authors of the research have distinguished budgets of amalgamated territorial communities. It is considered that co-operation of farmers with local power authorities, in such context, should probably make a positive impact on the external environment of the farming enterprise, i.e., the community. The order of investing of the innovations, funded from local budgets, can be beneficial for both parties, i.e., the farmer and the territorial community. Thus, within the above-proposed investment mechanism of reproduction of the production potential of farming enterprises on an innovative base, investment in the personal capital of farming enterprises should be done in a definite sequence of the following stages, particularly:

1. Determination of the investment directions. In the environment of farming enterprises, investments should be done in such urgent directions as introduction of new technologies, machines and equipment; reduction of the costs of animal breeding and support for sustainable levels of production; intensification of activity and increase of income; execution of ecological requirements.
2. Technical–economic argumentation for the necessity of investments should concern the following tasks, namely, assessment of the legislature in the field of production and consumption; evaluation of investment capabilities of farming enterprises with consideration of the level of economic development of the region of their placement; detection of maximum investments in the implementation of an investment project; setting of the resource and market focus; analysis of demand, supply and competition.
3. Production and technological fragments and the conception of marketing of an investment project should suggest development of a production program and determination of the scale of the production potential of farming enterprises; choice of the optimal volume of production capacities, kinds of technologies, equipment and know-how; obtaining of a complete right or social ownership of the technology; creation of an image of the farming enterprise and promotion of products, goods and service to the market; analysis of revenues with consideration of the forecast of raise or fall of prices; and sale amounts.
4. Financial analysis and assessment of investments: analysis of needs for long-term credits; calculations of unexpected material-financial expenditures, and setting of the payback period, profit rates.

A farming enterprise which claims a repayable financial assistance from the local budget should submit a prospective business plan with a clear financial–economic substantiation of its activity, and confirm that the planned activity meets economic goals, social conditions and the needs of the corresponding region. In the financial support, priority is given to the farming enterprises, which create new jobs. Funds from the budgets of amalgamated territorial communities should be supplied for definitely set goals, approved in the state economic programs.

8.5 CONCLUSION

The processes of reproduction on the fundamentals of innovative activity secure the result, which cannot be achieved under conditions of a usual type of operation. In the sector of farming enterprises, innovations are considered as new features and priorities, which orient production on narrow markets and specific needs of some individuals. Under conditions of farming enterprises, innovative activity aims to consolidate all necessary components of production potential into a general reproductive contour of growth of a new technological system, to create preconditions for modernization, economic growth and strengthening of the competitive capacity of farming enterprises.

Among the sources of investment in innovative projects by farming enterprises, the present research distinguishes budgets of amalgamated territorial communities. Use of that resource expects establishment of the appropriate legal base, which will be able to secure reimbursement of a share of loan for farmers, or interest rate from the funds of local budgets. Under improvement of the system of taxation and separation of family farms into a special group of single taxpayers, the product, obtained due to the introduction of innovative technologies, will secure additional revenues to the local budget. Thus, the state is obliged to create favourable conditions, i.e., to develop an efficient taxation system and privilege crediting, to secure the strong legal status of a farmer and a transparent mechanism of distribution of financial support for small farming enterprises, to stimulate development of animal breeding and co-operation, to contribute to substitution of the budget support with a project, etc.

Results of the economic–mathematic modelling suggest that farming enterprises of Category I are the most able to generate profit as a financial source of innovations. It is determined that at such enterprises, both in all natural climatic zones and in Ukraine generally, an increase of the elements of costs contributes to the increase of the figure of profit. That profit can be reinvested in the innovative development in the next cycle. On the other hand, family farms with under 20 ha of arable land mainly need to attract external sources of innovation funding. In the zone of Steppe, family farms demonstrate a clear regularity that an increase of costs for labour payments, payments for services and payments for land lease (an increase of the area of land use by means of extra lease) cause reduction of profit. Thus, innovations cannot be implemented without attraction of credit means, as well as state support funds in the environment of family farms. In Category III the opportunity of innovative development by means of internal sources of financing is also observed. The results of mathematic modelling confirm that the further growth of land use will contribute to the increase of the figure of profit at such enterprises and, consequently, will fuel their development on the innovative fundamentals.

REFERENCES

Bratchuk, L. M. (2016). Innovative activity: theoretical and methodological approaches to formation of an accounting object. *Economics of AIC*, 10, pp. 59–65.

Fedonin, O. S., Riepina, I. M. and Oleksiuk, O. I. (2004). *Potential of enterprises: formulation and assessment*. Kyiv: KNEU.

Grynko, T. and Gviniashvili, T. (2017). Organisational and economic mechanism of business entities' innovative development management. *Economic Annals-XXI*, 165, pp. 80–83.

Hnatyshyn, L. B. 2018. *Production potential of farming enterprises*. Lviv: Spolom.

Hoang, T. H. (2017). Credit constraint and household income: a quartile analysis approach. *Economic Annals-XXI*, 164, pp. 49–52.

Karpenko, L., Zalizko, V., Vdovenko, N., Starynets, O. and Mieniailova, H. (2019). Entrepreneurship as a basis for promotion of the strategy of development of polish industrial enterprises. *Journal of Entrepreneurship Education*, 22. Retrieved from: https://www.abacademies.org/articles/entrepreneurship-as-a-basis-for-promotion-of-the-strategy-of-development-of-polish-industrial-enterprises-8311.html (Access: 12.05.2020).

Koshkalda, I. V., Hnatyshyn, L. B., Prokopyshyn, O. S. (2019). Innovative-investment way of production factor reproduction as a factor of impact on the competitiveness of farming enterprises. *Agrarian economics*, 12, pp. 82–91.

Lesakova, L. (2019). Small and Medium Enterprises and Eco-Innovations: Empirical Study of Slovak SMEs. *Marketing and Management of Innovations*, 3, pp. 89–97.

Liubkina, O., Murovana, T., Magomedova, A., Siskos, E. and Akimova, L. (2019). Financial Instruments of Stimulating Innovative Activities of Enterprises and Their Improvements. *Marketing and Management of Innovations*, 4, pp. 336–352.

Lutsiv, O. M. (2008). *Production potential of the region: innovative aspect.* Lviv: Institute of Regional Researches of the NAS of Ukraine.

Malyarets, L. M., Babenko, V. O., Nazarenko, O. V., Ryzhikova, N. I. (2019). The Modeling of Multicriteria Assessment Activity in Enterprise Management. *International Journal of Supply Chain Management*, 8, pp. 997–1004.

Mazniev, H. Ye. (2014). Problems of financial support for innovative development of agrarian sector. *Economics of AIC*, 9, pp. 5–13.

Moldavan, L. V., Shchubravska, O. V. (2015). Investment priorities in the field of development of agro-industrial production of Ukraine and mechanisms of their fulfilment. *Economics of Ukraine*, 4, pp. 78–87.

Rossokha, V. V. (2005). Potential of agrarian enterprises: methodology of the research. *Economics of AIC*, 4, pp. 35–40.

Shumpeter, Y. (1982). *Theory of economic development: investigation of business profit, capital, credit and cycle of conjuncture.* Moscow: Progress.

Siekelova, A., Kovacova, M., Adamko, P., Stehel, V. (2019). Profit Management as an Instrument for SMEs Developing: the Case for Slovakia. *Marketing and Management of Innovations*, 3, pp. 285–296.

Zubar, I. V. (2015). Cooperational development of small farms on the basis of world experience. *Innovative economy*, 4, pp. 54–60.

Chapter 9

Information technologies as support for knowledge management

Małgorzata Kuraś

CONTENTS

9.1 INTRODUCTION

The issue of knowledge management, which dates back to the 1970s, is still the subject of extensive discussions among both academic researchers and management practitioners. The undoubted reason for this interest is knowledge itself, which is a unique resource for virtually every organization.

More and more enterprises are beginning to realize that knowledge is an organizational resource that needs to be managed, taking into account its intangible nature. Therefore, it should be developed, stored, made available and used at every level of the organization so that employees can make the right decisions based on both past experiences and a new insight into the future (ISO 30401:2018). Knowledge, considered in the context of an organization's resources, appears as the basic source of competitiveness and wealth of contemporary organizations, allowing them to undertake more and more effective activities (Skrzypek, 2001; Chluski & Dziembek, (2012)). Therefore, in enterprises more and more often activities aimed at creating, collecting and transferring knowledge are undertaken because they are considered the basis of innovation and the key to achieving a sustainable competitive advantage (Bootz et al., 2019; Soniewicki, 2017; Chugh et al., 2013).

Due to its complex nature, knowledge is a very specific resource that needs to be managed in a special way (Paliszkiewicz, 2007). The inclusion of knowledge management processes in the key processes taking place in the enterprise influences their improvement and is a chance for thorough reorientation in the way it operates. Hence, it is believed that knowledge management, as a basic element of integrated management systems in an enterprise, is the foundation of future management (Skrzypek, 2003). There is a belief in the literature that knowledge management is treated as a set of practices related to the use of knowledge as a key factor in creating value in an organization (Soto-Acosta & Cegarra-Navarro, 2016). One important issue to discuss is the role of information technology in relation to the success or failure in the implementation and functioning of knowledge management in the organization. The aim of the study is to present the most important issues related to knowledge management, with particular emphasis on the aspect of the use of information technology (IT). Information systems and tools enabling effective and efficient knowledge management in the organization are presented.

9.2 KNOWLEDGE IN THE CONTEXT OF AN ENTERPRISE RESOURCE

Knowledge is a complex concept rooted in many scientific fields. The high degree of abstraction of this issue makes it very difficult to provide a homogeneous definition of knowledge. This difficulty arises from the fact that, unlike data and information with quantitative and formal dimensions, it is intuitive. According to the triangle of the knowledge hierarchy of D.J. Skyrme, on the one hand, data forms the basis for the creation of information. On the other hand, information combined with experience and inference creates knowledge. The result of the optimal use of knowledge in combination with intuition is wisdom at the highest level in the hierarchical structure of knowledge (Skyrme, 1999). Knowledge is therefore defined as the seamless combination of experience, values, structured information and expert point of view that forms the basis for the evaluation and introduction of new experiences and information (Davenport & Prusak, 2000). It is created in the minds of people and used by them to solve problems. Unlike data and information, it is associated with a specific person (Davenport & Prusak, 2000; Probst et al., 2002). Knowledge is a catalyst for action, making people aware of the opportunity and the possibility of seizing it (Mikuła et al., 2002). It is "liquid" and at the same time formally structured. Due to its specific nature, it is difficult to capture in words and understand completely and logically (Krawiec, 2003). In relation to the organization, it may be included not only in documents and databases, but also in adopted procedures, processes and applied practices or standards (Davenport & Prusak, 2000).

The importance of knowledge as an essential resource of an enterprise has already been noticed by the creator of the neoclassical theory, A. Marshall. He took the position that knowledge was an element of the enterprise's capital, constituting the strongest drive of production (Nonaka & Takeuchi, 1995). F. Hayek and A. Schumpeter pointed to the unique character of knowledge as a resource, arguing that knowledge is subjective and cannot be considered as established once and forever (Nonaka & Takeuchi, 1995). Consequently, the benefits of the knowledge organizations possess vary depending on the circumstances. Knowledge is therefore specific to individual enterprises and is what distinguishes them from other similar entities (Nonaka & Takeuchi, 1995).

Currently, knowledge is perceived as the most important resource determining the company's competitive advantage. This approach is related to the arrival of the new economy, which A. Toffler described as the "third wave" (Toffler, 1980). In the 1980s, Toffler had already predicted that it was knowledge that would be the driving force behind this economy and a source of wealth for entrepreneurs. By definition, knowledge is dematerialized and elusive, hence knowledge-based capital is, in fact, symbolic capital relating to human thought and memory, and the contents of computers (Toffler, 1990). The emergence of the new economy—the economy based on knowledge—was also predicted by P. Drucker (Drucker, 1969). He pointed out that entering the era of the knowledge society, one should be aware that knowledge becomes the basic, or even the only, economic resource. Other resources are manufacturing factors complementary to knowledge (Drucker, 1993).

The specificity of the processes of acquiring knowledge, articulating it and increasing it may determine the uniqueness and competitive advantage of a given organization. This knowledge accumulated over time creates "specific company resources" (Penrose, 1966; Barney, 1991; Stonehouse et al., 2000) or constitutes its "key competencies" (Prahalad & Hamel, 1990), which are the key to understanding the company's strategy and results of the company's operations. The knowledge available to an organization at a certain time also affects learning capacity. Cohen and Levinthal (1990) introduce here the concept of "absorption capacity", i.e., the company's ability to recognize, create, store and reuse critical knowledge compared to the earlier level of its use. Over time, knowledge becomes the basis of action and is included in the established standards that contain the "forms, rules, procedures, conventions, strategies and technologies around which organizations are built and through which they operate" (Levitt & March, 1988).

Knowledge in the context of an enterprise resource has certain characteristic features that distinguish it from traditional resources. The most important are domination, inexhaustibility, simultaneity, non-linearity, variability and immeasurability. Domination refers to the role that knowledge plays in the organization—it integrates the remaining resources and therefore has strategic importance for the organization's functioning. Knowledge is a resource that is not subject to exhaustion; on the contrary, it increases with use. Simultaneity is associated with the possibility of knowledge being used simultaneously by many people in different places in the enterprise. On the other hand, the non-linearity results from the fact that there is no clear relationship between the number of knowledge resources held and the results achieved. Knowledge is a resource sensitive to changes because it can be updated or outdated at any time. Hence, when creating broad systems of knowledge accumulation, one should remember the danger of getting stuck in the layers of outdated knowledge. Immeasurability, on the other hand, is a feature resulting from the fact that knowledge is a resource difficult to measure, although, of course, attempts are made to quantify this phenomenon (Lis et al., 2017; Giju et al., 2010).

From the point of view of knowledge as the basis of the company's competitive potential, it must bear the characteristics of a strategic resource. Hence, the condition for gaining and maintaining a lasting competitive advantage is the knowledge that is valuable, diverse, rare, difficult to imitate and has no substitutes (Barney, 1991; Barney & Wright, 1998).

There are many types of knowledge, depending on the adopted classification criterion (Pavesi, 2003). However, thanks to I. Nonaka and H. Takeuchi and their theory of creating organizational knowledge, the most popular is the division of knowledge into tacit knowledge and explicit knowledge (Nonaka & Takeuchi, 1995). Explicit knowledge is the knowledge that is transformed into a formalized, structured, expressible form. It is included in the record of the past in libraries, archives, databases, etc. However, as M. Polnayi (1966) claims, most of the knowledge remains in a hidden form, deeply rooted in a specific context. This means that this knowledge is difficult to express, formalize or share formally. Tacit knowledge includes (Nonaka & Takeuchi, 1995):

- Cognitive elements – i.e., mental models such as schemas, paradigms, perspectives, beliefs that help individuals perceive and define the world in which they live
- Technical elements – containing specific knowledge of things (such as *know-how*), skills, qualifications

Tacit knowledge is intangible and difficult to follow, making it a potentially important asset for creating a competitive advantage (Barney, 1991). Formal (explicit) knowledge is knowledge that can be much more easily described and transferred through the use of documents, artefacts or software, as well as immediately communicated and shared. Tacit knowledge and explicit knowledge are not separated from each other, but complementary. Hence, knowledge in an organization is created through interactions between the presented types of knowledge.

9.3 KNOWLEDGE MANAGEMENT CONCEPTS

Knowledge management is an important element of integrated management systems in an organization and is treated as the foundation for future management. This concept provides an opportunity for a fundamental reorientation in the way enterprises think and operate. Incorporating knowledge management processes in the key processes of the organization should enable continuous improvement and indicate tasks for the future (Skrzypek 2003). The only right move leading to the integration of modern systems is grouping them into those that use knowledge in their activities (*knowledge intensive*) and those that rely entirely on it (*knowledge based*) (Janiec, 2002).

The complexity and multidimensionality of the knowledge management concept means that it is viewed and defined differently. One of the concepts defines knowledge management as a process that allows an organization to build wealth based on its intellectual assets or knowledge-based organizational assets. These assets are strongly associated with people or have their source in processes, organizational systems and culture regarding the organization's brand, the individual knowledge of its employees, intellectual property or knowledge-related structures (Bukowitz & Williams, 1999). Knowledge management is also defined as a business process as a result of which organizations create and use organizational or team knowledge (Mikuła et al., 2002). The concept is also referred to as established and systematic management of knowledge relevant to a given organization and the processes of its creation, acquisition, organization, diffusion and use to achieve the goals of that organization (Skyrme, 1999).

Published in November 2018, the international ISO 30401 standard defines knowledge management as a "holistic approach to improving learning and effectiveness through optimization of the use of knowledge, in order to create value for the organization. Knowledge management supports the existing process and development strategies. As such, it needs to be integrated with other organizational functions." (ISO 30401:2018). According to the standard, it is a discipline that focuses on how organizations create and use knowledge. At the same time, the standard emphasizes the fact of creating individual solutions in this area for each organization, taking into account their needs and specificity of operation. Based on the conviction that knowledge comes primarily from human experience and insights, it is clear that knowledge management should include interactions between people, supported by specific processes and technologies (ISO 30401:2018).

An effectively operating knowledge management system should, therefore, combine the management philosophy with modern IT techniques and technologies (Krawiec, 2003). Therefore, knowledge management should be considered in two aspects. The first refers to processes based on philosophical sciences and social psychology, and emphasizes the didactic aspects of knowledge management and learning processes. The other focuses on database management and knowledge distribution in a networked IT system (Sveiby, 2001). That is why the notions of behavioural and IT schools have been distinguished in the literature. The behavioural school is a view in which knowledge management requires knowledge and understanding of human behaviour. In this case, the effectiveness of knowledge transfer is based on the quality of the flow of knowledge between employees, and the key role in creating and transferring this knowledge is played by the so-called professional community. In turn, from the point of view of an IT school, knowledge is a collection of information included in an organization's IT system. In this approach, knowledge management is to ensure the efficient flow of knowledge and information through refining and improving IT systems (Fazlagić, 1999). These two ways of knowledge management are referred to as *people management* and *information management* and they are complementary to each other. They cannot be considered separately, but should be treated as mutually complementary.

In the case of knowledge management in the context of people management, knowledge is treated as a dynamic and constantly changing process based on the individual knowledge and skills of individual employees. In this approach, the achievements of psychology (at the individual level) and philosophy, sociology and management theory (at the level of the organization) are used to improve the individual skills of employees and the learning process, because the knowledge, competence and creativity possessed by people play a key role in the development of the enterprise. In this aspect of knowledge management, the actions taken are designed to stimulate and best motivate employees to share knowledge, which will result in using the intellectual and competency potential of employees as well as incorporating the individual knowledge into the knowledge of the organization (Sveiby, 2001; Wiig, 2002).

Information management perceives knowledge objectively, as a resource that can be identified and used in information systems. It mainly concerns data processing, i.e., data acquisition, storage or exchange. To implement these tasks, it is necessary to use modern IT tools to improve the flow of information and prevent communication chaos. They also regulate the excess or scarcity of data and information in individual areas of the enterprise (Kozarkiewicz-Chlebowska, 2001). Information management includes, among other things:

- Analysis of information solutions
- Improvement of data management systems
- The use of concepts related to the development of artificial intelligence
- The use of the software used by a dispersed group of co-operating users (groupware)
- Analysis of processes taking place within a given organization and in relations with its partners and customers (re-engineering) (Jabłoński, 2003)

In the development of the concept of knowledge management, four generations (stages) can be distinguished. The first one focused primarily on improving the ability of an individual (employee) to obtain, share and use their own knowledge in the best possible way. In the next stage, the focus was on the acquisition and codification processes in order to expand the knowledge management skills of the individual (employee) to increase organizational effectiveness. The further development of the concept of knowledge management resulted in the focus of the third generation on collaboration within the field of knowledge and creating social networks (social networking). This enabled organizations to implement innovation and generate knowledge in different functional disciplines and silos. Today, knowledge management is moving to the fourth generation, which uses artificial intelligence (AI), machine learning, data analytics, the Internet of Things (IoT) or other modern developments (Liebowitz & Paliszkiewicz, 2019).

With each stage of the development of the knowledge management concept, the growing role of information technology can be seen. Hence the development of information and informative networks enabling access to data, dialogue or discussion, as well as specialized knowledge bases and expert systems are now inseparable attributes of knowledge management in an enterprise.

9.4 INFORMATION TECHNOLOGIES VERSUS KNOWLEDGE MANAGEMENT

As previously stated in the concept of information management, knowledge is perceived as objects (data) that can be identified and included in information systems. Thus, it mainly concerns so-called formal (explicit) knowledge. Formal or "codified" knowledge is information that is transformed into a formalized, structured and expressible form. It can, therefore, be described and transferred by means of documents or software and immediately communicated. In order for these processes to be implemented, the support from the IT technologies (Chugh et al., 2013; Drosos et al., 2016) underpinning the operation of Management Information Systems is necessary. They are referred to as formal and computer systems created to provide, select and integrate current information essential in the decision-making process. Their task is, therefore, to support the management and integration of organizational structures (Kiełtyka, 2002). Integrated information systems include a wide range of software containing complex support systems. They are becoming a more and more indispensable element in the functioning of modern enterprises, also in the field of knowledge management (Cupiał et al., 2018). Information technology is considered an essential part of knowledge management as it provides the means to create, share and capture knowledge. The rapid development of information technology and the development of new and improved technological tools now allow for the creation of knowledge bases of any size, as well as enable the provision of the necessary knowledge at the right time and in the right form (Plebańska, 2016; Liebowitz & Paliszkiewicz, 2019). Such knowledge management support provides opportunities for faster performance of tasks and supports knowledge exchange. As a consequence, it increases the efficiency of knowledge workers and the entire organization (Sarka et al., 2019; Soto-Acosta & Cegarra-Navarro, 2016). It is noted that, in parallel with the use of appropriate information technology, IT professionals should be aware of the different knowledge management processes. This enables successful implementation and realization of knowledge management projects in the organization. An important aspect is also the right selection of knowledge management tools so that IT becomes a sustainable and integrated part of the knowledge management system in the enterprise (Chugh et al., 2013).

In the era of the rapid development of information technology, there is a very wide range of IT systems and tools used in knowledge management. They include both computer network environments and services functioning within them and specific applications as well as their entire classes. Taking into account the needs of implementing knowledge processes, among the most important IT systems and tools we can distinguish (Cupiał et al., 2018; Chugh et al., 2013; Kozioł, 2010; Kulej-Dudek & Dudek, 2010; Jashapara, 2014; Wallis, 2011) are:

- *Document management systems* – thanks to them it is possible to collect and classify documents; these systems also facilitate the search for documents and access to them, and the recording of work performed on these documents (e.g., monitoring of the changes made);
- *Correspondence management systems* – allow companies to automate the process of sending information to employees of the enterprise as well as to clients;
- *Workflow systems* – help and improve the implementation of document handling procedures. These systems ensure that the activities undertaken in a given organization will be carried out in accordance with the adopted work procedure: each stage of work will be carried out by a specific person, at a specific time and on the basis of specific data. In other words, the system assigns individual tasks to employees and manages the schedule for their implementation;
- *Group work support systems* (*groupware*) – allow for an unrestrained flow of knowledge and knowledge sharing. The basic goal of this type of system is to provide employees with harmonious co-operation by facilitating communication between both teams and their individual members;
- *Decision support systems* – are interactive computer systems that perform advisory and decision-making roles. The most widely used systems here are the expert systems.

Using them consists of comparing the current situation with the knowledge of experts included in the base of knowledge on a similar issue occurring in the past and inferring the possibilities of solving it. In other words, the use of these systems gives the opportunity to draw conclusions based on known facts, which leads to confirmation of hypotheses or to drawing new conclusions (Simiński, 1997).

- *Expert systems* – are computer programs supporting planning and decision-making functions. Their aim is to include in the system advanced information in the selected field. Thanks to this, with the same input data and under certain conditions, the systems can replace a real person in making routine decisions. Expert systems include such elements as knowledge base, base of data and facts, inference mechanism and explanation of decisions made, as well as the user interface (Michalik, 2014).
- *Remote learning systems (e-learning)* – are tools for transferring knowledge using a computer and all available electronic media (e.g., internet, intranet, satellite broadcasts). They are primarily used to educate employees online. E-learning gives the opportunity to independently choose the preferred format for providing knowledge and the pace of its transfer.
- *Data warehouses* – are complete databases that are used for multidimensional data recording and forming as well as for their quick and easy retrieval (Kubiak & Korowicki, 2004). Data warehouses enable formulating new queries, creating reports or analyzing the use of resources. Their goal is to integrate the best elements that made up former decisions (Kiełtyka, 2002);
- *Customer Relationship Management (CRM) systems* – are programs that enable the management of the relationship with customers. Their task is to integrate technologies and operational processes in such a way as to achieve continuous readiness to meet customer requirements.
- *Corporate portals* – are platforms for effective communication and co-operation, both inside and outside the organization. They constitute a unified work environment, integrating with one user interface, which is a Web browser, various data sources and applications. Corporate portals allow efficient and easy access to data and information gathered in the organization, which improves the effectiveness of the knowledge management system (Lewandowski & Kopera, 2006);
- *Intranet* – is an internal, local network of a given organization, using the infrastructure and internet standards. It is a controlled work environment, designed for a specific group of users, with short access times (Kiełtyka, 2002). Although the intranet limits access to external information, it ensures speed and reliability as well as greater security of data and information flow;
- *Extranet* – a tool, similar to the intranet, that is created to facilitate communication with external partners. It is accessed by specific people who know the system access code.

Creating an unambiguous and clear classification of tools to support knowledge management is not a simple task. The reason is the classification of the tools themselves as well as the classification of their functionality. On the one hand, the naming of tools often coincides with the naming of their functionality; on the other hand, the functionality of the tool designed for the implementation of a particular process is equipped with a different tool (Plebańska, 2016). M. Plebańska points out that the mechanisms supporting knowledge management are based on three essential technologies: database, networking and Web technology. The first concerns the physical and logical structuring and storage of data. It is based on database mechanisms and software language systems. The second is understood as a set of network connections, mechanisms responsible for coordinating processes related to the exchange of data. It distinguishes the hardware layer in the form of servers, network connections and tools related to network synchronization, and a layer associated with the software that makes it possible to perform the above steps, whereas Web technology means a technology that combines database technology with network technology. Its implementation is carried out by websites and mechanisms related to the representation of data on websites. Web technology makes it possible to exchange information and knowledge on websites equipped with appropriate applications (Plebańska, 2016).

As already mentioned, the concept of knowledge management has evolved over time. Knowledge management initiatives, which often to a significant extent involved centrally managed knowledge repositories, have changed. And while the basic needs of knowledge management continue to address the issue of the ability to capture, share, apply and create knowledge, the development of information technology allows for the application of new solutions in this area (Von Krogh, 2012; Liebowitz & Paliszkiewicz, 2019). Referring to the previously presented division of technologies supporting knowledge management, it is important to point out social media, which are now increasingly important in the activities of enterprises (Aichner & Jacob, 2015). It is "a group of Internet-based applications that build on the ideological and technological foundations of Web 2.0, and that allow the creation and exchange of User Generated Content." (Kaplan & Haenlein, 2010). The potential of social media makes it possible to create and share knowledge through interactions between employees and other stakeholders. Social media technologies can take different forms. Among them, one can distinguish corporate social networks, discussion forums, social networks and blogs (Soto-Acosta & Cegarra-Navarro, 2016; Aichner & Jacob, 2015). They differ from traditional knowledge management technologies by offering open, ubiquitous and mobile information and communication technology solutions (ICT). They are an effective communication tool, which greatly affects the processes of acquiring, storing and sharing knowledge (Von Krogh, 2012; Soto-Acosta & Cegarra-Navarro, 2016; Liebowitz & Paliszkiewicz, 2019).

9.5 USE OF IT SYSTEMS AND TOOLS IN KNOWLEDGE MANAGEMENT

The literature proposes a division of the use of IT systems in knowledge management in an instrumental approach. This approach indicates a set of research and application tools used in diagnostic works, in designing knowledge management systems and in their implementation. The determinants and elements of the knowledge management system in this aspect include (Kowalczyk & Nogalski, 2007):

- Strategic analysis
- Benchmarking
- Co-operation with other enterprises and institutions
- Practices, internships, studying literature, extracting resources
- Internal fusions, networking
- Documents, databases, best practices, knowledge maps, individual and collective memory, communication
- Internal training, teamwork, mailing lists, knowledge brokers, knowledge fairs, mentoring programs
- Learning through action, after-action review, implementation of process and product innovations
- Internal entrepreneurship (intrapreneurship)

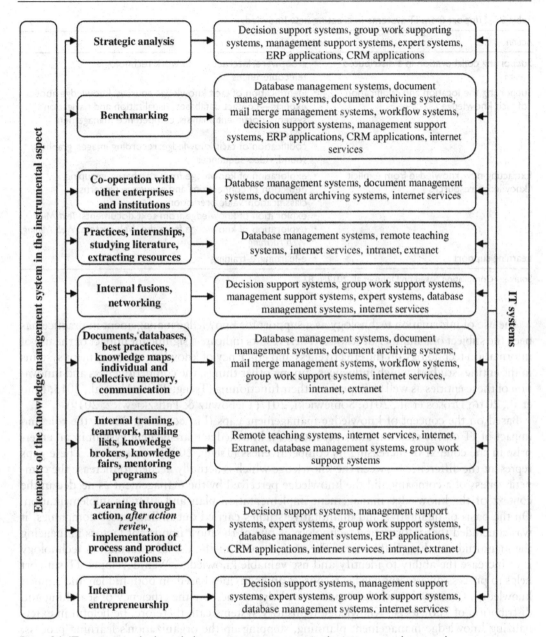

Figure 9.1 IT systems in the knowledge management system in the instrumental approach

Source: Compilation based on: Kozioł, M. 2010, p. 41.

The above elements have been assigned (indicated) IT systems that can be used in each of them. These proposals are presented in Figure 9.1.

Typically, the functioning of IT systems is identified primarily with the issue of acquiring, updating, storing and sharing explicit knowledge. Here, primarily document management systems, database systems, data warehouses and expert systems are used. However, IT systems can also be used to create new knowledge based on that already accumulated. Examples of solutions supporting the creation of new knowledge are presented in Table 9.1.

Table 9.1 Support from IT systems in creating new knowledge

Action	Support
Supporting collaboration in a distributed team	• groupware, internet group work technologies, teleconferences
Supporting the location and codification of tacit knowledge	• identification of tacit knowledge sources: knowledge about experts—contact databases, visualization and navigation systems, document analysis, competence management systems • codification of tacit knowledge: recording images, graphics, sound, video sequences
Extracting new knowledge from explicit knowledge resources	• exploration of knowledge from databases: grouping, detection of connections and sequence patterns, classification, value prediction • exploration of knowledge from text documents: *Text Mining;* • exploration of knowledge from the Web system: *Web Mining, Web Farming*
Learning support	• e-learning, e-training

Source: Compilation based on Dohn et al., 2012, p. 87.

The use of information technology as a support for knowledge management in practice has been the subject of a number of studies. Their results indicate a significant impact of the use of information technology on the effectiveness and efficiency of knowledge management systems in the entities studied, which influences, among other things, the competitiveness and innovation of these entities as well as improving their functioning (Tseng, 2008; Ali et al., 2015; Mao et al., 2016; Drosos et al., 2016; Soniewicki, 2017; Liebowitz & Paliszkiewicz, 2019).

Based on the concept of knowledge management gaps (Lin & Tseng, 2005), the role and impact of IT on the creation and operation of a knowledge management system in an enterprise in the context of increasing its competitiveness (Tseng, 2008) was studied. These gaps represent the difference between the knowledge which is actually needed to increase the competitiveness of a company and the knowledge perceived by the management as needed in the context of the knowledge management implementation plan and after its implementation. On the basis of qualitative and quantitative studies carried out in Taiwanese companies, it was concluded that information technology is one of the most important factors influencing the magnitude of these differences. The main benefit of the use of information technology is to increase the ability to identify and use valuable knowledge. Well-developed IT support helps to process diverse knowledge resources and activities based on both hidden and explicit knowledge. Creating knowledge repositories helps to increase the efficiency of searching and distribution of knowledge. Knowledge repository systems can, therefore, be helpful in externalizing knowledge management planning, stepping up the organization's learning process, and improving planning and decision-making. A very important issue in the case of repositories is the need to constantly update knowledge, which has a positive effect on the processes of socialization, externalization, pooling and internalization of knowledge; that is, it increases the efficiency of the creation of organizational knowledge. IT systems and tools also play a significant role in supporting communication, co-operation and coordination among the organization's employees. The use of software for group work, decision support systems, workflow systems, video conferencing and intranets has a positive effect on the internal exchange of information, group discussions or communication in organizations. In turn, virtual communities, email, electronic bulletin boards, distance learning systems or an extranet facilitate inter-functional communication, external information retrieval and knowledge transfer between the internal branches of the company (Tseng, 2008).

A similar scope of IT technology support in knowledge management in the context of competitiveness is indicated in the studies carried out in Polish construction companies (Soniewicki, 2017). The first phase of research aimed to determine the intensity of the use of information technology for knowledge management. It was found that in the companies investigated were mostly used technologies known as basic technologies, including the internet, email, word processors and spreadsheets. Data storage systems such as, for example, systems that collect, share and manage documents and data, CRM and data warehouses were also widely used. A relatively large number of the entities studied as support for knowledge management used information and communication technologies, such as corporate portals, intranets, corporate forums or newsgroups. On the other hand, low intensity of use was observed in the case of group co-operation systems and decision support systems or expert systems (Soniewicki, 2017). The overall level of use of information technology was not affected by the size of the companies studied. Nevertheless, when considering the use of technologies according to their types, it has become apparent that large enterprises (more than 250 employees) are very active in the use of basic information technologies and storage systems. On the other hand, IT communication systems were more commonly used in medium-sized enterprises (from 50 to 250 employees) and small enterprises (from 10 to 49 employees) (Soniewicki, 2017).

Further studies concluded that the higher the use of the information technologies indicated in the companies studied, the higher their level of competitiveness. Companies where the overall use of IT support in knowledge management was low were the least competitive ones. Companies with relatively high use of the technologies in question were more competitive than their closest competitors, but this difference was not large. On the other hand, those with the most intensive use of IT support showed the highest level of competitiveness among respondents (Soniewicki, 2017). Taking into account the different types of information technology used, it turned out that companies using IT communication systems and group work systems more intensively were more competitive than those where this intensity was low. The most competitive companies, on the other hand, were those that made intensive use of the decision-support and expert systems. It can, therefore, be concluded that the higher the intensity of the use of more advanced information technologies in the companies studied, the higher the level of competitiveness of those companies (Soniewicki, 2017).

The above-mentioned studies point to the important role of support for the knowledge management system in the company by information technology. Of course, they are not a key element in building competitive advantage, nor are they the foundation of knowledge management. Nevertheless, a lack of support for them can be a certain impediment to achieving the desired level of competitiveness. At the same time, they are an excellent tool to support the implementation and operation of the knowledge management system in the enterprise (Soniewicki, 2017; Tseng, 2008).

Of course, support for information technology knowledge management is not limited to companies. Examples include higher education institutions (Ali et al., 2015; Drosos et al., 2016).

Using the SECI model created by I. Nonaka and H. Takeuchi (1995), the role of information technology in knowledge management in universities (Ali et al., 2015) was indicated. It has been proposed to use specific IT tools and systems for specific ways of converting the knowledge included in the SECI model (Table 9.2).

The application of information technology is therefore primarily intended to improve the functioning of the knowledge management system and thus to support the knowledge-making process. In the case of universities, this is particularly important as it can have a positive impact on improving teaching and learning processes.

But support from information technology in knowledge management at universities can be used beyond the field of education. The university should also be seen as a modern

Table 9.2 IT support for different ways of converting knowledge in the SECI model

Method of converting knowledge	Information technologies	Examples of applications
Socialization	video conferencing, electronic discussion forums, electronic bulletin boards, internet – the community of practice	conducting distance lectures, distance communication, conducting exams, exchanging questions and answers on lectures, creating a network of experts among lecturers within practice communities
Externalization	knowledge repositories	recording and storing lectures, storing and sharing research reports, student discussion results during workshops; for lecturers and researchers the possibility of collecting and storing publications from university conferences, publications from journals, etc. as well as theses or projects; repositories can also be used to collect and store specific rules, procedures and policies in force at the university in the academic, research as well as administrative field
Combination	blogs, portals, document management systems	creating their own portals by lecturers to capture their notes, syllabuses, tasks or references for individual courses; use of blogs by lecturers to share their experiences in the context of solving problems of students
Internalization	electronic discussion forums, blogs, social media	used for co-operation, discussion, exchange of knowledge, experience, opinions, ideas, solutions, etc.

Source: A compilation based on Ali et al. 2015, pp. 59–67.

organization where business processes take place (Drosos et al., 2016). Therefore, IT can be a support in the academic field (research, lectures, distance learning) as well as supporting the business needs of universities.

What are widely used by universities are websites. However, universities provide static information and do not provide personalized services to their students. University Web portals can be helpful in this regard, by supporting both business process management (finance, recruitment) and academic services (e-learning, library). This can be a source of key information to help you make decisions for potential students (Drosos et al., 2016). Knowledge management initiatives are essential to increase student satisfaction by providing personalization in the services offered by the university. To achieve this, the support from information technology, which aims to increase the efficiency and effectiveness of these processes, would be helpful. IT ensures proper communication and collaboration between users, which in turn supports the knowledge-sharing process.

In conclusion, from the point of view of knowledge management, the key task of information technology is to support interpersonal communication, and enable employees and other users to access distributed data sources and their classifications, and search for them. They allow both the creation of knowledge bases and data collection as well as the quick and effective allocation of these resources to individual parts of the enterprise. However, what is particularly valuable is the use of modern information technologies, which gives the opportunity to create new knowledge in the enterprise.

9.6 CONCLUSION

The efficient functioning of modern enterprises without proper support from information technology is, in practice, impossible. Especially when it concerns enterprises for which knowledge and information constitute their basic resource. IT systems allowing access to data, enabling dialogue and creating knowledge bases, as well as the use of expert systems, improve knowledge management in particular in the context of information management. Among the many measurable benefits of implementing IT systems, we can point to the following:

- Improving the extraction of necessary data and information from existing resources
- Improving knowledge creation on the basis of an already existing system
- Preventing loss of knowledge in the event of an employee leaving the enterprise by formalizing the knowledge the employee has provided and including it in knowledge bases
- Improving communication between employees, thereby facilitating the sharing of knowledge and experience

The proposals for various IT systems and tools presented in the study do not exhaust the large and ever-increasing number of possible solutions. Each organization must, therefore, choose the most appropriate ones taking into account the information needs and the specificities of its operation.

This study has repeatedly highlighted the importance and role of information and communication technologies in supporting information technology management. And there is probably no one who would not agree with these considerations. Nevertheless, it should be remembered that knowledge and knowledge management is first and foremost the domain of people. Therefore, the initiatives taken in this area should focus to a large extent on human and organizational issues (Antonova et al., 2006). Many authors like Davenport and Prusak (2000); Kaplan (2002), Senge et al. (1999), pointing to the key role of information technology for the collection and distribution of information, emphasize that only people are capable of capturing and storing knowledge.

REFERENCES

Aichner, T., Jacob, F. (2015). Measuring the Degree of Corporate Social Media Use. *International Journal of Market Research, 57(2)*, pp. 257–275.

Ali, N., Sulaiman, H., Cob, Z. C. (2015). The Role of Information Technology for Knowledge Management Paradigm in Higher Education. *Journal of Information System Research And Innovation 6*, pp. 59–67.

Antonova, A., Gourova, E., Nikolov R. (2006). *Review of technology solutions for knowledge management*. Conference Paper of 2nd IET International Conference on Intelligent Environments, pp. 39–44.

Barney, J. (1991). Firm Resources and Sustained Competitive Advantage. *Journal of Management, 17(1)*, pp. 99–120.

Barney, J. B., Wright P. M. (1998). On Becoming a Strategic Partner: The Role of Human Resources in Gaining Competitive Advantage. *Human Resource Management, 37(1)*, pp. 31–46.

Bootz, J. P., Durance, P., Monti, R. (2019). Foresight and knowledge management. New developments in theory and practice, *Technological Forecasting & Social Change, 140*, pp. 80–83.

Bukowitz, W. R., Williams, R. L. (1999). *The knowledge management fieldbook*. London: Financial Times Prentice Hall.

Chluski, A., Dziembek, D. (2012). *Pozyskiwanie wiedzy w organizacji wirtualnej*. In: D. Jelonek (ed.), *Wybrane problemy zarządzania wiedzą i kapitałem intelektualnym*. Częstochowa: WWZPCz.

Chugh, M., Chugh, N., Punia, D. K., Agarwal A. (2013). *The role of information technology in knowledge management*. In: X. Luo (ed.), *Advances in Intelligent Systems Research*. Proceedings of the Conference on Advances in Communication and Control Systems-2013 (CAC2S 2013), pp. 668–693.

Cohen, W. M., Levinthal D. A. (1990). Absorptive Capacity: a New Perspective on Learning and Innovation. *Administrative Science Quarterly, 35(1)*, pp. 128–152.

Cupiał, M., Szeląg-Sikora, A., Sikora, J., Rorat, J., Niemiec, M. (2018). Information technology tools in corporate knowledge management. *Ekonomia i Prawo. Ecomomics and Law, 17(1)*, pp. 5–15.

Davenport, T. H., Prusak L. (2000). *Working Knowledge. How Organizations Manage What They Know.* Boston: Harvard Business School Press.

Dohn, K., Gumiński, A., Zoleński, W. (2012). Czynniki determinujące opracowanie systemu informatycznego wspomagającego zarządzanie wiedzą w przedsiębiorstwie produkcyjnym. *Organizacja i Zarządzanie, 1*, pp. 81–96.

Drosos, D., Chalikias, M., Skordoulis, M., Mandalenaki, M. (2016). *The Role of Information Technology and Knowledge Management In Higher Education.* Proceedings of 2nd International Conference on Lifelong Education and Leadership for All (ICLEL 2016). Liepaja, pp. 395–403.

Drucker, P. F. (1969). *The age of discontinuity: Guidelines to our changing society.* New York Harper & Row.

Drucker, P. F. (1993). *Post-Capitalist Society.* New York: Harper Business.

Fazlagić, A. (1999). Geneza zarządzania wiedzą. *Global Business, 14(59)*.

Giju, G. C., Badea, L., Lopez Ruiz, V. R., Nevado Pena, D. (2010). Knowledge Management – the key Resource in the Knowledge Economy. *Theoretical and Applied Economics, 6(6(547))*, pp. 27–36.

ISO 30401:2018 Knowledge management systems – Requirements. Retrieved from: https://www.iso.org/standard/68683.html (Access: 22.04.2020).

Jabłoński, M. (2003). O sukcesie decyduje wiedza. *Personel, 17*, pp. 18–20.

Janiec, M. (2002). *Wprowadzenie do zarządzanie wiedzą.* Kraków: Wydawnictwo Akademii Ekonomicznej.

Jashapara, A. (2014). *Zarządzanie wiedzą.* Warszawa: PWE.

Kaplan, A. M., Haenlein, M. (2010). Users of the world, unite! The challenges and opportunities of Social Media. *Business Horizons, 53(1)*, pp. 59–68.

Kaplan, S. (2002), KM the right way. Retrieved from: www.cio.com/archive/071502/right.html. (Access: 05.02.2020).

Kiełtyka, L. (2002). *Komunikacja w zarządzaniu. Techniki, narzędzia i formy przekazu informacji.* Warszawa: Agencja Wydawnicza PLACET.

Kowalczyk, A., Nogalski, B. (2007). *Zarządzanie wiedzą. Koncepcja i narzędzia.* Warszawa: Difin.

Kozarkiewicz-Chlebowska, A. (2001). *Koncepcja zarządzania wiedzą – jej geneza, zastosowanie i perspektywy.* In: L. Piaseczny (ed.), *Polska w Europie 2000 – polskie nauki o zarządzaniu wobec wyzwań XXI wieku. Dorobek Szkoły Letniej "Warszawa 2000".* Warszawa: Wyższa Szkoła Przedsiębiorczości i Zarządzania.

Kozioł, M. (2010). Informatyzacja systemu zarządzania wiedzą w przedsiębiorstwie. *Zeszyty Naukowe Uniwersytetu Ekonomicznego w Krakowie, 838*, pp. 35–49.

Krawiec, F. (2003). *Strategiczne myślenie w firmie.* Warszawa: Difin.

Kubiak, B. F., Korowicki, A. (2004). *System zarządzania wiedzą w rozwoju współczesnej organizacji.* In: J. Kisielnicki, J. S. Nowak, J. K. Grabara (eds.), *Informatyka we współczesnym zarządzaniu.* Warszawa: Wydawnictwo Naukowo-Techniczne, pp. 81–93.

Kulej-Dudek, E., Dudek, D. (2010). *Przegląd narzędzi i systemów wspierających zarządzanie wiedzą w przedsiębiorstwie.* In: L. Kiełtyka (ed.), *Rozwój i doskonalenie funkcjonowania przedsiębiorstw.* Warszawa: Difin 2010, pp. 346–366.

Levitt, B., March, J. G. (1988). Organizational Learning. *Annual Review of Sociology, 14*, pp. 319–340.

Lewandowski, J., Kopera, S. (2006). Systemy informacyjne w zarządzaniu zasobami ludzkimi. *Zarządzanie Zasobami Ludzkimi, 3-4*, pp. 45–53.

Liebowitz, J., Paliszkiewicz, J. (2019). The next generation of knowledge management: Implications for LIS educators and professionals. *Online Journal of Applied Knowledge Management, 7(2)*, pp. 16–28.

Lin, C. H., Tseng, S. M. (2005). Bridging the Implementation gaps in the knowledge management system for enhancing corporate performance. *Expert Systems with Applications, 29*(1), pp. 163–173.

Lis, T., Tomski, P., Kuraś, M., Kuraś, P. (2017). Knowledge of the Organization and the Effectiveness of Decisions in the Strategic Dimension. *Zeszyty Naukowe Politechniki Częstochowskiej. Zarządzanie, 28*(2), pp. 7–15.

Mao, H., Liu, S., Zhang, J., Deng, Z. (2016). Information technology resource, knowledge management capability, and competitive advantage: The moderating role of resource commitment. *International Journal of Information Management, 36*, pp. 1062–1074.

Michalik, K. (2014). *Systemy eksperotwe we wspomaganiu procesów zarządzania wiedzą w organizacji.* Katowice: Uniwersytet Ekonomiczny.

Mikuła, B., Pietruszka-Ortyl, A., Potocki, A. (2002). *Zarządzanie przedsiębiorstwem XXI wieku. Wybrane koncepcje i metody.* Warszawa: Difin.

Nonaka, I., Takeuchi, H. (1995). *The knowledge-creating company*, New York: Oxford University Press.

Paliszkiewicz, J. (2007). Knowledge management: An integrative view and empirical examination. *Cybernetics and Systems, 38*(8), pp. 825–836.

Pavesi, S. (2003). *Enabling knowledge processes in innovative environments*, Ph.D. thesis, Twente University Press.

Penrose, E. T. (1966). *The theory of the growth of the firm.* Oxford: Blackwell.

Plebańska, M. (2016). Technologiczne narzędzia zarządzania wiedzą a innowacje w przedsiębiorstwach sektora MSP. *Zeszyty Naukowe Uczelni Vistula, 51*(6), pp. 105–117.

Polnayi, M. (1966). *The Tacit Dimension*, London: Routledge & Kegan Paul.

Prahalad, C. K., Hamel, G. (1990). The Core Competencies of the Corporation. *Harvard Business Review, May-June*, pp. 79–90.

Probst, G., Raub, S., Romhardt, K. (2002). *Zarządzanie wiedzą w organizacji.* Kraków: Oficyna Ekonomiczna.

Sarka, P., Heisig, P., Caldwell, N. H. M., Majer, A. M., Ipsen, C. (2019). Future research on information technology in knowledge management. *Knowledge and Process Management, 26*, pp. 277–296.

Senge, P., Kleiner, A., Roberts, C., Ross, R. G., Smith, B. (1999). *The Dance of Change: The Challenges to Sustaining Momentum in Learning Organizations.* New York: Currency/ Doubleday.

Simiński, R. (1997). Sztuczna inteligencja w systemach zarządzania. In: *Systemy informatyczne zarządzania, 25–31.* Częstochowa: Wydawnictwo Politechniki Częstochowskiej.

Skrzypek, E. (2001). Wpływ zintegrowanego systemu zarządzania na efektywność gospodarowania w przedsiębiorstwie. In: E. Skrzypek (ed.), *Metody i narzędzia doskonalenia zarządzania przedsiębiorstwem.* Lublin: Wydawnictwo UMCS.

Skrzypek, E. (2003). Wpływ zarządzania wiedzą na innowacyjność przedsiębiorstwa. In: H. Brdulak, T. Gołębiowski (eds.), *Wspólna Europa – innowacyjność w działaniu przedsiębiorstw.* Warszawa: Difin.

Skyrme, D. J. (1999). *Knowledge networking. Creating the collaborative enterprise.* Oxford: Butterworth-Heinemann.

Sojkin, B. (2009). *Informacyjne podstawy decyzji marketingowych.* Warszawa: PWE.

Soniewicki, M. (2017). Znaczenie wykorzystania technologii informatycznych w procesach zarządzania wiedzą przedsiębiorstw budowlanych, *Prace Naukowe Uniwersytetu Ekonomicznego we Wrocławiu, 496*, pp. 135–149.

Soto-Acosta, P., Cegarra-Navarro, J. G. (2016). New ICTs for Knowledge Management in Organizations. *Journal of Knowledge Management, 20*(3), pp. 417–422.

Stonehouse G., Hamill, J., Campbell, D., Purdie, T. (2000). *Global and transnational business: strategy and management.* New York: Wiley

Sveiby, K. E. (2001). What is knowledge management? Retrieved from: https://www.sveiby.com/files/ pdf/whatisknowledgemanagement.pdf (Access: 05.02.2020).

Toffler, A. (1980). *The third wave.* New York: Morrow.

Toffler, A. (1990). *Powershift: Knowledge, Wealth, and Violence at the Edge of the 21st Century*, New York: Bantam Books.

Tseng, S. M. (2008). The effects of information technology on knowledge management systems. *Expert Systems with Applications*, *35*, pp. 150–160.

Von Krogh, G. (2012). How does social software change knowledge management? Toward a strategic research agenda. *Journal of Strategic Information Systems*, *21(2)*, pp. 154–164.

Wallis, A. (2011). Systemy informacyjne w zarządzaniu wiedzą w przedsiębiorstwie. *Zeszyty Naukowe Uniwersytetu Szczecińskiego. Ekonomiczne problemy usług*, *68(2)*, pp. 580-588.

Wiig, K: M. (2002). *Knowledge Management Has Many Facets*. Knowledge Research Institute, Inc. Retrieved from: http://www.krii.com/downloads/Four_KM_Facets.pdf, (Access: 07.02.2020).

Chapter 10

Information technologies for the industrial management of objects in an innovative economy under conditions of instability and development of Industry 4.0

Sultan Ramazanov, Vitalina Babenko
and Oleksandr Honcharenko

CONTENTS

10.1 INTRODUCTION

Humankind is facing the biggest challenge during its existence. Humanity enters into "Industry 4.0," where the physical world is connected to the virtual world. Information technology, telecommunications and production are merging, and at the same time, the means of production are becoming more independent. It is still impossible to say exactly what the "smart factories" of the future will look like. Scientists from all over the world and specialists from all scientific fields are called upon to find answers to thousands of challenges of the new world in the conditions of Industry 4.0 and the digital economy. The term "digital economy" appeared in the scientific literature not so long ago, at the end of the twentieth century, and became widespread. Digital technologies at the beginning of the twenty-first century are developing rapidly and have a major impact, not only on the economy, but also on the development of society.

The favorites of "Industry 4.0" will be biotechnology, nanotechnology, robotics and mechatronics, new medicine and new environmental management, development and use of personality, and team capabilities at a new, higher level. This is about development, reforms, modernization, innovative technologies and what the world is transitioning to today, moving to the sixth technological way, that is, to the NBIC (*nanotechnology, biotechnology, information technology, cognitive technologies*) [Ramazanov, 2020; 2019; Ramazanov & Petrova, (2020); Ramazanov et al., 2019; Ramazanov et al., 2020). And socio-humanitarian technologies (SHT) refer to a person, to practice, to society ... to morality, to culture. And this is more of a philosophical problem. That is, now we have to focus on NBIC + SH - technology. From here it is clear which executives we need, what personnel we need to prepare. Yes, those who can organize and secure this breakthrough in the future.

We are on the threshold of a new revival in science and technology, based on a comprehensive understanding of the structure and behavior of matter from the nanoscale to the most complex of open systems, the human brain. The unification of science, based on the unity of nature and its holistic study, will lead to technological convergence and a more effective social structure to achieve human goals. The phrase "convergent technologies" refers to a synergistic combination of the four major "NBIC" (*nano-bio-info-cogni*) fields of science and technology, each of which is currently progressing rapidly.

Thus, on the basis of a synergistic approach, the issue of exacerbation of global crises generated by technogenic civilization is considered, and the question arises: Is it possible to overcome these crises without changing the basic system of values of technogenic culture? This value system will have to change that; overcoming global crises will require a change in the goals of human activity and its ethical regulations. *Humanity has a chance to find a way out of global crises, but it will have to go through an era of spiritual reformation and the development of a new value system.*

The modern paradigm of the global community's transition from a systemic crisis and the transition to a secure and sustainable development is, first and foremost, an innovative way of development based on modern innovative, information and convergent technologies, based on new knowledge as the main resources of development, based on socio-humanitarian technologies, as well as on the basis of active transition according to the 6th, and then to the 7th technological way of development and Industry 4.0.

Technological foundations of Industry 4.0: Cyberphysical systems (CPS), warning systems, process management, automation, smart grid-efficient power supply; informatization of production and logistics, communication "Machine–Machine" (M2M); design principles in Industry 4.0, interoperability, virtualization, decentralization, real-time data collection and analysis, oriented services, modularity, parametric design, personalized products; Computer-integrated systems (CIS), computer-integrated production, application systems: CAD, CAE, CAM, CAPP and others. Digitalization of industry, communicating robots; strategies for creating integrated systems, integration criteria, conceptual models.

Business and Industry 4.0: change in business models, cloud services, data analysis and evaluation, 3D simulation of production, a sharp reduction in time from the idea to the market, flexibility and individualization of mass production, remote management and maintenance of facilities; creation of Smart production and services, intelligent factories, industrial infrastructure, integrated production, industrial restructuring, industrial internet infrastructure; principles of creating a new type of firms in digital industrial production, assistive and service technologies are key production technologies (communicating robots, remote support systems, 3D printing); effects of Industry 4.0, collaboration between various business functions, various product lines, technologies and stakeholders, organizational forms; virtual marketing. Integration of consumers through the internet; Management/ Management in Industry 4.0. Market implementation of innovative products (IP), intellectual property; education; nonlinear processes, systems analysis and applied synergetics; synergetic, geopolitical and geoeconomic analysis of the problems of targeted development.

10.2 INTEGRATION AND INTELLECTUALIZATION OF ECONOMIC–MATHEMATICAL MODELING PROCESSES AND AUTOMATIZATION OF INDUSTRIAL SYSTEMS MANAGEMENT AND OBJECTS

10.2.1 Concept, creation principles and structure of modeling systems and control in "Industry 4.0" (systems of type "X")

The current ecological economic situation in the transition to market relations requires a new approach to the planning, management and monitoring of production–transportational complexes (PTC) and processes. This approach affects all aspects of the PTC economy: organization of production and marketing, requires the integration of all monitoring, management and decision-making processes in a new unstable informational environment. Such integrated computerized systems will make it possible to make various managerial decisions more quickly and flexibly, deliver to the market products of the appropriate quality, at lower cost and, which is more, to take into account the environmental situation in the industrial production zone.

The integrated intelligent computerized system (name it a *system of the type "X"*) proposed in this paper is an information system built on the basis of the principles of a system approach and the concept of 4 "I" (Ramazanov 2008, 2014), i.e., with maximum integration, intellectualization, individualization and a single information base, the principle of maximum consideration of "NO- and MANY-" factor synthesis, as well as the maximum possible greening of production processes (the concept of "4" and "+ 2"). Systems of type "X" belong to the class of large and complex logistics systems.

The principal directions of integration of subsystems in a system of type "X" are as follows:

- Integration of databases and knowledge and the creation of a single data bank with distributed processing
- Technical integration and the creation of a heterogeneous local informational-computer network of AWPs and workstations
- Mathematical, algorithmic and software integration across hierarchy levels

The directions and levels of intellectualization in the system are:

- Intellectualization of AWPs of all levels
- Intellectualization of regulators based on active expert systems with a mixed knowledge base, including unclear
- Intellectualization of system software package interfaces
- Intellectualization of the tasks of designing, control and diagnosing PTC objects

The structure of the control system PTC. The structure of the factory management system undergoes appropriate changes, arising from the operational management criterion. OF as an object of management still remains three levels, with the corresponding spheres of management: organizational and economic activity, production in general, and technological processes.

To control PTC an integrated automated control system (ICS) should be used, the lower level of which is formed by ICS technological processes (ICSTP), the middle by an automated system of operational dispatch control (ASODC), economic and environmental management system of a factory (ASOE and EC). General management of technological processes, including monitoring the operation of equipment, diagnosing its condition, alarm, start, stop, etc. functions are carried out by intelligent control systems (ISC), which are the top level of the hierarchy in relation to local automatic control systems (ACS). ISCs use the experience and intuition of specialists in the management of processes (complexes) that are formed in the knowledge base. Thereby, operators of low qualification can manage the processes at the top level. As experience accumulates, the knowledge base can be updated and adjusted. The technical base of the ISCs are various PCs (or workstations). All the automated workplaces and stations (AWP) are integrated into a local computational network (LCN). The AWP of the factory dispatcher is connected to the same network, carrying out general production management and coordination of the functioning of individual areas and industries. ISC makes technological processes management and decision making with fuzzy information about their condition possible. For each process, the ISCs take the role of a hybrid regulator. Such control systems are effective at any level of processes equipment with automatization.

In the vast majority of cases, technological processes (TP) PTC are equipped with automatic regulators of particular simple functions, and the quality of final products depends on several mode parameters. In such cases, the decision maker plays the role of a quality regulator, using local ACS to achieve the control goal, acting on the setters. In case of absence of local ACS, control actions are carried out by the operators of the corresponding processes. If more advanced systems for automatic control of the quality of final products function, the role of the decision maker (DM) is to monitor the work of ACS and equipment, and to intervene if the conditions for the normal functioning of the equipment are violated or fail. The dispatcher of PTC controls the production in real time through the operational staff of the factory and partly directly routes and launches lines of technological equipment (for example, a flow-transport system). All AWPs of the organizational and economic management subsystem are integrated into a local computer network, which forms a common computational network of the factory with LCNs of the lower and middle levels. The environmental monitoring subsystem, which performs the functions of controlling pollution of the atmosphere, water and soil, takes into account harmful emissions that are to be controlled by environmental authorities, forms a database on environmental issues, automates the preparation of documents of statistical reporting, monitors the implementation of the action plan for improving technology and improving environmental safety is one of the main subsystems in here.

10.2.2 Integrated system for monitoring, modeling and control of PTC

Functional structure of the upper level ICS PTC. The structure of the automated system of organizational and economic management is formed by the AWPs of the director, chief engineer, economist, accounting service, chief mechanic, chief energy engineer, human resources department, marketer, ecologist and ICS service. The main characteristics of AWPs are given in (Ramazanov 2014, 2008).

The concept of creation and the structure of the local system of environmental and economic monitoring (SEEM) PTC. The generalized structural diagram of the synthesized

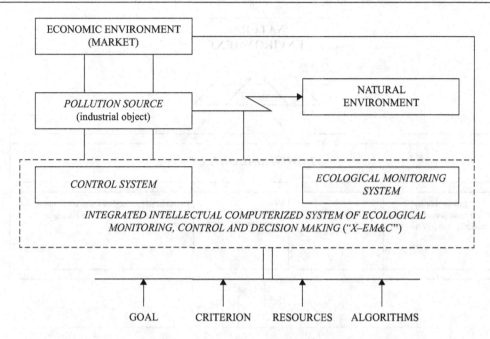

Figure 10.1 Generalized block diagram of the pollution source control system

system of environmental–ecological management of industrial pollution sites of OPS is shown in Figure 10.1.

The system includes subsystems for automation of accounting, planning, management, monitoring, control and diagnosis, as well as the design of coal processing technology objects.

An integrated environmental and economic management system for an industrial facility presented as an integrated system (Figure 10.2).

It includes an integrated subsystem of management and PR support, which is based on environmental monitoring, management with elements as environmental marketing and environmental audit.

10.3 INTELLIGENT MANAGEMENT IN ICS PTC IN MIXED UNCERTAINTY

10.3.1 The structure of the environmental management system in conditions of mixed information uncertainty

The degree of complexity of the management and decision-making system depends on the level of information certainty, and its quality is higher when accounting for mixed information uncertainty: stochastic (I_s), multiple (I_M) and fuzzy (I_f).

Let the structure of the environmental management system in the case of mixed information uncertainty in the form of Figure 10.3.

Here, as membership functions $\mu_{X_0}, \mu_{V_0}, \mu_{G^*}$ and others, functions with the properties of "Gaussianity" are accepted, i.e., functions of the form:

$$\mu_\Omega(\omega) = \exp(-\omega^T R \omega), \mu_\Omega(0) = 1, \lim_{\|\omega\|\to 0} \mu_\Omega(\omega) = 0$$

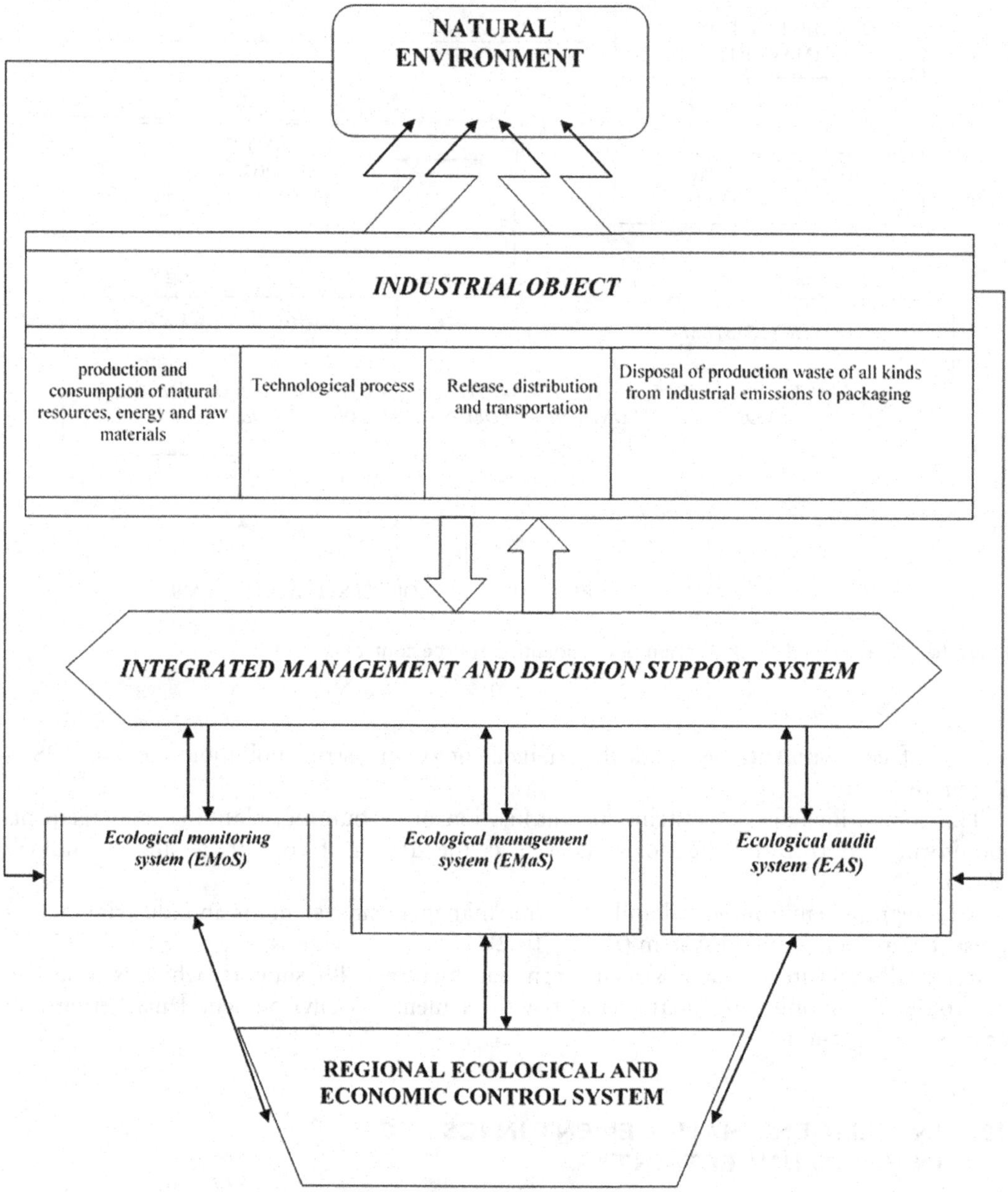

Figure 10.2 Integrated environmental and economic management system for an industrial facility

Then the TP (OU) model can be represented as F0: U x W ---> X, measuring channels in the form:

$$F\{C1\}: X \times V_X \to Y, \quad F\{C2\}: C \times V_C \to \tilde{C},$$

where X is the space of states, Y is the space of output TP variables, U is the set of all admissible controls, $C, \tilde{C}$ are the sets of pollutions and their measurements, respectively, W, V_x, V_c are the corresponding sets of disturbances and interference of measurements,

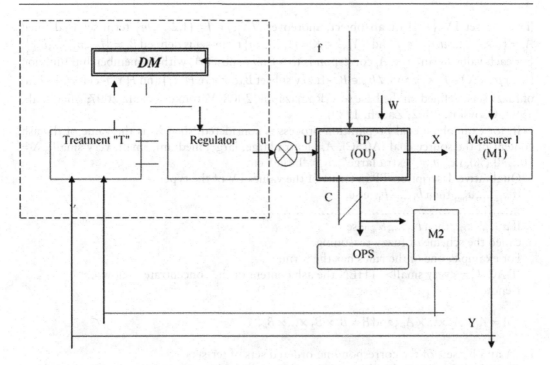

Figure 10.3 The structure of the environmental management system in mixed information uncertainty

and here $I_c = \{p(w), p(v_x), p(v_c)\}$ - is the information field of stochastic uncertainty; - $I_u = \{w \in W, v_x \in V_x, v_c \in V_c\}$ - information field of multiple uncertainty;

$I, = \{\mu_{X_0}, \mu_{V_0}, \mu_{G^*}\}$ - fuzzy information field. Mixed informational uncertainty can now be described as a tuple: $I_0 =\rangle I_C, I_M, I_H \langle$. Moreover, a single database and knowledge of ICS OF consists of combining 3 databases (B0, B1, B2) of all levels of the hierarchy $I =\rangle B_0, B_1, B_2 \langle$, taking into account possible information uncertainty.

Note that in Figure 10.3 $g \in G^*, G^*$ - the set of possible and fuzzy tasks, $X \supset X_0$ - the fuzzy set of the target, $U \supset U_0$ - the fuzzy set of restrictions on the control vector, and $C \subset \bar{C}$ - the set of MPE parameters.

Thus, in conditions of mixed uncertainty, the task of environmental management and decision-making is reduced to solving the following optimality problem:

$$u = \arg\max M_w \left\{ \mu_d(x, w) \right\} = \arg\max_{u \in U} M_w \left\{ \mu_{X_0} \left(F0(u, w) \right) * \mu_{V_0}(u) * \mu_{G^*}(g) \right\} \text{ for } C \in \bar{C}.$$

Here M_w is the symbol of mathematical expectation (for average), and * is the symbol of composition (merging).

In Figure 10.3 also accepted designations: $U = \left[u, r + \varepsilon_{\cdot, p} \right]$ - the decision, made by the DM, where r is the refinement of the control u, $\varepsilon_{\cdot, p}$ is the error of the DM; $\hat{x}$ and $\hat{C} \in \hat{\bar{C}}$ - estimates obtained after processing "T", f - controlled DM effect on TP.

This paragraph considers the most appropriate options for environmental modeling and TP management in a fuzzy information environment.

Logical and linguistic description. Consider a description of the functioning of a complex object (a technological process of hardware and PTC) in a fuzzy environment.

Let there be sets of informative input parameters $X = \{X_1, X_2, ..., X_m\}$ (i.e., the set of input linguistic variables (LV) $\{X_j\}$) and sets of input parameters $Y = \{Y_1, Y_2, ..., Y_n\}$

(i.e., the set LV $\{Y_k\}$) of an object, moreover $\forall X_j, j \in J = (1,2,...,m)$ term-set is defined $A_j = \{a_{1j}, a_{2j},...,a_{pj}\}, j \in J$ and $\forall Y_k, k \in K = (1,2,...,n)$ term-set is defined $B_k = \{b_{1k}, b_{2k},...,b_{qk}\}$. For each value (term) $a_{ij} \in A_j$ corresponds to a fuzzy subset $\tilde{A}_{ij}$ with its membership function (MF) $\mu_{\tilde{A}_{ij}}(X) \in F(X_j)$, and $\forall b_{ik} \in B_k$ - fuzzy subset $\tilde{B}_{ik}$, where $F(X_j)$ and $F(Y_k)$- class (algebra) of fuzzy sets, defined on the base sets (Ramazanov, 2008; Voronkova et al., 2007; Aliev et al., 1990; Osovskiy, 2002; Zadeh, 1989).

If, for example, a coal preparation process is considered, then X_j is the value of the ash content of the source coal (ACSC), A_j= {extra large, large, medium, small, very small}, X_j= 10...90 (%), i.e., a_{1j}= "extra large", a_{2j}= "large" etc.

Qualitative description TP in terms of the values LV of the type:
If $a_{11},...,a_{1m}$, then $b_{11},...,b_{1n}$ else,

....

If $a_{p1},...,a_{pm}$, then $b_{q1},...,b_{qn}$ else
called the scheme of fuzzy reasoning.
For example, one of the rules has the form:
IF ACSC = <very small>, THEN the ash content of the concentrate = <low>.
Denote by

$$A = A_1 \times A_2 \times ... \times A_m, \text{and } B = B_1 \times B_2 \times ... \times B_n,$$

i.e. A and B - sets of the corresponding ordered sets of ter-sets.
Then the behavior of the object (TP) is characterized by function $F : A \to B$ (in terms of term-sets), or some function

$$\tilde{F} : F(X_1 \times X_2 \times ... \times X_m) \to F(Y_1 \times ... \times Y_n),$$

which can be obtained as a fuzzy match for all

$$\mu_{\tilde{A}_{ij}}(X) \in F(X_j), \mu_{\tilde{B}_{ik}}(Y) \in F(Y_k), \tilde{F} : \bigcup_{i \in I}\left(\mu_{\tilde{A}_i} \times \mu_{\tilde{B}_i}\right),$$

where $\mu_{\tilde{A}_i} = \underset{j \in J}{X} \mu_{\tilde{A}_{ij}}, \mu_{\tilde{B}_i} = \underset{k \in K}{X} \mu_{\tilde{B}_{ik}}$.

If we now define a fuzzy ratio: $R = \{\mu_R(x,y) | (x,y) \in X \times Y\}$, then, to determine certain output parameter of the TP B_i, it is necessary to determine the composition of the fuzzy subset A_i, that affects the input of the TP, and the ratio R, i.e.,

$$\mu_{\tilde{B}_i}(Y) = \mu_{\tilde{A}_i}(X) \circ R(X,Y).$$

For example, in terms of "AND-OR" we get

$$\mu_{\tilde{B}_i}(Y) = \underset{x \in X}{V}\left\{\mu_{\tilde{A}_i}(X) \wedge \mu_R(X,Y)\right\} = \underset{x \in X}{\max}\min\left\{\mu_{\tilde{A}_i}(X), \mu_R(X,Y)\right\}$$

This is the fuzzy inference algorithm in this case.
The general algorithm of fuzzy modeling. The fuzzy process modeling algorithm can be represented as:

1. The allocation of the main technological (system) parameters: input (x), control (u), output (y), disturbing (w).

2. Definition (formation) of linguistic variables (LV), i.e. their names, term-sets and carriers of fuzzy sets (FS) corresponding to terms, as well as their universal sets for the main technological parameters.

3. Formation of the rule base: $(j) \underbrace{IF\, A = T_i^A}_{antec_i}$, THEN $\underbrace{B = T_k^B}_{conveg_k}$ where j - is the number of products, and each product can be assigned a tuple (j, DT, <author>, <date>, <explanation>), where DT is the degree of truth of the rule: DT $\in$ [0,1]; <author> - expert identifier - the author of the rule; <date> - the date the rule was entered in the BM; <explanation> - text of the author's explanation of the rule.

    Note that $antec_i \underset{=}{\Delta} A_{i1} \wedge A_{i2} \wedge ... \wedge A_{ip}$, $conveg_k \underset{=}{\Delta} B_{k1} \wedge B_{k2} \wedge ... \wedge B_{kq}$.

4. The formation of a matrix of fuzzy relationships:

$$R_s = \int\limits_{A \times B} \mu_{R_s}(a,b) | (a,b), \quad S = \overline{1, n}$$

5. Combining these matrices: $R = \bigcup\limits_{S=1}^{n} R_s$, where $\mu_R(a,b) = \max(\mu_{R_1}, ..., \mu_{R_n})$.

6. Organization of logical conclusion (LC) according to a certain scheme, for example, according to the modus ponens rule, i.e., the compositional rule of L. Zadeh (Osovskiy, 2002; Zadeh, 1989).

Note that, although there are other composition rules (Aliev et al., 1990; Osovskiy, 2002; Zadeh, 1989), this option is the most convenient to use and implement.

Intelligent management system. Objects and processes in coal preparation technologies relate to complex production and transportation systems, which are characterized by instability, nonlinearity, multiconnectedness, significant delay in flows and uncertainty in the context of various decisions.

10.4 PHASE-NEURAL SYSTEMS OF HYBRID CONTROL OF A MULTIDIMENSIONAL INDUSTRIAL AND ECONOMIC OBJECT

In the process of managing complex industrial facilities, the decision maker in most cases is based on his perception of possible and random information and its expression through linguistic concepts and discourse. Such information is poorly structured in practice, and is of a qualitative and nonnumerical nature, which leads to its fuzziness. The theory of possibilities and fuzzy sets enables the representation and control of fuzzy information in a quantitative meaning, which makes it possible to create fuzzy active expert systems (Osovskiy, 2002). On the other hand, the practical application of neural networks shows that they also have a feature of fuzziness, mainly due to their distribution. This leads to the need of hybrid intelligent control systems development, i.e. fuzzy self-learning control systems based on neuromodelling (Figure 10.4).

Knowledge in the neural network is represented as a distributed system with weighting factors between the blocks and nodes of the network as complexes of the form: "Learning + Calculations + Processing". Processing knowledge implies the insurance of the same behavior of the neuro system under equal external conditions and influences. This property of systems is an important feature for many applications, in particular for active expert systems.

To develop an algorithm for deriving a solution for any new situations, not described in the database: So, let there be a set of L rules of the form: RULE[1] ALSO RULE[2]......ALSO RULE[L], where RULE[J] has the form: IF X_1 is A_1^j and X_2 is A_2^j and ... and X_n is A_n^j THEN Y_1 is B_1^j and Y_2 is B_1^j... and Y_m is B_m^j. Here $X_1, X_2, ..., X_n$ are the input linguistic variables

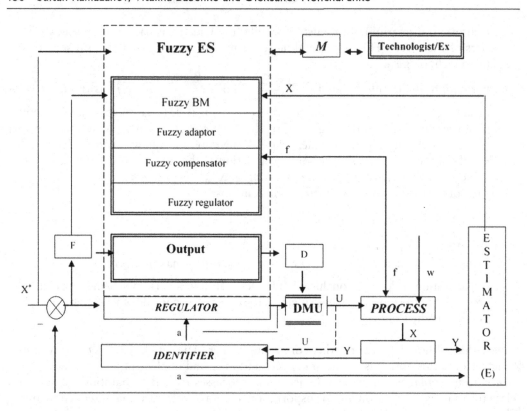

Figure 10.4 Block diagram of a hybrid intelligent controller

in the part of IF, i.e., variables that take values from universal sets $U_i=(U_{i1}, U_{I2}, ..., U_{in})$, and $Y_1, Y_2....Y_m$ - output linguistic variables in THEN part, i.e., variables that take values from universal sets $V_k=(V_{k1}, V_{k2},...,V_{km})$. The input data is given in the form: X_1 is C_1, AND X_2 is C_2, ..., X_n is C_n, and the output as: Y_1 is D_1, AND Y_2 is D_2, ..., И Y_m is D_m, where A_j^j, C_i, B_k^j, D_k are fuzzy subsets that are defined in accordance with universal sets and represent some terms of the type: high, low, normal, medium, etc. For solving this problem, as a quantitative measure of the estimation of the output, let's apply membership functions of the form:

$$A_i^j (U_i): U_i \to [0, 1], C_i (U_i): U_i \to [0,1], B_k^j(V_{k)} : V_k \to [0,1], D_k (V_k): V_k \to [0, 1]$$

The output mechanism is obtained in the form of: determining the measure of possibility β_i^j for each i on the right side of IF; definition of the general measure $\beta^j=\Lambda_1^n \beta_i^j$; definition of the composition $\beta^j \phi\beta^j (v)= \beta^j \Lambda \beta^j (v)$.

If more than one rule is used in the derivation of the solution, but with different β^j (i.e., all the rules satisfy the condition $\beta > \beta_o$), then they can be combined by using the operator.

Thus, the general equation of the approximate output mechanism is obtained in the following form: $D^j(v)= \bigcup\limits_{k=1}^{K} \left\{ [\bigcap\limits_{i=1}^{n} \beta_i^k] \cap \beta^k (v) \right\}$, where K is the total number of rules used in decision making under the condition $\beta > \beta_o$. Here β_o is the threshold value set by the expert when choosing dominant rules.

The proposed version of the output mechanism uses a multilayer neural network, namely the BNN (Back-propagation Neural Network) network.

Answered the following questions, related to the use of the BNN neural network: How many layers are sufficient for the network used? How many processing nodes are needed for

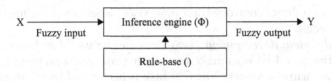

Figure 10.5 A simplified diagram of a fuzzy system

each hidden (internal) network layer? How much and what information is required when implementing a mapping (input–output model) in a neural network for an approximate output mechanism? The results obtained in this work can be used in a process control system for coal preparation, metallurgy, cement production, etc.

Knowledge Engineering in Management. In the design of fuzzy control systems and their realization of the procedure of representation of knowledge, reasoning and the acquisition of knowledge play a fundamental role. Since we use a rule-based model, that is, a production structure, the release of the knowledge representation has a definite meaning on how linguistic rules can be represented numerically using fuzzy subsets and fuzzy correlation, or fuzzy implication. There are two approaches for creating a rule base in fuzzy systems: 1) A set of rules, extracted from an experienced expert, can be expressed as a set of linguistic rules with the form IF <Condition> THEN <Action>, that links the measured variables to control the variable; 2) The synthesis of the rule base, based on the recognition algorithm, directly using a controlled (investigated) process.

Two types of fuzzy systems. A fuzzy system can represent itself as an element of active control or as a function of approximation (for modeling the process).

For the first: let it assume that for a certain system the set of inputs X and the output Y are known, the rule base is obtained from an accessible source containing a set of rules connecting X with Y using predefined linguistic notation. The fuzzy system at the linguistic level can be installed as shown in Figure 10.5.

For X_0, $Y_0 = \Phi (\Psi_{x}^{y}, X)$. The mechanism works as follows: the output process, at first, performs the correspondence procedures between X <condition> and IF parts of the rules; performs the corresponding "THEN" action, based on the result of compliance with the THEN parts of the rules using a fuzzy output strategy. To execute a fuzzy system in computational form, one of the algorithms has to create a correlation matrix from the available rule base, and the reaction at the output Y is calculated by the equation of the relation Y = XoR, where o - logical operator that performs the composition of the output.

The second execution of a fuzzy system is as a function of approximation, i.e., process modeling. At the same time, the system interacts with the environment through two procedures, namely: phasification (FZ), dephasing (DF) (Figure 10.6).

In Figure 10.6 Y = F (X), y = f (x), x ∈ $\bar{X}$ in y ∈ $\bar{Y}$.

With this system model, we can represent a known or unknown function, linear or non-linear (which is very important). The execution of a fuzzy algorithm in an active control

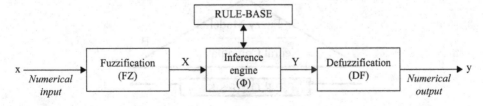

Figure 10.6 Phasing–dephasing procedure

system can be either a direct controller or a supervisor, where the function of a fuzzy system is in a low level circuit.

Hybrid control system development. Two ideas can be used for develop of a fuzzy neural control structure: the first is to make the existing fuzzy system neural, the second is to "blur" the existing neural network. The first task is performed by mapping a fuzzy system into neural networks, functionally or structurally.

As usual, the following management issues arise: process specified for management may be uncertain and obscure; the ability to allow a description, for example, by a reference model, a mathematical function of value, an index table, or fuzzy goals; specifying a set of limiting conditions imposed by the characteristics of the physical system; using existing knowledge about the process and technologies, create a controller so that the centralized control system behaves as expected, provided that these characteristics are satisfied and maintained.

The solution to the problem above using a fuzzy neural approach is formulated as follows: for a given process (object) P, a set of restrictions Q and a goal R, select the structure of the controller S and the computational algorithm T, using the previous knowledge of U and learning algorithms V to create S so as to achieve R under condition Q, i.e., for the control problem (P, Q, R), our task is to create (S, T) using (U, V). By fuzzy neural control, we usually mean the following: a controller has a structure resulting from a combination of a fuzzy system and neural networks; the final control system consists of a fuzzy system and a neural network as independent components that perform various tasks, and hybrid design methodologies for constructing appropriate controllers, derived from the ideas of fuzzy and neural control. The decision output process can be competing (alternative) or combining, depending on the corresponding reasoning algorithm. After defining the structure of a fuzzy neural system with an appropriate computational algorithm, attention must be paid to the role of this system in solving the control problem. To represent knowledge and its acquisition, we use a back propagation neural network (BNN), the implementation of the approximation algorithm of which is described in Figure 10.7, and an anti-proliferation network (CPN), which simplifies the fuzzy control algorithm and is presented in Figure 10.8.

When a fuzzy system and a neural network are considered as two different computing elements, they can be configured at the system level in a hierarchical way: a fuzzy system will be a supervisor or a neural network; a low-level controller is directly controlled

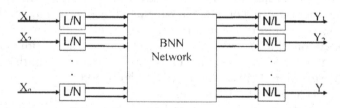

Figure 10.7 Backward propagation NN scheme

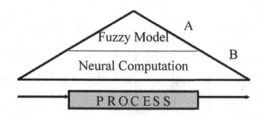

Figure 10.8 The simplified structure of mixed management

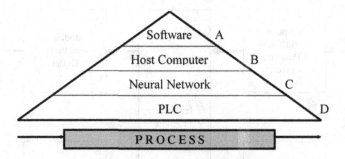

Figure 10.9 Hierarchical system with distributed control functions

by an industrial facility. The second level is the process variable controller itself. [Neural Networks + Programmable Logic Controller (PLC)] (Figure 10.9).

The second type of integration between neural networks and a fuzzy system is in the sub-level, selecting one to the other functionally or structurally.

As a result of the merger and integration of a fuzzy system with neural networks, we get a fuzzy neural system, which may be called the "Hybrid Control System." Hybridization is caused by the fact that, on the one hand, diffuse systems deal with qualitative information, and, on the other hand, neural networks deal with quantitative (numerical) information. The main idea and advantage of implementing such a system is that a fuzzy system has tremendous potential in representing linguistic and structured knowledge using fuzzy sets and performing fuzzy reasoning in fuzzy logic in a qualitative way (using the experience of experts in the problem domain); on the other hand, neural networks are especially suitable for representing nonlinear mappings in a computational way; they are created by themselves mainly through sampling learning algorithms.

Obviously, it is easy to comprehend the behavior of fuzzy systems due to their logical structure and step-by-step input/output procedures; neural networks usually act as a black box. The basic configuration structure of a hierarchical system with distributed logical functions of measurement, regulation and control is shown in Figure 10.9. In Figure 10.9 A + B is supervisor level, and C + D is control level.

Dispatch control consists of collecting and storing information about the values of the parameters of the controlled process and alarms, and evaluating performance, operating time and other statistics, etc. The dialogue procedure and reporting procedure for each con-trolled process variable in an analog or digital form is called a "point," and for each point there is a so-called "point technological map." The set of technological maps of the point corresponding to all adjustable process variables at any time contains complete information about the operational state of the process (Figure 10.10).

Therefore, the functional structure and algorithm of the blurry neural system (hybrid) for real-time control of a multidimensional industrial facility was developed. Such a system can be used, for example, in a process control automation system in a production system, i.e., PINT.

10.5 INTELLIGENT MANAGEMENT AND DECISION SUPPORT SYSTEM DIAGNOSTICS OF THE CRISIS STATE OF AN INDUSTRIAL FACILITY

Industrial facilities belong to the class of complex production and economic systems (PES), which in the process of their purposeful or predetermined functioning are dynamic and are subject to influences of both controlled and uncontrolled causes, i.e., the state of PES

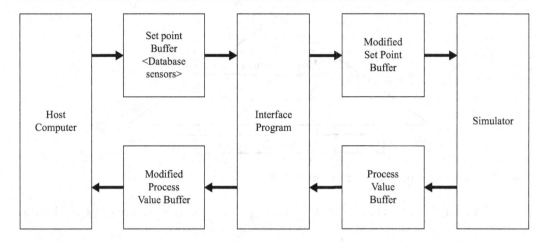

Figure 10.10 General management scheme

undergoes certain changes over time. Therefore, it is necessary to organize monitoring and diagnostics in order to give PES normal (desired) functioning, taking into account economic and environmental parameters. Issues of organizing diagnostic procedures, building object models, developing algorithms and designing specific automated diagnostic systems are widely known in foreign and domestic literature (Ramazanov, 2008; Voronkova et al., 2007; Aliev et al., 1990; Osovskiy, 2002; Zadeh, 1989). Note that the diagnosis of PES is associated with significant difficulties due to a number of features. Due to the need for diagnostic procedures directly during the operation of PES, methods of functional diagnosis are more often used. Significant difficulty in the implementation of diagnostic procedures is the inertia of many connections (relationships). The complex functional connection of the parameters is manifested in the fact that a change in the value of a parameter can be caused by a number of reasons.

A significant role in this is also played by management errors due to both the difficulties of providing continuous monitoring of the state of PES and the need to store, collect and process in real time a large amount of information, while taking into account many different factors for diagnosis, which often exceeds the capabilities of the operator dispatcher. Analysis of such features of the process of diagnosing complex technical and economic systems, such as: many alternatives for interpreting events; the need for joint consideration of many events; the formation of algorithms for recognizing the root cause of a violation more often as a set of rules than as a control system as well as the need to use heuristic methods for identifying the most probable solutions and their areas of existence, indicates the possibility of increasing the efficiency of diagnostic procedures when using the methods of the theory of artificial intelligence.

Thus, based on the foregoing, we can conclude that it is necessary to create hybrid (integrated) intelligent computer systems (HICS) for diagnostics of PES, combining the properties of traditional systems using "hard" models and algorithms, and such signs of intelligent systems (systems, based on knowledge), such as the presence of a knowledge base (KB), a friendly interface, output, self-learning. Moreover, the greatest effect can be obtained by integrating these two approaches into a single system (Ramazanov, 2008). In the process of diagnosing the technological state of PES in environmental monitoring, the procedure for finding the causes of violations in sets of uncontrolled disturbances that differ in the presence of uncertainties is advisable to implement using artificial intelligence methods. The lack of sufficient statistical data for establishing objective relationships between the values of signs and probabilistic diagnoses leads to a heuristic description of these relationships.

Problem formulation. In general, the model of the diagnostic object and information transmission channels can be represented in the form of the following operator equations:

$$F(x,u,w,a,t) = 0 \,, y(t) = G(x,u,\xi_0,v,b,t)\,, \tag{10.1}$$

where $x \in R^n$ is state vector; $u \in R^r$ - control vector; $y \in R^m$ - vector of output variables; w,v - vectors of perturbations and interference (included in equation (10.1) both additively and multiplicatively) (Ramazanov, 2008); a,b - vectors of undefined parameters, $\dot{a}(t) = 0$ and $\dot{b}(t) = 0$ and; F,G - some given operators (differential, both ordinary and partial derivatives, integral, integro-differential, matrix, etc.).

In particular, as (10.1), stochastic differential equations (linear or non-inear, continuous or discrete), partial differential equations can be used, for example, for taking into account the territorial location of production facilities.

Practically feasible models for processing and identification are:

$$\dot{x}(t) = A(t,\theta)x + B(t,\theta)u + W(t), \, y(t) = C(t,\theta)x + V(t)\,, \tag{10.2}$$

or, in the discrete case $y(k+1) = H(k)x(k) + V(k)$,

$$x(k+1) = \Phi(k+1,k,\theta)x + \Psi(k+1,k)u(k) + W(k)\,. \tag{10.3}$$

The control condition (scheme) of diagnosis is usually a ratio of the type:

$$\mu(E(t)) < \delta\,, \tag{10.4}$$

where $\mu(\cdot)$ - given metric, for instance, the Euclidean norm; δ - allowable threshold value that is set; $E(t)$ - discrepancy (deviation) of either the output from the norm, or the assessment of the state from the standard, or the estimation of parameters from the nominal, or the characteristics of the estimates from the possible (for example, covariance of the updating processes in the Kalman filter), etc.

For example, $E(t) = \Phi(y^T, q^{-1}y^T, ..., q^{-k}y^T, u^T, q^{-1}u^T, ..., q^{-k}u^T)$ where Φ is operator, and k - order of the control circuit, which must be determined (a priori).

Then the condition for the absence of defects will be of the form: $E(t) = 0, t = 0,1,2,...,$ and condition (4) can be rewritten as follows: $\|E(t)\| \le \delta$.

Attention should be paid to the fact that the task can be solved both in the case of deterministic, which is rare, and in conditions of stochastic and multiple uncertainty.

Intellectualization and integration of a diagnostic system. As noted in the introduction, to improve the efficiency and quality of diagnosing complex technical systems, which include PES, it is necessary to create intelligent and integrated computer systems based on both traditional methods and new information technologies.

Formulation of a problem of diagnosis in the conditions of fuzzy information. Let $X_1,...,X_n$ be a series of signs, based on specific values of which judgments are made about the subjective probability of diagnoses from a predetermined series of diagnoses $D_1,...,D_k$. Each of X_i, $i = \overline{1,n}$ takes a value from the set $X = \{x_{i1},...,x_{im_i},...,x_{ip_i}\}$. At the moment t, the state of the object is described by a feature vector:

$$X(t) = \left[X_1(t),...,X_n(t) \mid X_i(t) = X_{im_i} \right]^T, \, m_i = \overline{1,p_i}\,, \tag{10.5}$$

where $X_i(t)$ is the implementation of the feature X_i at the current moment t.

It is required to determine an estimate of the probability (possibility degree) of diagnoses $P_{\permil}(j)$:

$$\forall j = \overline{1,k} : m_{\permil}(j) = m_{\permil}\left(D_j / X(t)\right), \tag{10.6}$$

where $P_{\permil}$ is the symbol of subjective probability.

Forms of representation of expert knowledge in the system. To solve this problem, an important issue is the way of presenting expert knowledge.

The first way. Expert knowledge is presented in the form of the following system of rules:

$$\forall i = \overline{1,n}, \forall j = \overline{1,k} : X_1 = x_{1m_i},\dots,X_n = x_{nm_i} \Rightarrow$$
$$\Rightarrow P_{\permil}\left(D_j \mid X(t)\right) = P_{\permil s}\left(D_j \mid \left(x_{1m_1},\dots,x_{nm_n}\right)\right) \tag{10.7}$$

where x_{im_i} is a specific value X_i from the set $\left\{x_{im_i}\right\}, m_i = \overline{1,p_i}, p_i = card\left\{x_{im_i}\right\}; P_{\permil s}$ - s-th value of the probability estimate from the set of possible values $\{P_{\permil s}\}, P_{\permil s}$ [0,1], $s = \overline{1,m}$.

The second way. The second possible type of presentation of expert knowledge is a system of rules described under the same notation as follows:

$$\forall i, \forall j, \forall m_i : x_i = x_{im_i} \Rightarrow P_{\permil}\left(D_j \mid X_i\right) = P_{\permil s}\left(D_j \mid x_{im_i}\right). \tag{10.8}$$

Both methods of presenting expert knowledge considered have different properties, and the processing algorithms for these forms of information are also different.

Linguistic way. The most convenient form for the expert to represent knowledge of an implicative form is linguistic, which is the most familiar for a person. In this case, the expert operates with fuzzy categories, such as:

"If the value X_i is very large, then the probability D_j is small." Therefore, a linguistic approach based on the theory of fuzzy sets by L. Zadeh can be applied to the compilation of a model of fuzzy information (Osovskiy, 2002; Zadeh, 1989).

In the fuzzy diagnostic algorithm, signs $\{X_i\}$ and probabilities $P_{\permil}$ are represented by linguistic variables (LP) defined by tuples:

$$\rangle X_i,T_i,V_i,G_i,M_i\langle, i = \overline{1,n} \tag{10.9}$$

$$\rangle P_{\permil},P,U,S,Q\langle, \tag{10.10}$$

where $X_i,P_{\permil}$ - name of the respective LV; T_i,P- term-sets of variables X_i and $P_{\permil}$ accordingly, i.e., the sets of their linguistic meanings, representing the fuzzy variables names (NV): $A_{if_i}\left(f_i = \overline{1,p_i} / p_i = cardT_i\right)$ and $B_r\left(r = \overline{1,m} / m = card\,P\right)$ with values from universal sets V_i and U; G_i,S- syntactic rules generating the names A_{if_i} and B_r values of variables X_i and $P_{\permil}$; M_i,Q- semantic rules that make it possible to turn each new meaning of LV into a VN, VN A_{if_i} and B_r, in turn, are representable in the form of corresponding tuples:

$$\rangle A_{if_i},V_i,\tilde{C}_{if_i}\langle, i = \overline{1,n}, \tag{10.11}$$

$$\rangle B_r,U,\tilde{E}_r\langle, r = \overline{1,m}, \tag{10.12}$$

where, A_{if_i}, B_r – names of VN; V_i and U are the same as above;

$$\tilde{C}_{if_i} = \bigcup_{v \in V_i} \mu_{\tilde{C}}(V) / V \text{ and } \tilde{E}_r = \bigcup_{u \in U} \mu_{\tilde{E}}(U) / U$$

- fuzzy subsets (FS) of the sets V_i and U, that describe the restrictions on the possible values A_{if_i} and B_r of VN; $\mu_{\tilde{C}}(\cdot)$ and $\mu_{\tilde{E}}(\cdot)$ - membership functions (MF) for $\tilde{C}_{if_i}$ and $\tilde{E}_r$. For example, for a certain block of PES diagnostic signs $\{X_1, X_2, X_3, X_4, X_5\}$ are associated with following LV:

$\rangle X_1, T_1, [\,\cdot\,,\cdot\,], G_1, M_1 \langle;$

$\rangle X_2, T_2, [\,\cdot\,,\cdot\,], G_2, M_2 \langle;$

....

$\rangle X_5, T_5, [\,\cdot\,,\cdot\,], G_5, M_5 \langle;$

where term-sets $T_1 = ... = T_5 =$ {increased slightly, increased, increased slightly, decreased slightly, decreased, decreased much, did not change}.

Probability estimation is presented by the same named LV $P_{\%0}$, and the term-set P consists of the following linguistic values of the variable: B_1- excluded, B_2- almost improbable, B_3 - very improbable, B_4- lowly probable, ..., B_m - absolutely accurate.

The question of constructing MF for $\tilde{C}_{if_i}$ and $\tilde{E}_r$ can be solved using the recommendations presented in (Aliev et al., 1990; Osovskiy, 2002).

Therefore, expressions (10.7) and (10.8), according to the notation (10.9) - (10.12), can generally be written as follows:

$$\forall i, \forall j : \text{IF } X_1 \text{ IS } A_{1f_1}, ..., X_n \text{ IS } A_{nf_n},$$

$$\text{THEN } P_{\%0}\left(D_j / (X_1, ..., X_n)\right) \text{IS } B_r \tag{10.13}$$

$$\forall i, \forall j, \forall f_i : \text{IF } X_i \text{ IS } A_{if_i}, \text{THEN } P_{\%0}\left(D_j / X_i\right) \text{IS } B_r \tag{10.14}$$

Note that the presentation of information in a model of type (10.14) requires further additional procedure of obtaining, for each diagnosis, a comprehensive probability estimation $P_{\%0}\left(D_j / (X_1, ..., X_n)\right)$ by generalizing, according to a certain rule, independent estimates $P_{\%0}\left(D_j / X_i\right)$, obtained by individual criteria.

Model (10.13) does not have this drawback, but has a larger dimension. Rules of the type (10.13) can also be represented as:

IF X_i IS A_{if_i}, THEN D_j with probability B_r.

Therefore, the fuzzy production model (fuzzy knowledge base) consists of diagnostic rules ("dispatcher-expert"):

IF X_i IS A_{if_i}, AND

IF X_2 IS A_{2f_2}, AND

....

IF X_n IS A_{nf_n}, THEN D_j with probability B_r

Based on a set of rules, a matrix of fuzzy relations is constructed:

$$X_i R D_j \text{ or } R = \bigcup_{x \in X \in D} \mu_R(x, d) / (x, d).$$

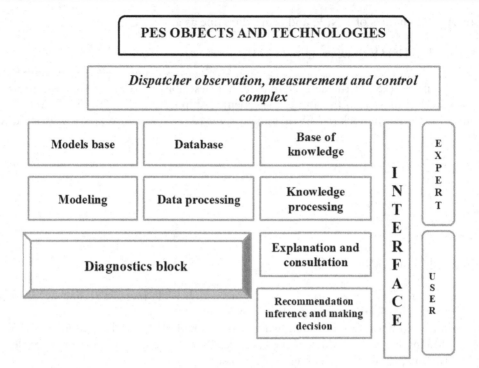

Figure 10.11 Hybrid system for diagnosis of the state of PES

The general structural diagram of the system of functional diagnostics of PES can now be represented in the form (Figure 10.11).

Software realization of formation of databases and knowledge of the diagnostic system PES. A program has been developed for an interactive mode of operation (i.e., an expert system) with interface menu system that includes items: "Knowledge Base," "Database," "Modeling," "Expert," "Service," "Exit." Each of the items has an additional pop-up menu. The items in the "Knowledge Base" pop-up menu are: "Description of components," "Description of connections," "Description of inputs," "Description of outputs," "Synthesis of filters," "Synthesis of frames," "Synthesis of representations," and "Synthesis of rules." This makes it possible to build a description of the system "Object - Diagnostic System" in the form of related databases, model databases and knowledge bases.

Therefore, the mathematical and software of an intelligent system for diagnosing a crisis state of PES is proposed.

10.6 INTELLIGENT SYSTEM OF MODELING AND CONTROL IN CONDITIONS OF ENVIRONMENTAL AND ECONOMIC RISK

10.6.1 Introduction

The problem of quick and accurate detection and assessment of the risk situation (RS) in the conditions of transformation of the economic structure of society, i.e., in the absence of amount of information required, informational unsteadiness, uncertainty and fuzziness, the problem has become quite relevant at the present stage, when the main environmental, economic, social and technological parameters are in the catastrophic zone. Important issues in this situation are classification, recognition and determination of the dynamics of RS.

The importance, versatility and applied prevalence of the recognition problem have led to the fact that a large number of decision rules have been created for decision-making in recognition problems in a wide variety of applied areas (Ustenko, 2019; Aliev et al., 1990; Osovskiy, 2002; Zadeh, 1989). However, many existing methods and approaches for which they were created were not suitable for solving other problems related to the high efficiency, adequacy and extremeness of solutions. Therefore, the modern theoretical level, the information–instrumental and technical base make it possible to develop and apply new and more advanced technologies in solving problems of identification and recognition of complex processes and objects. It is natural to use modern approaches and principles when creating new methods, namely, fuzziness and confusion of information and elements of intelligence; hybridization of information (a priori and a posteriori), models (formal and qualitative) and criteria/decision rules: linear, nonlinear, expert, hierarchical, etc.; self-organization (synergistic aspect); adaptability, learnability, speed and parallelism of the algorithm (neural network); the distribution of model parameters, etc.

Methods obtained in this way can naturally be called hybrid, and the process of creating them is called hybridization, similar to how nature uses viable biological species that have proved themselves successful, although under different conditions, for creation of biological species for new conditions.

Particular important issues that arise when solving the problem of creating intelligent modeling systems, and environmental and economic risk management (IMSRM) can be formulated as follows:

- Various modifications for the development and improvement of technologies for solving the problems of assessment (identification), recognition and management of environmental and economic risks (EER) based on modern theories (hybridization, intellectualization, self-organization, adaptability and training, etc.)
- Taking into account mixed multiplicatively additive random disturbances (noises) in dynamic system models and observation channels

Certain possible approaches in pattern recognition (objects, images, etc.) that are applicable in solving problems of economic and environmental monitoring of complex systems are considered below.

10.6.2 Fuzziness, information confusion and intellectualization of a solution

One of the development directions of automatic classification and pattern recognition methods in the last 20–30 years is associated with the use of the theory of fuzzy sets. As L. Zadeh (1989) notes, "the deep connection between the theory of fuzzy sets and pattern recognition is based on the fact that most real classes are naturally fuzzy in the sense that the transition from membership to non-membership for these classes is more rather than spasmodic." Using fuzzy classification algorithms makes it possible to take into account the complexity of the structure of classes of objects, non-statistical uncertainty of the objects' affiliation to certain types, the presence of objects of an "intermediate" nature.

When constructing probabilistic decision rules in the problem of pattern recognition, the goal is to restore the degrees of reliability of the affiliation of objects to classes. This task differs significantly from the task of blurry pattern recognition, despite their outward similarity. Indeed, the probabilistic formulation of the recognition problem is based on the assumption that each object belongs to the same class, the available information about the objects does not give grounds for unambiguously assigning them to one or another class.

Use of the probabilistic approach for constructing algorithms for recognizing blurry patterns does not seem appropriate, since each object here can belong (with varying degrees) to two or more fuzzy classes, and this fact is fundamental; it is not associated with a lack of a priori information about objects.

Currently, dozens of papers have already been published in which various approaches to the construction of classification algorithms are set out, with the aim of determining the degrees of belonging of objects to classes—fuzzy sets. However, recognition algorithms (classification with training) of blurry patterns are much less developed.

Analysis of numerous human–machine recognition systems for objects with a high degree of risk (such as industrial facilities with old and worn equipment, etc.) showed that classical models and methods have reached a certain limit in performance improvement. There is a well-known contradiction between the increase in the quality indicators of human-machine systems due to the complexity of their models and software and hardware basis and a decrease in fault tolerance. Intelligence degree increase of the control system of these objects can significantly overcome this contradiction.

In a pattern recognition system (PRS) and diagnosis, built using the methodology of artificial intelligence, the main core—the knowledge base (KB), the most convenient way to organize is based on a production model of knowledge with a construction type

« IF < sign>, THEN < result > »

The main requirements for intelligent PRS are: ability of online work; adaptability; quick adaptability to specific situations, compact implementation; ability to be embedded.

The most appropriate class of PRSs that meet the above requirements are PRSs, based on neural fuzzy networks (NFN) with a mixed base (Aliev et al., 1990; Osovskiy, 2002; Zadeh, 1989).

KB is implemented on the basis of neural networks (NN), so the construction of the desired knowledge base is equivalent to the task of determining the rational architecture and matrix of weights of the synthesized NN. Architecture of the developed NN is a three-layer feed-forward structure. The first layer includes input neurons (nodes), the middle is made of hidden neurons, and the last one is made of output nodes.

The input signals $y_j, j = \overline{1, n}$, when they appear at the input (synapses) of the j-th neuron, are converted to dendritic signals according to a nonlinear function $f\left(w_{ji}, y_i\right)$. Here w_{ji} are synapse weight coefficients. The resulting signal is obtained as a result of a combination (in particular, summation) in the neuron body of all dendrite signals according to a nonlinear function $u_j\left(f_{ji}\right)$, $i = \overline{1, n}$. This signal enters through the axons to the inputs of other nodes.

Synthesis of PRS based on NN is as follows. Let there be a set of production rules that describes the reference behavior of the synthesized PRS in the form:

$$
\left.
\begin{aligned}
&IF \quad g = g_1 \quad and \quad x = x_1 \quad THEN \quad \dot{x} = \dot{x}_1, \\
&IF \quad g = g_2 \quad and \quad x = x_2 \quad THEN \quad \dot{x} = \dot{x}_2, \\
&\text{...} \\
&IF \quad g = g_n \quad and \quad x = x_n \quad THEN \quad \dot{x} = \dot{x}_n
\end{aligned}
\right\}
\tag{10.15}
$$

Reference model of pattern (recognition object) is $\dot{x}_m = h\left(x_m, g_m\right)$.

Representation of this knowledge in the KB of the developed PRS lies in learning NN, i.e., for learning NN, a mismatch (error) is used between the outputs of the network and the reference (image), i.e., determining the matrix of weights w_{ij} and thresholds of neurons p_j so that in the moment of each current situation (g_i, x_i) appearance at the system input, the corresponding response at its output is obtained according to (10.15)

Note that in automating the recognition process, it is necessary to deal with the uncertainty of the initial information and the operating mode of the system. Moreover, the nature of this uncertainty is so that the use of PRSs with deterministic and stochastic bases does not provide the required quality of recognition processes. Therefore, there is a need to create intelligent systems –IMSRM, that take into account the uncertainties of a fuzzy nature, inherent in recognition processes.

Let the recognition object (RO) be described in dynamics in the form of the following differential equation:

$$\dot{x}^* = f\left(x^*, u^*\right),\ x^* \in X,\ u^* \in U \tag{10.16}$$

or as a combination of fuzzy products:

$$\left.\begin{array}{l} IF\ u^* = O\text{Б}\ and\ x^* = M3\ THEN\ \dot{x}^* = nM\ ELSE \\ IF\ u^* = OC\ and\ x^* = n3\ THEN\ \dot{x}^* = mM\ ELSE \\ \cdots\cdots\cdots\cdots\cdots\cdots\cdots\cdots\cdots\cdots\cdots\cdots\cdots\cdots\cdots\cdots \\ IF\ u^* = \Pi C\ and\ x^* = M3\ THEN\ \dot{x}^* = nM\ ELSE \end{array}\right\} \tag{10.17}$$

where $x^*, \dot{x}^*, u^*$ - basic variables, respectively, of fuzzy sets of signs, their changes and parameters (control); NL- negatively large; NA - negatively average; NS - negatively small; Z - zero; PS - positively small; PA - positively average; PL is positively large.

The reference transition process of the synthesized system is given in the form:

$$\left.\begin{array}{l} IF\ g^* = O\acute{A}\ and\ x^* = \hat{I}\tilde{N}\ THEN\ \dot{x}^* = \hat{I}\hat{I}\ ELSE \\ IF\ g^* = \hat{I}\tilde{N}\ and\ x^* = \hat{I}\tilde{N}\ THEN\ \dot{x}^* = \hat{I}\hat{I}\ ELSE \\ \cdots\cdots\cdots\cdots\cdots\cdots\cdots\cdots\cdots\cdots\cdots\cdots\cdots\cdots\cdots\cdots \\ IF\ g^* = \ddot{I}C\ and\ x^* = \ddot{I}\acute{A}\ THEN\ \dot{x}^* = \hat{I}\hat{I}\ ELSE \end{array}\right\}. \tag{10.18}$$

The task is to synthesize IPRS with fuzzy NN for identification and recognition of the object (10.17), which provides the desired fuzzy characteristic (10.18) of the system. The fuzzy recognition system is built on the basis of fuzzy NN, the architecture of which is adopted in the form of a three-layer "feed-forward" structure.

Input term-sets of linguistic variables e and $\dot{e}$ after scaling with coefficients $k_e, k_{\dot{e}}$ go to the phaseifier, at the output of which fuzzy variables $\tilde{y}, \tilde{y}'$ with a representation of the LR-type are obtained. These signals, after being multiplied by fuzzy weight coefficients $\tilde{w}_{ij}$, are then summed to form the resulting signal; $\tilde{w}_{ij}$ is represented in the adopted model as a fuzzy number with an LR-representation. NN limit, unlike normal neurons, is adopted as min. Fuzzy neurons of the other two layers function similarly. Now it is necessary to determine fuzzy values $\tilde{w}_{ij}$ so that, as noted above, the characteristic of the designed control system coincides with wanted (10.18). For this, the NN is trained using an algorithm that is based on fuzzy arithmetic. All fuzzy arithmetic is implemented for fuzzy numbers $(L - R)$ - type (Aliev et al., 1990; Osovskiy, 2002).

10.6.3 Hybridization: Information, models and criteria for decisive rules

Let's represent the recognizing decisive rule in the form of a transformer F of a formal description of an object X into the name of its image (class): $y = F\,(X)$. The source material for the synthesis of the decision rule F is information that is divided into two types: a priori information J about the structure of the decision rule (the source of this information is usually a person); a posteriori information I or training sample $I =\rangle X_i, y_i \langle \ (i = 1,...,N)$, where X_i- description of the i-th object of the sample, and y_i is its belonging to one of the images (classes), i.e., the name of the image to which belongs X_i.

The decisive rule in the general case is a result of the transformation of the information by a Φ synthesis algorithm: $F = \Phi(J,I)$. Thus, the problem of synthesizing any decision rule is reduced to creating an algorithm Φ that can effectively take into account both types of initial information: a priori J and a posteriori I.

For hybridization, which is a process of synthesis of F, ready-made decision rules are used. Two types of recognizing decisive rules are considered as initial blocks: rules without training, the structure and parameters of which cannot be changed, i.e., $y = f(X)$, trained rules, the structure and parameters of which can be changed by changing the learning sample I, i.e., $y = f'(X,I)$.

The convenience of the rules also lies in the simplicity of their synthesis, which is usually called learning. The process itself is usually used for parametric decision rules of the form: $y = f''(X,C)$, where $C = (c_1,...c_k)$ is a vector of parameters whose values are determined at the training stage: $C = L(I,f'')$. Here L is the operator of determining the parameters of C for the rule f'' and the training sample I. In the training mode, the operator L is recursive and realizes the selection of a change in the parameters C_l after which the inequality $f''(X_i,C_l) \neq y_i$, for example, turns into equality or the inequality defect of the equation decreases when changing $C_l \to C_{l+1}$, where l is the number of the learning step.

Thus, the initial decisive rules for hybridization can be either unchanged or mutable, which means adjusted by a given training sample.

It consists of the use of the given initial (basic) decisive rules $F_1,...,F_q$ so that the properties of obtained hybrid decisive rule exceed the properties of the original decision rules, that is, the "descendant" (hybrid) of these rules would be in a certain given sense better than each of its "parents."

With $R(X)$ denote the hybrid rule. It can be represented in the form: $R(X) = \varphi(F_1(X),...,F_q(X))$, where $F_i(X)$ is the i-th basic decisive rule, $F_i \in \{f,f',f''\}$; φ- hybridization algorithm for the rules. Moreover, hybridization makes sense only when $R \succ F_i \ (i = 1,...,q)$, where the preference sign $\succ$ is determined by the goals of hybridization, i.e. by creating a rule that minimizes a given performance criterion $Q = Q(F)$, which reveals preference $R \succ F_i$, if $Q(R) < Q(F_i), (i = 1,...,q)$.

As the criterion, it is natural to choose the probability functional of the erroneous classification. It is generally accepted that objects $X_i \ (i = 1,...,q)$ and their affiliation y_i (class number) appear independently and randomly in accordance with distribution density $P(X,y)$. Then the probability of an erroneous classification by rule F is determined by the average risk functional: $Q(F) = \int_{X,y} k(y - F(X))P(X,y)dX,dy$, where function k is given by the obvious expression $k(z) = \begin{cases} 0, & z = 0, \\ 1, & z \neq 0. \end{cases}$

However, density $P(X,y)$ is usually unknown a priori and the use of the corresponding criterion requires its reconstruction on the basis of training sample I, which is ineffective in the real case of a limited length N of this sample.

Therefore, the empirical risk functional that determines the frequency of erroneous classification is used as an efficiency criterion:

$$Q_3(F) = \frac{1}{N} \sum_{i=1}^{N} k(y_i - F(X_i)).$$

Most formal (nonexpert) decisive rules of p-class problem recognition can be represented as: $y = sig\Psi(X)$, where the decisive function sig has a stepwise form:

$$sig\,v = \begin{cases} 0, & v < a_1, \\ i, & a_i \leq v < a_{i+1}\ (i = 1,...,p-2), \\ p-1, & a_{p-1} \leq v, \end{cases}$$

and limits $a_1 < ... < a_{p-1}$ are parameters of the rule, and class numbers are obvious: $y \in \{0; 1; ...; p-1\}$.

Now, for formalized decision rules of the form (10.18), hybridization can be represented in as: $R(X) = sig\,\psi(\psi_1(X),...,\psi_q(X))$, where $\psi(...)$ is the scalar function of the hybrid factorization of variables, and the synthesis problem of the hybrid decision rule is reduced to constructing functions, and $\psi_i(X)$ is the factorization of the i-th rule $F_i(X) = sig\,\psi_i(X)$ $(i = 1,...,q)$.

Therefore, hybridization as a method of synthesizing new decisive rules on the basis of existing ones is a procedure for synthesizing the factorization of decisions that make up the hybrid, or the rules that generated these decisions.

So, the hybridization problem in solving the recognition problem comes down to the synthesis of a new rule $R(X)$, which processes not only data about the object X, but also how other available rules $F_1(X),...,F_q(X)$ relate to this object, moreover, the initial information for such a synthesis is the training sample I and a priori data J, which make it possible to determine the composition of the initial rules, the efficiency criterion of the hybrid rule, and other circumstances important for effective hybridization, i.e., we get $R = \Phi^\partial(J, I)$, where Φ^∂ is the hybridization algorithm, and I and J - information necessary for such hybridization:

$$J = \{F_i(X),...,F_q(X), Q(R),...\},$$
$$I = \rangle X_i, y_i \langle (i = 1,...,N).$$

Hybrid decisive rules synthesis can be based on very transparent analogies, borrowed from the field of collective decisions, made in human groups. Note also: hybrid decision rules make possible the usage of the rules created earlier to solve other recognition problems for solving specific problems; hybrid rules have a distinct continuity with traditional recognition methods; collective hybrids allow to combine informal recognition rules (experts), simulating the work of a group of experts; hybrid recognition rules make it possible to solve a number of important practical problems with an accuracy exceeding traditional recognition methods.

10.7 CONCLUSIONS

1. The concept of creation of a local environmental monitoring system for an industrial facility (using coal processing plants as an example) based on a systematic approach and the principles of maximum integration, intellectualization, individualization, widespread use of modern information technologies and accounting for uncertainty, nonlinearity, nonstationarity, fuzziness, etc., as well as multidimensionality, multicriteria, etc., i.e., taking into account "NOT and MANY" - factors when making managerial decisions at all levels.

2. To control the complex processes of the production and transport complex, the necessity and importance of using hybrid intelligent regulators for TP and intelligent AWPs based on a fuzzy knowledge base for the upper levels of PTC control in SEEM is substantiated.
3. A methodology and algorithm for creating hybrid intelligent systems that operate under conditions of mixed uncertainty and allow combining traditional quantitative with difficult formalizable qualitative information in the form of linguistic and fuzzy variables has been developed.
4. An intelligent control system and decision support for diagnosing the crisis state of an industrial facility is proposed.
5. Intelligent system of modeling and control of production systems in the conditions of environmental and economic risks was presented in the current work.

REFERENCES

Aliev, R.A., Abdikeev, N.R., Shahnazarov, M.M. (1990). *Planirovanie proizvodstva v usloviyah neopredelennosti.* Radio i svyaz.

Osovskiy, S. (2002). *Neyronnyie seti dlya obrabotki informatsii.* Moscow, Russia: Finansy i Statistika Publ. 2002.

Ramazanov, S., Babenko, V., Honcharenko, O., Moisieieva, N., Dykan, V. (2020). Integrated Intelligent Information and Analytical System of Management of a Life Cycle of Products of Transport Companies. *Journal of Information Technology Management, 12(3),* pp. 26–33. DOI: 10.22059/jitm.2020.76291.

Ramazanov, S., Petrova, M. (2020). Development management and forecasting in a green innovative economy based on the integral dynamics model in the conditions of "Industry - 4.0". *ACCESS Journal: Access to Science, Business, Innovation in Digital Economy, 1(1),* pp. 9–31.

Ramazanov, S.K. (2008). *Instrumentyi ekologo-ekonomicheskogo upravleniya predpriyatiem.* Donetsk: OOO Yugo-Vostok, Ltd.

Ramazanov, S.K. (2014). *Modeli ekologo-ekonomicheskogo upravleniya proizvodstvennoy sistemoy v nestabilnoy vneshney srede.* Lugansk: Ph EUNU.

Ramazanov, S.K. (2019). *Information and innovative management technologies in ecological and economic systems.* Kyiv: KNEU, 220 p.

Ramazanov, S.K. (2020). Future Production Systems (Green Innovation Economy of the Future). *ACCESS Journal: Access to Science, Business, Innovation in Digital Economy, 1(1),* pp. 6–8.

Ramazanov, S.K., Stepanenko, O.P., Tishkov, B.O., Honcharenko, O.G. (2019). Problem of forecasting and innovation economics control based on integrated dynamics model. In: I. Linde, I. Chumachenko, V. Timofeyev (eds.), *Information systems and innovative technologies in project and program management.* Riga: ISMA, pp. 91–106.

Ramazanov, S.K., Zablodska, I.V., Zablodska, D.V. (2019). Integrating model for sustainable development. *Economics and Law, 4(55),* pp. 124–139.

Ustenko S.V. (2019). *Intelligent management of a technogenic industrial facility in conditions of mixed uncertainty.* Kyiv: KNEU, pp. 271–292.

Voronkova, A.E., Kozachenko, A.V., Ramazanov, S.K., Hlapenov, L.E. (2007). *Sovremennyie tehnologii upravleniya promyishlennyim predpriyatiem.* Libra.

Zadeh, L. A. (1989). Knowledge representation in fuzzy logic. *IEEE Trans. Knowledge And Data Engineering, 1,* pp. 253–283.

Chapter 11

The role of organic brand in the development of farmers' association
Evidence from Ukraine

Iryna Koshkalda, Liudmyla Bezuhla,
Olena Nihmatova and Tetiana Ilchenko

CONTENTS

11.1 INTRODUCTION

The outstanding social and environmental role of organic farming explains the constant scientific attention to problems of its development, therefore consolidating the intellectual potential of leading researchers and practitioners in this field (Reganold & Wachter, 2016). Many of them argue that organic farming should be considered as an innovative agricultural sector because of a specific: the environmentally friendly technology involved. The organic methods and technologies, they said, follow the best traditions of agricultural innovation. Hyundo Choi (2016) defines organic farming as a new food system that generates agro-innovations used by farmers to maintain sustainability in the agricultural sector.

However, researchers consider innovations in organic farming not only in terms of new technological solutions but also through institutional changes taking place in its market: "Local actors rely upon social values (e.g., trustworthiness, health (nutrition and safety), food sovereignty, youth development, farmer and community livelihoods) to adapt sustainable practices to local contexts and create new market outlets for their products, which are core components of institutional innovations" (Loconto et al., 2016, 92). These innovative market structures are grasped based on different concepts, namely "alternative food networks" (Mestres and Lien, 2017), "local food network" (Favilli et al., 2015), "local food supply chain" (Seyfang, 2004), participatory guarantee systems, and community supported agriculture. These market structures are associations of stakeholders interested in the development of organic farming and creating the food system, which includes smallholder farmers and other supporters of organic farming, such as local authorities, consumers, etc. This system is an alternative to industrialized food supply.

Institutional innovations develop within the activities of smallholder farmers, which form the basic economic group in the organic market due to the inherent characteristics of their economic activity which are predisposed to comply with agricultural practices of organic farming (Cen et al., 2020; Morshedi et al,. 2017). Smallholder farmers' associations play an important role in the organic market, namely address the problems in marketing:

consolidating consignments, reducing storage and transportation costs (Grigaliūnaitė & Pilelienė, 2017).

These institutional innovations, in particular, contribute to the creation of wider communication between producers and consumers of organic products. The genesis of such structures shows that partnership between farmers and consumers play a crucial role in them. Terziev and Arabska (2014) argue that market innovation is primarily the process of forming new relationships between producers and consumers. These "market innovations" are necessary, first of all, because partial changes in design, packing, positioning, and pricing of organic products are not enough. The use of new market approaches to achieve a strong communication between producers and consumers is important in this context. Other studies have suggested that it is economically feasible for farmers' associations to create synergies with consumers to accelerate sales (Michelsen et al., 2001; Pickard, 2016).

However, the peculiarities of the organization and support of relations between producers who collectively carry out economic activities and consumers have not received sufficient recognition in the specified concepts. These relations were not examined, and therefore are unreachable to further scientific exploration and development. At the same time, in marketing literature, one could find the concept for these relations, namely, the concept of a brand.

Therefore, it is necessary to extract the theoretical content that deals with the relationship between producers and consumers from the abovementioned concepts by using the concept of a brand. We assume that the brand formation within the organic farmers' associations is an innovation that serves as a basis for the development of the organic market. The main goal of this study is to address the lack of research of the smallholder farmers' associations and the formation within them of the relationships with consumers based on the brand, which should be created using the information about the characteristics of organic products, and organic farming in general. To this end we study brand formation by smallholder organic farmers' association and run a consumer survey in Ukraine.

11.2 LITERATURE REVIEW

Allison Marie (Loconto et al., 2016) argues that innovations in organic farming are both technological and institutional in nature. The authors define an institutional innovation as the process in which people or organizations mobilize other stakeholders at the strategic level through network relationships in order to redesign or change the business situation. Scholars examine a form of local association of organic market participants, which illustrates the example of institutional innovation, namely participatory guarantee systems (PGS). PGS' are networks which are created within local communities, including farmers, researchers, local authorities, suppliers, and consumers. These market structures create a food supply chain that goes beyond the classical type and provides a unique, close relationship between producers and consumers, based on knowledge exchange, the consumer trust in production methods, and the products, and presupposes active consumers' participation in its distribution, which ensures the development of sustainable practices.

Terziev and Arabska (2014) examine the concept of alternative food networks as necessary market innovations in the development of organic farming. The authors argue that there are different approaches to the study of market structures like these. They give an example of a marketing approach such as community-supported agriculture (CSA), which has been spreading since the 1960s in Switzerland, Japan, and since the 1990s in Europe and North America. Within the CSA, consumers, searching for health food, team up with farmers, who in turn obtain stable markets. Therefore, consumers pay in advance for their food order, and farmers provide them seasonal fresh produce, thus the risks, in this case, are shared among key market participants. The shared risk separates this market structure from the industrial food system: "CSA integrates local farmers and society members to work together as partners and create a sustainable local food system" (Terziev & Arabska, 2014, 6). It takes time to build a trusting relationship with consumers within this structure. Douadia Bougherara et al. argue that this long-term relationship between farmers and consumers is an institutional innovation (Bougherara et al., 2009).

In the scientific literature, consumer support of organic producers and the formation of long-term trust between them is investigated based on different concepts. Favilli et al. (2015) argue that innovations in agriculture are carried out not only in the form of technology but also through environmentally friendly production practices, which are possible only on the basis of collective action, including "a range of actors in building relationships and facilitates the generation, exchange and exploitation of new knowledge." Collective action is organized into different types of networks, one of which has recently become, as the authors note, "an organizational model that is able to achieve objectives of sustainability," including organic agriculture at the local level (Favilli et al., 2015). The local organic food network is described as a food system that consists of smallholder organic farmers and enthusiasts (who use organic farming methods), and have a specific distribution system (alternative forms of trade, such as farmers' markets) and relationships with consumers.

Mestres and Lien (2017) conceptualize the association in organic agriculture as an alternative food network. They define it as "an arena for consumer activism that bypasses the conventional markets" and as "forms of food provisioning with characteristics deemed to be different from, perhaps counteractive to, mainstream modes which dominate in developed countries." Alternative food networks include "different producer–consumer alliance options that seek to overcome traditional distinctions in the capitalist commodity chain (between production, distribution and consumption). Through cooperation, these initiatives link small local organic food producers with a variety of activists' and/or consumers." The main feature of alternative food networks is the establishment of trusting, friendly relations between the participants, aimed at the development and dissemination of the ideals of nonmarket, the ecological relations between people and "social and environmental sustainability." The alternative food network is a noncommercialized cooperation between organic producers and consumers, in which the differences between these two participants are erased through coordinated production and marketing activities, and conscious control of the conditions of exchange. Consumers, as members of various forms of such networks (associations, consumer cooperatives, etc.) are directly involved in supporting producers (volunteering, gifts, assistance, participation in joint projects, use of a personal property as communal property (machines, land, tools), etc.), the establishment of fair prices (the use of "social currency," the value of which is determined by the level of trust and involvement in the network), quality control of organic products (consumers provide feedback on products directly to farmers).

Johannes Michelsen et al. (2001) define an organic agriculture "as a social movement, initiated by persons and organizations, which are not part of the mainstream agriculture segment." The key characteristic of the social movement, they write "that it includes the development of special perceptions and worldviews opposing dominant views, which are criticized," and the goal of this movement is to change the nature of agriculture. Furthermore, organic farming is a social movement because it develops through the efforts of many social groups in accordance with their interests (consumers, traders, scientists, etc.). He argues that the interaction between producers and various social groups, including consumers, are not based on the commonality of their material interests, but the commonality of certain values. In this context, the author considers the socio-political side of the associations between producers and consumers.

Thus, from the point of view of the above-mentioned authors, institutional innovations in the organic market can be generally understood as a way of exercising economic, socio-environmental, and political interests of organic market participants through their collective action. The interaction between producers with consumers in the framework of such associations is an extremely necessary process in the context of sales growth, overcoming competition with conventional agriculture, and expanding the organic market.

Now turn to the studies of brand in the context of organic farming. This concept helps to understand the interaction between producers and consumers. The scientific literature indicates that the interaction between producers and consumers can be most effectively developed through using brand as a marketing tool, the main content of which is to inform consumers about the values of organic products, referring to the uniqueness of organic farming, and give them the motives for consumption of organic products (Richetin et al., 2016). Researchers who study the problem of brand formation and development in the organic market point to various reasons that necessitate initiating brand activities by farmers.

First of all, they indicate the existence of barriers to the uninterrupted, efficient marketing of organic products, and chief among those are high prices and low level of consumer awareness about the characteristics of organic produce and the importance of its consumption (Nikodemska-Wolowik 2009). Most organic products quickly deteriorate or lose some product qualities, because they do not contain preservatives and are not treated with, for example, wax for long-term storage, hence the importance of their rapid sale (Ulyanchenko & Bezus, 2016). The problem with marketing is exacerbated by the opportunistic behavior of conventional companies that, for example, name or label conventional foods as "organic" and sell overpriced produce to unsuspecting consumers. This situation, in turn, reduces the level of consumer trust in organic products, even if the organic labeling requirements are fully respected (López & Álvarez, 2005).

Stanton and Guion (2015) think that "<...> the goal of brand development is to create a name that carries meaning beyond the individual products associated with that name, thereby communicating a consistent, confident message to consumers" (123). Natalia Stepanenko (2013) considers brand as an image of a social object as "the result of interaction between individuals and the interaction between individuals and groups," which is an integrating element of the marketing communications system of the agricultural enterprise and "a necessary condition in the implementation of its product policy, with the main imperative is the innovative value of the product" (318). For organic farming, branding is a tool for revaluation of values by consumers and producers, the rural community as a whole, which presupposes "<...> the formation of a stable positive attitude towards the brand in the recipient and a favorable situation for its implementation in consumer behavior, <...> motives, <...> and the emergence of positive emotions" concerning the environmental friendliness of the product, the characteristics of organic farming, the principles of management, the pricing of organic product (Stepanenko, 2013, 320), etc.

Recent studies indicate that organic farming technologies are innovation, and the organic brand gains its uniqueness through the communication of this innovativeness in the process of promoting organic products. The organic brand development implies, as the researchers claim, the creation of its attributes (name, logo, packaging), the implementation of an advertising campaign that centers on certification of organic products and communicate their uniqueness—high quality, exceptional taste, environmental friendliness, status consumption, and safety—as well as informing consumers about organic farming principles, pricing, and points of sale (Janssen & Hamm, 2012; Bauer et al., 2013; Larceneux et al., 2012; Fifita et al., 2019; Asioli et al., 2018). Moreover, the word *organic* in the laws and standards has the status of a brand. That is, the organic brand not only communicates to consumers the characteristics of its particular use–value but also disseminates information about organic farming as a whole through certification: "not an individual product or brand but a type of product that is also sold under many brand names" (Stanton & Guion, 2015, 135). Conversely, since the organic produce is a brand on the level of certification, farmers need to convey this to consumers in order to create brand value in their minds.

Information about organic agriculture, its differences from its conventional counterpart as well as beneficial attributes of organic products for human health and sustainable agricultural development, is the essence of brand communications. This information directly affects consumer purchasing behavior, reduces the information asymmetry and the possibility of opportunism in the food supply chain (Anisimova & Sultan, 2014). The main function of the brand as a marketing tool is to inform consumers about the values of organic products based upon the essence of organic farming and to create consumption motives. Branding helps to overcome the problem of high prices for organic products: if consumers know about the huge benefits of "organic," then the price is a secondary concern for them. As Michelsen et al. (2001) point out, consumers need a justification for the high price of organic produce based on relevant knowledge.

At the same time, consumers' knowledge of organic products and environmental issues in general does not directly lead to the purchase of organic produce (Eckhardt et al., 2010). Consumers' awareness of conventional agriculture as harmful to health and the environment does not automatically lead to supporting organic cause. Other scholars believe that consumer trust in organic farmers is a crucial condition for creating assurance in buying a truly organic product. It should be noted that present-day consumers' perceptions of quality differ significantly from those of two decades ago. In the past, consumers thought of quality in terms of the taste, freshness, color, that is, the internal characteristics of the product. Today, the quality of a product is determined by the production process (environmental, work and safety policies, etc.), the entrepreneur's personality (brand), and the region of production. Consumers understand the quality on the basis of certain characteristics of the production and the producer, but not the products themselves. Trust in quality not only implies the positive experience of consumption, but also the knowledge of how the products were made. In this aspect, consumers' interaction with the producer through brand communications is imperative (Schreer & Padmanabhan, 2019).

An important problem for the organic market as a whole, and farmers' associations in particular, are inconsistent, contradictory messages about the values of organic farming, which reduce the consumers' ability to identify "organic" and undermines their trust (Seufert et al., 2017; Dayoub & Korpela, 2019). In this regard, there is a need for a collective brand communication strategy of organic farmers, which aims to raise consumers' awareness about organic farming and create shared positive associations with "organic." Building and strengthening relationships with consumers, according to scholars, should be based on creating and managing a collective local brand. The researchers highlight the need to create synergies between farmers' associations and consumers in order to enable the latter to demonstrate their support for community and environmentally friendly practices in agriculture through civic activism.

Given the importance of the producers' association and branding in the organic market, it is necessary to study from the point of view of cooperative producers the conditions of brand development as a marketing tool to spread ideas about organic farming and increase consumer demand. There is an urgent need to develop a theory of brand from the standpoint of outlining the place of branding in the formation of competitive advantages of smallholder organic cooperative producers, as well as to create a methodological approach (conceptual basis) for its introduction.

To achieve this goal, we will use statistics and analysis of the organic market in Ukraine, as well as the following research methods.

11.3 RESEARCH METHODS

Following the principles of the dialectical research and a systematic approach to the study of economic and social phenomena, the study used the following methods:

1. The data analysis method was used to structure the theoretical knowledge about the characteristics of the organic brand with the subsequent integration of previously disconnected concepts and findings into a qualitatively new concept.
2. The survey method based on questionnaires was used for collecting data on educational attainment, the attitudes of Ukrainian consumers to organic products. This information underpins the formation of scientific hypotheses. ABC analysis was applied to the data of the survey in order to identify the most significant factors that influence consumers' choice of organic produce. The information about these factors could be used for the effective promotion of organic products as the main content of the brand building. The survey was conducted among 384 respondents at specialized agricultural fairs, exhibitions of organic products, in Kyiv, Ukraine. The choice of these places was motivated by the need to reach the target audience—actual organic consumers. Statistical analysis was done using Excel.
3. The content analysis is the method used to determine the types of brand communications of organic producers by way of studying virtual textual content (information about organic production, producers of organic products, the content of consumer information), graphic content (use of certification marks, trade signs, video and photo materials about organic production and products, specific manufacturer, links to social media sites).
4. Expert survey is a method used to identify the main problems of the marketing activities of smallholder organic producers. During an expert survey of managers from 32 organic farms, members of smallholder producers' associations and cooperatives, we proposed they assess the main marketing problems in the Ukrainian market of organic products and choose one of these answer options: "very concerned," "somewhat concerned," "not at all concerned" and "not sure," and indicate what problems their farms face.
5. The dialectical method presupposes the understanding of two concepts—phenomena in contradictory interrelationships of opposites, which leads to resolving contradictions by the interpenetration of opposites in a new synthetic concept-phenomenon. This method helped to understand the interrelationship between individual organic farmers' brands and collective associations as two different, opposing practices of interactions with consumers, which can only fully develop their potential through the interpenetration of opposites: creating a collective brand on the basis of an association. The need for synthesis is due to the contradiction of individual brand identity in, on the one hand, the focus on creating a unique concept of "organic," which blurs the consumer's understanding of "organic" as such, and on the other, the desire to establish contact with the consumer through brand communications. A collectivity of smallholder organic farmers' associations is also an internal contradiction: the desire to represent the general interest of producers does not lead to the conceptualization of "organic," and the possibility of wider communication with consumers is not supported by using brand communications.
6. The method of scientific modeling enables the creation of simplified representations of economic phenomena and respective relations. This method was used in the development of the conceptual framework of the business model of the brand association and the algorithm for its implementation.

11.4 RESULTS AND DISCUSSION

Knowledge and trust are two basic conditions for the creation of an organic brand. They could be formed in the process of constructing social relationships between the main market actors, namely between consumers and producers. Concerns about the quality of conventional food are an objective prerequisite for the development of such relationships, the creation of the organic brand. At the same time, as it was stated, consumer loyalty for organic produce is the result of awareness about the benefits of organic food over conventional. Branding helps farmers keep the price high due to increased demand for organic products, even if a number of producers start to grow. These characteristics determine the uniqueness of the organic brand, the development of which yields benefits to both farmers and consumers.

The benefits of a brand for consumers lie in the fact that while exercising a certain environmentally friendly lifestyle, they create new meanings in the field of healthy living and environmental protection, and disseminate information about organic products, consumption experience, and positive attitude among other potential consumers by way of reflecting upon material practices of interaction with other consumers and producers, thus attracting new consumers to buy organic products.

It can be argued that close relationships between producers and consumers—the formation of the consumer as a co-producer—are the evidence of the fundamental transformation of the structure of relations between the key actors of organic agriculture and its market: they are no longer understood and practiced as relations between antagonistic economic agents, but as relations of social cooperation between the subjects of social activity wanting to transform agriculture in general. Therefore, the process of building relationships between consumers and producers should be treated with special attention because of their paramount importance and foundational role in the formation of all other relationships in this market. The consumer is one of the key actors of market relations and not only as the one who buys products, but in addition has special interests and is exercising social activity in the market (interested in the use value of products, etc., and protects own rights to its quality).

Thus, the organic brand is the result of joint efforts of the farmer's brand communications and the activities of environmentally conscious consumers. Organic brand values forming through co-created meanings of organic farming, its positive attitude to nature (and to humans as part of nature), the exercising of practical activities based on these values, as well as the formation of new ideas, meanings, and images of organic products and spreading them in the public at large (Hatch & Schultz, 2010). In the process of acquiring knowledge about organic production technologies, which are environmentally friendly, consumers are provoked to reevaluate their values and priorities in life, transform themselves into planetary-conscious beings who can take responsibility not only for their own lives, but the lives of all living things in general. The organic brand encourages the consumer to think not in terms of what the world does for him/her, but what he/she does for the world, thus forming a special culture and ethics of consumption. Thus, the organic brand development involves mutually beneficial two-way communication between producers and consumers.

This approach to branding, unlike others, provides an opportunity to identify additional sources of profit growth during the creation of a brand of smallholder organic businesses through an in-depth understanding of consumers' activities, namely the co-creation of new ideas, meanings, and images of organic products.

Therefore, it should be argued that the organic market is developing faster when organic producers interact with consumers, spreading knowledge about the characteristics and benefits of produce, and demonstrating its production sites and technologies. Thus, the brand in this sense promotes the sale of organic products at a premium price in order to obtain economic benefits and achieve social and environmental goals (see Figure 11.1).

Companies should constantly carry out marketing research to know about the preferences of consumers and their values, and also conduct advertising campaigns and improve product quality. These activities could be done by using third-party organizations: consulting firms and marketing agencies. But the cooperation of smallholder farmers with such organizations might not be carried out on an ongoing basis, given the high cost of their services. At the same time, in the process of continuous interaction with consumers, smallholder farmers can study their tastes and preferences, and receive feedback and respond immediately without any help, which is more effective than conducting one-sided expensive research.

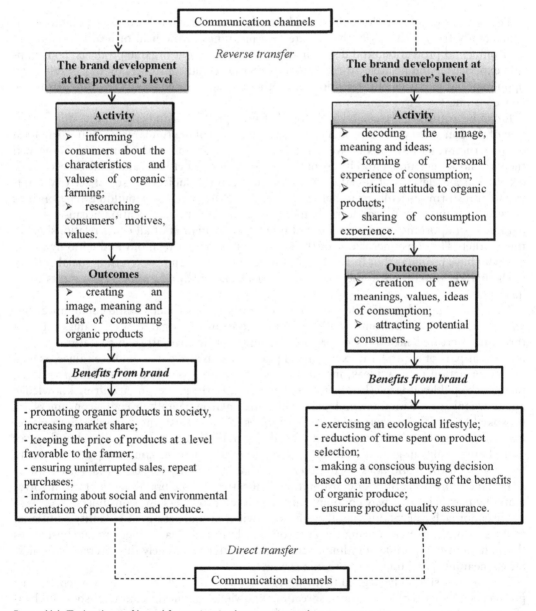

Figure 11.1 Technology of brand formation in the organic market

According to data from *The World of Organic Agriculture* statistical yearbooks, organic certified agricultural land in Ukraine increased almost 2 times over the period 2002–2018, from 162,4 thousand ha to 309,1 thousand ha, and the number of organic farms has risen 9,8 times, from 31 to 304. At the same time, the share of organic land in the total agricultural land of the country in 2017 was equal to 0,72%. Ukraine has repeatedly been included in the top twenty ranking lists of leaders among European countries in terms of organic land. This country ranked 20th in 2018 among 178 countries of the world where organic production has been introduced. Cereals are the most-grown crops on the Ukrainian organic lands; therefore, the production of vegetables, potatoes, melons, fruits, and medicinal plants is limited.

The most significant feature of the Ukrainian organic market lies in the fact that it serves as a source of organic raw materials of plant origin to Western European consumers. The largest part of organic products is being exported (Milovanov 2018). The domestic organic market is characterized by limited demand. Its share in 2018 was only 0,22% of the domestic food market. However, the sales of organic products increased by 600% over the period 2005–2018, from 0,2 to 33,0 million euros, respectively. Sales of organic products in the domestic market are carried out through large and small specialized retail chains. However, the retailers' activities in terms of promotion of organic products and the amount of professional advice are insufficient, as they often do not take into account the specifics of the use value of "the organic" and the peculiarities of its production. Therefore, the brand development is a relevant thing and a great advantage for organic producers, which would provide an opportunity to spread the information about organic products, their values in close cooperation with consumers, and in result, increasing demand. Though, at the same time, the brand development is associated with rather high costs.

Our studies have shown that the use of branding by Ukrainian organic producers is not popular at all. Only a fraction, namely, less than 5%, or 14 companies out of 304 (data for 2017), carry out brand communications: have a trademark, website, Facebook page, hold events (field trips to production sites, organize festivals), take part in festivals, fairs, give interviews to journalists, publish own magazine, etc. However, it should be noted that these 14 companies interact with consumers in a piecemeal fashion, unsystematically at best. This is supported by the fact that most companies do not use all types of brand communications at once (see Table 11.1).

Although almost all companies have websites and social media presence, these resources have not been updated for months or, in some cases, for years, indicating a lack of communication with customers.

Only 3 large companies—LLC "Organik Milk," LLC "Etnoprodukt," and PE "Agroekologia,"—systematically and painstakingly carry out brand communications aimed at sales promotion: have a trademark, conduct field trips, organize holiday events, and communicate on websites and social media. Besides, it should be noted that these enterprises provide local patronage and sponsorship. "Etnoprodukt" LLC repairs and builds playgrounds. PE "Agroekologia" financed the construction of a local church and the reconstruction of the dacha of the writer V. G. Korolenko, and sponsors the local Korolenko holiday. Furthermore, the company publishes the research and production magazine "*Agroeko.*" LLC "Organik Milk" sponsors some large-scale fairs. These companies occupy a significant market share and are popular among organic consumers, who firstly mention them in opinion polls (Savchuk, 2016).

The export of domestic organic products to Europe at premium prices stimulates at the current stage the organic market development in Ukraine. Large national business structures perform the functions of the state in the absence of centralized comprehensive support, spreading eco- and socio-oriented agriculture, stimulating integration processes in the organic sector, endorsing small business development through promoting the conversion of

Table 11.1 Marketing activities of Ukrainian organic producers, aimed at brand development

Organic producers	Types of brand communications					
	Trademark	Website	Events	Fairs, festivals	Social media	PR
PE "Galeks-agro"	+	+	+	+	+	+
PE "Agroekologiya"	+	+	+	+	+	+
LLC "EtnoProdukt"	+	+	+	+	+	+
"Firma Diamant Ltd"	+	+	–	+	+	+
Agrofirm "Hermes"	+	–	–	+	+	+
LLC "GALS"	+	+	–	+	+	+
Farm "Blagodatna ferma"	+	+	–	+	+	–
Farm "GADZ"	+	+	–	+	+	–
PJSC "Kvark"	+	+	–	+	–	–
PE Scientific Selection and Seed Company "Soyevij"	+	+	–	+	–	–
PJSC "Femili Garden"	+	+	–	+	+	–
PJSC "Dzherela Karpat"	+	+	–	+	+	–
LLC "Organik milk"	+	+	+	+	+	+
TM "Skviryanka"	+	+	–	+	+	–

Source: Authors' investigation of official sources of organic producers.

small conventional farms within cooperative groups (in 2018 there were 9 grain, legume, fruit, and berry cooperatives) to form large export shipments. Eight public associations have been operating in the market since 2002. They are created mostly by large producers, aiming to facilitate the transition of conventional smallholder farmers to organic farming. But according to research conducted by the Ukrainian Association of Consumers and Ukrainian scientists, cooperatives created by large agricultural holdings do not have autonomy in their activities, which deprives their members of the right to vote and make independent decisions (Bezus & Bilotkach, 2018). Therefore, the need to increase self-sufficiency and to reduce the dependence of smallholder organic producers on unfavorable conditions of cooperation with large structures, led to the creation of their independent associations in the forms of public organizations and cooperatives, following the example of more experienced large companies. There are few independent small producers' associations in Ukraine: the agricultural service "Rodinniy Dobrobut" (eng. "Family Welfare") cooperative and the Public Association "Ukrayinskiy organichniy klaster (eng. "Ukrainian Organic Cluster"). They are stimulating sales in the domestic market, forming large shipments for retailers, reducing logistics costs, and sell a part of their products abroad.

Although guaranteed sales and higher export pricing for organic products are increasing every year, the domestic market offers for smallholder organic producers more favorable business opportunities for selling added-value products, given the following material preconditions. According to Ukrainian scholars, there is still untapped potential for demand for organic products, and the current volume of this market lags behind its potential volume. At the same time, opinion polls show that the Ukrainian population is more dissatisfied than in the past with the quality of food, and there is a trend of improving the culture of consumption. Ukrainian experts argue that organic consumers may constitute 5% of the population of large cities, based on their solvency and other socio-demographic factors (Voskobiynyk & Gavaza, 2013). Natalia Mamonova (2018) shows that 48% of patriotic Ukrainians (as opposed to 21% in 2012) associate the country's agricultural development with small-scale farming, which can ensure national food security.

Table 11.2 The main marketing problems and their urgency for organic producers

Types of marketing problems	Very concerned, %	Somewhat concerned, %	Not at all concerned, %	Not sure, %
Absence of shipment volume	59	15	12	14
Transportation problems	21	12	56	11
Lack of procurement organizations	35	25	25	15
Low demand for products	69	12	4	15
Low level of purchase prices	85	8	1	6

Source: Authors' own.

The activities of smallholder farmers' associations concerning the interaction with consumers are not systematic and persistent. Research of activities of Public Union "Ukrayinskiy organichniy klaster" and "Rodinniy Dobrobut" cooperative showed that they are only active in festivals and fairs both specialized and thematic. However, they do not have a trademark; websites and groups on social media are created but barely used. All other types of brand communications are not popular among the producers of these associations.

However, according to our expert survey of managers from 32 smallholder organic farms in these associations, conducted in November 2017, the marketing of organic products is considered as one of the key concerns for them. In the course of the survey, we offered to evaluate the proposed problems with marketing in the domestic organic market with one of the answers options: "very concerned," "somewhat concerned," "not at all concerned" and "not sure."

As can be seen in the Table 11.2, the most pressing problems for survey participants are low purchase prices (85%) and low demand for organic products (69%), which together do not contribute to the expanded reproduction. The low purchase price is the result of the almost monopolistic position of both large and small (specialized organic) retailers in the Ukrainian market, which dictates conditions that cannot always be satisfying to smallholder organic producers: most of these stores are interested in regular deliveries, a wide product range, and a short term of sale, after which, if the product is not sold, it returns to the farmer. It should be said that sales of organic products within such indirect sales channels are characterized by a lack of quality promotional work with consumers. There is a wide range of products from smallholder organic producers, members of the Public Union "Ukrayinskiy organichniy klaster" and "Rodinniy Dobrobut" cooperative, but these organizations do not always have the ability to meet the requirements of retailers concerning the volume and regularity of deliveries, as revealed by the survey.

The activities of these associations with consumers are unsystematic and scarce. One can say that the Public Union "Ukrayinskiy organichniy klaster" does not carry out such activities at all. The main interactions of "Rodinniy Dobrobut" cooperative with the client base is exercised in social media, thematic communities, and groups. However, these interactions, according to our observations, are non-systematic. The organization of marketing activities within these associations is the responsibility of management, not by special hired experienced professionals. Thus, it can be argued that brand-oriented activities with consumers are absent in these associations. The associations of producers—"Rodinniy Dobrobut" cooperative and the Public Union "Ukrayinskiy organichniy klaster"— do not integrate into their activities the owners of money, i.e., individual consumers who could protect the ideals and practices of organic agriculture through distribution of its values to the public. In other words, a producer association lacks a consumer approach that one could see in the brand practices of individual companies.

In contrast, according to our survey of Ukrainian consumers of organic products, 56% of respondents believe that there should be continuous feedback between them and producers,

Table 11.3 The level of awareness about organic products in Ukraine (according to the survey), %

Questions	Response options	Number of responses, %
Do you know about the characteristics of organic produce?	Yes, I know	69.2
	Yes, in part	12.6
	No, I do not know	13.1
	It's difficult to answer	5.1
Choose the main criteria you use while buying organic produce?	List of ingredients	9.1
	The name on the packaging	44.0
	Labeling	34.6
	Conclusions of state control bodies	12.3
Do you know this labeling?	Yes	16.4
	No	83.6

Source: Authors' own.

and 85% of respondents are not satisfied with the accessibility of information about the specific qualities of organic produce and the conditions of its production. Primary marketing information also shows a very low level of awareness of Ukrainian consumers about organic products: although 69.2% of respondents consider themselves aware of the characteristics of organic products, only 16.4% of them are familiar with organic labeling (see Table 11.3).

The main motivations for the consumption of organic products among those surveyed are concern for one's health (34,5%); exceptional taste (30,2%); a feeling of belonging to an environmentally conscious community (18,8%); aesthetic appeal, the appearance of the product (10,2%); following the example of friends, relatives, colleagues, opinion leaders (6,3%). In addition, the respondents mentioned a positive experience of buying and cultivating such products by themselves, and also personal acquaintance with the professional organic farmers. Thus, one can say that concern for one's health is the most important motivation for consumption.

ABC analysis of the factors that influence the choice of organic products by consumers showed which ones need to be addressed first (see Table 11.4). The most influential factors belong to Group A: product quality, fair prices, and professional staff members. Group B consists of such factors as the convenient location of a point of sales and the trademark reputation. Group C includes the country of origin and packaging.

Now turn to the characteristics by which the respondents determine the quality of organic products. These characteristics form the basis of the level of trust, which is the crucial element of brand building. The product quality for the domestic consumer is defined by the environmental sustainability of the region (70%); the technological process, which does not cause environmental damage (66,3%); product certification (57,5%); and local production about which respondents knew (43,8%). The quality of the product points to the freshness of the product (40%), the health benefits (35%), the small scale of production (30%), the exceptional taste (28,7%), and the safe transport of products to points of sale (23,8%). The aesthetic appeal and the appearance of the product indicate its quality in 12,5% of the responses and the quality of service at the points of sales in 11,3% of the responses.

Among the three types of online platforms, according to the survey, 52,44% of respondents considered the official pages of organic farmers on social networks to be very important,

Table 11.4 Cumulative evaluation of factors affecting consumers' choice of organic products (according to the survey), %

№	Factors	The importance of the factor, the number of respondents	The importance of the factor, %	Cumulative importance of factor, the number of respondents, (%)	The cumulative importance of the three factors, number of respondents (%)
1	Product quality	109	28.4	109(28.4)	Group A 242 (63)
2	Fair price	80	20.8	189(49.2)	
3	Professional staff members	53	13.8	242(63)	
4	Convenient location of a point of sales	52	13.5	294(76.5)	Group B 95 (24.7)
5	Trademark reputation	43	11.2	337(87.7)	
6	The country of origin	32	8.4	369(96.1)	Group C 47 (12.3)
7	Packaging	15	3.9	384(100)	
Total		384	100	384(100)	

Source: Authors' own.

36,34% fairly important, and 4,58% not important at all (see Table 11.5). The second most significant online platform for respondents is the website (38,32%). The blogosphere is not very popular with those surveyed (6,25%) but important (29,17%). Respondents are attracted to the events: for 19,14% they are very important and for 39,58% they are fairly important. Fairs, as a form of promotion, are not currently the most popular—only one quarter of those surveyed considered them important or fairly important. Respondents also do not consider publications (advertising) in the press about organic products important: for 2,78% of the surveyed this form of promotion is very important and for 27,08% it is fairly important, while for 36,11% it is not that important and 34,03% think it is not important at all. Telemarketing as a form of promotion is also not very popular.

The results of the survey show a low level of consumers' awareness, their desire to actively interact with producers, receive information that confirms the quality of products and get professional advice. The main communication channels should be (in order of importance) social networks, websites, and events through which producers establish close relationships with consumers and gain their trust.

Table 11.5 Marketing communication channels and assessing their importance for organic consumers (according to the survey), %

Marketing communication channels	Very important	Important	Equally important and not important	Not important
Thematic groups in social networks	52.44	36,34	6.64	4.58
Website	38.32	29.61	19.03	13.04
The blogosphere	6.25	29.17	39.58	25.00
Events (e.g., festivals, flash mobs, production tours, etc.)	19.14	39.58	6.25	35.03
Fairs	4.87	20.83	63.20	37.50
Environmental and social advertising in magazines, on television	2.78	27.08	36.11	34.03
PR	0.69	10.43	36.08	52.08

Source: Authors' own.

Therefore, associated smallholder organic farmers should take into account the results of our study, implement marketing activities based on branding, stimulate sales by establishing constant contact with consumers, and thus create a platform for their self-realization.

Establishing this kind of interaction requires knowledge, time, and money. In this regard, it is necessary to create collective brand communication by farmers in order to inform consumers about organic products and generate shared positive associations with "organic." Studies have shown that smallholder farmers' associations in Ukraine do not pay enough attention to consumers, and individual farmers' brands cannot reach a wider audience. That determines the necessity to create a business model of brand association. This model presupposes the synthesis of the principle of a collectivity of associations with the principles of systematic engagement and involvement of consumers based on individual farmers' brand practices.

However, this synthesis cannot be a mechanical combination of two opposing practices but will be the result of a rethinking of the organic market foundations, and thus the creation of a new basis for interpenetration, synthesis of associations, and brand principles.

The precondition for this rethinking lies in a structural change in the fundamental social relations of the market. The point is that in the contemporary economy, the consumer, as the owner of money, not only buys products on the market but additionally creates social relations about/around the products, disseminating information about them, sharing the values of their producers, etc. In other words, the consumer is a co-creator of products, their brands, which is accelerating turnover, reduces production and turnover costs, and leads to market expansion for the benefit of the producers. The organic market, as shown above, exists only in the form of a social movement and associations of farmers with consumers who support the peculiar nature of production, as well as corresponding worldview and values. Therefore the integration of brand tools in the organic producers' associations is merely a conscious organization of this movement, the result of the recognition of the inexhaustible potential of consumers' co-creation, which functions as a market force, together with producers.

This business model is designed specifically to bring together smallholder organic farmers and, on the one hand, to collectively use brand building activities which are impossible to handle individually due to lack of financial resources, and on the other hand, to implement marketing activities consistent with the characteristics (principles and, in general, philosophy) of organic farming. The brand association is the creation of a unique space for dialogue between organic farmers and consumers, and establishing close and systematic communication with consumers. Implementation of the brand association model involves awareness and acceptance by the members of the associations of the main tasks, goals, and principles of organic products marketing on the basis of brand development.

Therefore, the brand association is a business model that presupposes conducting brand building activities for smallholder organic farmers' associations to stimulate sales and minimize marketing costs. The brand association is the creation of a unique space for dialogue between organic farmers and consumers, and establishing close and systematic communication with consumers. The purpose of creating the business model of brand association is to solve marketing problems, increase organic area, support Ukrainian small farmers, and form mutual trust between business and the public (see Table 11.5). All members of a brand association, while implementing this business model, must share its core idea, which is a prerequisite for its effective implementation and operation.

The enactment of the business model of brand association is envisaged within the framework of the implementation of the marketing activity of existing associations (cooperative, civic association) in Ukraine. Smallholder organic farmers' lack of experience, management and marketing knowledge, and understanding the importance of long-term prospects is taking its toll. Hence, the initial investment of organic producers for the implementation of the

Table 11.6 The main functions of the marketing professional

The marketing professional
• Preparation and adjustment of the marketing program based on feedback from consumers • Planning and organization of events • Collection, study, and analysis of customer feedback • Replenishment of information material of an advertising nature • Assistance in creating a team of like-minded people among members of a public union, cooperative

Source: Own research.

business model should be aimed at the implementation of marketing activities, namely the involvement of a marketing professional. The main functions of the marketing professional are presented in Table 11.6.

Thus, the brand association in the organic market can be considered as an institutional innovation through which, it is proposed, to create long-term relationships between consumers and cooperated farmers. These relationships are especially important to explore for the development of emerging organic markets, including the Ukrainian market (see Figure 11.2).

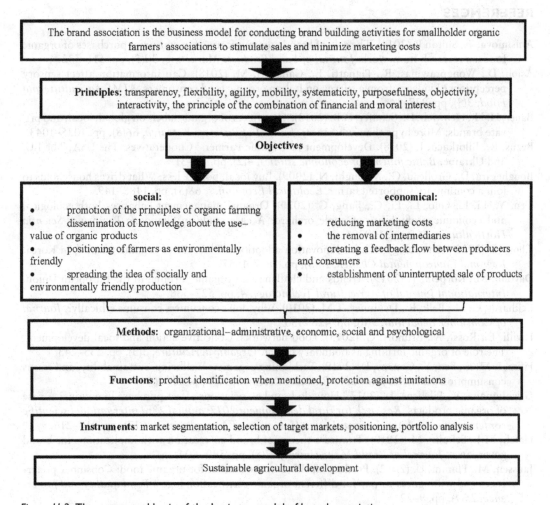

Figure 11.2 The conceptual basis of the business model of brand association

11.5 CONCLUSIONS

Expansion of the national market of organic produce in Ukraine leads to rural development and creates the possibility of providing the population with healthy products. Ukrainian consumers are concerned about food quality, which enhances the consumption culture in the country and creates material conditions for the sale of organic products. Research shows a low level of consumer awareness of organic products and consumers' desire to engage with producers. Meanwhile, smallholder organic farmers' associations are operating in the market, solving sales problems, forming consignments, and reducing logistics costs, while constantly experiencing the low demand for organic products in the national market. The problems related to the sale of organic products can be solved by creating a collective brand in the context of smallholder organic farmers' associations. The proposed business model of a brand association can be used as the conceptual basis for the formation of long-term relationships between consumers and cooperated farmers. Such relationships are especially important to create in the emerging organic markets, including the Ukrainian market.

REFERENCES

Anisimova, T., Sultan P. (2014). The role of brand communications in consumer purchases of organic foods: a research framework. *Journal of Food Products Marketing, 20(5)*, pp. 511–532.

Asioli, D., Wongprawmas, R., Pignatti, E., Canavari, M. (2018). Can information affect sensory perceptions? Evidence from a survey on Italian organic food consumers. *AIMS Agriculture and Food, 3(3)*, pp. 327–344.

Bauer, H. H., Heinrich, D., Schäfer, D.B. (2013). The effects of organic labels on global, local, and private brands: More hype than substance?. *Journal of Business Research, 66(8)*, pp. 1035–1043.

Bezus, R., Bilotkach, I. (2018). Development of Organic Farmers' Cooperatives: The USA, The EU, and Ukraine. *Baltic journal of economic studies, 4(2)*, pp. 24–31.

Bougherara, D., Grolleau, G., Mzoughi, N. (2009). Buy local, pollute less: What drives households to join a community supported farm?. *Ecological Economics, 68(5)*, pp. 1488–1495.

Cen, Y., Li, L., Guo, L., Li, C., Jiang, G. (2020). Organic management enhances both ecological and economic profitability of apple orchard: A case study in Shandong Peninsula. *Scientia Horticulturae, 265*, pp. 109201.

Choi, H. (2020). A typology of agro-innovation adoptions: The case of organic farming in Korea. *Regional Environmental Change, 16(6)*, pp. 1847–1857.

Dayoub, M., Korpela, T. (2019). Trends and challenges in organic farming in the European Union. *International Journal of Agricultural Technology, 4*, pp. 527–538.

Eckhardt, G. M., Belk, R., Devinney, T.M. (2010). Why don't consumers consume ethically?. *Journal of Consumer Behaviour, 9(6)*, pp. 426–436.

Favilli, E., Rossi, A., Brunori, G. (2015). Food networks: Collective action and local development. The role of organic farming as boundary object. *Organic agriculture, 5(3)*, pp. 235–243.

Fifita, I. M. E., Seo, Y., Conroy, D. (2019). Fashioning organics: Wellbeing, sustainability, and status consumption practices. *Journal of Business Research, 117*, pp. 664–671.

Grigaliūnaitė, V., Pilelienė, L. (2017). How do brand associations affect purchase intentions? A case of organic products. *Research for rural development 2017: annual 23rd international scientific conference proceedings. Jelgava: Latvia University of Agriculture, 2(2017)*, pp. 210–216.

Hatch, M.J., Schultz, M. (2010). Toward a theory of brand co-creation with implications for brand governance. *Journal of Brand Management, 17(8)*, pp. 590–604.

Janssen, M., Hamm, U. (2012). Product labelling in the market for organic food: Consumer preferences and willingness-to-pay for different organic certification logos. *Food quality and preference, 25(1)*, pp. 9–22.

Larceneux, F., Benoit-Moreau, F., Renaudin, V. (2012). Why might organic labels fail to influence consumer choices? Marginal labelling and brand equity effects. *Journal of Consumer Policy*, *35(1)*, pp. 85–104.

Loconto, A. M., Poisot, A. S., Santacoloma, P, Vicovaro, M. (2016). Institutional Innovations in Ecological Organic Agriculture in Africa. In: A. Meybeck, S. Redfern (eds.), *Food and Agriculture Organization of the United Nations*. Rome: Hal.

López, R.C., Álvarez, H.A. (2005). Información asimétrica y activos específicos en la agricultura orgánica: una interpretación neoinstitucional. *Compendium, 8(14)*, pp. 21–37.

Mamonova, N. (2018). Patriotism and food sovereignty: changes in the social imaginary of small-scale farming in post-Euromaidan Ukraine. *Sociologia Ruralis, 58(1)*, pp. 190–212.

Mestres, S. G., Lien, M. E. (2017). Recovering food commons in post industrial Europe: Cooperation networks in organic food provisioning in Catalonia and Norway. *Journal of Agricultural and Environmental Ethics, 30(5)*, pp. 625–643.

Michelsen, J., Lynggaard, K., Padel, S., Foster, C. (2001). *Organic Farming Development and Agricultural Institutions in Europe: A Study of Six Countries*. Stuttgart-Hohenheim. Retrieved from: https://orgprints.org/8488/ (Access: 28.02.2020).

Milovanov, E. (2018). History of the concept of Organic 3.0 and prospects for its further development in Ukraine. *Balanced nature using, 3*, pp. 15–25.

Morshedi, L., Lashgarara, F., Farajollah Hosseini, S.J., Omidi Najafabadi, M. (2017). The Role of Organic Farming for Improving Food Security from the Perspective of Fars Farmers. *Sustainability, 9(11)*, p. 13.

Nikodemska-Wolowik, A. M. (2009). Organic farming brand identity: Meeting trends, building trust. *Pecunia: revista de la Facultad de Ciencias Económicas y Empresariales, 8*, pp. 263–275.

Pickard, D. (2016). Collective forms of social action: the case of organic farming in Bulgaria. *Organic Farming in Bulgaria (1990–2012). Sociological interpretations*. Sofia: St. Kliment Ohridski University Press, pp. 153–185.

Reganold, J. P., Wachter, J. M. (2016). Organic agriculture in the twenty-first century. *Nature plants*, *2(2)*, pp. 1–8.

Richetin, J., Mattavelli, S., Perugini, M. (2016). Increasing implicit and explicit attitudes toward an organic food brand by referencing to oneself. *Journal of Economic Psychology, 55*, pp. 96–108.

Savchuk, V. A. (2016). Marketing management in the market of organic agri-food products. *Bulletin of Khmelnytsky National University. Economic Sciences, 5(1)*, pp. 150–156.

Schreer, V., Padmanabhan, M. (2019). The many meanings of organic farming: Framing food security and food sovereignty in Indonesia. *Organic Agriculture, 1–12*. Retrieved from: https://link.springer.com/article/10.1007/s13165-019-00277-z (Access: 28.02.2020).

Seufert, V., Ramankutty, N., Mayerhofer, T. (2017). What is this thing called organic? – How organic farming is codified in regulations. *Food Policy, 68*, pp. 10–20.

Seyfang, G. (2004). *New initiatives for sustainable food: a case study of an organic producer cooperative*. CSERGE Working Paper EDM, No. 04-11, 2004. Retrieved from: https://www.econstor.eu/handle/10419/80233 (Access: 28.02.2020).

Stanton, J. V., Guion D. T. (2015). Perceptions of "organic" food: A view through brand theory. *Journal of International Food & Agribusiness Marketing, 27(2)*, pp. 120–141.

Stepanenko, N. (2013). Innovation of value as an objective modality of organic produce branding. *Collection of scientific works of the Tavrida State Agrotechnological University (Economic Sciences), 1(2)*, pp. 317–322.

Terziev, V., Arabska, E. (2014). Innovations in organic agriculture for assuring food quality and safety and healthy living environment. *Proceeding of International scientific and applied conference Role of economic sciences in society development*. UFA, AETERNA, 2014, pp. 3–11. Retrieved from: https://www.aeterna-ufa.ru/sbornik/EC-24.pdf#page=3. (Access: 28.02.2020).

Ulyanchenko, O., Bezus, R. (2016). Problems and tendencies of development of organic vegetable growing and fruit-growing in Ukraine. *Bulletin of KhNAU. Series: Economic Sciences, 2*, pp. 23–32.

Voskobiynyk, Y., Gavaza, E. (2013). Capacity of the organic products market in Ukraine. *Agroincom*, 4-6, pp. 7–10.

Chapter 12

Economic security management

Innovative leadership

*Iryna Markina, Valentyna Aranchii, Dmytro Diachkov,
Yuliia Romanchenko and Mykola Syomych*

CONTENTS

12.1 INTRODUCTION

Currently, the most of the mighty countries of the world are in the process of forming the knowledge society: the innovation type of economy is actively being formed and their transition to the sixth technological mode is taking place. In Ukraine, the third and fourth technological modes are predominant in most sectors of the economy, while in certain sectors the fifth technological mode is being actively formed, which shows a significant lagging behind the national economies of the world leading economies (Ioda, 2009; Semenov & Kozin, 2010). In these situations, Ukraine must correspond to the world economy's trends to save and reinforce its position on the world stage, both politically and economically, and also to strengthen national security by raising the level of innovation practice.

The main component of economic security is the formation of economic independence, ensuring the sustainability and stability of the national economy and its further development. The ability to self-develop and progress is directly related to innovation ability, the creation of a favorable investment and innovative climate, and the development of the intellectual sphere. A constantly growing economy is able to withstand internal and external threats. Economic security and the growth of the national economy are directly associated with the development of innovative activity. Innovations become the most important product of the national economy and contribute to the economic security of the country, as qualitative technological changes are one of the keys for ensuring economic growth.

The impact of scientific and technological advances on economic development and society is constantly growing. The use of the up-to-date technologies, the protection and development of science and technology, as well as production potential, which is able to ensure the production of competitive domestic products, are the main factors determining the state of scientific and technological security of the country. The renewal of fixed assets, the level of technological infrastructure of enterprises, and the degree of competitiveness of domestic products significantly depend on the results of scientific and technical, and innovative activities of companies. Introduction of scientific research, engineering, scientific and technical, and other developments into the production process should ensure the transition of the national economy to an innovative path of development and the scientific and technological security of Ukraine. Scientific and technical security is closely connected with the scientific, economic, and political spheres: it cannot be developed separately. At the same time, this relationship is reversed, because even these areas cannot make progress without effective scientific and technical activities. Modern society has a high technological level of development. Therefore, production technology, management systems, and information support must have a strong scientific basis that will guarantee their competitiveness.

Economic security is determined by the state of productive forces, and social and economic relations, and the level of using the results of scientific and technological progress. In this regard, it can be noted that economic security of the country is based on the development of productive forces—it provides expanded economic reproduction. The world practice shows that economic security is only possible under conditions of the transition of the national economy to an innovative path of development; the accelerated development of the national economy should be done through intensifying investment and innovative activities aimed at modernizing production and increasing the competitiveness of domestic producers. To achieve these goals, it is necessary to create the appropriate conditions to increase the interest of entrepreneurs in modernization and the creation of their own production based on the latest technologies. Ukraine needs to overcome the lack in technology and the development gap with mature economies and create the conditions for the growing intellectual capital and adapting to the processes of economic globalization (Oleksyuk, 2012).

With a significant list of normative acts that are relevant to the country's innovation development, there is no long-term policy of innovation security of the economy and security of certain territories. The urgency of these problems is becoming more significant under globalization, as both traditional and nontraditional threats require a powerful innovative sector of the economy, relevant institutions, mechanisms, models, tools, etc. for their elimination or neutralization (Markina et al., 2018; Naumov et al., 2018).

The reliable and efficient system of economic security and its important component—innovation security guarantees the sovereignty and independence of the country, the protection of national economic interests under the existing of internal–external threats, increasing dynamics, uncertainty of the external environment, and the influence of barely foreseen factors.

12.2 LITERATURE REVIEW

In different states, research has been conducted for decades on aspects of forming an effective economic security. Moreover, the innovative component in these studies is considered as its main component. Noting the importance of the developments on security issues, it should be determined that systematic research on the problem of securing economic security in terms of innovation development has not been carried out until now. This is especially true concerning the processes of ensuring the interconnection of economic security and innovation activity, forming the concept of innovation safety, and its implementation in practice.

Management scientists and practitioners define the new concepts in science, engineering and technologies as innovations, and they identify innovation safety with research–technical or technological security, which is formed as a set of conditions in the scientific and technical areas that ensure the fulfilling of the requirements of economic and, first of all, research–technical security. In this case, security is determined as the security of the state in industry, scientific–technical and technological sectors of the economy, referring to innovation component in scientific–technical progress (Kopylenko et al., 2018; Sakovich & Brovka, 2016).

Another group of scientists highlights the investment security as the economic security subsystem that ensures the level of reliability and safety of innovation processes (Sizov, 2004).

The place of the innovation component implies its entry into the system of economic security (Skrydlov, 2012), and it is argued that "in the system of economic security, innovation activity is manifested in the form of rather complex components of its elements ..." (Bulavko et al., 2009).

Some scholars introduced the term of *innovation security*, understanding it as a "state of economic security, which would ensure the competitiveness of R and D results and products manufactured on the national and international markets, the ability of the economy to ensure sustainable development and counteract the negative factors that take place on the global markets" (Burmistrov, 2015). That is, actually, innovation security is again limited to scientific–technical security.

Ukrainian researchers of innovation security consider it, on the one hand, as a minimum permissible level of developing a scientific–technical base, providing the opportunities of at least simple reproduction of scientific–technical potential and guaranteeing its effectiveness at the expense of its own intellectual resources, defense sufficiency, and technological independence in case of any negative changes (such as external political and economic conditions). On the other hand, innovation security is assessed from the perspective of the economy's openness. Moreover, innovation security "must be based on the criteria, which are contrary to autonomy, autarkicity, and closeness—on the maximum inclusion in the international division of labor in the sphere of science, machinery, and production." (Pankova, 2015).

12.3 THE PURPOSE AND METHODS

All the above-mentioned facts determined the statement of the article purpose: to analyze the country's innovation activity, its influence on economic security's level. However, for the proper forming and solving the problems of ensuring the economic security based on innovation leadership the following main tasks were determined:

- Analyzing the development of Ukrainian's innovation and the countries-leaders of innovations
- Determining the relationship between innovation activity and the level of the economic security
- Developing the conceptual solutions to growth of innovation and economic security of Ukraine

12.4 RESEARCH METHODOLOGY

12.4.1 The analysis of innovation increase of Ukraine and the EU innovation leaders

Under modern conditions, introducing innovations is the main source of economic growth. Modern business entities create new technologies and set the pace of development of the national economy, whose effective functioning through the creation and implementation of innovations increases the level of economic security of the state and its stability. In the transformational conditions of our country's functioning there are a lot of unresolved problems that determine the competitiveness of products and economic security of the country. In spite of this, the important task remains the formation and implementation of an innovation policy that will focus on increasing the level of economic security (Nikoliuk et al., 2017; Syomych et al., 2018; Samoilov et al., 2014).

According to most economic models, sustainable security and constant growth are determined by a set of investments, human capital development, and the level of basic production technologies. Every component is important here. The development of technology as a function of scientific, technical, and innovative activities of society plays an important role in developed industrial and especially post-industrial societies. Ensuring a close and continuous relationship between a fundamental applied science and innovative practice is a determining factor of the effectiveness of scientific and technical activities of economic sectors and innovative development of the country (Filipets, 2015).

Under such conditions, ensuring the national economic security is a priority task of the state, which seeks to fully integrate into the global economy. But for the complete integration into the world economy it is necessary that the country's economy is at the advanced stage of development, guided by advanced achievements in science and technology. That is why, at present, the innovation activity has turned into the main resource of the state, the efficiency of which determines the dynamic and progressive development of the national economy. Activation of innovation development within the national economy, its branches, levels, and subjects of activity is a necessary condition for realization of the national interests of the country within the framework of economic security. It should be mentioned that innovation activity is the whole complex of actions aimed at obtaining the results of scientific–technical research and developments, and their use in solving the following problems: saving resources, reducing financial and labor costs, increasing the volumes of production, improving product quality, population growth, and ensuring the preservation of the environment (Kuzaeva, 2009).

The problem of security in the modern economy of Ukraine has become especially urgent due to the negative consequences of economic reforms, the tendency to domination of fuel and energy components in export, and preferences for food and consumer goods in import. This list can be extended by the weakening of scientific and technological potential of the country, reduction of research in strategically important areas of scientific and technological development, outflow of specialists and intellectual property abroad, and imbalance between mining and processing industries, as well as different degrees of readiness of regions to operate under a market economy by taking into account the opportunities available to them (Bilyk, 2016).

Today, the developed countries are in the process of rapid transition from 5th to 6th technological waves. Examples include some of the numerous breakthroughs in aerospace, machinery manufacturing, biotechnology, and artificial intelligence systems (creating computers that can beat people at chess, compose music, and write books); space and aviation industries are mastering the technology of the continuous support of information and a product life cycle. In contrast, the Ukrainian economy has a significant technological gap, which creates a threat to its economic security. Ukraine is characterized by low values of key indicators of innovative activity of domestic enterprises, which is the evidence that their products are mostly non-innovative and, therefore, uncompetitive. From the total volume of industrial products sold, only 9.8% have innovative features, while this number exceeds 75% in the European Union. Ukraine's lag in the quantity of innovations poses a serious threat to economic independence and, consequently, to the country's security. However, this is not the only risk factor. Another one is the low quality of innovation. According to experts, 75% of investments are directed to the 3rd wave and only 20% and 4.5% to the 4th and 5th technological waves, respectively. The 3rd technological wave also dominates in the technological part of capital investments (technical re-equipment and modernization) – 83%; only 10% is accounted for the 4th wave (Petrova, 2013). Thus, low-tech industries belonging to low-science industries, such as mining and fuel sectors (0.8-1%), food industry, light industry, and agroindustry (1.2%), dominate in the Ukrainian economy. In general, the reproduction of the production of the 3rd technological wave (mining, metallurgy, railway transport, multi-ton inorganic chemistry, etc.) prevail in Ukraine. As a result, almost 95% of domestic products belong to the productions of the 3rd (60%) wave and 4th (35%) technological wave. GDP growth due to the introduction of new technologies in Ukraine is estimated at only 0.7–1% (Zadnipryana, 2011). This causes the need to overcome the technological lag in order to replace outdated technological waves, a high level of depreciation, and a lag in domestic production through the continuous process of search, preparation, and implementation of innovations.

Issues of measurement, diagnostics, and characteristics of innovation security, in particular, innovation activity as the basis for the formation of economic security, remain important.

The Global Innovation Index is the global study of the International business school INSEAD at Cornell University and the World Intellectual Property Organization. The study analyzes the level of introducing innovations in institutions, education, infrastructure, and business and makes the corresponding rating. Last year 126 countries were rated (see Figure 12.1).

Regional indices measured by average points show that North America is the best in terms of innovation development, it is followed by Europe, Southeast Asia, East Asia and Oceania, North Africa and West Asia, Latin America and the Caribbean, Central and South Asia, and, finally, Sub-Saharan Africa.

The first region, the USA and Canada, is among the most effective regions for the formation and implementation of innovations with an average indicator of the Global Innovation Index of 56. The US fell to 6th place, due to lower incoming and outgoing innovations, human capital growth, narrowing innovation infrastructure, and less creative results.

The second region comprises the countries of Europe. The growth of the Global Innovation Index in 2018 in the European countries with an average indicator of 47 is to be noted. Most of the countries with a high level of innovation development are the countries of the European Union. Among the Top 10, according to the analyzed ratings, are Netherlands – 63.3, Sweden – 63.1, United Kingdom – 60.1, Finland – 59.6, Denmark – 58.4, Germany – 58.0, and Ireland – 57.2. New economies with lower than average incomes, which joined the top 10 most efficient economies in the European region this year, are the Republic of Moldova and Ukraine.

Third, in terms of development, is a region that unites Southeast Asia, East Asia, and Oceania. The average indicator for this region for the Global Innovation Index in 2018 was 44. The direction of the development of innovation activity is the ASEAN countries. The highest values show Singapore – 59.8, Republic of Korea – 56.6, and Japan – 55.0

The fourth region is North Africa and West Asia with an average of 34. The most impressive is the level of innovation development of Israel – 57.2, Cyprus - 47.8, and the United Arab Emirates – 42.6.

Latin America and the Caribbean is the fifth region in terms of innovation development, with an average of 30. Chile continues to lead the region with a value of 37.8. Costa Rica has a value of 37.5, Mexico - 35.5.

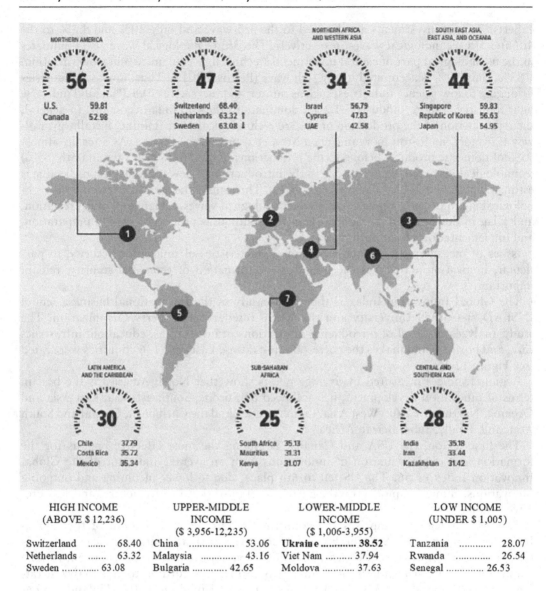

HIGH INCOME (ABOVE $ 12,236)		UPPER-MIDDLE INCOME ($ 3,956-12,235)		LOWER-MIDDLE INCOME ($ 1,006-3,955)		LOW INCOME (UNDER $ 1,005)	
Switzerland	68.40	China	53.06	**Ukraine**	**38.52**	Tanzania	28.07
Netherlands	63.32	Malaysia	43.16	Viet Nam	37.94	Rwanda	26.54
Sweden	63.08	Bulgaria	42.65	Moldova	37.63	Senegal	26.53

Figure 12.1 Top innovation regions by GII score

Source: Data from: Dutta S., Lanvin B., and Wunsch-Vincen S. (2019).

The sixth region is Central and South Asia with an average of The Global Innovation Index 2018–28 (Dutta, Lanvin &Wunsch-Vincen, 2019). Among the countries that have made significant advancements in innovation and research activities: India – 35.2, Islamic Republic of Iran – 33.4, and Kazakhstan – 31.4.

The seventh region is Sub-Saharan Africa with an average of 25, despite the high indices of innovation activity in separate countries. South Africa, with a value of 35.1, Mauritius – 31.3 and Kenya – 31.1, have significant growth in this group.

In 2018, Ukraine was the 43rd in the Global Innovation Index. This is 7 items higher than in 2017 when we took the 50th place. It is also expedient to distinguish the top 5 countries with low income. They are Ukraine, Vietnam, Moldova, Mongolia, and India (see Table 12.1).

Table 12.1 Innovation achievers countries: Classification of group income, region and years of achievement

Country	Classification of group economy income	Region	Years of achievements (total)
Moldova, Rep.	Lower-middle income	Europe	2018, 2017, 2016, 2015, 2014, 2013, 2012, 2011 (8)
Viet Nam	Lower-middle income	South East Asia, East Asia, and Oceania	2018, 2017, 2016, 2015, 2014, 2013, 2012, 2011 (8)
India	Lower-middle income	Central and Southern Asia	2018, 2017, 2016, 2015, 2014, 2013, 2012, 2011 (8)
Kenya	Lower-middle income	Sub-Saharan Africa	2018, 2017, 2016, 2015, 2014, 2013, 2012, 2011 (8)
Ukraine	Lower-middle income	Europe	2018, 2017, 2016, 2015, 2014, 2012 (6)
Mongolia	Lower-middle income	South East Asia, East Asia, and Oceania	2018, 2015, 2014, 2013, 2012, 2011 (6)
Malawi	Low income Sub-Saharan	Africa	2018, 2017, 2016, 2015, 2014, 2012 (6)
Mozambique	Low income	Sub-Saharan Africa	2018, 2017, 2016, 2015, 2014, 2012 (6)
Rwanda	Low income	Sub-Saharan Africa	2018, 2017, 2016, 2015, 2014, 2012 (6)
Georgia	Lower-middle income	Northern Africa and Western Asia	2018, 2014, 2013, 2012 (4)
Thailand	Upper-middle income	South East Asia, East Asia, and Oceania	2018, 2015, 2014, 2011 (4)
Montenegro	Upper-middle income	Europe	2018, 2015, 2013, 2012 (4)
Bulgaria	Upper-middle income	Europe	2018, 2017, 2015 (3)
Madagascar	Low income	Sub-Saharan Africa	2018, 2017, 2016 (3)
Serbia	Upper-middle income	Europe	2018, 2012 (2)
costaRica	Upper-middle income	Latin America and the Caribbean	2018, 2013 (2)
South Africa	Upper-middle income	Sub-Saharan Africa	2018 (1)
Tunisia	Lower-middle income	Northern Africa and Western Asia	2018 (1)
Colombia	Upper-middle income	Latin America and the Caribbean	2018 (1)

Source: Dutta, Lanvin & Wunsch-Vincen, 2019

According to the calculated subindexes for the countries with lower-middle-income economies, Ukraine was the first in GII rating and the fifth as to the index of introduced innovations (the 75th place in the general rating), the country was the first in the subindex of issued innovations (the 35th in the general rating) and the first relative to the efficiency coefficient of innovations (the 5th in the general rating) (see Table 12.2).

The basis of Ukrainian innovation's competitiveness is human capital. As compared with 2017, this index rose at the growth of expenditures of government on education (the 22nd place in 2017; the 26th place in 2018) and science. Concerning the "human capital" subindex Ukraine was the 43rd in 2018 as compared with the 41st in 2017. A low level of R and D spending (the 50th in 2018) is the factor that restrains innovation development, which stipulates the searching of other sources of financing and migration of scientists from Ukraine.

In 2018, as to the subindex "Institutions," Ukraine occupied the 107th place, including the political environment index – the 122nd place (the 122nd place in 2016), the regulatory environment – the 78th (the 82nd place in 2017), and the state of business environment – the 100th place (the 78th place in 2017).

Table 12.2 Top 10 economies for sub-index GII: Lower-middle-income economies (30 in total)

Global innovation index	Innovation input sub-index	Innovation output sub-index	Innovation efficiency ratio
Ukraine (43)	Georgia (53)	Ukraine (35)	Ukraine (5)
Viet Nam (45)	India (63)	Moldova, Rep (37)	Moldova, Rep. (6)
Moldova, Rep. (48)	Viet Nam (65)	Viet Nam (41)	Armenia (15)
Mongolia (53)	Mongolia (66)	Mongolia (47)	Viet Nam (16)
India (57)	Ukraine (75)	Armenia (50)	Mongolia (30)
Georgia (59)	Tunisia (77)	India (57)	Kenya (41)
Tunisia (66)	Moldova, Rep. (79)	Georgia (62)	Egypt (45)
Armenia (68)	Philippines (82)	Tunisia (63)	Pakistan (46)
Philippines (73)	Morocco (84)	Kenya (64)	India (49)
Morocco (76)	Kyrgyzstan (85)	Jordan (67)	Jordan (50)

Source: Based on Dutta, Lanvin & Wunsch-Vincen, 2019; Innovation statistics, Eurostat. March 2017, 2018.

By the degree of infrastructure development, our country ranked 89th in the ranking, compare to the 90th in 2017. Innovative markets of Ukraine received a high rating, which corresponds to the 89th position.

As to the subindex "Business Experience," Ukraine rose by 5 items and took the 46th place (the number of intellectual workers – the 41st place, innovation relations – the 63rd, knowledge acquisition – the 75th).

Concerning the research efficiency, Ukraine was the 27th in 2018 as compared with the 32nd place in 2017, including the index of knowledge creation – the 15th place, knowledge impact – the 40th, knowledge spreading – the 53rd place.

As to the subindex "Creativity," Ukraine improved its position, moving from the 49th place to the 45th, including the index of intangible assets – the 13th place, creative goods and services – the 86th place, online creativity – the 43rd.

In order to properly innovate the country's economic system, the task of finding ways to solve the key problems of the national economy based on innovation growth, not only in the internal but also in the external security spheres of the country, arises in order to increase the value of the state at the regional and world levels, before the theory and practice.

The state's security under the conditions of modern transformation changes is a complex, multifaceted concept. However, most scholars and practitioners agree that economic, food, technological, social, defense, psychological, military, and political and geopolitical security are integral parts of national security. Consequently, like other factors, the level of the GII of the country's economy has a link with other elements of the system of components of national security. It should be noted that the impact on some components is stronger and more obvious, while others are less obvious, but not less significant.

In the process of influencing the innovation activity on the country's economies, and in particular on economic security, most authors proceed from the fact that the level of innovation of the state's economy directly affects the level of economic security (the state of the protection of the economy from internal and external threats, which provides long-term sustainable development) (Gureeva, 2016).

It has been previously established that innovation and innovative security are a form of economic security of the state; the Global Innovation Index and the Index of Economic Freedom hypothesis of interdependence has been adopted in this study. To this end, the indicators of the most progressive countries qualifying to the GII index of different regions are taken for analysis and the Index of Economic Freedom (IoEF) 2018 for these countries is determined (see Figure 12.2).

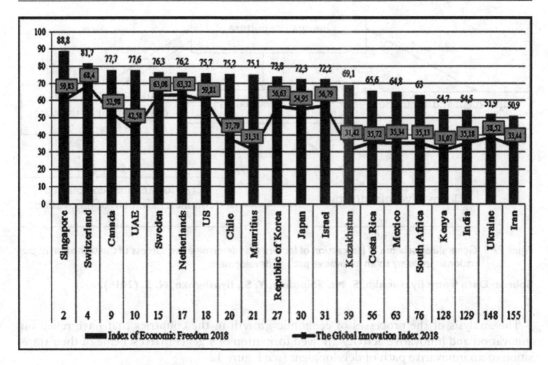

Figure 12.2 The assessment of the GII and the IoEF in 2018

Source: Data from: Dutta S., Lanvin B., and Wunsch-Vincen S. (2019); 112.ua (2018); European Innovation Scoreboard. (2018).

There are complex relationships between the indicated factors, so their impact is complex, but it is not simply the sum of isolated influences.

Correlation–regression analysis enables us to assess the extent of factors' influence without taking into account the impact of other factors. It is known from practical experience that this type of dependence is described by the linear production type function.

The calculated dependence index r = 0.91 illustrates a nearby connection between the GII and the IoEF.

The value of the paired correlation coefficient indicates that there is a close relation between the factors. As $\chi^2_{po3p} > \chi^2_{\kappa p}$, Xi2 calculation is (10.14)> Xi2kp (7.79), the conclusion can be made that the total multicollinearity factors is absent.

To determine the quality of the calculated model it is necessary to analyze the statistical characteristics of the F- criterion of Fisher and the general correlation coefficient. In this case, Fcalc = 7.41 and Ftab = 6.12, then the linear econometric model with reliability P = 0.95. Thus, a linear econometric model that has a reliability value of P = 0.95 is adequate to the experimental data. On the basis of a definite model and the correlation equation, it is possible and appropriate to carry out analysis and forecasting. Note that the correlation coefficient r = 0.91 asserts that the model is of sufficiently high quality.

Ukraine ranked 44th in Europe, and ranked 150 among 186 countries in the ranking of the annual IoEF. Ukraine scored 51.9 points out of 100 possible. Last year Ukraine's index rose by 3.8 points owing to positive changes in 8 of 12 indices. Significant changes have affected the monetary freedom and the freedom of investment, according to the Center site. Ukraine was the last among 44 countries of Europe, and its rating was lower than the regional and general global indices.

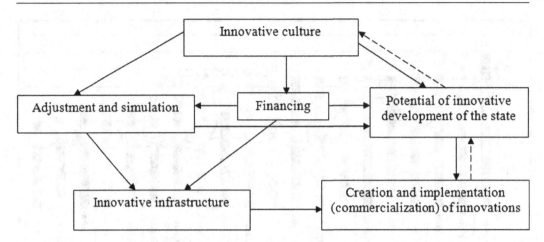

Figure 12.3 Generalized scheme of interaction of factors that determine the success of the transition of the national economy to an innovative path of development

Source: Data from: Ilyashenko, S. M., Shipulina, Y. S., Ilyashenko, N. S. (2015).

The analysis of the processes of economic growth in the countries that have relied on innovation and innovative activity allowed formation of a generalized scheme of their transition to an innovative path of development (see Figure 12.3).

As the figure shows, the formation of preconditions for the transition of the national economy to an innovative path of development is based on its innovative culture. Its main subsystems and their elements, as well as the assessment of their conditions in Ukraine, are presented in (Ilyashenko et al., 2015). According to the scheme, the effectiveness of innovation largely relies on the level of potential for innovative development, which is considered to be a set of resources and capabilities to implement them for the country's development through the creation and implementation of innovation in various fields of human activity. In the process of creating and commercializing innovations, the potential of innovative development intensifies, which in turn affects the development of innovation culture (directions of influence are given in Figure 12.1 by dotted lines). The potential of innovative development of an economic entity with different levels of generalization (an enterprise or institution, region or industry, national economy as a whole) includes three potentials of the subsystem:

1. The market potential as the presence of market competitive advantages or the ability to form them in order to meet consumer needs backed by their purchasing power;
2. The production and marketing potential as the technical capacity and economic feasibility to produce and promote innovations in national and international markets, which will strengthen the position of the country (its enterprises and institutions) in these markets, will ensure its economic security. In fact, in the process of interaction of the factors indicated in Figure 12.3, an innovative favorable environment is created and developed, which results in the intensification of the activity aimed at the creation and implementation (commercialization) of innovations; this activity leads to the growth of the economic security level of the country;
3. The innovation potential as the ability to create innovative developments and implement them in new products, technologies, management methods, etc., which meet consumer needs and allow the competitive advantages of economic entities to be realized.

Thus, in the process of ensuring the economic security of Ukrainian enterprises, the following instruments of the country's innovation policy should be used:

1. Programs of technological development, which are formed to solve the problems of system-forming enterprises and industries that help identify the points and poles of economic growth, as well as technological re-equipment of those industries that can provide the maximum effect for the economy;
2. Individual innovative projects with a high degree of commercialization giving an economically significant effect on specific enterprises, usually with a rapid turnover of capital and a mobile variable range of production;
3. The legislative framework focused on the state support and incentives for investors who invest in science-intensive, high-tech production, as well as a system of targeted tax benefits, state guarantees and loans.

The results of innovative activity are manifested in the following forms:

1. New (modernized) products (goods or services) that meet the needs and demands of consumers better or form new needs and demands;
2. New (modernized) technologies of production and sale of products that are more efficient than traditional ones;
3. New methods of managing the activities of enterprises or institutions that are more effective than traditional ones;
4. New methods of governing the country and its regions, which are more effective than traditional ones;
5. New methods of organizing the life of society, which improve the quality of people's lives.

They contribute to the formation and implementation of relative competitive advantages and the transition to the path of innovative development in line with the concept of innovative advancement, and as a consequence, they result in an increased level of economic security of the country.

The study of economic management experience of the developed countries in the market environment with global competition, the analysis of issues concerning national security of advanced economies prove the well-known fact that the technological revolution is one of the factors that have ensured these countries stable development. This development at the beginning of the twenty-first century can be provided only through the innovative activities of the enterprise. Under conditions of global competition, the innovation factor determines the paradigm of economic development and the essence of the concept of economic security.

12.5 THE DEVELOPMENT OF CONCEPTUAL SOLUTIONS OF RAISING THE LEVEL OF INNOVATION AND ECONOMIC SECURITY OF UKRAINE

The investigation of the potential for the growth of economic security of Ukrainian enterprises revealed its average level, which is determined by a high degree of efficiency of production of innovative goods (works, services) and a low level of efficiency of technological innovations. The average level of growth potential of Ukraine's economic security is due to a high level of efficiency of production of innovative goods (works, services) and low level of efficiency of costs for technological innovations. The relatively stable efficiency of production of innovative goods (works, services) and costs for technological innovations determines the sustainability of effective development of innovative activity in Ukraine (Bilyk, 2016). Thus, to increase the growth potential of economic security of Ukrainian enterprises, it is necessary to optimize the costs of technological innovation while maintaining or proportionally increasing the efficiency of production of innovative goods (works, services) (Ivanov, 2011).

A low efficiency of costs for technological innovations reflects the natural dynamics of enterprises in the depressed region aimed at "simple" renewal of fixed assets through obsolete equipment and technology. The result of this trend is the loss of competitive advantage in the most capital- and labor-intensive sectors, such as mechanical engineering and machine-tool manufacturing, while maintaining the competitiveness of the chemical, electrical engineering, and instrument-making industries. Qualitative symbiosis of investments and innovations should create conditions for the manifestation of innovative metamorphoses in the sectoral structure of the region's economy by preserving the morphology of the regional economy, i.e., the opportunities for economic security of Ukrainian enterprises through the influence on the morphogenesis of the regional economy are revealed (Kosenko, 2010).

Thus, in the process of ensuring the economic security of Ukrainian enterprises, the following instruments of the country's innovative policy should be used:

1. Programs of technological development, which are made to solve the issues of system-forming enterprises and industries that help identify the points and poles of economic growth, technological reequipment of those industries that can provide the maximum effect for the national economy;
2. Individual innovative projects with a high degree of commercialization, which provide an economically significant effect on specific enterprises, as a rule, with a rapid capital turnover and a mobile variable range of production;
3. The legislative framework focused on the country's support and incentives for investors who invest in science-intensive, high-tech production, as well as a system of targeted tax benefits, state guarantees and loans.

According to the instruments of the national innovation policy, the process of solving the issue of economic security in the region should be realized through a reasonable sequence of operations, which consist at least of three stages:

1. Problem statement, which includes the following stages: meaningful problem statement (problem definition and formulation), system analysis of the problem (an object is presented as a system), system synthesis (the process of constructing a mathematical model of the object and determining methods (algorithms) for obtaining a solution to the problem);
2. Development of the program for solving a problem;
3. Implementation of the model and obtaining results. A key element in ensuring the economic security of Ukrainian enterprises should be a mechanism for consolidating positive trends in the scientific and technical complex and the introduction of effective methods to use innovations in production. The mechanism should be based on the national innovation policy, which on a single scientific and methodological basis integrates the strategy and methodology for implementing a set of investment process and innovative activity, as well as a legal framework that allows to materialize society's needs for innovation (Mikhailovskaya, 2009).

To solve the problem of financing research and development, it is necessary to implement the following actions:

1. Use the principle of division of funding;
2. Budget allocations for science should be structured in two main areas: firstly, basic research, which should be fully funded by the state; secondly, applied developments, which should be encouraged by placing government orders with the mandatory involvement of equity participation of direct consumers of the final scientific product;
3. Intensify the work on finding and attracting alternative financial sources, specifically from the funds of industrial enterprises, banks, and international scientific, social, and humanitarian organizations, as well as individuals;
4. Introduce tax and other financial benefits for enterprises and organizations that invest in R and D and innovative projects, in particular, by making appropriate amendments to the regional regulatory and legal framework;
5. Create conditions for competitive distribution of funds for research programs and projects (Yatsenko, 2016).

To ensure the development of the innovation subsystem of Ukraine it is necessary to:

1. Create an optimal combination of instruments of the national innovation policy, which takes into account the potential of the region's economy
2. Increase the efficiency of the innovation subsystem of the regional economy
3. Provide conditions for intensification of innovation and investment activity at Ukrainian enterprises
4. Achieve a high share of innovative products of regional manufacturers
5. Provide conditions for the effective use of the country's intellectual potential
6. Create conditions for strengthening the economic basis of municipalities in the region
7. Legislatively support the development of small businesses focused on the creation of innovative products (Saenko, 2011)

The conducted analysis shows that in the process of ensuring innovation, various factors reduce the security of the social and economic system of the state, in particular: the created national systems of innovation development, which replace the functioning state economic systems of the traditional economy and, thus, upset the established order and the balance of forces; the government management systems, not adapted to innovation development; the systems and information protection mechanisms of innovative processes; large financial expenditures and commercial risks; the countries that have moved to the innovation way of development and significantly strengthened their competitive position on the world market; heavy-handed actions of competitors as a result of raising the competitiveness of innovative products.

Taking into account the defined, the formation of the system of economic security requires the development of a number of directions for ensuring innovation security and innovation activity (see Table 12.3).

To develop the innovative potential it is necessary to implement the above mentioned measures, the using of which will stipulate the system development of innovation activity and raise the level of innovation and economic security. Summarizing the positive world experience, Ukraine needs to create an individual model of an innovative system of economic security, since the existing provides for a consistently linear character, a network form of

Table 12.3 The directions of strengthening innovation security of Ukraine

The direction of strengthening the innovation security	Ways of implementation
Institutional-legal	• regulatory–legal and methodological support of monitoring and evaluating the level of economic and innovation security • the development of state research and scientific–technological organizations, which will carry out the effective coordination of research • the improvement of activity coordination between the government institutions, which regulate innovation activities
Economic	• the creation of new productions, economic sectors of advanced technological modes, intensive technological renovation of basic sectors of the economy • the upgrading of the quality of education and researchers' training • development of an innovative market, which presents creative products and services • the stimulation (using direct and indirect methods) of enterprises' innovation activity • the support of patent-licensing activities of inventors and enterprises • development of international cooperation on the basis of joint participation in international innovation projects • formation of high-tech exports, participation in scientific and technical cooperation • the development of the government-private innovation partnership • provision of targeted financing of priority directions of scientific and technical development • the formation of innovation clusters
Information–analytical	• creation of a system of representative indicators of innovation security • the establishing of the monitoring of innovation security state and open publishing calculations' results • the determining of real and potential threats (risks) to innovation security • the determining of the optimal ways to eliminate the identified threats and making the programs of their implementation • the organizing and ensuring of the control over implementing the measures to overcome or neutralize the threats to innovation security

Source: Based on (Gordunovsky, 2014; Nagorny, Sager & Sigida, 2017; Pisarenko & Kvasha, 2018)

organization for the industrial societies, and is deeply integrated in the state, economic, and social processes.

Instead, the proposed new model should aim at self-organization, and modernization of internal and external trends in the development of the scientific and technological component of the country, which would lead to the transformation of the state economic security management system to adequately respond to exogenous challenges and stimulate endogenous factors (see Figure 12.4).

The suggested model of an innovative system of economic security has the necessary and sufficient number of elements for the implementation of its functions, and is a convenient tool for preparing strategic decisions on optimizing the national innovation system in Ukraine. The model allows us to carry out systematic studies of the influence of specific subsystems, elements of subsystems, the strength of the links between them on the result of functioning and, in particular, to ensure the safe functioning of the country.

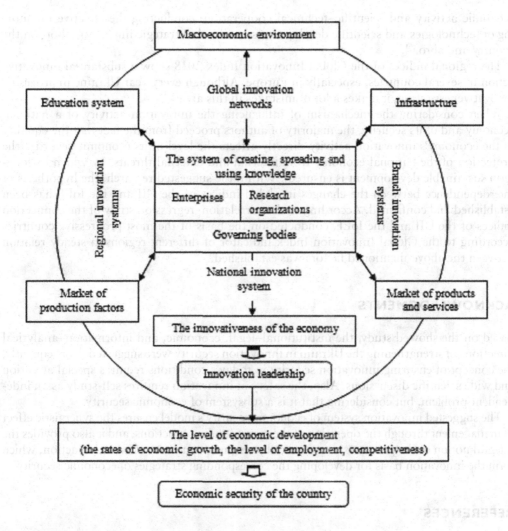

Figure 12.4 The model of the innovation system of economic security
Source: Data from: Bodrunov, S. (2015a, 2015b).

12.6 CONCLUSIONS

Innovation leadership of the country is one of the major factors of its economic development and ensuring innovation and as a result, economic security. Therefore, innovation security is considered as part of economic security, aimed at achieving the position of high-technological, sustainable, and economically efficient, confirming the state's economy and social sphere with innovations and also creating conditions for modernizing branches of industry, forming and implementing the policy of the country's sustainable social-economic development. A high level of innovation security contributes to the reliability of reproducing the national scientific–technical, technological, and production potentials; the change of the priority directions of search, important, and functional research, technical and technological developments to confirm the effectiveness of the state economic condition; the participation on the world markets of high-tech products, which promotes scientific, technical, and technological developments; the justification of intellectual goods, chiefly of external economic activity and scientific–technical cooperation; conducting the effective monitoring of technologies and scientific developments having the strategic importance both in the country and abroad.

The regional indices of the Global Innovation Index 2018 show a substantial innovative action in several countries, especially in Europe. Although every year Ukraine improves its innovativeness rating, it makes a lot of mistakes in this area.

When considering the mechanism of influencing the innovation activity of a national economy and of its security, the majority of authors proceed from the fact that the equality of the economy's innovation activity directly affects the level of its economic security (the protection of the national economy from internal and external threats, by which its long-term sustainable development is ensured). Within the suggested research, the hypothesis of interdependence between the changes in global indices of the GII and the IoEF has been established and confirmed. According to the correlation–regression study of the connection indices of the GII and the IoEF, conducted on the basis of the most progressive countries according to the Global Innovation Index indicator of different regions, a steady relation between the above-mentioned factors was established.

ACKNOWLEDGMENTS

Based on the showed study, the institutional–legal, economic, and information–analytical directions of strengthening the Ukrainian innovation security were suggested. Consequently, the concept of ensuring innovation security in today's conditions requires special attention and wide scientific discussions. Also, the safety of innovation requires self-study as an independent problem, but considering that it is a subsystem of economic security.

The suggested innovation system of economic security's model ensures the synergistic effect of management through the operation of the corresponding functions, and it also provides the integral notion of the processes, resources, objects (infrastructure) of invention action, which form the innovation basis for developing the corresponding strategies of economic security.

REFERENCES

112.ua. 2018. Economic freedom rating—2018: Ukraine ranked last. *Without taboo*. Retrieved from: https://beztabu.net/rejting-ekonomicheskoj-svobody-2018-ukraina-zanyala-poslednee-mesto_n37697 (Access: 02.03.2020).

Bilyk, V. V. (2016). Characteristics of innovative-investment component of economic security of enterprises of Ukraine. *Scientific bulletin of Uzhhorod national university, 10* (1), pp. 35–38.

Bodrunov, S. (2015a). Innovative development of industry as the basis of technological leadership and national security of Russia. *Scientific report. Scientific reports of the Institute of new industrial development (INIR). SPb.: INIR, 55.*

Bodrunov, S. (2015b). Innovative development of industry as the basis of technological leadership. Retrieved from: https://beztabu.net/rejting-ekonomicheskoj-svobody-2018-ukraina-zanyala-poslednee-mesto_n37697 (Access: 28.02.2020).

Bulavko, V., Nikitenko, P., Solodovnikov, S., Shakhotko, L., Gusakov, V., Ilina, Z., Batova, N., Enchik, L., Kondratenko, S., Kulakov, G., Tsilibina, V., Levkevich, V., Piletskaia, K. & Ivanov, F. (2009). Economic security: Theory, methodology, practice. *Minsk: Law and Economics*, pp. 397–399.

Burmistrov, T. (2015). Problems of Innovation Security in Russian Economy. *For a Responsible Power*. Retrieved from: https://beztabu.net/rejting-ekonomicheskoj-svobody-2018-ukraina-zanyala-poslednee-mesto_n37697 (Access: 28.02.2020).

Dutta S., Lanvin B., Wunsch-Vincen S. (2019). Global Innovation Index 2018 (2019). Energizing the World with Innovation. 11th Edition. *Editors Geneva, Switzerland, by the World Intellectual Property Organization (WIPO), and in New Delhi, India, by the Confederation of Indian Industry (CII).* Retrieved from: https://www.globalinnovationindex.org/gii-2018-report (Access: 28.02.2020).

European Innovation Scoreboard. (2018). *European Commission.* Retrieved from: https://beztabu.net/rejting-ekonomicheskoj-svobody-2018-ukraina-zanyala-poslednee-mesto_n37697 (Access: 28.02.2020).

Filipets, Z. B. (2015). Features of scientific and technological development of Ukraine in the context of economic security. *Bulletin of the Association of Doctors of Philosophy of Ukraine. Retrieved from:* http://aphd.ua/publication-37/ (Access: 28.02.2020).

Gordunovsky, O. (2014). The current state and directions of enhancement of Ukraine's innovation security. *Financial Space,* 2(14), pp. 23–29.

Gureeva, M. (2016). Scientific and technical security of Russia at the present stage. *Innovation Science,* 3-1(15), pp. 77–82.

Ilyashenko, S. M., Shipulina, Y. S., Ilyashenko, N. S. (2015). Innovative culture of society as a socio-cultural mechanism activation of innovation activity. *Problems and prospects of innovative economic development: Proceedings of the XX International scientific-practical conference, Odessa, September 7-11, National Academy of Sciences of Ukraine, Institute for Research of Scientific and Technical Potential and history of science named after AHEM. Dobrova NAS of Ukraine, Kyiv-Odessa, Vol. 1. Part 1,* pp. 138–143.

Innovation statistics. (2018). Eurostat. March 2017. Retrieved from: http://ec.europa.eu/eurostat/statisticsexplained/index.php/Innovation_statistics (Access: 02.03.2020).

Ioda, Yu. (2009). Innovation and economic growth: an assessment of development factors. *Bulletin of the University of Tambov. Series: Humanities,* 5, pp. 189–195.

Ivanov, M. (2011). Increasing the efficiency of functioning of regional economic systems on the basis of activation of innovation and investment activities. *East: special issue,* 1(108), pp. 79–82.

Kopylenko, O., Gryshova, I., Diachenko, O. (2018). Leading institutional mechanism of the state regulation and the shadow economy. *Proceedings of the 2nd international conference on social, economic and academic leadership (ICSEAL 2018), Advances in social science, education and humanities research,* 217, pp. 60-68. Doi: 10.2991/icseal-18.2018.10.

Kosenko, A. (2010). Innovation and investment component of the formation of the competitiveness of the national economy. *Official site of the Volodymyr Vernadsky National Library.* Retrieved from: http://www.nbuv.gov.ua (Access: 02.03.2020).

Kuzaeva, T. (2009). Innovative development of the region as a factor in ensuring its competitiveness (on the example of the Orenburg region). *Bulletin of the Orenburg State University,* 9, pp. 58–61.

Markina, I., Voronina, V. Aksiuk, Y. (2018). Marketing information for holding leading positions in the market segment of the grain processing enterprises. *Proceedings of the 2nd International conference on social, economic and academic leadership (ICSEAL 2018),* 217, pp. 193–201.

Mikhailovskaya, O. (2009). Substantiation of the system of innovation and investment. Stock

Nagorny, Ye., Sager, L., Sigida, L. (2017). Comparative analysis of the indicators innovative activity of Ukraine and other countries of the world. *Scientific Herald of the International Humanitarian University,* pp. 23–27.

Naumov, O., Gryshova, I., Rozsa, Z. (2018). Leadership in Energy Efficiency of Agro-industrial Production: Regional Aspects. *Leadership for the future sustainable development of business and education. springer proceedings in business and economics.* Cham: Springer, pp. 579–590.

Nikoliuk, O., Gryshova, I., Shestakovska, T. (2017). The organic production in the context of improving the ecologicalsafety of production of the food industry. *Food Science and Technology,* 11(4), pp. 103–111.

Oleksyuk, V. M. (2012). Innovative development as a component of economic security of the state. *Investments, innovations in the economy. Bulletin of the Chernivtsi Trade and Economic Institute. Economic Sciences,* 3, pp. 111–116.

Pankova, L. (2015). Technological safety: an innovative component. *Russian technological leadership forum "Technodoctrin".* Retrieved from: https://vpk.name/news/124757_tehnologicheskaya_bezopasnost_innovacionnaya_sostavlyayushaya.html (Access: 28.02.2020).

Petrova, I. L. (2013). Formation of the market of innovations in the context of economic security of Ukraine. *Effective economy, 8*. Retrieved from: http://www.economy.nayka.com.ua/?op= 1&z=2221 (Access: 28.02.2020).

Pisarenko, T., Kvasha, T. (2018). The state of innovation activity and activities in the field of technology transfer in Ukraine in 2017: analytical background. *Kyiv.: UkrISTEI, 98*

Saenko, O. (2011). Improving the institutional system in the context of strengthening the economic security of Ukraine. *Bulletin of the Chernivtsi Trade and Economic Institute, 41*. Retrieved from: http://www.nbuv.gov.ua/portal/Soc_Gum/ (Access: 28.02.2020).

Sakovich, V., Brovka, G. (2016). Innovative safety: basic concepts, the essence. *Science and technology, 15(2)*, pp. 144–155.

Samoilov, P., Semenova, I., Matevich, I. (2014). The influence of innovative activity on the economic security of the country. *Investments and Innovations Bulletin of Samara State University of Economics, 4(114)*, pp. 119–122.

Semenov, E., Kozin, S. (2010). Technological structures in the economy and the innovative potential of development of Russia. *Bulletin of the Irkutsk State Technical University, 5(45)*, pp. 327–331.

Sizov, Yu. (2004). Economic security of the region: regionalization, business continuity, strategy. *Moscow, Nauka, 310*.

Skrydlov, I. (2012). Innovative Component of Economic Security of Russia. *St. Petersburg, 157.*

Syomych, M., Markina, I., Diachkov D. (2018). Cybercrime as a leading threat to information security in the countries with transitional economy. Proceedings of the 2nd International conference on social, economic and academic leadership (ICSEAL 2018). Retrieved from: https://www. atlantis-press.com/proceedings/icseal-18/25904333 (Access: 20.03.2020).

Yatsenko, O. (2016). Directions of development of investment and innovation activities of enterprises. *Collection of scientific works of ChSTU, 21*, pp. 92–197.

Zadnipryana, T. S. (2011). Conditions for creating an innovative model of economic development of Ukraine. Retrieved from: https://www.kpi.kharkov.ua/archive/2011/7/7_2011_3.pdf (Access: 20.03.2020).

Chapter 13

The impact of social media communication on the company's reputation

Nada Soudi, Yasmine Kabli,
Chams Eddoha Mokhlis and Mounia Sbihi

CONTENTS

13.1 INTRODUCTION

Nowadays, new technologies are radically redefining communication. Businesses must act, produce, sell and communicate differently. This requires great flexibility and agility. Social networks are at the heart of technological, economic and communication changes; taking the measure of these changes is necessary to understand their impact on the company and its reputation. In addition, consumers express the need to be more in touch with brands on social media. Digital marketing software Hubspot surveyed 569 people and said 60% to 94% of respondents expect brands to be on Facebook and to listen to their customers on digital platforms. Marketing managers are the first ambassadors for this change. Mark Jarvis, Dell's marketing director, said it clearly: "Listening to our customers is the most perfect form of marketing."

13.2 STATE OF THE ART

Different concepts will be mobilized such as brand, reputation, social media and the link between reputation and social media, which we can now call social reputation.

13.2.1 Brand

In her book "the brand," Chantal Lai (2009) defined the brand according to two different approaches: the etymological approach and the legal one.

According to the etymological approach, the word came from the Old High German, *brin-nan* and Old English *byrnan*, *biernan* and *brinnan* via Middle English as *birnan* and *brond*.

This concept first appeared in the United States at the time when cattle were branded to identify the owner. It's a distinctive symbol burned into the animal's skin with a hot branding iron. According to the legal approach and the intellectual property code, the brand is "a sign of graphic representation used to distinguish the products or services of a natural or legal person" (Lai, 2009). This legal definition is focused on the distinctive side of the brand as an intellectual property or as a factor of differentiation from competition (Kotler, 2015).

The brand can also be defined through spontaneous associations that stand in the customer perception (Aaker, 1991), or simply the major asset of the company (Kapferer, 2007).

The brand can sum up all the communications made by all the subjects (individual and collective) involved in its creation (Semprini, 1995). The brand would therefore be, above all, a speech co-produced by the company, its customers and its influencers (Lewi & Lacoeuilhe, 2012). It summarizes different approaches and defines brands as a mental landmark in a market that relies on tangible and intangible values.

In an interview, Bruno Botton (2019), holder of a diploma in marketing from Paris-Dauphine University and a graduate of Skema (a French business school), explains the roles of a brand:

- For the company, the brand has mainly a role of appropriation and authentication: it certifies the origin of the product or the service.
- It is an instrument for rallying and building customer loyalty to the products/services.
- It is also a means of increasing the value of a product or service in the eyes of consumers and therefore of selling it at a higher price.
- And a tool to protect the capital of the company.
- Many concepts are related to the brand, such as brand reputation.

13.2.2 Reputation

Several authors and managers have studied the keys of a company's competitiveness. Besides the classic criteria—physical assets, financial resources and competent human resources—companies gain in competitiveness by being better than their peers and by having a great reputation.

Thus, managers would develop a strategic advantage by generating favorable perceptions in the minds of their stakeholders. In the first issue of *Corporate Reputation Review*, Fombrun and van Riel (1997) deplored the lack of studies on the reputation of companies: "It is surely because reputations are rarely noticed until the companies feel threatened." Today, it is impossible to attest that companies' reputations are underestimated.

According to Cambridge, reputation is "The opinion that people in general have about someone or something [...] based on past behavior or character: The company worldwide reputation is linked to the quality of products."

Reputation is generally seen as the result, not the cause:

- The result of actions carried out by "someone or something"
- The result of the interpretation of the signs understood by the individual transformed into opinion

A "good" reputation increases the intention to buy a service (Yoon et al., 1993); it also acts as a guarantee that influences consumer behavior and affects the confidence placed in new products. Fombrun (1996) defines reputation as "the overall company assessment by stakeholders, which is expressed by their affective reactions." However, it isn't clear why only affective reactions are allowed and why cognitive components are excluded.

Then again, Gray and Balmer (1998) define the reputation of the business as "a stakeholder assessment of the attributes of a company," which almost completely excludes the affective reactions. Hall (1992) combines both cognitive and affective components: "a company's reputation is made up of knowledge and emotions held by individuals". For Bromley (1993), reputation is "a collective system of knowledge, beliefs and opinions that influence the actions of stakeholders."

Reputation can have a positive or a negative value and it can be specified based on attributes or traits (Bromley, 1993). Dowling (2002) specifies that reputation relies upon the attributed values (honesty, integrity, authenticity and responsibility) that individuals attribute to organizations when they hear their names. Reputation is considered as an important intangible asset that results of both strategic and marketing work. The Marketing Science Institute considers reputation as one of the "Gold Research Priorities" (Boistel, 2014). Unlike the image, Argenti and Druckenmiller (2004) proposed a classification of questions that clarify the distinction between these two concepts:

- Image: What do stakeholders think of who you are and who you tell them you are?
- Reputation: What do all stakeholders think about who you tell them you are and what you have done?

Kitchen and Laurence (2003) conducted a study to rank stakeholders according to their level of impact on the company's reputation. The results are shown in Table 13.1.

For Harpur (Mishra, 1978), a good reputation is acquired when there is an ideal match between the values, objectives, intentions, actions of the company and the expectations of the stakeholders. To keep up a good reputation, leaders must consider expectations and achievements.

A positive reputation has three major benefits (Balmer and Greyser, 2003):

- A preference for the company when quality and prices are considered the same as competitors'
- Company's support in times of controversy
- Better stock market valuation

Reputation is also considered as a strong barrier to competition entry since it becomes difficult to imitate the company. It discourages competition imitation when a solid and

Table 13.1 The stakeholders ranking according to their influence degree

	Score
Clients	4.58
Employees	3.92
CEO Reputation	3.70
Press Relations	3.24
Shareholders	3.05
Internet	2.90
Industry specialist	2.87
Financial specialist	2.78
Regulator/ Government	2.64
Diffusion Medias	2.29
Union Leaders	2.29

Source: Kitchen and Laurence (2003)

Emotional Appeal	**Workplace Environment**
- Good feeling about the company	- Is well managed
- Admire and respect the company	- Looks like a good company to work for
- Trust the company	- Looks like it has good employees
Products and Services	**Financial Performance**
- Stands behind products/services	- Record of profitability
- Offers high quality products/services	- Looks like a low risk investment
- Develops innovative products/services	- Strong prospects for future growth
- Offers products/services that are good value	- Tends to outperform its competitors
Vision and Leadership	**Social Responsibility**
- Has excellent leadership	- Supports good causes
- Has a clear vision for the future	- Environmentally responsible
- Recognizes/takes advantage of market opportunities	- Treats people well

Figure 13.1 Element that measure reputation quotient

Source: Fombrun (2000)

lasting positioning is adopted (Weigelt and Camerer, 1998). The reputed product or service is difficult to imitate: researchers have found that a solid reputation increases customers' confidence in products and services, advertising claims and the buying decision. With customers' loyalty, companies can get premium prices and higher purchase rates. According to Caminiti (1992), a solid reputation assists companies in attracting talent and fosters employee retention. Companies with a good reputation have better access to the financial markets, which reduces investment costs and supply rates. It is now clear that the profitability of a company, all other factors being equal, increases with a better reputation. To overcome these weaknesses, Fombrun and colleagues (2000) developed a conceptual reputation model that represents an empirical theory-based assessment of reputation. The result has been the development of a reputation instrument that the authors have called the reputation quotient (Fombrun et al., 2000), which includes economic and non-economic measures of reputation (see Figure 13.1) in six areas.

These six areas can be classified into two big categories: rational appeal and emotional appeal. The first dimension, "rational appeal," includes traditional economic attributes—financial performance, products and services, vision and leadership—as well as noneconomic environmental attributes and social responsibility. The second dimension, called "emotional appeal," includes larger non-economic reputation measures, such as respect and trust in the company.

It seems likely that different groups of stakeholders will value these factors differently. A company investor or a shareholder may be more concerned about the rational attractiveness of companies as a factor of the companies' reputation than an "ethical investor," a worker or a potential customer might be.

13.2.3 Social media

There are three versions of the Web (Sharma, 2018). The social Web brings a set of socio-technical devices (blogs, wikis, bookmarking, etc.) allowing internet users to communicate, learn and even socialize. Today, organizations are strongly encouraged to take advantage of this new resource to promote their marketing communication actions.

These devices are commonly grouped under the name of "social networks" or "social media," such as Facebook, Instagram, Twitter. Social networks are platforms where internet users develop public or semipublic profiles, which they then connect to those of other internet users.

In 1995, 1% of the world population was online. From 1999 to 2013 the number of internet users increased tenfold. Today more than 4.1 billion people have an internet connection and the number is growing at a rate of around 10 people a second.

The top 3 platforms in 2019 (active users) were: Facebook: 2.45 billion per month, YouTube: + 2 billion and WhatsApp: + 2 billion.

Here is what goes on in a single minute of internet time (Desjardins, 2019):

- 18.1 million text messages sent
- 188 million emails sent
- 3.8 million Google searches
- 1 million Facebook logins
- 694,444 hours watched on Netflix
- 4.5 million videos watched on YouTube
- 390,030 apps downloaded on the Apple App and Google Play combined
- 41.6 million messages sent on WhatsApp and Facebook Messenger
- 1.4 million swipes on Tinder
- 87,500 people tweeting
- 2.1 million Snapchats sent
- 347,222 scrolls on Instagram
- 1 million dollars spent online

All of these numbers have surely increased for 2020, a year marked by a lockdown period. New uses specific to this period have arrived and are upsetting habits, since lockdown requires finding activities that do not require going out.

Social networks can also reassure users: finding that everyone is in the same situation can help. They seem to be the refuge of populations to keep in touch during this pandemic period and to support lockdown more easily.

13.2.4 Social reputation

Organizations speak of "e-reputation" to refer to online reputation. Social reputation is an e-reputation specifically on social media. E-reputation becomes a term widely used to designate all the factors and actions aimed at developing and ensuring the reputation of an organization through the web. E-reputation is an extension of reputation on the Web.

E-reputation is defined by Paquerot et al. (2011) as "A built reputation from the set of stakeholder's perceptions about the object and from any piece of information circulating on the Net". E-reputation is an element of reputation emanating from all forms of contact on the web. Frochot and Molinaro (2008) suggest the following definition: "E-reputation, called cyber reputation, digital reputation or even Web reputation, is the image that internet users have of a company or a person according to the information disseminated about him on the Web, it's what is said by others and messages broadcasted by various Internet users."

Therefore, e-reputation is the redocumentation of traces and information generated by internet users (Zacklad, 2006) but also documents that recorded knowledge related to the existence and behavior of organizations. In short, e-reputation constitutes the image that internet users have of a brand present on the Web.

13.3 EMPIRICAL STUDY

13.3.1 Study problem

In today's digital world, social media are part of our daily life. Hence, it is important to analyze the impact of digital trends on consumers' behaviors and perception of brands. Is it a positive or a negative impact? Strong or light?

Thus, the problem of the study is:

"What is the impact of social media on the company's reputation?"

The study focuses on understanding the attitude and the consumers' point of view on companies' digital presence and social reputation. The purpose is still to quantify and measure, through the resulting statistics and figures, social media impact on company reputation.

It can be classified by three main objectives:

- Know the importance of social networks in relation to the perception of a brand
- Evaluate the impact of social networks on the image perceived by internet users
- Define the impact of content and community management on the image perceived by internet users

13.3.2 Study methodology

The objective of the quantitative study is to quantify attitudes, opinions, and behaviors, to define other variables and to generalize the results over a larger sample. The survey is intended for the general public according to simple random sample. The administration of the survey lasted two weeks (end of May 2020), it was a confinement period due to the Covid virus. So persons used more social media and were more willing to answer questions.

We administered the online questionnaire using Google Forms: practical, especially in this period, easy to design and very synthetic in terms of data analysis; 360 responses were collected. The following analysis was performed via Google Forms and SPSS to cross the variables.

The collected sample is distributed as below:

- 12,5% men and 87,5% women
- 6,4% are under 18 years, 88,3% are between 19 and 29 years and 5,3% above 30 years
- 99.7% of respondents use social networks especially Youtube, Facebook and Whatsapp

13.3.3 Study results

Respondents use social media mainly to communicate with their loved ones and to follow the news. The results are presented in Figure 13.2.

Objective 1: Know the importance of social networks (see Figure 13.3) in relation to the perception of a brand.

Almost 70% believe that social networks influence their perception of a brand.

Ninety-five percent of the respondents consult the opinions (see Figure 13.4) shared on social networks at different frequencies to learn about a brand.

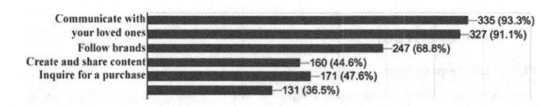

Figure 13.2 Why are you using social networks?

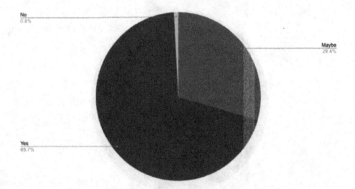

Figure 13.3 Are social networks influencing your perception of brand?

| | | **If yes, how often?** | | | |
		Sometimes	Rarely	Always	Total
Do you consult opinions		1	0	0	0	1
on social networks	No	14	0	3	0	17
to learn about a brand?	Yes	0	159	24	159	342
Total		15	159	27	159	360

Figure 13.4 Do you consult opinions on social networks to learn about a brand? If so, how often?

Most of the respondents believe that social networks influence their perception of a brand through shared opinions and comments of internet users, which they usually check during their purchasing process.

Objective 2: Evaluate the impact of social networks on the image perceived by internet users.

80% of the respondents change their consumption habits (see Figure 13.5) when checking internet users' opinions.

62% of respondents have already expressed their opinions (see Figure 13.6), positive and negative, on a brand on social media

However, rumors influence less than the "trustworthy" opinions of internet users. The results are shown in Figure 13.7.

80% of the respondents have already changed their consumption habits when checking online opinions and comments, including 62% who have already expressed their opinions on a brand, positive and negative.

Objective 3: Define the impact of content and community management on the image perceived by internet users.

As it can be noticed in Figure 13.8, 75% of respondents think that a brand's e-reputation is "shaped" mainly by their content and 70% think that reviews are also an important influencing factor.

The majority of respondents agree or strongly agree with these statements. Indeed, respondents think that the presence of a company on digital platforms is important (see Figure 13.9) and that its content must be well taken care of since it reflects the brand and we can easily judge a brand based on it.

For the respondents, a "digital" company is, above all, a company closer to its customers but also more modern and more innovative. The results are shown in Figure 13.10.

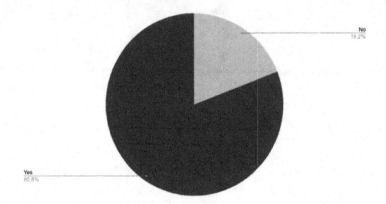

Figure 13.5 Have you ever changed your consumption habits towards a brand because of an opinion on social networks?

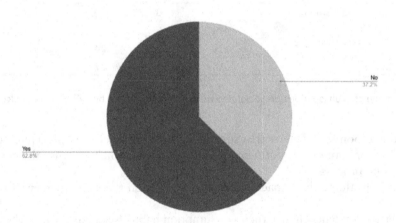

Figure 13.6 Have you already expressed your opinion about a brand on social networks?

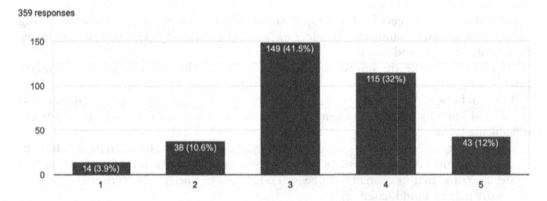

Figure 13.7 How much do rumors on social media affect your perception of a brand?

	Strongly disagree	Disagree	Undecided	Agree	Strongly agree
For you: [The content published on social networks allows you to judge the company products]	4,43%	8,58%	23,54%	48,19%	14,95%
For you: [The interest shown by a brand in the opinions of Internet users influences your vision about it]	4,15%	7,47%	20,22%	39,33%	28,53%
For you: [Up-to-date and credible content influences your opinion of the company]	2,21%	6,92%	14,40%	46,53%	29,63%
For you: [Digital communication is important and allows more interactivity between the company and its customers]	3,04%	3,87%	8,31%	36,56%	47,92%
For you: [The type of content published influences your perception of a brand]	3,32%	5,81%	15,78%	48,47%	26,31%

Figure 13.8 For you, the brand image on social networks is shaped by:

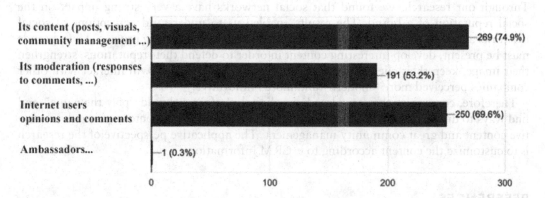

Figure 13.9 For you, the companies present on the digital platforms and which adopt a digital communication are:

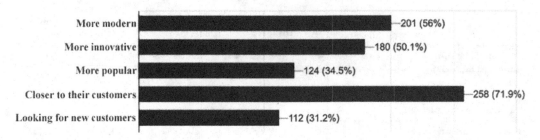

Figure 13.10 For you, the companies present on the digital platforms and which adopt a digital communication are:

Most of the respondents think that the main factors that influence e-reputation are the brand's digital presence, its content and the reviews about its products. They also think that a "digital" company is closer to its customers, modern and innovative.

To summarize, this statistical test has allowed us to prove that social media have a strong impact on brand reputation:

Social networks are widely used for common reasons such as communicating with loved ones, following the news, looking for a job... but also consulting opinions in relation to brands and their products.

A digital presence for a brand is crucial and allows it not only to get closer to its customers and have a modern image but also to increase its notoriety and to strengthen its brand image.

In addition, the published content as well as community management are very important and directly impact a brand's e-reputation. Beware of the opinions and comments on the "recommendation groups," particularly on Facebook, which are now more and more numerous and where consumers are more sensitive, demanding, but above all easily influenced.

Finally, overall, we can see that the opinions of the interviewees generally go in the same direction.

13.4 CONCLUSION

Through our research, we found that social networks have a very strong impact on the social reputation of a brand. The results enabled us to understand perceptions of social networks and their impact on social reputation during the purchasing process. Thus, brands must be present, develop interesting content in order to defend their reputations, strengthen their image, keep their clients and attract others. Otherwise, they will interact with other companies perceived more "modern" and more "innovative."

Therefore, companies that are already on digital platforms should "play the game" and find ways to distinguish and differentiate their brands and digital contents through innovative content and great community management. The applicative perspective of the research is to customize the content according to e-CRM information.

REFERENCES

Aaker, D. (1991). *Managing brand equity.* New York: The Free Press
Argenti, P., Druckenmiller, B. (2004). Reputation and the Corporate Brand. *Corporate Reputation Review*, 6, pp. 368–374.

Balmer, J.M.T. & Greyser S.A. (2003). Revealing the corporation: perspectives on identity, image, reputation, corporate branding, and corporate-level marketing: an anthology. Routledge.

Boistel, P., (2014). Réputation : un concept à définir. *Communication & Organisation*, 46, pp. 211–224. Retrieved from: https://journals.openedition.org/communicationorganisation/4796 (Access: 20.06.2020).

Botton, B. (2019). La marque: un élément essentiel de la stratégie commerciale. CCI Business Builder. Retrieved from: https://business-builder.cci.fr/guide-creation/les-strategies-operationnelles/la-strategie-commerciale (Access: 20.06.2020).

Bromley, D. B. (1993). *Reputation, image, and impression management*. Wiley.

Caminiti, S. (1992). The payoff from a good reputation. *Fortune, February 10, 125(3)*, pp. 74–77.

Desjardins, J. (2019). What Happens in an Internet Minute in 2019? Visual Capitalist.com. Retrieved from: https://www.visualcapitalist.com/what-happens-in-an-internet-minute-in-2019/ (Access: 20.06.2020).

Dowling, G. (2002). *Creating Corporate Reputations: Identity, Image, and Performance*. Oxford University Press.

Fombrun, C. J. (1996). *Reputation: Realizing Value from the Corporate Image*. Harvard Business School Press.

Fombrun, C. J., Gardberg, N. A. & Server J. M. (2000). The Reputation QuotientSM: A multi-stakeholder measure of corporate reputation. *Journal of brand management*, 7, pp. 241–255.

Fombrun, C. J., van Riel, C.B.M. (1997). The Reputational Landscape. *Corporate Reputation Review*, 1(1/2), pp. 5–13.

Frochot, D., Molinaro, F. (2008). *Le livre blanc sur l'e-réputation*. Paris: Les Infostratèges.

Gray, E., Balmer J. (1998). Managing Corporate Image and Corporate Reputation. *Long Range Planning*, 31(5), pp. 695–702.

Hall, R., (1992). The Strategic Analysis of Intangible Resources. *Strategic Management Journal*, 13(2), pp. 135–144.

Kapferer, J-N. (2007). *Les marques, le capital de l'entreprise –créer et développer des marques fortes*. Groupe Eyrolles.

Kitchen, P. J., Laurence, L. (2003). Corporate Reputation: An Eight-Country Analysis. *Corporate Reputation Review*, 6(2), pp. 103–117.

Kotler, P. (2015). *Marketing Management*. Pearson.

Lai, C. (2009). *La marque*. Dunod.

Lewi, G., Lacoeuilhe, J. (2012). *Branding management: la marque, de l'idée à l'action*. Paris: Pearson.

Mishra, V.C. (1978). Charles Harpur's Reputation 1853-1858: The Years of Controversy. *Australian Literary Studies*, 8(4). Retrieved from: https://www.australianliterarystudies.com.au/articles/charles-harpurs-reputation-1853-1858-the-years-of-controversy (Access: 21.06.2020).

Paquerot, M., Queffelec, A., Sueur, I., Biot-Paquerot, G. (2011). L'e-réputation ou le renforcement de la gouvernance par le marché de l'hôtellerie?. *Management & Avenir*, 45(5), pp. 280–296. DOI: https://doi.org/10.3917/mav.045.0280.

Semprini, A. (1995). *The brand marketing*. Oniro.

Sharma, M. (2018). Web 1.0, Web 2.0 and Web 3.0 with their difference. *GeeksforGeeks.org*. Retrieved from: https://www.geeksforgeeks.org/web-1-0-web-2-0-and-web-3-0-with-their-difference/ (Access: 20.06.2020).

Weigelt, K., Camerer, C. F. (1998). Reputation and Corporate Strategy: A Review of Recent Theory and Applications. *Strategic Management Journal, September*. DOI: https://doi.org/10.1002/smj.4250090505.

Yoon, E., Guffey, H. J., Kijewski, V. (1993). The effects of information and company reputation on intentions to buy a business service. *Journal of Business Research*, 27(3), pp. 215–228.

Zacklad, M. (2006). Une approche communicationnelle et documentaire des TIC dans la coordination et la régulation des flux transactionnels. Retrieved from: https://archivesic.ccsd.cnrs.fr/sic_00113272/document (Access: 20.06.2020).

Chapter 14

Higher education as a development actor

The case of Morocco

Asmaa Elmortada and Chams Eddoha Mokhlis

CONTENTS

14.1   INTRODUCTION

The university is an institution that has a particularly prestigious place among citizens. It not only presents itself as the main component of the higher education system where the creation and reproduction of learned culture is practiced daily, but it crystallizes in particular the vision of society towards the desired socio-economic development. It is highly requested, i.e., it is in increasing numbers of requests.

It is in this context that Morocco is increasingly making education one of its priorities through the pursuit of a double strategy that focuses, on the one hand, on increasing the number of higher education institutions to meet the growing demands of university integration, while it works, on the other hand, on the adequacy of the required training with the needs of the labor market.

Such a context prompts us to question the quality of Moroccan university training in the presence of frequent policies to change the education system, as it increases concerns about approaches to recruiting graduates whose number is increasing annually.

14.2 THE MOROCCAN UNIVERSITY

14.2.1 First structuring

As early as 1958, the government aimed to train young people capable of occupying jobs in the administrations and public enterprises (Elmortada et al, 2014). Within the framework of this vision, the Ministry of Education set itself, in the first stage, two major objectives: to generalize primary education, and to orient young people towards the different disciplines of higher education that was organized in three faculties—of letters, sciences and law—heirs of the French protectorate system (medical studies and engineering studies aside).

These decisions were intended both to reduce income margins and to train a skilled work-force to achieve the desired growth. They also had the objective of encouraging the departure of French executives from the public service as well as from the private sector.

On the other hand, Morocco is committed to encouraging young people to continue their university studies. Indeed, the government implemented the scholarship offer system, as it provided information regarding interesting career prospects in administration, and public and parapublic enterprises. The university then became a safe gateway to prestigious employment in the public sector. It also constituted a channel of strong social recognition for young people from the working class.

However, in this first phase, the evolution of the vocational training system is subject to several constraints: those related to its overall improvement from a quantitative and qualitative point of view, those linked to the internal structuring of this training, and finally, those linked to employment and the state of the national economy. Indeed, the vocational training system was characterized by instability at the level of its structures given the separation between technical education and vocational training from the 1970s (1974: appearance of the office of professional training and work promotion named the OFPPT).

As a result, the vocational training system continues to present multiple shortcomings: duality, if not crumbling of training according to the training departments, while the employment environment suffers from an imbalance in the supervision rates, with a manifest shortage of supervisors

14.2.2 The reform of the education system

During the 1980s, and under the influence of a number of economic difficulties, the Moroccan government moved towards the liberalization of the economy as a program of structural adjustment. The aim of this strategy was to reorganize the public sector (privatize viable companies and make unprofitable ones disappear).

Such a policy subsequently put a new challenge before the Moroccan state. Indeed, the growing demand for highly qualified labor has guided those responsible for the education system towards the evolution of operationalized training. This presented itself, at the time, as a miraculous solution bringing Moroccan education closer to its socio-economic environment through the channeling of the pressure of educational demands, the fight against unemployment, the modernization of businesses and ensuring their competitiveness.

In this context, the reform of the vocational training system started in 1984, focused on the coordination of qualification hierarchies, the increase in the numbers of young people accommodated by educational institutions, as well as the adequacy of the training provided, with the needs of the job market.

A second remarkable roadmap for Moroccan education reforms is that enacted in 1999. This is the National Charter for Education and Training. As part of this, a program to change the Moroccan education system is implemented through:

14.2.3 Convergence towards the European LMD system

Based on modular study programs, the LMD (License-Master-Doctorate) educational system was established in Morocco in 2003–2004 with the support of France and for a short time. Like the European LMD, the semester is validated when the modules constituting it are validated. The diploma is then acquired after validation of all semesters. However, unlike the European LMD, Morocco has not adopted the same aspect of the system for validating credits (hourly equivalents) that can be capitalized and transferred; instead, it is oriented towards promoting bridges between training institutions, namely between the OFPPT centers and the faculties.

14.2.4 Governance reform in favor of university autonomy

Until 2009, the Moroccan University enjoyed little autonomy vis-à-vis its own management, so even the presidents of universities were not allowed to pursue strategies specifically adapted to their institutions. As a result, the faculties became isolated institutions with little motivation to achieve the major goals of the university.

In necessary reactivity to this situation, Morocco has followed a new strategy. It is the establishment of the Emergency Program enacted in 2009, the main result of which is the assurance of the autonomy of the university. As a result, each university is free to manage the global grant from the Ministry of Finance offered to it to achieve its contractually determined objectives.

In 2014, Morocco carried out a review of its education system based on the 2012 government program. The axis of this government program *Rayonnement de l'université marocaine en termes de formation et de recherche scientifique*" indeed provided in its level 4 (strengthening and implementation of social programs) to proceed with "the overall assessment of Let us train to improve the quality of higher education, particularly through the reform of the undergraduate cycle. The objective was to strengthen the skills and personal aptitudes of the students by providing them with mastery of languages, communication and information technologies as well as the transmission of the culture of entrepreneurship ..." (INESEFRS, 2018).

Over the 2012–2016 period, this same program also promoted "support for the autonomy of universities within the framework of a renewed contractualization between them and the State, based on accountability and results-based management, with a view to implementing devolution and decentralization" (INESEFRS, 2018). In 2014, the government created the National Agency for Evaluation and Quality Assurance of Higher Education and Scientific Research (ANEAQ) whose mission was operationalized in 2016.

Despite the fact that these changes made it possible to denounce the deviations and abuses resulting from practices at work within universities concerning the conditions of access to master's degrees, the payment of these training courses, the granting of diplomas by nepotism, ...; the 2014 revision was purely technical and mainly concerned modifications to the National Pedagogical Standards Notebooks (CNPN) of the license, as confirmed by INESEFRS (2018).

14.2.5 Diversification of training through the development of private education

The policy initiated by the Moroccan state, the aim of which is to reduce public deficits, has led to a drop in spending on education. Particularly with the increasing increase in the annual numbers of baccalaureate holders, this policy then affected the quality of education

Table 14.1 Evolution of the number of higher establishments in Morocco (2017–2019)

	2017–2018	2018–2019
University education (public)	126	129
Training for executives (public)	71	73
CCP Institution (Public / Private Partners)	28	31
Private higher education	171	163
Total	396	396

Source: Data from Cour des comptes (2018)

in public universities, from which the relay was subsequently transferred to the private sector for the development of employment and private schools. In 2011, the Ministry of National Education received around ten requests for the designation "private university."

To date, there are 163 universities and private institutions in Morocco as shown in Table 14.1.

14.3 THE MOROCCAN LANDSCAPE OF HIGHER EDUCATION TODAY

14.3.1 Result of the established LMD structuring

The reform carried by the LMD was introduced in Morocco with the aim of generalizing it to all universities. Since 2004, the first phase concerned the conversion of the existing license forms into the new system. Since 2006, the revision has affected the master's cycle, and finally reestablished the doctoral cycle in 2008. Thus, in the space of a little over a decade, the LMD system has acquired a certain maturity.

In fact, the following table shows that students in training under this system within universities reached 720,849 students in 2016-2017, i.e. 92.2% of the total of university students. The maturity of the system also crystallizes in terms of training. Indeed, Table 14.2 shows a great diversity of the training offer whether it is undergraduate, master or doctorate.

According to INESEFRS, another indicator of the maturity of the LMD system is based on the development of "professionalizing" training with, in total, nearly 380 vocational training courses including science and technical licenses (LST) and nearly 260 in specialized masters in 2016–2017. However, these streams only welcome 6.2% of bachelor and master students (2016–2017 data).

Table 14.2   The LMD system in figures at the Moroccan university (2016-2017)

Cycle		Number of students in the LMD system	Number of accredited courses
Bachelor	Fundamental studies	623370	311
	Professional studies	32821	378
Master's degree	Academic master	24799	467
	Specialized Master	10212	257
Doctorate*		29647	229
Total		720849	1642

*Not including the specialty diploma in dentistry

Source: Data from INESEFRS (Instance Nationale d'Evaluation du Système de l'Education, de la Formation et de la Recherche Scientifique) (2018)

If quantitatively the LMD system is in the maturity phase, it also includes several other achievements at political, organizational level and also in terms of mobilization of actors, particularly teachers and students.

14.3.2 At the level of professional training

The Moroccan higher education model is characterized by the juxtaposition of universities with other non-university establishments and establishments dependent on post-baccalaureate vocational training.

According to INESEFRS (2018), until 2016-2017, post-baccalaureate vocational training was made up of 1,937 public and private establishments welcoming, 142,999 trainees preparing a diploma of specialized technician (TS). In 2016-2017 alone, 558 public establishments trained 114,468 trainees (i.e. 80% of total TS).

Unlike the other components of higher education, post-baccalaureate vocational training is distinguished by training at the Specialist Technician level which they provide in establishments that also offer training at the secondary technician level. The concomitance of these trainers in the same establishments has the advantage of bringing a territorial proximity (geographic) for the benefit of trainees of different levels of diplomas and areas of specialization. However, it makes it difficult to integrate – even gradually – these establishments into universities, along the lines of the Higher Schools of Technology (EST), which are immediately part of the university.

Their non-integration into universities cannot prevent them from being considered as an integral part of a potentially unified higher education system. Indeed, the establishment of formalized bridges between the university and the post-baccalaureate vocational training component will be likely to encourage exchanges between: on the one hand, TS training and the Professional License; and on the other side the common core (DEUG, DEUP) and the TS.

However, according to the CSEFRS (2019), it should be noted that the dropout rate at the level of university higher education (open access) is 25% during the first year of studies, 40.2% after two years and 20.9% after three years of study in this system.

14.3.3 Private higher education

Private higher education has grown rapidly, creating a great deal of dispersion and heterogeneity in terms of the number of training courses provided and in terms of quality. Indeed, the number of students at the higher level has evolved and reached 960,741 students enrolled in all types of higher education in 2019 as shown by Table 14.3.

Private higher education in Morocco is also characterized by a diversification of the training offered as shown in Figure 14.1.

Although the number of students enrolled in private institutions has increased in the past two years and has increased from 47,272 students in the 2017–2018 academic year

Table 14.3 Evolution of the overall enrollment of students in Morocco at the higher level (2017–2019)

	2017–2018	2018–2019
University education	820430	876005
Training for executives	25634	35452
Higher private institutions	47272	49284
Total	893336	960741

Source: Data from ENSSUP (2019)

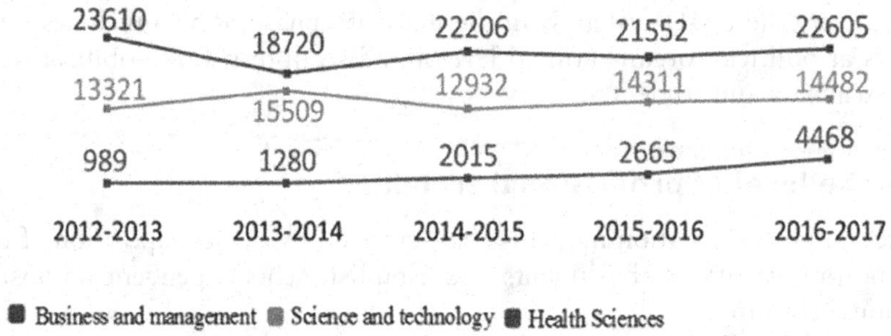

23610	18720	22206	21552	22605
13321	15509	12932	14311	14482
989	1280	2015	2665	4468
2012-2013	2013-2014	2014-2015	2015-2016	2016-2017

■ Business and management ■ Science and technology ■ Health Sciences

Figure 14.1 Evolution of the number of students in private training by disciplinary field

Source: **Data from INESEFRS (Instance Nationale d'Evaluation du Système de l'Education, de la Formation et de la Recherche Scientifique) (2018)**

to 49,284 students in 2018–2019, the largest number of registered students remain in the public sector with 876,005 students in 2018–2019. This highlights, according to Abdous (2020), the open access institutions that have a nonselective system and the default choice that students face when accessing these institutions which are free but do not necessarily offer education quality, hence the large number of students enrolled.

Another problem for Morocco is that the expansion of private education, with its different models existing in parallel with a dysfunctional public sector, has created a multispeed education system that widens social inequalities and undermines social cohesion. Upper and middle class students who attend French schools, other foreign institutions and relatively high-quality private schools have different life experiences and are exposed to a different value system than that of the working class and poor students who attend private schools at low prices and public schools. As a result, today's students who are tomorrow's active citizens are increasingly alienated from each others' life experiences, depending on the type of school they attend.

14.3.4 The scientific research

Over the past two decades, Morocco has paid particular attention to the promotion of scientific and technological research, by putting in place various provisions to this effect. At the institutional level, the establishment of the Permanent Interministerial Committee for Scientific Research and Technological Development (2001), the revision of the law relating to the CNRST (2001), the creation of the Hassan II Academy of Sciences and Techniques (2006), the reform of the doctoral cycle and the Centers for Doctoral Studies (2008), the development of the national strategy for the development of scientific research by 2025 (2006), mark the will of the State to grant importance to research. In terms of resource allocation, a report published in 2019 by the CSEFRS (2019) indicates that the increase in the share of GDP devoted to research, which has gone from 0.3% in 1998 to around 0.8% currently, and Research Support programs also go in the same direction.

These various programs and other initiatives have not, however, impacted national research commensurate with the efforts made and therefore call for a rethinking of the national research and innovation system so that it is more coherent and efficient and fully plays its role—engine of the economy. Figure 14.2 shows the evolution of the global share (%) of scientific publications of Morocco in comparison with other countries according to a bibliometric study that was carried out by the National Center for Scientific and Technical Research published in 2019 (CNRST- IMIST, 2019; INESEFRS, 2018).

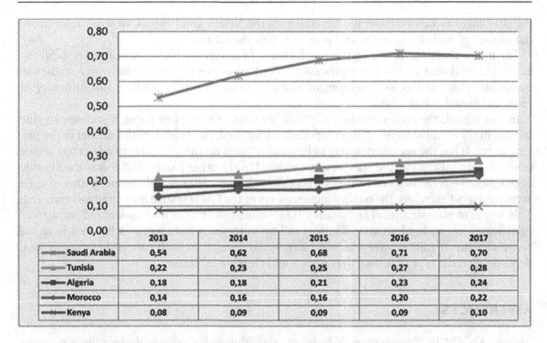

	2013	2014	2015	2016	2017
Saudi Arabia	0,54	0,62	0,68	0,71	0,70
Tunisia	0,22	0,23	0,25	0,27	0,28
Algeria	0,18	0,18	0,21	0,23	0,24
Morocco	0,14	0,16	0,16	0,20	0,22
Kenya	0,08	0,09	0,09	0,09	0,10

Figure 14.2 Evolution of the global share (%) of scientific publications by country

Source: CNRST-IMIST (Centre National pour la Recherche Scientifique et Technique - Institut Marocain de l'Information Scientfique et Technique), 2019

One of the imperfections in the arsenal of research and innovation initiatives and actions over the past two decades is the inadequacy noted in governance and the lack of coordination both at the central level (ministerial departments) and at the level of research operators. This negatively impacts the functioning of structures and the production of research.

In addition, the evaluation conducted by the National Instance of Evaluation (INE) of the doctoral cycle in Morocco, in particular in terms of an international comparative analysis, noted that despite many assets capitalized, in particular following the restructuring after the LMD reform, some dysfunctions still limit its scope as a cycle of transition from a state of "acquisition" of knowledge to a state of "production."

Thus, it is necessary to institute an effective framework for research and to establish good governance so that the doctoral cycle must be oriented and framed by a national policy of scientific research to meet the needs of higher education in teacher–researchers and for the development of research and innovation. In other words, the model of the doctoral cycle in the Moroccan context must be one that makes it contribute to the development of the country while participating in the progress of knowledge. The Doctoral Study Centers of universities must reflect for each university its differentiation in terms of scientific research policy within the framework of national policy, the display of its centers of excellence, and its particularities in relation to the specific needs of the region (CSEFRS, 2019).

14.4 CONCLUSION

Higher education in Morocco is evolving in a context where both national and international requirements intersect. After almost two decades, and in the aftermath of the Strategic Vision for 2030, it is imperative to identify the gains and the constraints. The goal is to see the challenges to be overcome in implementing the Vision and beyond, to work to improve the quality of higher education and project it into the future.

The major challenge posed by the development of university higher education is to fill the accumulated deficit and create a process that enhances the quality of university studies to overcome what hinders its development and give hope to young graduates in difficulty of recognition and perspectives.

In this regard, the reality remains relatively dualistic. On the one hand, it secretes an elite formed in the establishments of its components: regulated, managerial training, and in the private sector. It has the necessary assets to be quickly hired on the job market and occupy senior positions administration and state organizations. On the other hand—and this is the flip side of this model—is the mass of students who follow the basic license training programs of open access universities, where the quality requirements of the LMD system have gradually relaxed. This leaves in play structural constraints (low management rates and undersized infrastructure) which are so burdensome. We thus end up with today's students—who constitute the active citizens of tomorrow—who are increasingly foreign to each others' life experiences, depending on the type of school they attend and their social classes.

REFERENCES

Abdous, Kh. (2020). *Privatisation de l'éducation au Maroc. Un système d'éducation à plusieurs vitesses et une société polarisée.* Brussels: Recherche de l'Internationale de l'Education.

CNRST (Centre National pour la Recherche Scientifique et Technique) (2001). Dahir n° 1.01-170 du II Joumada l 1422 (1er aout 2001) portant promulgation de la loi n° 80-00 relative au centre national pour la recherche scientifique et technique (CNRST).

CNRST- IMIST (Centre National pour la Recherche Scientifique et Technique - Institut Marocain de l'Information Scientfique et Technique) (2019). *Production Scientifique Nationale en comparaison avec d'autres pays.* Gouvernement du Maroc.

Cour des comptes (2018). *Evaluation de la formation initiale dispensée par les universités.* Retrieved from: http://www.courdescomptes.ma/upload/_ftp/documents/22.%20Formation%20initiale_universités.pdf (Access: 20.06.2020).

CSEFRS (Conseil Supérieur de l'Education, de la Formation et de la Recherche Scientifique) (2019). *Réformes de l'enseignement supérieur: perspectives stratégiques.* Gouvernement du Maroc.

Elmortada, A., Mokhlis, A., Elfezazi, S. (2014). Le Maroc actuel: la relation université/employabilité. In: *Proc. Colloque international sur l'Employabilité et l'Innovation dans les Universités du Maghreb.* Faculté des Sciences Juridiques Economiques et Sociales de Kénitra, Les 20, 21 et 22 Novembre 2014, Marocco.

ENSSUP (2019). *L'Enseignement supérieur en chiffres 2018-2019.* Gouvernement du Maroc. Retrieved from: https://www.enssup.gov.ma/sites/default/fles/STATISTIQUES/5341/brochure_2018-2019.pdf. 2019. (Access: 20.06.2020).

INESEFRS (Instance Nationale d'Evaluation du Système de l'Education, de la Formation et de la Recherche Scientifique) (2018). *L'enseignement supérieur au Maroc, efficacité, efficience et défis du système universitaire à accès ouvert.* Gouvernement du Maroc.

Chapter 15

Extra-financial assessment of the immaterial capital (Case of large service company)

Chams Eddoha Mokhlis, Yamadou Diop and Asmaa Elmortada

CONTENTS

15.1 INTRODUCTION

The frenetic race of global dynamics is pushing companies to follow suit, to move forward, to equip themselves to take advantage not only of the opportunities offered by the environment but also to overcome its problems. Conservatism can thus play tricks on those who refuse to live according to the prevailing realities. This dynamic to which we are referring is an unprecedented transformation of the composition of the value of enterprises. It is common knowledge today that the overall value of an enterprise is essentially composed of intangible elements.

The 25-year evolution of the price-to-book ratio on the New York Stock Exchange shows that companies had a market value roughly equal to their book value at the end of the 1970s. This ratio is now around 3 (Fustec & Marois, 2006). This new reality imposes new methods, new ways of doing things, because of the inability of traditional techniques and tools to grasp the realities of the current enterprise. (Bounfour, 1998) shows that, in general, physical goods and equipment tend to diminish in importance in favor of intangible activities, that is, the ability of enterprises to combine the knowledge of their members and networks. We want to make it clear, at this level we are talking about immaterial capital at the level of enterprises, because some of them deal with it at the territorial level and others at the individual level.

This reversal of the market value/book value ratio is due to the marginalization of what used to be the key to the competitiveness, that is, physical capital. The term *immaterial* will therefore be forged to designate something that we know exists but which we cannot otherwise grasp. It will therefore be expressed in opposition to what is physical, palpable, that is immaterial, intangible.

Immaterial capital has been present since companies existed; however, as we have indicated, it was marginal and had a lesser importance in relation to physical assets. Intuitively and empirically, financial markets have long valued immaterial capital (Fustec & Marois, 2006). Part of this immaterial capital has been assimilated into goodwill, which is composed of intangible elements but not considered as such because it does not meet the requirements of IAS 38 (international accounting standard, Thésaurus Bercy, 2011). There are more and more attempts today to formalize immaterial capital and make it a rigorous discipline. Hence the development of tools to evaluate and manage this capital in the image of the one we will use in this paper. There is, therefore, a desire to move from the "indeterminate" specific to the intangible to the "determined" specific to accounting (Dupuis, 2015).

This research is part of a nonfinancial perspective that consists of noting immaterial capital, as do, for example, rating agencies Moody's and Standard and Poor's the in United States. The extra-financial evaluation is no less important than a financial evaluation because before talking about the price of a thing, you have to check its performance. This leads us to formulate our research question, which is as follows: How can an external financial assessment of the immaterial capital of an enterprise be carried out? To answer this question, we deployed the "Thesaurus capital immaterial" methodology (extra-financial component). The particularity of this method compared to traditional approaches, such as balanced scorecard, is that it offers a rating scale by associating a score to each indicator. Thus, it is possible to obtain a score at the end of the evaluation.

15.2. LITERATURE REVIEW

15.2.1 Definition of immaterial capital

Immaterial capital is now considered to be the main determinant of the performance and competitiveness of organizations. This is the gaseous part of the company's assets, according to the concept of extended balance sheet (Thésaurus Bercy, 2011). This parallelism with gas is not insignificant in so far as this immaterial capital, like gas, is difficult to grasp, to control, because it is volatile. This immaterial capital has emerged in the current debates, due to the change of the economic model. This latter is no longer based on the means of physical production and therefore on physical goods. The growing tertiarization of the economy and the popularization of the means of production have moved value creation elsewhere.

According to the OECD (2006) (Organisation for Economic Co-operation and Development), there is no definition and classification of immaterial capital generally accepted by all practitioners and academics. However, several authors have given their views and definitions of immaterial capital. According to the French Intangible Capital Observatory, intangible capital represents all the assets of an organization that are neither financial or materials often excluded from the balance sheet, although they are creators of value, distinctive, competitive and sustainable. (Pierrat, 2009) defines in more detail the intangible asset; according to this author, an intangible asset is part of the value of the enterprise which simultaneously presents several characteristics, namely: absence of physical substance; indefinite lifetime; uniqueness, or at least high specificity; considerable uncertainty about future benefits; not separable from other assets. (Lev, 2001) considers intangible resources to be those that can generate future value without being physical or financial. Analytical models that have emerged in recent years break down the company's intangible capital into three components, human capital, structural capital and relational capital (Bounfour, 2011). Nowadays, we need competent and skillful human resources, not just executants like in Taylorism. Employees leave the status of expenses to that of assets that are essential determinants of the perenniality of organizations. In the management sciences, the School of Human Relations has developed precisely from the awareness of the importance of personnel that is no longer considered as a mere factor of production. The company is not self-sufficient; to move forward, it must forge partnerships with the major players in its environment that can influence its activities. Indeed, value is not created only within organizations but also outside. A loyal supplier granting long settlement times, a bank that allows overdrafts, a recruitment agency that always provides qualified staff, associations promoting a good image of the company as a result of sponsorship actions—these are concrete examples of how good relations can enable the objectives set by the company to be achieved. The organization is this capital, which makes it possible to channel the energies of all the staff and to adapt to changes. It helps to create good dynamics and synergy in order to converge the efforts of all actors. This is a real asset, allowing efficiency and rigor in the execution of tasks. If employees know what they need to do and what part of the chain they are in, the performance would be better. (Edvinson & Madone, 1999) proposes the metaphor of the tree to grasp the importance of immaterial capital. The tree is assimilated to the enterprise; the trunk, the branches, the leaves, the fruits only inform about the present. The knowledge of what is happening in its roots is much more relevant to imagine the health of the tree in the future. The roots, therefore, correspond to immaterial capital. In the measurement of immaterial capital, there are two main currents, one quantitative, concerning financial investment in human, structural and relational capital, the other concerning the development of nonfinancial indicators (Fustec, 2016).

15.2.2 Assessment of immaterial capital

Several methods were proposed by the researchers to evaluate the intangible capital of the company. A synthesis of the methods used was carried (Ramanauskaitė & Rudžionienė, 2013). These two authors classify into four categories as presented in the Table 15.1 below.

- *Thésaurus capital immaterial method*

Thesaurus Capital immatériel is a method of financial and non-financial assessment of immatériel capital that can be adapted to both small and medium-sized enterprises and large groups. The financial evaluation is used in transaction (merger, sale, etc.); while the extra financial evaluation is carried out for management purposes in order to know the degree of performance of immaterial capital. The extra-financial view falls into the fourth category known as (Scorecard Methods). This method compared to other approaches of this same

Table 15.1 Classification of immaterial capital assessment methods according to general principles

N	Group of methods	Features
1.	Market Capitalization Methods – MCM	Based on the calculation of the difference between the market value of an enterprise and its assets, which is equal to the value of intellectual capital. These methods are hard to apply in nonprofit entities or enterprises of the public sector (e.g., market to book values, Tobin's q, Investor's assigned market value, etc.)
2.	Return on Assets Methods – ROA	Based on pretax average income versus average capital unit calculation. Afterwards, the obtained result is compared with the average value of the industry branch, and the result is treated as the average of return on intellectual capital. Part of these methods are based on discounted cash flow calculation and do not avoid some errors (e.g., CIV, EVA, VAIC, knowledge capital earning, etc.)
3.	Direct Intellectual Capital Methods – DIC	Based on evaluation of intellectual capital in monetary units by identifying the specific components or elements (e.g., technology broker–IC audit, total value creation, the value explorer, citation-weighted patents, accounting for the future, etc.)
4.	Scorecard Methods – SC	Based on identification of various components of intellectual capital and attribution of specific indicators or indices to measure these components. The difference from the first type lies in the fact that this type does not seek evaluation in monetary units (e.g., Skandia navigator, IC index, intangible assets monitor, etc.)

Source: Compiled by Ramanauskaitė and Rudžionienė (2013), according to Engström et al. (2003); Lev et al. (2003); Müller (2004); Wall et al. (2004); Sitar & Vasic (2004); Westnes (2005); Kok (2007); Pukelienė et al. (2007); Vaškelienė (2007); Jurczak (2008); Kuzmina (2008); Sveiby (2003); Znakovaitė & Pabedinskaitė (2010); Salman & Mahamad (2012).

category such as for example: the balanced scorecard, the Skandia navigator, the value chain scoreboard has a particularity. It concerns the providing of a rating scale by associating a rating to each indicator. Thus it is possible to obtain a score at the end of the evaluation hence the choice of this method.

After the evaluation, effective capital will be strengthened and capital with deficiencies will be corrected. In this paper we focus on extra-financial evaluation. Thesaurus capital immaterial considers that the company has ten immaterial capital assets, namely: societal capital, natural capital, human capital, information system capital, organizational capital, knowledge capital, brand capital, partner capital, customer capital, shareholder capital. Each type of capital is considered a complex entity that can be divided into several components called criteria. The latter in some cases may have subcriteria. Each final criterion or final subcriterion is associated with an indicator, to which it is assigned a score of twenty that depends on the reality of each company. Some notes can be multiplied by a coefficient. This model may undergo some adaptations while maintaining its relevance. For instance, the client capital can be divided into enterprise client (business to business) and final consumer client (business to consumer). These two categories of customers can then be broken down into criteria as previously indicated. Also, the indicators in the model can be replaced by other indicators, deemed more relevant depending on the context of the company.

15.2.3 Non-financial information

There are two visions of nonfinancial reporting (Erkens et al., 2015). The first concerns another definition of performance that is not limited to the classic measures of financial performance. With this, performance is linked to governance, strategy, operational efficiency and quality management. It is, therefore, based on non-financial indicators. The second approach refers to financial performance. However, the disclosure of this information is done through other means than the traditional channels, such as the annual report, etc. The first vision is much more dominant in literature. Because of this, managers and investors need to know what is beyond the accountant in order to be able to make the right decisions. Nonfinancial information gives private and institutional investors a longer-term view of their investment strategies. As a result, the stock market supervisory authorities have become pioneering bodies in promoting the communication of nonfinancial information (Gauvin et al., 2006). The balanced scorecard is precisely one of the first initiatives in this direction, in addition to those the classical financial indicators propose to integrate: the customer axis, internal processes, organizational learning. Thus, any important aspect of the life of the organizations will be neglected. Nonfinancial information is considered to be information not taken from accounting. It makes it possible to compensate the lack of accounting information needed to assess certain assets, particularly intangible assets (Protin et al., 2014). It is therefore precisely in this vision that a nonfinancial rating of immaterial capital is needed to be perform. A holistic vision of this capital will be acquired.

15.3 METHODOLOGY

Following the literature approach, an empirical research was carried out in 2018, relying on the Thesaurus Capital Immaterial method. This study aims to conduct an extra-financial assessment of the immaterial capital of a large service company operating in Business to Business, which is the local subsidiary of an international firm located in Morocco.

To conduct this study, we have developed a questionnaire based on the indicators of the Thesaurus Capital Immaterial method. This is a Likert-type questionnaire, therefore having proposals for responses going from one extreme to another. This method makes it possible to identify the different subtleties of a phenomenon to be studied. The scale used consists of five levels with a score out of twenty. A high score is attributed to proposals that support the measured dimension and a low score to proposals that are unfavorable. The best score being twenty out of twenty for the best proposal, this score decreases by five points as we go down the scale to zero out of twenty for the last level.

It is important to remember that we simply formulated the questions knowing that the associated indicators, the possible answers and the corresponding notes to each answer are provided by the Thesaurus capital immaterial.

The data collection was carried out by submitting questionnaires to 25 people of different hierarchical levels and functions: 5 members of the Board of Directors, 5 members of the Management Committee, 5 heads of departments, 5 heads of services and 5 managers.

This method has to be adapted to the context of the company and it is in this context that we decided to evaluate only nine capitals, excluding brand capital. This exclusion is explained by the fact that this capital is not relevant to the company since it is not in a market where it must make itself known, put forward a name or a logo to have market shares. Indeed, it receives an annual budget (theoretically considered its sales revenue) from the group to which it is attached in order to carry out its work. The group to which the company is attached is its only client; it was created only for it. Some of the criteria recommended by the method were deliberately omitted, because they were not applicable in this case. This method of evaluation is generic and must be contextualized while maintaining the fundamentals. The valuation of each capital is done in the form of a tree of criteria.

Table 15.2 Evaluation results

Immaterial capital	Scores	Weighting	Weighted scores	Average
Human capital	17.9	3	53.7	
Customer capital	14.37	3	43.11	
Knowledge capital	17.5	3	52.5	
Information system capital	17.85	2	35.7	
Organizational capital	15.64	2	31.28	
Shareholder capital	20	1	20	
Partner capital	17.03	1	17.03	
Natural capital	10.62	1	10.62	
Societal capital	13.33	1	13.33	
Total		17	277.27	16.31

Source: The authors

15.4 RESULTS

The rating scale is (A) for scores of 16 and above, (B) for scores of 12 and above, (C) for scores of 8 and above, (D) for scores of 4 and above, and (E) for scores of 0 and above. Table 15.2 presents the summary of the results. The different immaterial capital don't have the same weight in the value creation process. Their relative importance depends on the sector of activity of the enterprise. A classification into three groups of the different immaterial capital was proposed in the Thesaurus Capital immaterial method, of course, according to the sector to which the enterprise belongs. The company's activity is classified in the Business Operational Services sector. For example, in this sector, leading capital include human capital, client capital, knowledge capital and brand capital. Supporting capital includes information systems and organization, and third-tier capital comprises shareholders, suppliers, and natural and societal capital.

We decided to associate a coefficient of three (3) with the leading capital, two (2) for the supporting capital and one (1) for the third-tier capital. The division of capital into classes is provided in the method. The objective of weighting is to give more weight to the most important assets in the value creation process. Leading capital benefit from the highest weighting; this decreases as they move to smaller capital classes. In this case the weighting does not have a large effect, since the weightless mean, which is 16.03, is roughly equal to the weighted mean, 16.31. The simple average is obtained by dividing the total score by the number of capital, whereas the weighted average is obtained by dividing the total score weighted by the total weighting factor.

15.4.1 Human capital

The summary of human capital evaluation is shown later in Figure 15.4. The assessment grid proposed by the French framework for measuring immaterial capital divides human capital into three subsets and this is more relevant to the measure. These three subsets are:

- *General Manager*: its function is to manage the company in a global way. It engages the company and is therefore responsible for all of its results whether they are good or bad. As shown in Figure 15.1, the criteria measured are many; it turns out that the general manager has demonstrated the qualities of strategist and management by making good decisions in the long and short term, according to reports of the 5 members of the Board of Directors and 5 members of the Management Committee. The score of 13.33

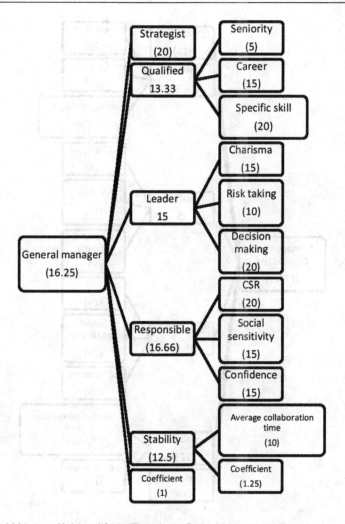

Figure 15.1 General Manager (Adapted from Thésaurus Capital Immatériel: French government)

Source: The authors

at the competence level is explained by the fact that the executive officer has only held this position for two years. Apart from the criterion of seniority at the post, the competence criterion would have been 17.5 considering only the career and competence on the different areas of activity. The executive officer must also be a leader and have good managerial skills and the confidence of the employees. On the criteria previously defined, the leader gets off with a score of 15.83/20 (average: leader and responsible). The assessment of the executive management must also take into account the stability of the individuals in this position. In our case it is only on average 5 years, hence the score of 10/20, which denotes a low stability.

- Management Committee: These are the functional directors who support the executive officer in managing the company. The criteria used for their assessment are the same as those of the executive officer which are leadership, competence, responsibility, ability to be a good strategist. The summary score obtained is 17.41/20. The evaluation criteria are shown in Figure 15.2.

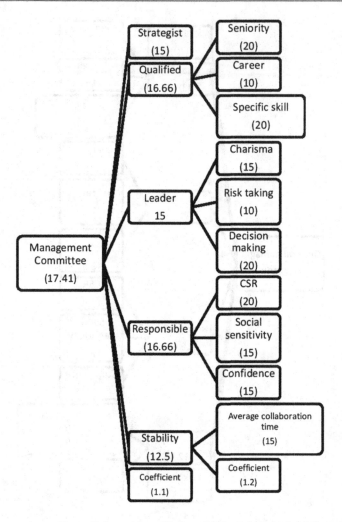

Figure 15.2 Management committee (Adapted from Thésaurus Capital Immatériel: French government)

Source: The authors

- *Staff:* This group is composed of all the other employees; it is the workforce of the company. The criteria measured in this case are more related to operational issues such as:

  - The competence: the indicators at this level are the state of the replacement system (20/20), the notes to the individual interviews (15/20), the diversity (20/20) and the share of the payroll devoted to training.
  - The commitment and serenity are measured by the rate of turnover, absenteeism, the state of the social climate, the level of stress. The coaching rate is 30% in this case. Finally the loyalty is measured, because good human capital is also capital that is stable and not volatile. The assessment of the staff corresponds to Figure 15.3.

The leader's rating is calculated by averaging between the general manager and Management Committee ratings. A final average is made with the result of the last operation and the staff rating to obtain the full human capital rating. The assessment is presented in Figure 15.4.

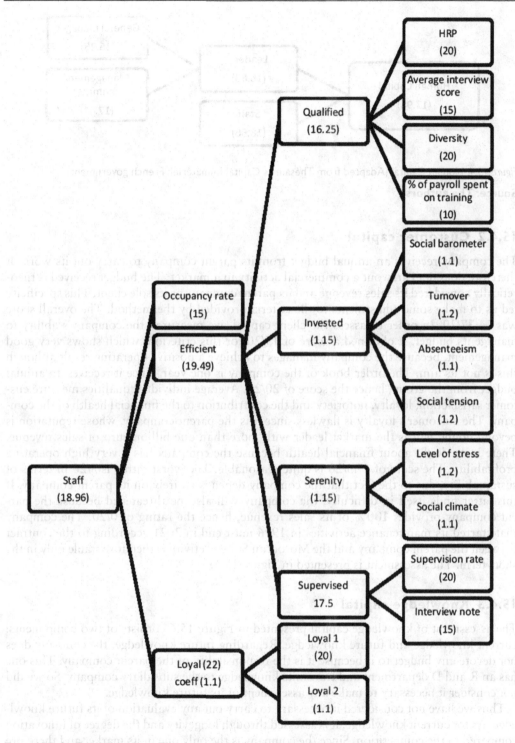

Figure 15.3 Staff (Adapted from Thésaurus Capital Immatériel: French government)
Source: The authors

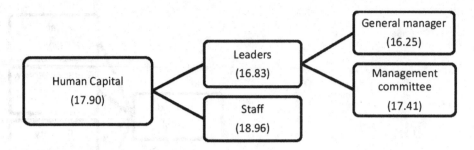

Figure 15.4 Human Capital (Adapted from Thésaurus Capital Immatériel: French government)

Source: The authors

15.4.2 Customer capital

The company receives an annual budget from its parent company to carry out its work. It therefore does not carry out a commercial activity in a market. The budget received is theoretically considered its sales revenue and its parent company as its sole client. This specificity led us to make some adjustments to the criteria provided by the method. The overall score was 14.37/20. In order to assess the client capital, we measured the company's ability to manage its budget. It obtained a score of 15/20 for this criterion, which shows very good management, because the company manages to achieve a positive operating result although this is not its aim. The order book of the company is one year, since it receives an annual budget from the group, hence the score of 20/20. Average individual qualities measure customer satisfaction, loyalty, notoriety and the contribution to the financial health of the company. The customer's loyalty is flawless since it is the parent company, whose reputation is beyond doubt as it is the market leader with more than one billion euro of sales revenue. There is no doubt about financial health because the company has a very high operating profitability. The score of 17.5/20 is quite reasonable. The worst rating is 5/20 in terms of sustainability, due to the fact that the company depends entirely on its parent company. If this latter finds itself in difficulty, the company will also be threatened because the parent company provides 100% of its sales revenue, hence the rating of 0/20. The company that started its maintenance activities in 1996 must end in 2021 according to the contract between the parent company and the Moroccan State. Activity is therefore stable only in the short term. The assessment is presented in Figure 15.5.

15.4.3 Knowledge capital

The assessment of knowledge capital presented in Figure 15.6 consists of two components: current knowledge and future knowledge. Regarding future knowledge, the company does not devote any budget to it because it is the responsibility of the parent company. This one has an R and D department and transmits knowledge to the subsidiary company. So we did not consider it necessary to make any assessment of its future knowledge.

Thus we have not considered it necessary to carry out any evaluation of its future knowledge. As for current knowledge, it is assessed through longevity and the degree of innovation compared to the competition. Since the company is the only one in its market and therefore a natural leader, the ratings of intensity and competitive advantage can only be 20/20. The company brings some process innovations on certain functions, hence the rating of 15/20. Longevity refers to the continuity, the duration in time of such knowledge. Certified according to ISO 9001 standard, the company has developed a quality management system and

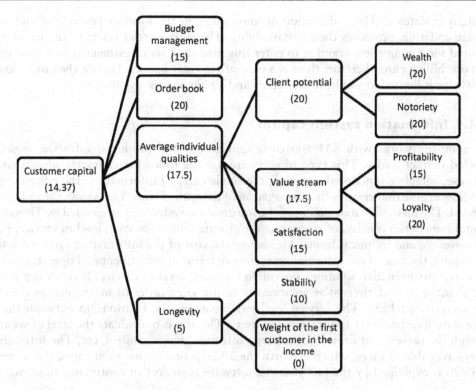

Figure 15.5 Customer Capital (Adapted from Thésaurus Capital Immatériel: French government)

Source: The authors

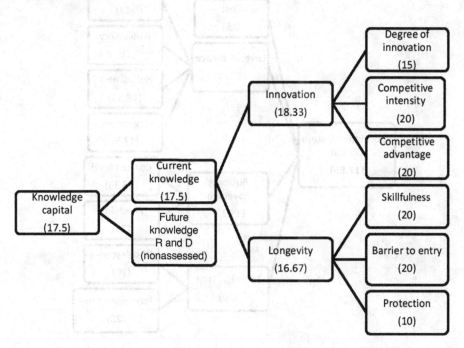

Figure 15.6 Knowledge Capital (Adapted from Thésaurus Capital Immatériel: French government)

Source: The authors

regularly updates it. The codification of knowledge, in the form of procedures and their regular updating, promotes their sustainability. The entry barrier refers to the investment required for a competitor wanting to enter this market. This investment is valued at more than one billion euro, therefore there is a very strong entry barrier. Finally, the protection of knowledge is limited to a culture of secrecy and a fight against espionage.

15.4.4 Information system capital

The company works with SAP (systems, applications and products) software, which is a global market leader. This type of software has the following characteristics: a single database, complete functional coverage, the single entry of information, the presence of a workflow engine that ensures the propagation of data, etc. Figure 15.7 shows the indicators assessed. The method of assessment of the information system recommended by Thésaurus Capital immaterial consists of evaluating the criteria relating to cost, level of service, business coverage and technical limits. Measuring the cost of the information system consists of assessing the cost of the information system in terms of investment and operating costs, compared to alternative solutions providing the same level of service. It turns out in our case that the cost of alternative solutions is in the same order of magnitude as the current software package. The service level part concerns the relationship between the IT (information technology) application and users. The aim is to evaluate the level of security through the presence of firewalls, antivirus software, access control, etc. The software is always available to users, which is worth the 20/20 score. As for robustness, this score of 18.33/20 is explained by the fact that the software is subject to continuous improvement

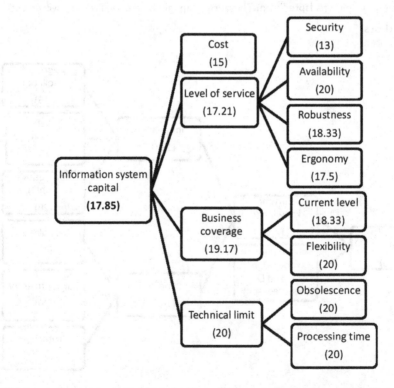

Figure 15.7 Information system capital (Adapted from Thésaurus Capital Immatériel: French government)
Source: The authors

and innovation. Finally, on the ergonomic level, the user interface is comfortable to use and the response time is instantaneous in all circumstances. As for business coverage, SAP brings together all of the company's functions and is easily flexible—only a few days are needed to adapt it to changes. At the technical limit level, the power of the SAP software package is such that it obtains a 20/20 rating when it comes to assessing its technical limits. The SAP software, as well as the basic software, are world standard and are far from being obsolete.

15.4.5 Organizational capital

According to Thésaurus Capital Immatériel, the organization of an enterprise is based on a set of elements, which are the structure, the position of the enterprise in relation to its partners, the level of completeness of the processes, the ability to adapt to change and its degree of control over project management. The assessment, as illustrated in Figure 15.8, focused on the relevance of the organizational chart in its updating and its ability to highlight the various strategic functions of the company.

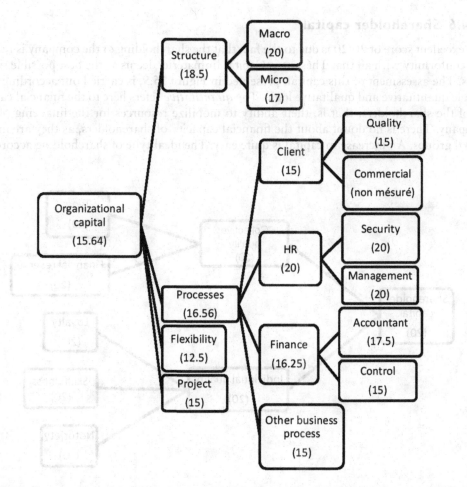

Figure 15.8 Organizational capital (Adapted from Thésaurus Capital Immatériel: French government)

Source: The authors

Business processes are the framework around which the whole organization is built. They distribute the various tasks to the employees concerned. Thus, the diagnosis of these processes concerned mainly the processes:

- Customer about the level of maturity of the quality policy, regarding this aspect the company is certified ISO 9001 version 2015.
- Human resources in relation to human security, as well as management style. The 20/20 score at this level is not surprising, as the company is certified OHSAS (Occupational Health and Safety Assessment Series) 18001 for the occupational health and safety management system and Empresa saludable (healthy company) for health, safety and well-being at work.
- The finance process is related to the maintenance of accounting and control, which is greatly facilitated by the SAP software.
- In terms of flexibility, this score of 12.5/20 is explained by the fact that the company is centralized, the decisions being taken at the headquarters. The maintenance centers dispersed throughout the country enjoy only a small autonomy.
- The company often carries out projects that result from the objectives it sets.

15.4.6 Shareholder capital

The excellent score of 20/20 is due to the fact that the shareholding of the company is in perfect conformity with all that Thésaurus Capital Immatériel deems as the best possible situations. The assessment of this capital, presented in Figure 15.9, is carried out according to a double quantitative and qualitative logic. The *quantitative* refers here to the financial capacity of the shareholders, that is, their ability to mobilize resources for the financing of the company. There is no doubt about the financial capacity of shareholders, as they are major global groups. An increase in capital is quite easy. The ideal type of shareholding according

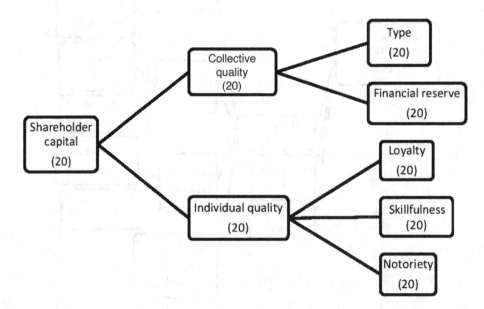

Figure 15.9 Shareholder capital (Adapted from Thésaurus Capital Immatériel: French government)

Source: The authors

to Thésaurus Capital Immatériel is when the company is controlled by its managers. That is, the cases of the present company, hence the score of 20/20. As for individual qualities:

- Loyalty refers to shareholder stability, which has been the case since the start of operations.
- Competence refers to the level of expertise of shareholders in the company sector.
- There is no doubt about the notoriety because the company is owned by multinationals, which inspires confidence.

15.4.7 Partner capital

The external relations of the enterprise are of strategic importance, because their quality strongly influences the activities of the enterprise. There is a strong interdependence between the economic actors. This dependence implies making wise choices of association in order to guarantee its own survival. The choice is not final, however, in the sense that the partners must be evaluated periodically. They must always meet the criteria for which they were chosen. We therefore applied to the company, as far as possible, the evaluation grid of partners (suppliers) proposed by Thésaurus Capital Immatériel. This evaluation examined, among other things:

- The level of service provided. The note of 16.25/20 is explained by the fact that there are rarely defects on delivery (good or service) and delays are rare. Another explanation is claims after delivery are taken into account and the solution is rarely delayed.
- The price quality ratio is rated 15/20. The products are of reference because the suppliers are registered and the price is the average of the market.
- The quality of the relationship is good.
- The partnership at more than 10 years. The robustness of the supplier portfolio focused on, a supplier rating as well as the degree of the risk of supply breakdown. The indicators are presented in Figure 15.10.

15.4.8 Natural capital

Natural capital refers to the living environment, that is, the climate, the quality of the air, the water, the geography, the living environment. The average score of 10.62/20 at this level could be predicted due to the crossing of large desert areas by the pipeline. The 0/20 score, for geography, is due to the fact that the company is located in regions where few people want to settle. The climate is semi-arid over most of the route of the pipeline with significant sunshine. Despite these conditions, access to good quality water is continuous and guaranteed. Several wells have been dug by the company. Air quality is acceptable. The score of 10.62, despite being average, must be nuanced. Indeed, it could not be otherwise because the pipeline cannot be next to houses, where the living environment would be better. It is therefore obliged to take desert routes for its own preservation and security of the population. Figure 15.11 is the presentation of natural capital assessment.

15.4.9 Societal capital

Considering only the city of the headquarters (Tangier), one might think that the company has a very good societal capital: potential local human resources, infrastructure and proximity of public services, etc. However, Tangier only covers a small part of the scope of the company. With its 1400 km, the pipeline crosses various regions and landscapes. As it passes

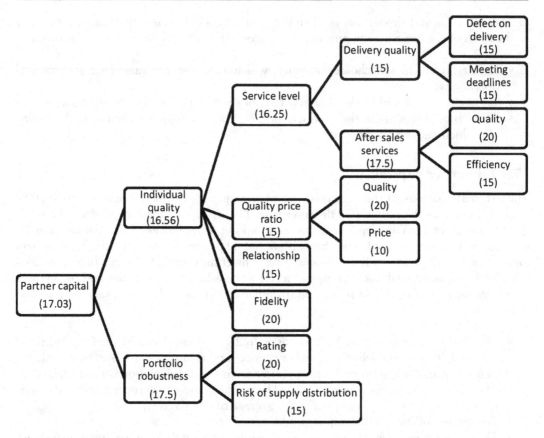

Figure 15.10 Partner capital (Adapted from Thésaurus Capital Immatériel: French government)

Source: The authors

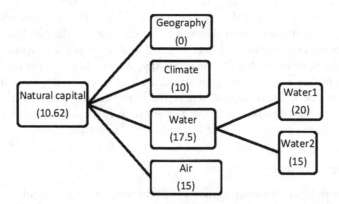

Figure 15.11 Natural capital (Adapted from Thésaurus Capital Immatériel: French government)

Source: The authors

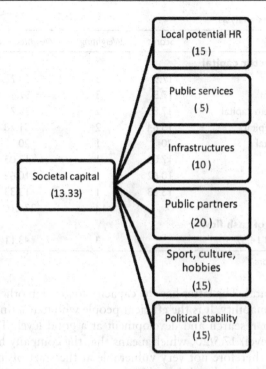

Figure 15.12 Societal capital (Adapted from Thésaurus Capital Immatériel: French government)
Source: The authors

through some medium-sized cities such as Taza and Ouazzanne, the recruitment of staff can pose some slight problems. The pipeline crosses large desert areas that constitute most of its route, where public services are very limited. On the infrastructure side, the airports and railway stations are not always close to the company's sites, but it still has access to the highway. The company's head office in Tangier is very close to the public partners: tax authorities and social agencies. The company's employees have access to fun activities. As an example, in the area of the Algerian border the company has built a large residence for its employees with multiple playgrounds. The country is relatively stable politically, despite the protest movements in 2011 or, most recently, the demonstrations of the HIRAK (Rif People's Movement) in late 2016 and 2017. Figure 15.12 presents the societal capital assessment.

15.5 DISCUSSION AND RECOMMENDATIONS

As presented in Table 15.3, for the analysis, Thesaurus Capital Immatériel proposes to classify the capital in two categories. The first is reserved for the client capital, which is the recipient of products or services and the issuer of sales revenue. The second includes all the other capital, which are the issuers of products and services, and receivers of sales revenue. The cash-collecting capital, and thus the issuers of products and services, obtained a score of 16.73/20, which corresponds to a (A+ level). The capital source of cash obtained a score of 14.37/20 (B+ level). The capital-issuing products and services are better rated than the capital-receiving products. This means that the company has the ability to satisfy the current customer and even find new customers. The excellent 17.9/20 score obtained by human capital is very meaningful. The immaterial capital of yesterday, today and even tomorrow

Table 15.3 Results analysis

Immaterial capital	Scores	Weighting	Weighted scores	Average
Cash flow collector capital				
Human capital	17.9	3	53.7	
Knowledge capital	17.5	3	52.5	
Information system capital	17.85	2	35.7	
Organizational capital	15.64	2	31.28	
Shareholder capital	20	1	20	
Partner capital	17.03	1	17.03	
Natural capital	10.62	1	10.62	
Societal capital	13.33	1	13.33	
Total		14	234.16	16.73
Capital source of cash flow				
Customer capital 14.37		3	43.11	14.37

Source: The authors

depends on human capital. The latter has the capacity to develop other capital, and its good score is a sign of sustainability. It is the efficient people who maintain the organization, the information system, or research and development at a good level. The knowledge capital corresponds to a (A+ level) 17.5/20, which means that the company has good management of its knowledge. It is therefore not very vulnerable at the start of its human capital. The knowledge is formalized, stored and shared in the enterprise as corporate memory. Its development is largely attributed to the quality management system in place. The score of the information system, 17.85/20 (A+), only confirms this result because it serves as a tool for storing and sharing knowledge. The shareholder capital perfectly meets all the criteria of excellence of Thésaurus Capital Immatériel 20/20 (A+). Shareholders can very easily inject money into the company. They are legal persons with international reputations and expertise in the field of the enterprise studied. The rating of 10.62/20 (C+) at the level of natural capital is not very alarming. This is explained by the geographical issues of desert areas. The rating at the level of societal capital 13.33 (B+) is also attributable to the situation of the company.

It can't move the pipeline through the middle of the cities where the societal and natural capital would have had better scores. That capital escapes the company to some extent. The points of improvement consist in adopting good practices, as for example, an attractive pay system, the creation of infrastructures and a pleasant working environment.

15.5.1 Customer capital

In order to improve the customer capital rating of 14.37 (B+), the company should optimize the management of its budget. It might reduce the significant gaps existing between forecasts and achievements. The ideal would be for the gap between forecast and realization to be zero. The B+ rating is largely attributable to the fact that the contract for which the company was incorporated is soon to expire. This therefore raises the question of the continuation of its activities. The parent company must find common ground with the Moroccan State for the continuation of activities.

15.5.2 Knowledge capital

The first recommendation regarding knowledge capital consists in the creation of a research and development department, in order to improve and optimize these operational maintenance processes. The company must be up-to-date, in terms of knowledge and research and development, as this constitutes the company's future knowledge. Another advantage of the research is to be able to carry out certain maintenance carried out so far by external providers. The company will thus increase its skills and autonomy. Current and future knowledge will need to be protected through patent filing if necessary. The introduction of a system of knowledge management can make it possible to strengthen this capital considerably.

15.5.3 Societal and natural capital

These are two types of capital that the company suffers more than it controls. The levers that can influence this type of capital are out of its control. Nevertheless, for the good of its activities, it could invest more in this type of capital. The case at the level of Ain Benimathar (housing for employees, construction of wells, recreational area) is an example. On top of that, they could build a field hospital or schools, build a whole ecosystem where it would be good to live.

15.5.4 Organizational capital

Organizational capital scores are generally acceptable. The rating is 15.64 (B+). The company must, however, decentralize, so that those who are far from the upper hierarchy can make decisions while applying the rules. The ideal would be for the company, to be decentralized with small autonomous units, in order to bring more flexibility and agility to the company.

15.5.5 Information system capital

With a score of 17.85 (A+), the results obtained at the capital level Information System are very satisfactory. However, there are a few areas where data protection can be improved. It is better to introduce a data encryption system in addition to passwords. The system must also be regularly subjected to intrusion tests in order to evaluate its resistance to external attacks. Those are the criteria of excellence of Thésaurus Capital Immatériel.

15.5.6 Partner capital

The supplier is a leading partner. Its current state is more than acceptable with a score of 17.03 (A+). Improvement points exist, so the company must be careful to choose suppliers that meet their commitments in terms of price, quality and deadlines. The relationship with the supplier must not only be good but also a partnership.

15.5.7 Human capital

Human capital and all its components (executive management, management committee and staff) obtained the best possible rating (A+). The position of executive officer suffers from a certain instability (only 5 years on average). The career of the executive officer must be 100% in line with his or her function. Moreover, the company would benefit from investing in the professional training of its employees. The setting up of a system of remuneration and good career management will motivate them and attract top talent. Finally, the company must try to integrate the top 10 companies where it is good to work. By doing so this rating would only improve.

15.6 CONCLUSION

In this article, we have tried to shed light on the question of the extra-financial valuation of intangible capital. After defining the concept of immaterial capital, we presented the methods proposed by researchers to evaluate it. The literature review revealed the difficulty of carrying out this evaluation due to the diversity of the constituent elements of this capital.

Then, we conducted an extra-financial assessment of the immaterial capital of a large service company using the Thésaurus Capital Immatériel referential. Our main results showed that the overall immaterial capital score was (16.31/20), which is the maximum level of the scale. The capitals that contributed most to this rating are two leading assets: human capital (17.9/20) and knowledge capital (17.5/20). In addition to these two assets, are added an asset of the second plan, which is the information system capital (17.85), and two third-tier assets, shareholder (20/20) and partner capital (17.03/20). Organizational capital (15.64) occupies a median position between the highest and lowest scores. Capitals with low ratings are customer capital (14.37), because of the dependence on a single customer and the short-term stability of the company's business, societal capital (13.33) and natural capital (10.62), due to the pipeline passing through desert areas.

Finally, the analysis of these results allowed us to inform the company about the state of its intangible capital, to propose recommendations addressed to the leaders, so they can make the necessary managerial decisions. This extra-financial assessment reveals the reality of the state of immaterial capital. A state that we are not able to know by simply considering its monetary value. A high price to book does not necessarily reflect the good condition of the corresponding immaterial capital. This study contributes to knowledge on the subject of the extra-financial evaluation of intangible capital, and to rising awareness of the crucial issue that its measure represents for managers.

This research focused on a single case. Future research could apply the Thésaurus Capital Immatérial method to several cases, using the latest version of this reference system. This study would benefit from analyzing the links between the results of the intangible capital rating and the firm's financial performance.

REFERENCES

Bounfour, A. (1998). *Le management des resources immaterielles. Maîtriser les nouveaux leviers de l'avantage competitif*. Dunod.

Bounfour, A. (2011). *Le capital organisationnel: Principe, enjeux, valeur*. Springer.

Dupuis, J. C. (2015). Économie et comptabilité de l'immatériel Enjeux du reporting non financier. *Méthodes & Recherches*.

Edvinson, L., Malone, M. (1999). *Le capital immatériel de l'entreprise Identification, mesure, management*. Maxima Mazar.

Engstrom, T. E. J., Westnes, S. F., Westnes, P. (2003). Evaluating IC in the hotel industry. *Journal of IC, 4*(3), pp. 287–303.

Erkens, M., Paugam, L., Stolowy, H. (2015). Non-financial information: State of the art and research perspectives based on a bibliometric study. *Comptabilité - Contrôle - Audit, 21*(3), pp. 15–92. DOI: https://doi.org/10.3917/cca.213.0015.

Fustec, A. (2016). Évaluation du capital intellectuel par des indices de notation, profitabilité et performances financières des entreprises. *Innovations, 51*(3), pp. 125–146. DOI: https://doi.org/10.3917/inno.051.0125.

Fustec, A., Marois B. (2006). *Valoriser le capital immaterial de l'entreprise*. Groupe Eyrolles Editions d'organisation.

Gauvin, E., Good, C. D., Bescos, P. L. (2006). *La perception des entreprises françaises en matière de diffusion d'informations non financières: une enquête par questionnaire.* Comptabilité - Contrôle - Audit 2006/2 (Vol. 12), pp. 117–142.

Jurczak, J. (2008). IC measurement methods. *Economics and Organization of Future Enterprise,* *1(1),* pp. 37–45.

Kok, A. (2007). IC management as part of knowledge management initiatives at institutions of higher learning. *The Electronic Journal of Knowledge Management, 5(2),* pp. 181–192.

Kuzmina, I. (2008). *Accounting of intangible assets in the context of a company's strategy.* Accounting and Finance in Transition, 5, pp. 209–229.

Lev, B. (2001). *Intangibles: Management, Measurement, and Reporting.* Washington DC: TBI, p. 216.

Lev, B., Abernethy, M. A., Wyatt, A., Bianchi, P., Labory, S. (2003). *Study on the Measurement of Intangible Assets and Associated Reporting Practices.* Europa: Enterprise, p. 277.

Müller, C. (2004). *The three Ms of IC – measuring, monitoring and managing.* Proceedings of the Fifth European Conference on Organizational Knowledge, Learning, and Capabilities, March 16–19, Innsbruck.

OECD (2006). *Actifs immatériels et création de valeur.* Paris: OECD.

Pierrat, C. (2009). Immatériel et comptabilité. In: Economica (ed.), *Encyclopédie de Comptabilité, Contrôle de gestion et Audit.*

Protin, P., Besacier, N.G., Disle, C., Bertrand, F., Périer, S. (2014). L'information non financière Clarification d'un concept en vogue. *Revue française de gestion, 5(242),* pp. 37–47.

Pukelienė, V., Palumickaitė, J., Matuzevičiūtė, K. (2007). IK matavimas ir vertinimas: teorinis aspektas. *Taikomoji ekonomika: sisteminiai tyrimai. VDU,1(1),* pp. 103–114.

Ramanauskaitė, A., Rudžionienė, K. (2013).Intellectual capital valuation: Methods and their classification. *EKONOMIKA, 92(2),* pp. 79–92.

Salman, R., Mahamad, T. B. (2012). IC measurement tools. *International Journal on Social Science Economics & Art, 2(2),* pp. 19–26.

Sitar, A. S., Vasic, V. (2004). *Measuring IC: lessons learned from a practical implementation.* Proceedings of the 5th International Conference of the Faculty of Management Koper, University of Primorska, pp. 337–351.

Sveiby, K.-E. (2003). Methods for measuring intangible assets. Retrieved from: http://www.sveiby. com (Access: 21.06.2020).

Thésaurus-Bercy V1 (2011). *Référentiel français de mesure de la valeur extra-financière et financière du capital immatériel des enterprises.* Ministère de l'économie, des finances et de l'industrie. Retrieved from: http://observatoire-immateriel.com/ (Access: 21.06.2020).

Vaškelienė, L. (2007). Development of organizational IC measurement methodology: problems and solutions. *Ekonomika ir vadyba Kaunas, Technologija,* pp. 165–173.

Wall, A., Kirk, R., Martin, G. (2004). *IC: measuring the immeasurable?* UK, Elsevier Ltd., p. 111.

Westnes, P. (2005). *What is IC? Defining and describing the concept.* Arbeitsnotat RF, No. 054, 59 p.

Znakovaitė, A., Pabedinskaitė, A. (2010). IK valdymas transporto sektoriuje. Mokslas – Lietuvos ateitis. *Vilnius, VGTU, 2(2),* pp. 126–133.

Chapter 16

Research of classification approaches of digital marketing tools for industrial enterprises

Anna Rosokhata, Olena Rybina, Anna Derykolenko and Viktoriia Makerska

CONTENTS

16.1 INTRODUCTION

In today's environment, the use of digital marketing tools is of great importance for domestic manufacturers, as it allows them to promote their products to world markets quickly, with a relatively small cost, to provide target audience influence, and to form and enhance their own image, as well as the image of their products, etc.

In our view, the pace of updating of all communication tools is accelerating. In turn, assessing their priority and the highest efficiency from application changes, as well as determination of the best becomes a constant, urgent task for each producer. From a technical point of view, the internet offers businesses an unlimited opportunity to implement image policies. No other type of advertising makes it possible to display the amount of textual, analytical, graphic and video information on an enterprise and its products that is necessary to create its positive image. As a means of communication, the internet is the best way to fully exchange information with clients and partners, and build a system of requests and data exchange (Verdenhofs & Tambovceva, 2019). The main advantage of online advertising is its low cost compared to other types of advertising. But when using promotion methods in the internet environment, some of its features must be taken into account. Since manufactured goods are not mass-marketed goods, bulk email advertising, banner advertising or image advertising on popular online portals will not work (Bozhkova et al., 2018). Special attention must be given to specialized forums that provide the opportunity not only to showcase products and find consumers, but also to communicate with colleagues Big Business Online Edition (2011).

16.2 BACKGROUND INFORMATION

This section is an overview of the concepts and definitions related to the proposed work. A brief description of the digital marketing tools for industrial promotion and internet Communication technologies are provided.

16.2.1 Digital marketing tools for industrial promotion

Analytics show that most Ukrainian producers are haphazardly formulating and implementing policy on the internet, which does not allow them to use its potential, and in many cases even denies the very idea of running an online business. In these circumstances, the task of systematizing the tools and methods of internet communications and developing recommendations on their effective use is relevant. This issue is particularly acute for industry, which determines the pace of development of other sectors of the national economy (Sinevicien et al., 2018; Yevdokimov et al., 2018).

The constant updating of the digital marketing tools and the disagreement among scientists regarding the systematization and classification of the objects of the digital environment need further consideration.

16.2.2 Internet communication technologies

Internet Communication technologies are communication technical (software) methods of creating a communication message, supporting information resources and bringing this information to the target consumer on the internet (Melnik et al., 2016). In the literature some scientists discuss a lot of questions about internet marketing communications; some of them are systematized in this research.

16.3 RELATED WORK

The question of researching digital marketing tools in the articles of foreign scientists is relevant, as evidenced by the results of their work (Karjaluoto et al., 2015; Setkute, 2018). The author (Taiminen, 2016) noted that the use of digital marketing tools should be considered as a comprehensive concept in which different digital channels can be applied at three different levels.

The authors (Nikunen et al., 2017) have proven that businesses use the tools they are researching through five elements of customer relationships. Research by (Thompson, 2005) aimed at identifying the extent to which Business-to-Consumer (B2C) businesses use and anticipate the effectiveness of various online marketing tools. The tools of industrial marketing communications and the role of digital channels are widely considered in Karjaluoto et al. (2015).

The author M. Abraham (2019) analyzes the impact of various marketing tools on fast-moving consumer goods at relatively low cost. The authors Gregori et al. (2015) explored the main issues and analyzed the needs of using digital tools for small and medium-sized businesses.

Based on bibliometric analysis of articles (published in journals included in the Scopus database) the authors have identified promising areas of research related to digital marketing for the period from 2010 to 2019. The main criteria for selection of scientific publications are language of the article - English; time horizon - articles published in 2010–2019 were taken into account; keywords - digital marketing tools. During this period, 2268 documents were analyzed. Using VOSviewer v. 1.6.10, the authors built a map of links between publications

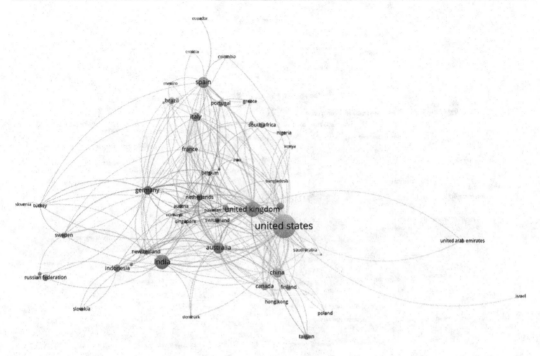

Figure 16.1 Map of publications by countries with the most active researchers 2010–2019 (developed by the authors on the basis of (VOSviewer v. 1.6.10, 2020)

by country. It is determined that the largest number of publications on the subject of the study is available in the United States (522), as well as in Great Britain (222), India (195), Australia (117), Spain (116), China (88), Italy (73), Germany (70), Canada (65) and France (53).

The analysis demonstrates nine clusters of research on the subject of Digital Marketing tools (Figure 16.1).

The obtained results confirmed the growing trend of works focusing on the analysis of digital marketing. Figure 16.2 shows the relationships between keywords and terms used in the research publications.

The problems of using digital marketing tools (including internet technologies, communication tools) for the promotion of industrial products were investigated in the works of Ukrainian scientists such as Glinenko L.K. & Dainovsky Yu. A. (2018), Zanori V.O. (2018), Ilyashenko S.M. and Ivanova, T.E. (2015), Litovchenko, I.L. & Pylypchuk, V. P. (2008), Mozgova G.V. (2013), Ruban V.V. (2017) and others. Their work discusses various aspects of promoting industrial products using the digital marketing toolkit, its basic methods and mechanisms.

16.4 PROPOSED SYSTEM

Ilyashenko S.M. & Ivanova, T. E. (2015) attributed to the latest forms of internet marketing communications:

- Email advertising
- Bulletin board services (BBS)
- Contextual (search) advertising
- Display (banner) advertising

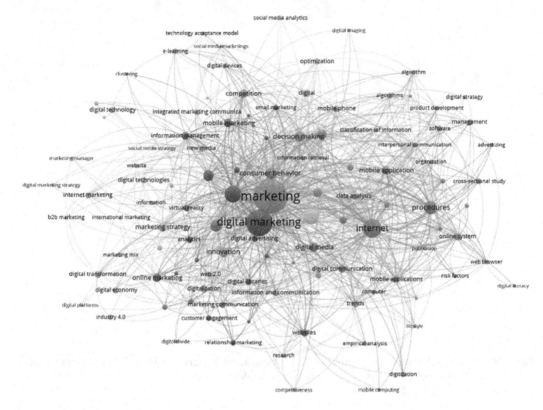

Figure 16.2 Map of the use of keywords in scientific publications 2010–2019 (developed by the authors on the basis of (VOSviewer v. 1.6.10, 2020)

- Video (digital) advertising
- Background advertising
- Rich media
- Lead generation
- Site sponsorship
- Targeting
- Search engine marketing (SEM)
- Search engine optimization (SEO)
- Site optimization for social networks
- Social media marketing
- Viral internet marketing
- Direct internet marketing

Litovchenko I.L. & Pylypchuk, V.P. (2008), along with the traditional tools of internet marketing communications (internet advertising, internet PR, sales promotion, direct marketing) distinguishes (defining them as special forms of communication):

- Online sales
- Search engine optimization
- Virtual communities (forums and chats, blogs, virtual networks, virtual games and worlds)

Mozgova G.V. (2013) identifies the following specific communication tools on the internet:

- Corporate site
- Contextual advertising
- Display advertising
- Advertising on widgets
- Product placement in online games
- Cross-branding
- Affiliate marketing
- SMM
- SEM
- Rating and comparison sites
- Podcasting
- Blogging
- Viral marketing
- Direct marketing
- e-CRM systems

Zanora, V.O. (2018), includes the following elements of internet marketing components: direct marketing, contextual advertising, display advertising, internet branding, viral marketing, marketing on social networks, search engine optimization, optimization for social networks, content marketing, email marketing. According to Ruban V.V. (2017) internet marketing includes such elements of the system as display advertising; contextual advertising; search engine marketing in general and SEO in particular; promotion in social networks: SMO and SMM; direct marketing using email, RSS, etc.; viral marketing; guerrilla marketing; internet branding.

Melnik Yu. M., Sager L. Yu., Illyashenko N. S. and Ryazantseva Yu. M. (2016) divide the internet marketing communications system into tools and technologies. They believe that the only means of communication on the internet is the website, but information (communication message) can be represented by various forms of internet communication: electronic media, banners, portals, rich media, blogs, forums, search engines, message boards, emails, articles, videos, cookies, personal pages, virtual communities and more. And the most popular internet communication technologies include SEO (search engine optimization), lead generation, product placement and targeting, as well as various types of marketing with their sets of rules, features and techniques: SMM (social media marketing), SEM (search engine marketing), viral marketing, content marketing, guerrilla marketing, horror marketing, provocative marketing, etc. (Melnyk et al., 2019). Systematic analysis and generalization of literature sources and practices of marketing activity in the internet environment gave us grounds to identify the main tools of digital marketing, as well as the main features of their classification, which distinguish domestic (Teletov et al., 2019; Saher, 2015; Baranchenko et al., 2019) and foreign scholars (Yeo et al., 2019; Isohella et al., 2017; Harsimrat, 2016; Išoraitė, 2016), as well as what we offer (Figure 16.3).

1. *By geographical feature:*
    - Local (target audience is limited by geographical location). These include local on-line marketplaces, sites and groups of cities/regions/countries in social networks
    - Global (target audience is not limited by geographical location). This is especially true of services such as site creation, design and more. These include aggregators

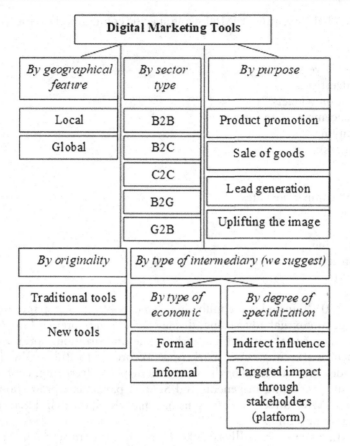

Figure 16.3 Classification of digital marketing tools

2. *By sector type:*
   - B2B (Business-to-Business). Communications between commercial partners—it is advisable to use personal site, registration in special forums, etc.
   - B2C (Business-to-Customer). Communications between the enterprise and consumers—it is advisable to use site, marketplaces, social networks, price aggregators, etc.
   - C2C (Customer-to-Customer). Communications between consumers (for example, the world-famous eBay and Amazon stock platforms)
   - B2G (Business-to-Government). Communications between business and government (government)—e-commerce systems (e.g., e-procurement systems)
   - G2B (Government-to-Business). A set of software and hardware for the online interaction of the executive and commercial structures to support and grow the business (e.g., government information websites, e-procurement systems, etc.)
3. *For the purpose of:*
   - Development, creation, improvement of the product and its promotion in the market (sites, advertising on the internet, forums, blogs of the producer)
   - Sale of products or services (It is advisable to create a website where the consumer will be able to buy/order the service directly.)

- Lead generation—attracting the target audience to the selling site by different methods: email, social networks, use of contextuality, banner or teaser advertising
- Enhancing image (It is necessary to monitor the reputation of the company on the internet by using only qualitative and unique content distributed in the internet environment.)

4. *By uniqueness:*
   - Traditional tools (advertising, public relations, direct marketing, sales promotion)
   - New tools [interactive communities (chats, discussion groups, communities); virtual marketing (internet word-of-mouth or gossip marketing), an online e-commerce platform (Amazon, OLX)]

5. *By type of mediation (we offer this feature):*
   5.1 *By degree of specialization:*
   - Tools of indirect influence (internet sites and other tools, and tools which contain multidirectional information, not specialized)
   - Tools of purposeful influence (through interested intermediaries—e-commerce systems, specialized portals, platforms)

   5.2 *By type of economic interest:*
   - Formal (defined and enshrined in special agreements for the provision of intermediary services)
   - Informal (used randomly, no cooperation agreements)

Separation of a new classification attribute "by type of mediation" helps further systematization of digital marketing tools, deepening understanding of the impact of different tools (indirect, focused), their degree of specialization and economic interest, which allows the most effective use of their various entities to be determined (Glinenko L.K. & Dainovsky Yu. A., 2018). E-commerce business models include the following: electronic showcase (manufacturer's website); online store; electronic bulletin board; e-shop/e-supermarket; price aggregator; electronic auction; electronic trading platform (platform); electronic marketplace; electronic ordering table.

We carried out a comparative analysis of the main digital tools. Table 16.1 summarizes their characteristics and specifies the application features of each of the digital tools listed above.

It should be noted that this classification is not exhaustive. The market for digital technologies and online resources is constantly changing. Every day creative developers, managers, marketers and other professionals add more tools to use for the promotion of goods and services.

First, one can say that the listed digital tools are basic, but there are also tools that simplify and assist in their utilization. Auxiliary (concomitant) Digital-tools include those that optimize, simplify, help to most effectively perform the tasks of basic Digital-tools.

Example of use of auxiliary (concomitant) digital tools is illustrated by the main tool, i.e., direct mail, when in order to form a database of emails marketers address the platforms for finding people and generating leads.

Depending on the purpose of the enterprise for which the data is collected, the data at the internet platform can be different. Some of the most popular platforms are LinkedIn.com, Insideview.com, Crunchbase.com, Builtwith.com and many more.

Also for the implementation of a digital tool—email—the main requirement is the availability of email addresses of recipients, but in the case of "cold contact" emails—i.e., the first contact—the company may not have these email addresses. In order to generate and

Table 16.1 Characteristics and features of major digital tools

Name of method/tool	Essence of the tool	Description features		Application features
		Pros	Cons	
1	*2*	*3*	*4*	*5*
Web site of the manufacturer	Site for placing information about the company, product catalogue, etc.	Ability to present it on any platform and declare its existence on the global market	Need to have a full-time professional to support the site	It is advisable to use a site such as "business card", "landing page"
E-commerce sites (platforms)	Site for placing information about the company/product/ service (placement)	Shareware information placement	Needs to be updated regularly (on average once a month)	It is necessary to install a UTM tag to track the traffic
Online storefront	Specialized site to sell custom-made products through own website	Ability to provide broad product information	Extra maintenance costs for manufacturer	Similar to online store
Electronic ordering table	Platform for communication between sellers and buyers	Provides certain property for use	Mostly temporary, short contact time, has usage fee	It is necessary to constantly analyse data
Electronic bulletin board	Website where businesses place promotional offers or sell products	Opportunity to submit various information for advertising	Need to constantly update ads	Need to use the services of a middleman
Price aggregators	Resources that specialize in collecting data on product availability/price, and providing this information to the buyer in an easy to compare and select form	Opportunity to present price advantages and better delivery or service conditions compared to international competitors	High placement rates, the need to constantly update the price due to the volatility of the exchange rate, etc.	Price aggregators only generate traffic to the site
Electronic marketplace	Platform for transactions between sellers and buyers	Specialization for the provision of certain types of services	Defined list of rules	Need to fulfil individual transaction elements (making payments, etc.)
E-shop	Sale of goods purchased from different manufacturers on their own behalf	Additional sales channel	Sale of products at middleman prices	Products are sold mainly from their own inventory

(Continued)

Table 16.1 (Continued) Characteristics and features of major digital tools

Name of method/tool	Essence of the tool	Description features		Application features
		Pros	Cons	
1	2	3	4	5
Online auction	Platform for communication between sellers and buyers for transactions	Opportunity to sell product for a good price	High competition	Buyer and seller set competitive price during the transaction
Direct email	Emailing	Targeted impact on a potential customer; opportunity to attract a potential customer for free	Unlimited response speed; the letter may be out of date	The content plan and purpose of the mailing list should be clearly defined
Social networks	Creating your own profiles, activities, thematic groups, and more	Depth of targeting, trusting influencers	Lots of unnecessary information; high cost for testing	Considered as a source of traffic to the main site or landing page
Forums	Web resource for discussing issues, topics in a specific area of activity	May be a supplement to the site	Minimum user profile information	Availability of administrators and moderators who can edit/delete user comments

verify valid email addresses, there are specialized digital resources, such as Guesser.email and Emailgenerator.io. These services help to create and select an existing email address in cases where the name and surname of the person and/or name of the company where the person works are known.

Another alternative to building an email address database for email distribution is searching for available addresses on the internet. Services such as Findanyemail.net, App.voilanorbert.com, App.anymailfinder.com and Neverbounce.com do not generate possible addresses and check them, but search for existing ones, collecting information and analysing from many internet sources on the search query of the person who potentially hit your mailing base. These services should also be attributed to the auxiliary tools, those that help in the organization of marketing digital communications.

Among the additional components in the implementation of direct mail, one can select services that are designed to verify email addresses. They most often act as an add-on, or extension, to the email in the browser from where the newsletter is distributed.

Examples of such services are Name2email.com, Rapportive.com and Mailtrack.io. These tools make it possible to track the stages and delivery status: whether the letter was delivered to the recipient, whether they opened it, and so on.

And, of course, focusing on direct mail, one should mention the platforms and resources where this procedure is carried out directly. At the moment, there are a comprehensive number of options to configure and perform emailing. These platforms are more or less known, depending on the country from where the distribution is made and depending on the language of the interface. In order to consider these tools in more detail, it should be said that they can also be classified on some criteria.

There are services for setting up direct mail from regular mail, platforms designed specifically for this (SendPulse, MailChimp, UniSender, GetResponse, etc.) and platforms that are multifunctional, aimed at performing many managing functions, including emailing.

Other auxiliary (concomitant) digital tools popular today are CRM systems. They are platforms, or programs, that primarily contain databases and help to optimize the relationship between the company and the client in order to collect, store and analyze information about partners, intermediaries, suppliers and existing and potential customers.

CRM systems designed as solutions that help to automate business processes are, i.e., Salesforce, PipeDrive, Oracle Siebel CRM, SAP CRM, Microsoft Dynamics CRM, ZohoCRM, OneBox and many more. One of the factors that classify CRM systems is the targeted use; according to this classification they are divided into:

- Strategic
- Operational
- Analytical
- For co-operation

Moreover, there are CRM systems that provide opportunities to meet all of the above goals. An example is the Salesforce platform, which is used by powerful global companies such as Dell, Google, Toyota and Cisco. The Salesforce platform consists of separate parts: Service Cloud (achievement of the operational purpose), Sales Cloud (achievement of the operational and analytical purposes), and Chatter (for performance of the strategic purpose), etc.

There are also a considerable number of CRM systems that are cloud or batch, individual or group, personalized for the purposes and needs of the companies and standardized. Depending on the specifics of each individual enterprise, it is advisable to use one or another type.

Depending on the main function, there are CRM management systems that operate:

- Contacts (call center, feedback)
- Marketing (surveys, analysis of results)
- Sales (online store, order by phone)
- Integrated

According to the logic of construction and purpose there are several fundamentally different types of information systems that belong to the class of CRM systems:

- CIF systems (Customer Information File)—systems for collecting reference data information about customers from disparate sources and providing this information to users and other information systems on request.
- SFA systems (Sales Force Automation)—systems for automating the operational processes of sales and marketing.
- Service desk—systems that provide support for operational customer service processes.
- Contact centre—contact processing systems with real and potential customers for the purpose of sales and service through any electronic channels of communication (language menus, IVR—interactive voice response, website, email, fax).
- Analytical CRM—systems based on data warehouses, designed for the accumulation, storage, aggregation and intelligent processing of chronological indicators collected on the basis of data from transactional systems.

Thus, as one can see, considering auxiliary (concomitant) digital tools, there are a considerable number of them, depending on the basic digital marketing tool that is being used. Therefore, each of the auxiliary (concomitant) digital tools has its own detailed classification. Referring to the basic digital tools, one should emphasize that each of them has its own characteristics and specifics of application for different areas and, accordingly, classification features.

Based on the main features of the classification (highlighted in Figure 16.1) and features (defined in Table 16.1), we propose the following definition of the scope of the above-mentioned digital tools (Table 16.2).

This concretization makes it possible to clearly define the scope of use of different digital tools and to use them more effectively in the practical activity of industrial enterprises (Karjaluoto & Ulkuniemi, 2015).

In the situation of a limited budget, it is not possible to use all digital tools at once (Ahuja, 2015), so we will determine the coefficients of the use of different means for promoting industrial products by the method of pairwise comparison (the basis of such analysis may become information about competitors' advertising campaigns) (Table 16.3).

As a result of the research we can offer five of the most effective digital tools for industrial enterprises nowadays. The five most essential tools are:

- Website
- An online platform
- Online store
- Electronic order table
- Electronic auction

Given the need to develop a unique advertising campaign, we suggest determining the important coefficient of digital tools by the formula:

$$W_I = 1 + I_I, \tag{16.1}$$

W_i – the coefficient of importance of the i-th digital tool

I_I – a relative measure of the weight of the i-th digital tool

Thus, the coefficient of importance of the above instruments will be, respectively, 1.16; 1.15; 1.13; 1.12 and 1.11.

Minimizing costs is not an end goal in itself for entrepreneurial activity that has tangible results in both natural and value measurements. Comparison of the latter with the costs is an argument when deciding on the implementation of new measures. However, not all activities at once (usually within one reporting period, usually a year) provide a target profit. Yes, creating your own website for the manufacturer (electronic storefronts, web pages, etc.) is an investment in the future.

At the stage of investing, we suggest introducing the coefficients of importance of internet funds from the perspective of their prospects (Formula 16.1). For example, long-term billboard rentals are less important to the manufacturer than any form of information dissemination on the internet.

Thus, when calculating the economic efficiency of using a certain digital tool we suggest taking into account its importance and adjusting by an appropriate factor:

$$Ef_i = \frac{E_i}{V_i} \cdot W_i, \tag{16.2}$$

Ef_i – the economic efficiency of using the i-th Digital Marketing tool

E_i – the economic effect of using the i-th Digital Marketing tool

V_i – a cost estimate of the cost of using the i-th tool during the billing period

W_i – the importance factor of the i-th Digital Marketing tool

The results of this study can be the basis for the selection of digital tools by specific industrial enterprises.

16.5 DATA COLLECTION AND ANALYSIS

To implement the proposed system, we collected and analyzed data to train and test our model.

16.5.1 Data collection

Let's carry out a comparative analysis of the use of different digital tools (video informer, static banner, carousel advertising). Consider, for example, a conditional Facebook advertising campaign with the following initial conditions for the middle industrial Ukrainian enterprise:

- Geography of location (cities): Kyiv, Odessa, Lviv, Kharkiv, Dnipro, Cherkasy, Kryvyi Rih
- The target audience: 22-45 years; positions: company director, commercial director, marketer, FEA manager, chief engineer, economy area: engineering industry
- Period: 5 weeks
- Quantity: const = 250000 (to allow comparison)

16.5.2 Data analysis

The initial data are presented in Table 16.4. According to the calculations, the use of static banner and carousel advertising on all pages of the site with video content have the highest economic efficiency (i.e., provide maximum coverage of the target audience representatives at

Table 16.2 Scope of digital tools

Classification		Internet platform	Electronic showcase	Online auction	Website	Price aggregator	Electronic order table	Online bulletin board	Electronic marketplace for specialist search	Online store	Direct mail	Social networks	Forums
By geographical feature	Local	+	+	+	+	+	+	+	+	+	+	+	+
	Global	+	+	+	+	+	+	+	+	+		+	+
By sector type	B2B	+	+	+	+	+	+	+	+	+	+	+	+
	B2C	+	+	+	+	+	+	+		+	+	+	+
	C2C											+	+
	B2G	+			+								
	G2B	+			+								
By purpose	Sale of goods	+	+	+	+	+	+	+		+	+		
	Lead generation	+	+		+			+	+	+	+		
	Uplifting the image	+			+							+	+
By originality	Traditional tools										+	+	+
	New tools	+	+	+		+	+	+	+	+			
By intermediary type	Direct	+	+	+	+	+	+	+	+	+	+	+	+
	Intermediate	+	+			+	+	+	+	+			

Table 16.3 The matrix of pairwise comparisons of digital tools

	Internet platform	Electronic showcase	Website	Price aggregator	Electronic order table	Online bulletin board	Electronic marketplace for specialist search	Online store	Online auction	Direct email	Social networks	Forums	Sum	Rank	The relative weight index (I)
Internet platform		1	0	1	1	1	1	1	1	1	1	1	10	2	0,15
Electronic showcase	0		0	0	0	1	1	0	0	1	0	0	3	8	0,05
Website	1	1		1	1	1	1	1	1	1	1	1	11	1	0,16
Price aggregator	0	1	0		0	1	1	0	0	1	1	1	6	6	0,1
Electronic order table	0	1	0	1		1	1	0	1	1	1	1	8	4	0,12
Online bulletin board	0	0	0	0	0		1	0	0	1	1	1	4	7	0,06
Electronic marketplace for specialist search	0	0	0	0	0	0		0	0	1	1	1	3	8	0,05
Online store	0	1	0	1	1	1	1		1	1	1	1	9	3	0,13
Online auction	0	1	0	1	0	1	1	0		1	1	1	7	5	0,11
Direct email	0	0	0	0	0	0	0	0	0		0	1	1	9	0,01
Social networks	0	1	0	0	0	0	0	0	0	1		1	3	8	0,05
Forums	0	1	0	0	0	0	0	0	0	0	0		1	9	0,01

Table 16.4 Output data of the digital tools on the Facebook network

Location	Digital Tool	Quantity, thousands	Units Cost, UAH, thousands	Coverage, thousands	Part of the target audience, %	Coverage of the target audience, persons	Demonstration, number of times, thousands	CTR, %	Clicks, number of times	Cost of 1000 impressions, UAH	Link cost, UAH	Cost coverage 1000 unique users, UAH
						Predicted values						
User News Feed	Video informer	250	150	125	72,2	90 250	250	0,25	625	600	240	1200
All pages of a video content site	Static banner	250	7,5	125	66,1	82 625	250	0,25	625	30	12	60
	Carousel advertising	250	6,25	125	95	118 750	825	0,25	2 062	7,58	3,03	50

the lowest cost). Guided by this approach, other digital tools will not be selected and used, which is a mistake, because when designing a unique advertising campaign it is the correction factor that will justify the use of important and promising tools (in our example, this is a video informer in the news feed). The results of this analysis can be used as a methodological basis in the development of an effective communication policy for enterprises in the internet space, especially when it comes to forming a system of instrumental support for its implementation.

Note: Price per Unit:

- Video informer: 0,6 UAH/15 sec. browsing
- Static banner: 30 UAH/1000 views
- Carousel advertising: 25 UAH/1000 views

16.6 CONCLUSION

Summarizing the above, we can draw the following conclusions:

- Further developed the classification of digital marketing tools in the division of the new feature "by type of mediation", which contributes to the further systematization of tools, deepening understanding of the impact of different tools (indirect, purposeful), the degree of their specialization and economic interest allows their application to different entities;
- The comparative analysis of the main digital tools is carried out: their characteristics are presented and the peculiarities of the use of each is determined;
- It is proposed to determine the importance factor of using each digital tool for promotion of industrial products by the method of pairwise comparison;
- It is suggested to take into account its importance when calculating the economic efficiency of using a particular digital tool.

The results of this study can be the basis for the selection of digital tools by specific industrial enterprises.

REFERENCES

Abraham, M. (2019). Responsiveness of Consumers on the Marketing Tools of Fast Moving Consumer Goods. *Journal of Information and Computational Science*, 9 (12), pp. 269–278.

Ahuja, V. (2015). Development of an optimal solution for digital marketing variables in an online tool. *International Journal of Internet Marketing and Advertising*, 9(1). Retrieved from: https://www.inderscienceonline.com/doi/pdf/10.1504/IJIMA.2015.068345 (Access: 27.03.2020).

Baranchenko, Ye., Aksom, H., Zhylinska, O., Firsova, S., Datskova, D. (2019). Inbound Marketing: Practical Aspects of Promoting Goods and Services in E-commerce. *Marketing and Management of Innovations*, 4, pp. 308–320.

Big Business Online Edition (2011). *The number of Internet users has grown to 2 billion people*. Retrieved from: http://www.bigness.ru/news/2011-01-26/internet/121281/ (Access: 27.03.2020).

Bozhkova, V. V., Ptashchenko, O. V., Saher, L. Y., & Syhyda, L. O. (2018). Transformation of marketing communications tools in the context of globalization. *Marketing and Management of Innovations*, 1, pp. 73–82.

Glinenko, L. K., Dainovsky, Yu. A. (2018). State and prospects of development of e-commerce of Ukraine. *Marketing and management of innovations*. 1. Retrieved from: http://mmi.fem.sumdu.edu.ua/sites/default/files/mmi2018_1_83_102.pdf (Access: 27.03.2020), pp. 83–102.

Gregori, G. L., Marinelli, L., Temperini, V. (2015). The use of digital marketing tools in SMEs: needs, problems and opportunities an empirical study in the Marche region. *International Journal of Sales, Retailing and Marketing*, 4(4), pp. 69–77.

Harsimrat, K. (2016). A Systematic Review on the Field of Digital Marketing. *International journal of technology and computing (IJTC)*, 2(12), pp. 539–543.

Ilyashenko, S. M., Ivanova, T. E. (2015). Problems and prospects of promotion of products of domestic enterprises on the Internet. *Bulletin of the Odessa National University. Series: Economics*, 20(1/2), pp. 101–107.

Isohella, L., Oikarinen, E.-L. Saarela, M., Muhos, M., Nikunen, T. (2017). Perceptions of digital marketing tools in new microenterprises. *Technology, Innovation and Industrial Management, International Conference*, Retrieved from: https://pdfs.semanticscholar.org/a11c/49ce2655c8b339f4a016b017dd75624124b5.pdf (Access: 27.03.2020), pp. 85–95.

Išoraitė, M. (2016). Raising brand awareness through the internet marketing tools. *Independent journal of management & production (IJM&P)*, 7(2), pp. 320–339.

Karjaluoto, H., Mustonen, N. and Ulkuniemi, P. (2015). The role of digital channels in industrial marketing communications. *Journal of Business & Industrial Marketing*, 30(6), pp. 703–710.

Karjaluoto, H. and Ulkuniemi, P. (2015). Digital communications in industrial marketing. *Journal of Business & Industrial Marketing*, 30. p. 6.

Litovchenko, I. L., Pylypchuk, V. P. (2008). *Internet marketing: a textbook. Center for Educational Literature*. pp. 170–184.

Melnik, Yu. M., Sager, L. Yu., Illyashenko, N. S., Ryazantseva, Yu. M. (2016) Classification of the basic forms and types of marketing Internetinternet communications. *Marketing and innovation management*, 4, pp. 43–55.

Melnyk, L., Derykolenko, O., Kubatko, O., Matsenko, O. (2019). Business Models of Reproduction Cycles for Digital Economy. *ICT in Education, Research and Industrial Applications. Integration, Harmonization and Knowledge Transfer: Proceedings of the 15th International Conference. Volume II: Workshops Kherson, Ukraine, June 12–15*, pp. 269–276.

Mozgova, V. G. (2013). Internet Marketing Tools and Their Benefits for Modern Ukrainian Enterprises. *Effective Economics*, 10. Retrieved from: http://www.economy.nayka.com.ua/?op=1&z=2429 (Access: 27.03.2020), pp. 79–86.

Nikunen, T., Saarela, M., Oikarinen, E.-L.; Muhos, M.; Isohella, L. (2017). Micro-Enterprise's Digital Marketing Tools for Building Customer Relationships. *Management (18544223)*, *12*(2), pp. 171–188.

Ruban, V. V. (2017). Digital marketing: the role and features of use. *Economic Bulletin of Zaporizhzhya State Engineering Academy*, 2(2). Retrieved from: http://nbuv.gov.ua/UJRN/evzdia_2017_2%282%29__5 (Access: 27.03.2020), pp. 20–25.

Saher, L. Yu. (2015). The methodic approach to the diagnostics of internal communications at the industrial enterprise. *Marketing and Management of Innovations*, 2, pp. 65–75.

Setkute, J. (2018). *In search of digital marketing communications success: the case of oil and gas industry B2B SMEs*. Robert Gordon University [online], PhD thesis. Retrieved from: https://openair.rgu.ac.uk (Accessed: 27.03.2020).

Sinevicien, L., Kubatko, O., Derykolenko, O., Kubatko, O. (2018). The impact of economic performance on environmental quality in developing countries. *International Journal of Environmental Technology and Management*, *21*(5/6), p. 222.

Taiminen, H. (2016). One gets what one orders: Utilisation of digital marketing tools. *The Marketing Review*, *16* (4), pp. 389–404.

Teletov, A., Teletova, S., Letunovska, N. (2019). Use of language games in advertising texts as a creative approach in advertising management. *Periodicals of Engineering and Natural Sciences*, *7*(2), pp. 458–465.

Thompson, S. H. T. (2005). Usage and effectiveness of online marketing tools among Business-to-Consumer (B2C) firms in Singapore. *International Journal of Information Management*, *25* (3), pp. 203–213.

Verdenhofs, A., Tambovceva, T. (2019). Evolution of Customer Segmentation in the Era of Big Data. *Marketing and Management of Innovations*, *1*, pp. 238–243.

Yeo, Z, Masi, D, Low, J. S. C., Ng, Y. T., Tan, P. S., Barnes, S. (2019). Tools for promoting industrial symbiosis: A systematic review. *Journal of Industrial Ecology*, *23*, pp.1087–1108.

Yevdokimov, Y., Melnyk, L., Lyulyov, O., Panchenko, O., Kubatko, V. (2018). Economic freedom and democracy: determinant factors in increasing macroeconomic stability. *Problems and Perspectives in Management*, *16*(2), pp. 279–290.

Zanora, V. O. (2018). Internet and Digital Marketing: Theoretical Foundations *Economics and Enterprise Management*, *36*, pp. 117–120.

Chapter 17

Innovations in internet marketing of enterprises in Ukraine on the example of biological products manufacturers

Aleksandr Teletov, Svetlana Teletova and Nataliia Letunovska

CONTENTS

17.1 INTRODUCTION

17.1.1 An industrial manufacturer of biologicals as an object of analysis

Enterprises producing biological products in Ukraine are participants in the market of socially responsible production, focused on strengthening the role of domestic producers in the production of environmentally friendly products. By manufacturing drugs for the prevention and diagnosis of dangerous animal diseases, they make a substantial contribution to increasing the profitability of livestock farms in Ukraine, and, as a result, help provide the population with high-quality livestock products.

The current market for veterinary drugs in Ukraine is continuously expanding in terms of quantity and quality. In recent years, it has become desirable as a business. Increasing the number of companies and the production of veterinary products increases market competition and encourages manufacturers to seek and use new strategies to enhance their image, gain consumers, and retain market share.

The market for veterinary products is divided into six main areas: chemical, biological, feed, disinfectants, and other veterinary preparations products. The most extensive distribution of the veterinary market is in biological industries (vaccines, medical sera, diagnostic products, nutrient mediums).

We have chosen Ukrainian producers of biological products as an object for analysis. We propose to consider internet marketing to improve the efficiency of their activities.

The specificity of bioproducts is that not all vaccines are single-use. Many vaccines are used throughout the life of an individual animal (revaccinations). The demand for products is seasonal. Most sales are in the spring when there is a need for additional immunity.

Vaccine buyers are veterinary laboratories, veterinary pharmacies, circus companies, zoos, farms, poultry farms, pig farms, cattle breeds, slaughterhouses, animal sports organizers, and pet owners.

The share of biological products in the value structure of the domestic market by pharmacotherapeutic groups is about 34.6% (vaccines for poultry, rabbits, pigs, cattle, bees, etc., test systems). Besides, under the influence of new lifestyles, the proportion of the pet segment (11–13.4%) is increasing every year (Gavryliuk, 2008). When segmenting the market of biological products in Ukraine, it is reasonable to say that this market is characterized by the lack of latest preparations developments, which is connected with the limited economic opportunities of Ukrainian manufacturers and buyers of preparations. Significant segments of the market are self-developed products (new preparations are having analogs (Vasutinska & Kuzminska, 2019)); new preparations for the domestic market, made in cooperation with foreign companies; and new generic preparations under their brand names for the domestic market. Generics are analogs of the original preparations that begin to be manufactured by other manufacturers after the patent protection of the original product has expired (Mykhailovskyi et al., 2008).

17.1.2 Innovative instruments of communication for enterprises: The role of internet marketing in the market activity of a manufacturer of biological products

In the context of farm-oriented trends, there is a need for primary processing of meat and milk directly near farms that can replace multi-ton refrigeration tanks. So the need for high-quality biological veterinary products is increasing for many agricultural professionals. The accessibility and ease of their acquisition should be supported by effective advertising. The relevance of innovative methods of promoting biological products is that only a few enterprises of this profile have an active online representation. Online activity shows how great a company is today. Modern instruments of advertisement are not used in the vast majority of enterprises in the bioproducts manufacturing field. It should be borne in mind that by 2022, more than 80% of a company's marketing budget will be spent on internet marketing tools, which should take into account manufacturers of any industry.

The purpose of the study is to substantiate general provisions and develop recommendations for innovative advertising management of enterprises producing biological veterinary preparations.

According to statistics, almost 80% of buyers start the process of buying by monitoring information online. The role of service as an element of competition is judged by the quality of communications in the B2B and B2C markets (mainly used by manufacturers of biological products).

Not many scientific works have been devoted to the problems of internet marketing in the biological products industry (Yeremiieva & Zozuliov, 2017), (Bushuieva & Ponomarenko, 2012), (Mogylna, 2017), (Gavryliuk, 2010), (Garvas & Muzyka, 2017), (Strus et al., 2019), (Rajkumar, 2016), (Napwora, 2015), (Sneeringer, 2019). Some information on this issue is being considered in professional print and online publications in Ukraine and abroad. Багато вчених приділили свої дослідження питанню інтернет-маркетингу у сфері B2B (Saher et al., 2018), (Melnyk et al., 2016), (Syhyda & Illiashenko, 2016), (Rosokhata, 2014). One paper (Holliman & Rowley, 2014) focuses on the formation of content marketing in the B2B sector. The authors identify important insight parameters that form the basis for successful interaction in this area. Another paper (Shaltoni, 2017) explores the problems of adapting internet marketing to use in emerging industries with a focus on certain tools. This study also examines if websites are used for basic marketing communications (brochureware) or for conducting advanced marketing activities. Authors Kwarteng et al., (2019) emphasize that companies should not only use some elements of internet marketing in their activities but also form an internal system of online management to ensure high competitiveness in the long-run perspective. Alnsour (2018) shows how the use of well-thought-out internet marketing communications makes it possible to establish highly effective market relationships. The focus is on the banking sector and building mutually beneficial business relationships between customers and a bank. According to the research, both biological products industry executives and internet marketing professionals are uniquely calling the site a major and integrated marketing tool, Figure 17.1 (Isaeva, 2016).

Having own website gives industrial companies unique opportunities for globalization and transition from "mass" marketing to customized marketing. The site is better than other tools; it provides qualitative information, supplementing it with interesting illustrative content. In addition to 24/7 accessibility, another advantage of the site is the ability to integrate all elements of the marketing mix. In this regard, we argue that the online marketing of bioproducts must always start with the site. It is appropriate to focus a large portion of your financial and time resources on it. The promotion of a corporate site should be supported by social networks. Interactive communication with consumers is facilitated by the existing registration process on a site, conducting surveys among clients, organizing email newsletters, implementing loyalty programs, etc.

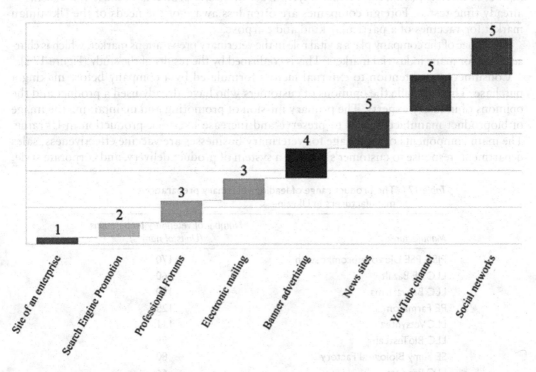

Figure 17.1 Survey results of the importance of major internet marketing tools in industrial communication with consumers, by rank

Sorted from the most essential tool to the least important in the respondents' opinion

The site allows companies to solve such issues as:

- Negative demand for biological products when a significant proportion of potential consumers refuse a specific type of product (due to lack of sufficient information). Site is the instrument of conversion marketing in this case
- Low demand when serving as an incentive marketing tool; site distributes necessary information about biological preparations, increasing interest in buying among potential consumers

17.2 RESULTS AND DISCUSSION

The leading domestic manufacturer of veterinary preparations in Ukraine is the O.L.KAR.-AgroZooVet-Service enterprise, which produces more than 1,000 items of various veterinary products. Other Ukrainian manufacturers are presented in Table 17.1.

In addition to Ukrainian manufacturers, more than 70 foreign companies—Bayer (Germany), INVESA (Spain), Biowet Pulawy (Poland), Pfizer (USA), Armavir Biofabrika (Russia), Huevepharma (Bulgaria), and Syva Laboratorios S.A. (Spain) occupy almost 95% of the foreign veterinary preparations market in Ukraine; 40 countries are represented in the market. Products of manufacturers from Belarus, the Netherlands, China, South Korea, and Slovenia are also presented. According to the results of the third quarter of 2019, domestic products occupied 54% of the market (Harvas & Kolodiichuk, 2019). The rest of the market is foreign production. Most buyers trust domestic products because the vaccine is already time-tested. Foreign companies are often less aware of the needs of the Ukrainian market for vaccines of a particular kind and purpose.

The image of the company plays a vital role in the veterinary preparations market, which is characteristic for many industrial markets. This is confirmed by the results of the study (Figure 17.2).

Consumers pay attention to external factors formulated by a company before making a purchase. These include the opinions of customers who have already used a product and the opinions of industry experts. The primary mission of promoting and maintaining the image of bioproduct manufacturers is to preserve and increase livestock production in Ukraine. The main components of the image for veterinary businesses are vaccine effectiveness, sales department, response to customer's queries, a system of product delivery, and corporate style.

Table 17.1 The product range of leading veterinary preparations manufacturers in Ukraine

Manufacturer	Number of veterinary preparations (Units of names)
PJSC PSE Ukrzovetprompostach	170
LLC PF Bazalt	160
LLC Brovafarma	130
PE Farmaton	125
LLC Vetsyntez	111
LLC BioTestLab	99
SE Sumy Biological Factory	80
LLC Product	66
LLC Urkvetprompostach	65
JSC Biofarm	49
SE Kherson Biological Factory	21

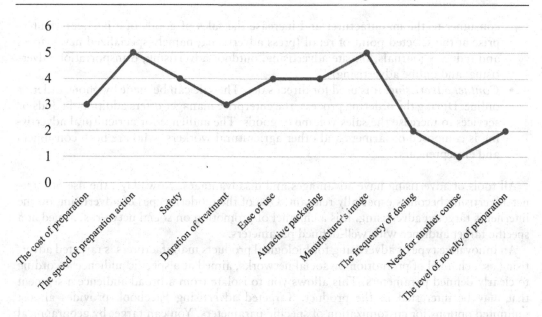

Figure 17.2 Results of the survey on the importance of various parameters that influence veterinary preparations purchase, in points (Harvas & Kolodiichuk, 2019)

5 – the most essential parameter; 0 – is not a significant parameter

Source: (Harvas, & Kolodiichuk, 2019)

The production department of an enterprise is responsible for the vaccine's effectiveness. The first contact of a client with a company occurs with sales consultants. Biological products are complicated, so the sales team always accompanies consumers. In creating an external image of a veterinary preparations manufacturer in today's changing environment with a focus on internet communications, the presence of a company's website and the effectiveness of its work play an important role (Syhyda, 2013).

Unlike in European countries, the Law of Ukraine "On Advertising" (Cedem, 2020) has no restrictions on the marketing of veterinary products.

Advertising of veterinary preparations, in particular biological products, is considered by us in the following directions:

- *Industrial advertising.* Brochures, advertising materials in professional journals, technical literature, and catalogs, industry exhibitions, technical demonstrations, and seminars. The largest industry exhibitions in Ukraine are Agroforum (exhibition of innovative products for agriculture), Agro2019 (the most significant agricultural exhibition in the country), Agrocomplex (exhibition of practical solutions for the agrarian industry), International Dairy Congress (veterinary dairy production exhibition), Agro Animal Show (international exhibition of productive livestock and poultry) and others. The most well-known professional thematic journals are *Animal Husbandry and Veterinary Medicine*, *World of Veterinary Science*, and *Veterinary Medicine, Animal Husbandry*, and *Nature Management Technologies*. Several universities hold annual seminars on veterinary research in Ukraine (Sumy National Agrarian University, Zhytomyr National Agro-Ecology University, National University of Bioresources and Environmental Management of Ukraine, etc.).
- *Retail advertising.* For veterinary medicine companies, it is a question of veterinary pharmacies. The objective of such advertising is to attract the attention of the potential

consumer to the manufacturer and increase the sales of goods of a particular enterprise at the selected point of retail (press advertising, namely specialized newspapers and industry journals, on-site advertising, outdoor advertising, transportation advertising, and online advertising).

- *Contact advertising.* It is used for direct sales. The sale can be made by phone order or online. During the ordering process, the enterprise manager offers additional goods or services to increase the sales volume of goods. The audience for agricultural advertising is composed of farmers and other agricultural workers, who are both consumers and entrepreneurs.

All tools of advertising have advantages and disadvantages. Nowadays, the use of internet advertising becomes especially relevant. One of the modern types of advertising on the internet is targeted advertising. It is a channel of promotion on social networks, aimed at a specific target audience with well-defined parameters.

An innovative type of advertising for biological products manufacturers is targeted advertising as a channel of promotion on social networks, aimed at a specific audience according to clearly defined parameters. This allows you to isolate from a broad audience a segment that may be interested in the product. Targeted advertising Facebook provides almost unlimited options for customization of specific parameters. You can target by geographical location, interests, time, socio-demographic characteristics, behavior, locality etc.

The most popular type of targeting is behavioral. It is a convenient and effective way to convey an advertising message to the target audience. It works based on knowledge about user behavior and actions. Using targeted advertising is expensive but effective.

Internet marketing activities in the company should be engaged in marketing services. It must advertise products that are in the sales season and those that are not in demand. Moderate demand for products does not require additional promotion measures.

So, we have highlighted the main types of advertising that are used in the marketing activities of modern veterinary product manufacturers in Ukraine. Consider the example of domestic producers of biological veterinary preparations in promoting their products on the market using internet marketing.

17.3 FINDINGS

We have found out that the main factor for evaluating a business in the modern world is its presence on the internet. There may be sites with an extensive product range for large enterprises, for the small ones with narrow product range, social networks are advisable. Concerning the veterinary field, lands are used mainly for intermediaries in the production of biological factories, i.e., veterinary pharmacies or hospitals.

Veterinary businesses have complex products, so it is more appropriate to choose a site for online business. All information on the site should be structured and understandable to potential customers. Most of those who know the effect of the products are veterinarians, but the site needs to be designed so that individuals without special education could understand what the issue is about.

We compare the sites of the main competitors in biological vaccine production in Ukraine: SE Sumy Biological Factory, SE Kherson Biological Factory, and LLC BioTestLab (Kyiv). Consider the basic criteria for competitive site analysis:

1. Usability
2. Site structure

3. Site indexing
4. Number of external pages
5. Total traffic
6. Behavioral factors: refusals, page depth, time spent on site
7. Traffic sources: direct, referrals, SEO, SMM, email marketing, and banner advertising
8. Adaptability to the mobile version

Usability criteria for veterinary business websites are color gamma, font, image placement, site load speed, and identity. Usability for biological product manufacturers is the primary indicator of keeping comparability between colors of a site and corporate style. SE Sumy Biological Factory uses a pastel-blue color scheme. Pictures posted on the site take some time to load, but all are of excellent quality. There are different fonts that are difficult to perceive. SE Kherson Biological Factory has a landing page that is very simplistic. The color scheme is unattractive. Too much green is present. Pictures are different in form and format. Almost 50% of the photos are downloaded from the internet. The fonts on the site are different. The site of LLC BioTestLab differs from competitors. It is the most organized. There is a fast and continuous playback video screensaver on the homepage. The site is made in the same style. There are a variety of colors, but for the most part, the site is presented in light green.

The structure of the site shows how convenient the primary tabs on site are, how easy it is to find the information you need. It should be ergonomic. Website of SE Sumy Biological Factory has an easy structure. It which consists of the following tabs: About the company, Product catalog, Cooperation, Contract production, Prices, and Contacts. The structure of the site of SE Kherson Biological Factory includes such tabs as: Main, Products, About us, and Contacts. The structure is concise. There is not enough information to make a decision. There is no price tab. The main page contains news dating back to 2017. If the company was presented as a landing, then it was necessary to provide the following basic information to potential customers: Information about product and its application, Prices, Company, and Contacts. Site of LLC BioTestLab has the following structure: Company, Infocenter, Production, Products, and Contacts. It is concise and understandable. The price tab is missing. New information about products is presented in the Infocenter tab.

Site indexing reflects the number of pages in the search engine. Google was chosen as the leading search engine for the study. The more pages, the more traffic we can get to a page on the internet.

External links are all sources that link to a specific site. In other words, they are called donors. The main donors may be suppliers of raw materials, resellers, potential customers, and clients. The more companies we can engage with online, the more potential customers will go to a particular site. You can interact and be a barter donor.

Total traffic shows the number of visitors to specific site over a given selected period. One user can visit the site several times, so the total traffic does not match the actual number of people who visited it. Consider the listed characteristics for competing sites in Table 17.2.

Table 17.2 Comparison of the sites of biological products manufacturers by page count, external links and total traffic

Enterprise	Domain	Number of pages in Google	Number of external links	Total traffic
SE Sumy Biological Factory	http://biofabrika.sumy.ua/	155	24	172
SE Kherson Biological Factory	http://khersonbiofabrika.com/	59	5	420
LLC BioTestLab	https://www.biotestlab.ua/	692	26	11,540

Table 17.3 Comparison of visitor behavior on competitors' sites

Enterprise	Behavior factors		
	Refusals	Depth	Time
SE Sumy Biological Factory	68%	3.1	34"
SE Kherson Biological Factory	66%	2.5	32"
LLC BioTestLab	59%	1.88	2'06"

The leader by the number of pages and total traffic is LLC BioTestLab. A large amount of traffic depends on factors such as the city where the enterprise is located (the capital of Ukraine), the number of registered farms nearby, the effectiveness of sales managers, etc.

There are three parameters to characterize behavioral factors: refusals, page depth, and time spent on the site (Table 17.3). A site refusal occurs when a user logs in to a site and visits only homepage without taking any action, that is, a click. Page depth displays the number of pages a user navigates.

The users' refusals on the sites of surveyed enterprises are quite favorable for the veterinary field as they do not have direct Buy or Order buttons. The depth of the site is the best in SE Sumy Biological Factory, which can be explained by the fact that the necessary information for consumers is many steps, or the consumer is interested in learning more about the factory. The best behavioral factor that shows how much a potential customer likes a site is their time spent. The most competitive by this parameter is LLC BioTestLab. Such statistics are caused by the interest of international counterparties who have visited the site and spent a long time on it. Not a deep site can indicate that all the necessary information is located in the least number of steps.

Consider all traffic sources for surveyed companies in Table 17.4.

The Sumy and Kherson factories use only half of the capabilities of a website's promotion tools to attract traffic. Direct actions can be an indicator of how loyal customers are to a particular business. All analyzed sites have an optimization that helps users to find them quickly.

About SMM, the best efficiency is observed in SE Kherson Biological Factory. Most often, the referrals are from social networking sites and resellers who post factory information in their social accounts. The close relationship is shown in the referral statistics. This shows the excellent relationships the factory has with its employees, resellers, suppliers, and customers. SE Sumy Biological Factory has no representation on social networks, although it has a high percentage of traffic sources. This situation can be triggered by discussions of targeted product customers on various social media pages.

The simplest of the elements of traffic sources is email marketing. It is aimed at legal entities present in the veterinary field. Email addresses of farms and veterinary pharmacies are not challenging to find and contact with a sales offer. Different messages should be made for each target buyer, depending on the species and the number of animals in the holding. Ukrainian farmers should actively develop under the conditions of administrative reform and creation

Table 17.4 Sources of traffic to competing sites

Enterprise	Sources of traffic, %					
	Direct entries	Referrals	SEO	SMM	Email	Banner advertising
SE Sumy Biological Factory	37.94	0	56.11	5.96	0	0
SE Kherson Biological Factory	0	25.85	48.3	25.85	0	0
LLC BioTestLab	14.72	0.22	84.36	0.7	2	0

of integrated territorial communities in rural areas [it is estimated that at the completion of the reforms in Ukraine, there will be about two thousand communities (Teletov et al., 2019). Today, there are more than 26 thousand farms in Ukraine, which is less than 10% of their possible number. The most efficient farming is focused on livestock products, the production and export of which is more stable, in line with crop production. The dairy cluster and the pig-breeding cluster are dominant here, and the lamb cluster is also promising.

Effective use of the internet to promote products is in LLC BioTestLab, which uses the maximum number of indicators. This company uses direct actions, referrals, SEO, SMM, and email marketing.

Developed sites generally contain all six traffic source metrics in their activity. The modern trend is that the use of smartphones to access the internet is gaining in popularity. Mobile phones account for almost half of the time people spend on the internet. It is important for the site of a biological products manufacturer to be customized for mobile use.

Veterinary businesses can be targeted on social networks for sales, but this is the next step after creating a friendly atmosphere between seller and buyer. Social networks have different target audiences. To orient business in the social space, you should first determine the target audience that will be most successful in promoting your product. Currently, in Ukraine, there are such popular social networks: Facebook (used by about 44% of respondents), Instagram (used by 18% of respondents), and Twitter (used by 5% of respondents). Other social networks account for 33% of the respondents' answers (Statista, 2019).

Facebook is the leading social network for the biological factories' promotion, as the target audience is over 25 years old. This audience already has an education and can independently decide on the purchase of such a complex product.

The stage of creating a page on a social network goes through the following stages: gathering information, choosing the way of sharing information (creating a page, group or account), creating a page/account/group under a company name, adding relevant information and contacts, creating and filling a page with content, and inviting potential customers. We compare the advantages and disadvantages of accounts, groups, and the page (Table 17.5). For industrial enterprises, it is better to create a social networking page because it has the best functionality for doing business.

The quality of images on a page requires specific parameters. Different types of photos fit into different geometric shapes, which is why you need to follow the rules of extension. For example, the main photo of a page fits in a circle. The cover fits in a rectangle. In order to provide better image quality to profile pictures, you should save them in PNG format. You can use the following resources to create the content yourself: https://www.canva.com and https://crello.com. These resources include free templates, but also available paid content. Some ideas for a veterinary business can be found in such tabs as Animals and Medicine.

One of the essential tools on a page in a social network is a survey. It helps to focus issues under consideration. It seems that the client's opinion is valuable and influences voting. For veterinary businesses, the following survey topics are possible: about farm animals, about pets, about vaccination and revaccination, about the weight of animals and others.

Searching for clients of veterinary businesses is not complicated. Engaging consumers on a Facebook social network page is possible by searching for similar groups or livestock accounts where a target audience is located. There are many veterinary referral pages on Facebook. A company can join other pages and groups and post on its behalf. The benefits of this search are:

- Publications are related to topics.
- Consumers are interested in such information.
- Page administration does not need to make new posts every day to keep the audience engaged.

Table 17.5 The advantages and disadvantages of presenting enterprises on the Facebook social network

Way of bringing information	Advantages	Disadvantages
Account	1. The ability to invite an audience in one step. 2. Easy of use. 3. New posts cover all friends. 4. Visibility in the news feed.	1. Lack of statistics control. 2. Only 5,000 people can be added to friends. 3. Administration may not allow an account with a suspicious name. 4. Advertising and sales are blocked by the administration.
Group	1. Group posts are visible in the group members' news feed. 2. Personal messaging (up to 5,000) is possible. 3. The ability to make a group "closed" (for VIP clients only).	1. Two steps are required to invite a potential audience (Add to friends – Invite to the group). 2. Groups cannot be advertised. 3. Visible only to that user who is invited or intentionally searches for a group.
Page	1. Ability to create an event and invite the target audience. 2. More functionality for visitors. 3. Ability to promote the page (targeting). 4. Statistics are available. 5. Unlimited audience. 6. Option to set the mode "not online"	1. Two steps are required to invite potential audiences (Add to friends – Invite to page). 2. Complex interface for use.

Practical application of targeting advertising. All Facebook advertising is done through Ads Manager. It lets view, edits, and tracks all created advertising campaigns, groups, and individual ads on Facebook. First, you need to determine the purpose of creating a Facebook advertising campaign. Topics for advertising a biological product business page can be directing people to a website, increasing conversions on a site, promoting posts, and page promoting. The main categories of choice for advertising campaigns for veterinary preparations manufacturers are awareness (brand awareness and audience reach) and views (traffic and audience engagement) (Figure 17.3).

Depending on the purpose, you need to choose where your potential audience will go: site views or messenger (Figure 17.4). A more effective parameter for optimizing your ad campaign is *Clicks on the tab*. Parameter *Shows* is less effective but has a broader audience. Optimization for displaying manufacturers' ads is better targeted at *Clicks on the link*.

Budgeting and evaluating the performance of targeting ads. You can install or not install the deadline for ads. In this case, the advertisement will be valid until there are no more funds in the account (Figure 17.5). It is essential to choose the duration of the advertisement, either daytime or full time.

For such a parameter as Location, one chooses the whole Ukraine or chooses a segment that we would like to enter into. If a business fully covers a particular locality, it may exclude it from the list. Delivery of the vaccine of studied enterprises can be made to any corner of Ukraine. Therefore, it is not appropriate to use the location tool. The best age to target with an ad campaign of biological products manufacturer is 30 years. When choosing a gender, one selects the parameter All, since both men and women can be buyers of products (Figure 17.6).

Interests that are most relevant to the target audience are farm animals, animal welfare, farming, rabbits, and more. For example, see Figure 17.7.

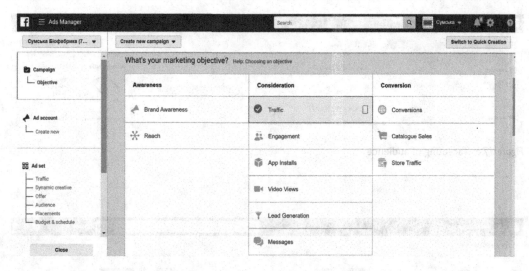

Figure 17.3 The first phase of a Facebook social networking campaign

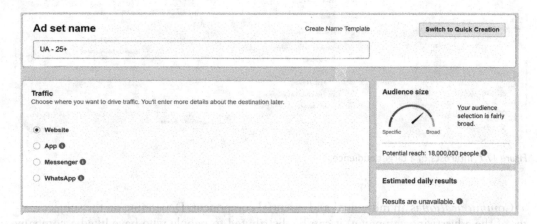

Figure 17.4 Choosing a traffic destination

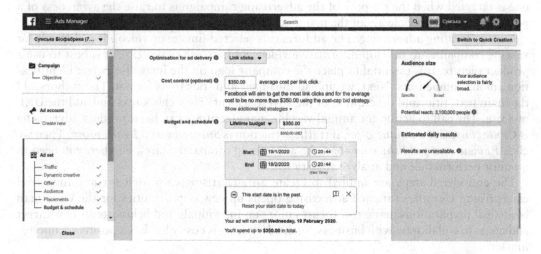

Figure 17.5 Targeted advertising budget

Figure 17.6 Targeting of audience

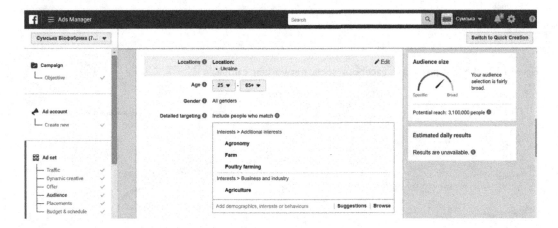

Figure 17.7 Interests of a target audience

Communication is an individual and essential component. Depending on the subject matter of the advertising campaign, it can be distributed to people who have liked a company page, friends of people who have liked the business page, all except for subscribers. The last one is targeted when the purpose of the advertising campaign is to raise the awareness of a potential group of people about the manufacturer.

Next is *creating advertising*. The ad format is selected (image or video). It is difficult for vaccine companies to develop informative videos and attract viewing, so it is best to use a product picture. It is essential to place the company logo on the image for better identification among competitors. Next, we upload the image and stick to its format. The authors add the main text, title, and description of the advertisement. They check text and add the URL of a site. The call to action for animal vaccine manufacturers can be: if product advertising is *Contact us, Get a unique offer,* if traffic attraction is *Subscribe* and *Learn more*. Then we click *Review and publish*; after that, the advertising campaign starts. Further, you need to monitor performance and analyze statistics.

The considered steps are unified to create an advertising campaign for any industrial enterprise in Ukraine. Targeted advertising opens up new opportunities for the Ukrainian biological preparations market. It focuses more on individuals and helps attract new target audiences to collaborate with business. Such advertising is costly but has a positive economic impact.

17.4 CONCLUSION

The study concludes that a significant effect of the online promotion of an industrial enterprise, in particular in the field of veterinary preparations, can be expected in the case of combined use of the site and a set of additional tools for its promotion, for example, the SMM promotion method.

In the context of the administrative reform of Ukraine in the countryside, communication support will create a positive perception of manufacturers of biological products, which will facilitate the impact of advertising management on the subjects of small and medium-sized agricultural businesses. A feature of veterinary products advertising is that it is aimed at reporting the existence of specific brands of goods for agricultural producers; ensuring the acceptance of advertised products by dealers; and forming a better attitude of farmers to a particular veterinary product by demonstrating how that product helps to increase efficiency, reduce business risk, increase profit margins, and more. The authors substantiate that the main components of the image for veterinary businesses are vaccine efficacy, reliability of sales service, prompt response, timely delivery, and corporate style. The image accompanies manufacturing companies throughout the process of production and sale of biological products. The factors considered are common to most veterinary businesses.

Almost every company has its competitive environment, relevant sites, etc., so the strategy of promoting a business on the internet involves regular analysis of them. The leading comparative indicators of competitive analysis of sites are determined. According to the authors' analysis, all Ukrainian producers of biological preparations for animals are represented on the internet.

Innovations in the advertising management of biological preparations include targeted online advertising. The stages of targeting advertising on the Facebook network are unified for the advertising campaign of any veterinary enterprise in Ukraine. The authors conclude that targeted advertising opens up new opportunities for the Ukrainian biological preparations market because it is more targeted at individuals who are not available to manufacturers and helps to find and engage a target audience in cooperation with an enterprise.

REFERENCES

Alnsour, M. (2018). Internet-Based Relationship Quality: A Model for Jordanian Business-to-Business Context. *Marketing and Management of Innovations*, 4, pp. 161–178. DOI: http://doi.org/10.21272/mmi.2018.4-15.

Bushuieva, I., Ponomarenko, M. (2012). Research and forecasting demand on the market of veterinary medicinal products. *Ukrainian Biopharmaceutical Journal*, 5-6(22-23), pp. 14–17.

Garvas, G., Muzyka, P. (2017). Clustering of production of veterinary preparations in the conditions of European integration. *Scientific Messenger of Lviv National University of Veterinary Medicine and Biotechnologies*, 19(81), pp. 118–122. DOI: 10.15421/nvlvet8121.

Gavryliuk, O. (2008). *Formation and state regulation the veterinary products market in Ukraine*. Candidate's thesis. Lviv.

Gavryliuk, O. (2010). *Ethical aspects of veterinary marketing*. Retrieved from: http://ena.lp.edu.ua:8080/bitstream/ntb/7532/1/05.pdf (Access: 25.03.2020).

Harvas, H., Kolodiichuk, V. (2019). Features of assessment of competitiveness of veterinary preparations. *Scientific Bulletin of LNUVMBT named after S.Z. Gzhytskyi*, 21(93), pp. 92–95.

Holliman, G., Rowley, J. (2014). Business to business digital content marketing: Marketer's perceptions of best practice. *Journal of Research in Interactive Marketing*, 8(4.7), pp. 269–293.

Isaeva, E. (2016). Basic internet marketing tools for industrial companies. *Bulletin of Omsk University. Series "Economics"*, 4, pp. 85–91.

Kwarteng, M.A., Jibril, A.B., Nwaiwu, F., Pilik M., Ali, M. (2019). Internet-Based Channel Orientation for Domesticated Services Firm: Some Drivers and Consequences. *IFIP Advances in Information and Communication Technology*, *558*, pp. 90–103.

Melnyk, Y. M., Saher, L. Y., Cherkas, I. Y. (2016). The transformation of marketing communications: non-traditional types. *Visnyk of Khmelnytsky National University. Economic science.*, *2(1)*, pp. 164–168.

Mogylna, L. (2017). Management of the quality of veterinary products of Ukrainian enterprises when entering the foreign market. *Economy and Society*, *8*, pp. 72–77.

Mykhailovskyi, V., Olenych I., Khariv I. (2008). Analysis of veterinary market segmenting criteria products relating to goods. *Scientific Bulletin of LNUVMBT named after S.Z. Gzhytskyi*, *1(36)*, pp. 297–301.

Napwora, M. P. (2015). *Marketing strategies adopted by veterinary pharmaceutical firms in Kenya to enhance performance.* Research project presented in partial fulfillment of the requirements for the award of the degree of Masters of business administration University of Nairobi.

Official site of CEDEM. Law of Ukraine "About advertising." Retrieved from: https://cedem.org.ua/library/zakon-ukrayiny-pro-reklamu (Access: 25.03.2020).

Rajkumar, G. (2016). Marketing authorization of veterinary products in Thailand. *International Journal of Drug Regulatory Affairs*, *4(1)*, pp. 21–23.

Rosokhata, A. (2014). The methodical apparatus formation forecasting of the industrial enterprise innovative activity directions. *Economics and Management*, *2*, pp. 115–121.

Saher, L. Yu., Melnyk, Yu. M., Niño-Amézquita, J. (2018). *The problems of development of an effective management system of internal communications and ways to overcome them.* Innovative Management: theoretical, methodical and applied grounds. 1st edition, Prague Institute for Qualification Enhancement: Prague, pp. 83–96.

Shaltoni, A. M. (2017). From websites to social media: exploring the adoption of internet marketing in emerging industrial markets. *Journal of Business and Industrial Marketing*, *32(7)*, pp. 1009–1019.

Sneeringer, S. (2019). Incentivizing new veterinary pharmaceutical products to combat antibiotic resistance. Retrieved from: https://academic.oup.com/aepp/advance-article-abstract/doi/10.1093/aepp/ppz022/5568261?redirectedFrom=fulltext (Access: 25.03.2020).

Statista (2019). Most used social networks in Ukraine in 2019. Statista. Retrieved from: https://www.statista.com/statistics/1057085/most-used-social-networks-ukraine/ (Access: 25.03.2020).

Strus, O., Polovko, N., Smetanina, K. (2019). Marketing aspects of the development of veterinary preparations based on peloids and products of their processing. *Socìalna farmacìâ v ohoronì zdorovâ*, *5(2)*, pp. 75–84. DOI: 10.24959/sphhcj.19.154.

Syhyda, L. (2013). Influence of enterprise's marketing environment on process of marketing distribution policy development. *Economic Annals-XXI*, *7*, pp. 28–32.

Syhyda, L., Illiashenko, S. (2016). The specificity of the marketing distribution policy; diagnostic procedures in the enterprise. *MIND Journal*, *2*. Retrieved from: https://mindjournal.wseh.pl/sites/default/files/article/03-17/the_specificity_of_the_marketing_distribution_policy_diagnostic_procedures_in_the_enterprise.pdf (Access: 26.03.2020).

Teletov, A., Letunovska, N., Provozin, M. (2019). *Social infrastructure of modern enterprises and territories.* Sumy: Trytoriia.

Vasutinska, Y., Kuzminska, N. (2019). Estimating the degree of novelty of a new product: innovative approach. *Marketing and Management of Innovations*, *2*, pp. 282–294.

Yeremiieva, N., Zozuliov, O. (2017). E-business features in the veterinary market. *Economic Bulletin of NTUU "KPI"*, pp. 299–306. DOIoi: 10.20535/2307-5651.14.2017.108740.

Index

Printed in the United States
by Baker & Taylor Publisher Services